Economics as Ideology and Experience

Ashok Mitra

ECONOMICS AS IDEOLOGY AND EXPERIENCE

Essays in Honour of Ashok Mitra

Edited by

DEEPAK NAYYAR

FRANK CASS
LONDON • PORTLAND, OR

First published in 1998 in Great Britain by
FRANK CASS PUBLISHERS
Newbury House, 900 Eastern Avenue
London, IG2 7HH

and in the United States of America by
FRANK CASS PUBLISHERS
c/o ISBS, 5804 N.E. Hassalo Street
Portland, Oregon 97213-3644

Website http://www.frankcass.com

British Library Cataloguing in Publication Data

Economics as ideology and experience : essays in honour of
Ashok Mitra
1. Economics
I. Nayyar, Deepak
330.1

ISBN 0 7146 4723 3 (cloth)
ISBN 0 7146 4273 8 (paper)

Library of Congress Cataloging-in-Publication Data

Economics as ideology and experience : essays in honour of Ashok Mitra
/ edited by Deepak Nayyar.
    p.   cm.
Includes bibliographical references.
ISBN 0 7146 4723 3 (cloth). -- ISBN 0 7146 4273 8 (pbk.)
1. Economics--Political aspects. 2. Economic policy. 3 India-
-Economic policy. 4. Ideology. I. Nayyar, Deepak.
HB74.P65E36   1997   97-17414
338.9--dc21   CIP

Printed in Great Britain by
Bookcraft (Bath) Ltd, Midsomer Norton, Avon

Contents

EXPERIENCE
The Indian Context

Contributors

AMIYA KUMAR BAGCHI taught in Presidency College, Calcutta; Department of Economics, Calcutta University; University of Cambridge; University of Bristol and the Roskilde University, Denmark. His books include *Private Investment in India, 1900–1939* (Cambridge: Cambridge University Press, 1972); *The Political Economy of Underdevelopment* (Cambridge: Cambridge University Press, 1982); *The Evolution of the State Bank of India: The Roots 1806–1876*, Parts I and II (Bombay: Oxford University Press, 1987); *Public Intervention and Industrial Restructuring in China, India and the Republic of Korea* (New Delhi: ILO-ARTEP, 1987); *The Presidency Banks and the Indian Economy 1876–1914* (Calcutta: Oxford University Press, 1989). He has also edited a number of books, the latest of which is *Democracy and Development* published by Macmillan, London. He is at present Director of the Centre for Studies in Social Sciences, Calcutta.

AMIT BHADURI, born in 1940, is a distinguished economist, known internationally for his unorthodox analysis of economic problems. Educated in Calcutta, MIT and Cambridge (where he received his Ph.D.), he has taught in many universities around the world. He has written nearly 50 articles in international journals and two books, translated into several European languages.

TERENCE J. BYRES is Professor of Political Economy at the School of Oriental and African Studies, University of London. He was a founder-editor of the *Journal of Peasant Studies*, and continues as one of its co-editors. His new book, *Capitalism from Above and Capitalism from Below* was published in 1996.

NIRMAL KUMAR CHANDRA has been teaching Economics at the Indian Institute of Management, Calcutta. His interests include the former USSR, China and, above all, India. He has published one book: *The Retarded Economies: Foreign Domination and Class Relations in India and Other Emerging Nations* (Bombay: Oxford University Press, 1988).

C.P. CHANDRASEKHAR teaches at the Centre for Economic Studies and Planning. His research interests include the industrialisation experience of developing countries and the economics of State intervention in the Third World.

PRAMIT CHAUDHURI is Reader in Economics in the School of African and Asian Studies at the University of Sussex and was Dean of the School from 1980 to 1984. He was educated at the Presidency College Calcutta; University College, Cardiff, and King's College, Cambridge. He has been a visiting lecturer/ Professor at the Delhi School of Economics, the People's University of China, Beijing, and the Department of Political Economy, University of Pavia, Italy. He was until recently Managing Editor and Book Review Editor for the *Journal of Development Studies.* His publications include: *The Indian Economy: Poverty and Development* (Crosby Lockwood Staples, 1979); *The Economic Theory of Growth* (Harvester Wheatsheaf, 1989); and as co-author, R. Cassen *et al., Does Aid Work?* (Oxford: Clarendon Press, 1994); he has also edited two volumes of readings on Indian economic development.

ARUN GHOSH took his M.A. in Economics from the University of Allahbad in 1944, and his Ph.D. from the University of London in 1949. He taught Economics at the University of Lucknow, and later joined the Government of India to work for Professor P.C. Mahalanobis. He retired in 1983 as Chairman of the Bureau of Industrial Costs and Prices. He was, thereafter, Vice-Chairman, West Bengal State Planning Board, and finally, Member of the Union Planning Commission. Dr Ghosh has written four books; *Prices and Economic Fluctuations in India* (1979); *West Bengal Landscapes* (1988); *Planning in India: The Challenge for the Nineties* (1991); and *India in Transition: Economic Policy Options* (1993).

JAYATI GHOSH is Associate Professor at the Centre for Economic Studies and Planning, Jawaharlal Nehru University, New Delhi. She obtained her Ph.D. from the University of Cambridge, England, and subsequently held a Fellowship at Darwin College, Cambridge. She has worked on land rent and agrarian relations, employment patterns, external debt of developing countries, domestic inter-sectoral relations, aspects of the international economy and structural adjustment policies. Her current research interests are historical aspects of international economics and the nature of India's integration with the world economy.

IQBAL S. GULATI, born in March 1924, is an academic of long standing. He has taught Economics at Baroda and Trivandrum and has written extensively on issues in public finance and international finance.

N. KRISHNAJI is a senior fellow at the Centre for Economic and Social Studies, Hyderabad. Earlier, he held academic positions at the Indian Institute of Management, Calcutta, the Centre for Development Studies, Trivandrum and the Centre for Studies in Social Sciences, Calcutta. His recent publications include a collection of essays entitled *Pauperising Agriculture* (Bombay: Oxford University Press, 1992).

T.N. KRISHNAN has held academic positions at the Indian Institute of Management, Calcutta and the Centre for Development Studies, Trivandrum. He has also worked at the United Nations, most recently for the United Nations Fund for Population Activities. He is, at present, co-ordinating a UNDP national project on the financing of human development in India.

DEEPAK NAYYAR is Professor of Economics at the Centre for Economic Studies and Planning, Jawaharlal Nehru University, New Delhi. Professor Nayyar is the author of *India's Exports and Export Policies* (Cambridge University Press, 1976), *Migration, Remittances and Capital Flows* (Oxford University Press, 1994) and *Economic Liberalization in India* (Orient Longman, 1996). He has also edited three books: *Economic Relations between Socialist Countries and the Third World* (Macmillan, 1977), *Industrial Growth and Stagnation: The Debate in India* (Oxford University Press, 1994) and *Trade and Industrialization* (Oxford University Press, 1997).

PRABHAT PATNAIK is a Professor at the Centre for Economic Studies and Planning, Jawaharlal Nehru University. He is the author of *Time, Inflation and Growth* (Calcutta, 1988), *Whatever Happened to Imperialism and Other Essays* (Delhi, 1995), and *Accumulation and Stability Under Capitalism* (Oxford, 1997). He has also edited two books: *Lenin and Imperialism* (Delhi, 1986) and *Macroeconomics* (Delhi, 1995).

UTSA PATNAIK has worked mainly in the area of development

problems, in particular the historical transformation of agrarian relations during industrialisation. Her publications include *The Agrarian Question and the Development of Capitalism in India* and *Peasant Class Differentiation: A Study in Method with Reference to Haryana.* At present she is Professor of Economics at the Centre for Economic Studies and Planning, Jawaharlal Nehru University, New Delhi.

RANJIT SAU is a Professor at the Indian Institute of Management, Calcutta, now visiting New Jersey Institute of Technology, Newark. He has taught in several universities in India and in the United States. Two of his books have been translated into Japanese in Tokyo: *Unequal Exchange, Imperialism and Underdevelopment* (Calcutta: Oxford University Press, 1978), and *Underdeveloped Capitalism and the General Law of Value* (Atlantic Heights, NJ: Humanities Press, 1984).

ABHIJIT SEN is a Professor at the Centre for Economic Studies and Planning, Jawaharlal Nehru University. He received his Ph.D. from the University of Cambridge, England, and has taught at the Universities of Sussex, Essex, Oxford and Cambridge. He has worked on the macroeconomics of developing countries, agriculture, employment and poverty.

REHMAN SOBHAN is at the Centre for Policy Dialogue, Dhaka. Earlier, he was Director General of the Bangladesh Institute of Development Studies. Dr Sobhan, who has a deep interest in development problems and public policy, has published several books and papers on these subjects.

A. VAIDYANATHAN is currently Professor Emeritus at Madras Institute of Development Studies, Madras. Educated at the Universities of Madras, Pittsburgh and Cornell, he has worked in the National Council of Applied Economics Research, New Delhi; the Perspective Planning Division of the Planning Commission; the Food and Agriculture Organisation, United Nations; the World Bank in Washington and the Centre for Development Studies, Trivandrum. He served as a member of the Planning Commission in 1990. The main focus of his research has been on various aspects of agricultural development and rural economy including analysis of agricultural growth, aspects of rural poverty, structure and trends in rural employment, water control and livestock. He has also contributed to the academic debates on the problems of overall planning.

Preface

Ashok Mitra is a man of many parts: academic, administrator, minister, parliamentarian, columnist and *littérateur*. However, this collection of essays in his honour is a tribute to him as an economist from colleagues and friends in the profession. The essays are marked by a discernible diversity. This was almost inevitable, for the interest and concerns of his friends, in economics as much as in life, range across a wide spectrum. Yet, there is a shared belief that ideology and experience, just as much as theory and policy, are inseparable in economics. This is, indeed, the common thread that runs through the essays.

This volume has been conceived and planned by an editorial committee consisting of Amit Bhaduri, Nirmal Kumar Chandra, N. Krishnaji, Deepak Nayyar, Prabhat Patnaik and Krishna Raj. A person like Ashok Mitra has so many friends and admirers that the volume could have been much larger. Inevitably, we had to be selective in inviting contributions. It was also inevitable that a few people who wanted to contribute were unable to do so because of other pressing commitments. We are grateful, none the less, that so many found the time to write papers.

I am indebted to my colleagues on the editorial committee for their help and unstinted support in this venture, and am grateful to the authors for their contributions to the volume. Many others have helped in a variety of ways, in particular Terence Byres whose help went much beyond the call of duty. Ananya Ghosh Dastidar provided valuable assistance in the preparation of the manuscript for publication.

Everyone associated with this volume would join me in expressing their sorrow at the death of Pramit Chaudhuri and that of T.N. Krishnan, who contributed to this volume but sadly did not live to see its publication. Both epitomised the liberal intellectual tradition and combined academic excellence with remarkable human qualities.

New Delhi   DEEPAK NAYYAR
October 1996

Ashok Mitra: A Biographical Sketch

Deepak Nayyar

Ashok Mitra was born on 10 April 1928 at Dhaka in what is now Bangladesh. He went to school and grew up in this quiet provincial town which was then the intellectual capital of East Bengal. He enrolled as an undergraduate in the Department of Economics at the University of Dhaka from where he obtained his BA Honours degree, on the eve of India's independence, in 1947. Dhaka was, at the time, a hub of intellectual and creative activity. Mitra became very much a part of this milieu. It was a period which marked the beginning of lifelong friendships, notwithstanding subsequent ideological differences, with A.K. Dasgupta and S.R. Sen under whom he studied economics. Around this time, outside the classroom, he met Sachin Chaudhuri (founder-editor of *Economic Weekly*), Budhadev Basu (novelist and literary critic), and Samar Sen (poet and political commentator). These relationships blossomed into friendships which went on to span lifetimes. It was also the beginning of his engagement with politics and ideology as he threw himself into communist student activism. After partition, he stayed on in Dhaka for a few months but then moved to Banaras Hindu University where his teacher A.K. Dasgupta became the University Professor of Economics. He completed his MA in Economics at Banaras in 1949. Thereafter, Mitra taught at the University of Lucknow for a couple of years. Lucknow, then, had stalwarts like the two Mukherjis, Dhurjati Prasad and Radha Kamal, as well as the latter's brother, Radha Kumud Mukherjee. It was a period of learning for the young Mitra which sharpened his academic inclinations.

The years from 1951 to 1954 were spent at The Hague in the Netherlands working on his doctoral dissertation under the supervision of Jan Tinbergen (the first Nobel Laureate in Economics). His thesis, *The Share of Wages in National Income,* which was published by the Netherlands Centraal Planbureau in 1954, and reprinted by Oxford University Press in 1980, gained wide recognition as an important contribution. It was characterised by a combination of rigorous theorising, careful sifting of empirical evidence, and a passion for political economy. Mitra set out a critique of Michal Kalecki's theory of income distribution which he described as tautological. There was a novel attempt to measure the degree of monopoly for the economy as a whole (as distinct from the usual industry-wise degree of monopoly) over a long period, based on an empirical analysis of income distribution in the United Kingdom from 1870 to 1938. Introducing a number of other factors, Mitra endeavoured to develop a theory of income distribution in a capitalist economy to reach a conclusion which was exactly the opposite of that reached by Kalecki. He found that an increase in the price of raw materials will increase and not lower the share of wages in national income. This debate has not been pursued in the subsequent literature on the subject but has some significance in the real world. Should trade unions in the industrialised countries, for instance, support or oppose the attempts by developing countries to form cartels among exporters of primary commodities so as to improve their terms of trade?

The next dozen years were spent almost entirely on research and teaching. Yet, it was a period which provided the foundations for Ashok Mitra's shift from theory to policy in subsequent years and from economics to politics later in life. On his return from the Netherlands, Mitra worked for one year in the Ministry of Finance in New Delhi and for another year at the Economic Commission for Asia and the Far East in Bangkok. This was followed by two years of research at the National Council of Applied Economic Research in New Delhi and four years of teaching at the Economic Development Institute of the World Bank in Washington DC. Mitra then moved to the Indian Institute of Management in Calcutta, which had just been established, where he spent three years as Professor of Economics.

During this phase of research and teaching, Mitra was engaged in debates on planning and development, particularly with reference to the Indian experience. In 1957, he wrote a note on 'The Concept of Subsistence' which was published in the *Economic Weekly*. Considering the interminable debate on the subject, his conception was startlingly simple: it was the absence of a surplus. Thus, the subsistence farmer is one who produces just as much as the family consumes with nothing left for savings. In this approach one need not worry either about the nutritional threshold of poverty (which is difficult to measure) or about the social and cultural factors affecting living standards. When the standard of living goes up, so does the subsistence level. This conception was different from Lassale's 'iron law of wages' where wages never exceed the physiological subsistence minimum. It was more consistent with Marx's idea that the wage level is determined by convention just as it was consistent with a major premise of classical political economy that savings in a capitalist economy come from non-wage incomes. There were also contributions to the debate on planning, such as his critique of optimality in the Mahalanobis model which developed the Shigeto Tsuru critique further. Such academic research was combined with an orientation towards policy as Mitra was associated with advising the world's first elected communist government in the State of Kerala during the late 1950s.

The transition from the ivory tower of academia to the real world of policy formulation, when it came, therefore posed no problems for Ashok Mitra. It was soon apparent that he had an equal flair for both. Mitra moved from Calcutta to Delhi when he became Chairman of the Agricultural Prices Commission in 1966. This tenure of three years, Mitra was to reflect later, was not only enjoyable as it yielded close friendships, such as the one with Dharam Narain, but also productive as it shaped his later work on the significance of inter-sectoral terms of trade in the process of economic development. In 1969, he was appointed Chief Economic Adviser to the Government of India in the Ministry of Finance. During his tenure, Prime Minister Indira Gandhi's government took three major policy decisions in which Mitra exercised an important influence. First, commercial banks in the private sector were nationalised. Second, priority sector lending, for agriculture and small-scale industries, was introduced. Third, a structure of differential rates of interest, which distinguished between borrowers and uses, was put in place. There were such successes. But there were also problems. Mitra became increasingly disenchanted with the emerging political situation and resigned in 1972. He left Delhi and returned to Calcutta.

For the next three years, until 1975, he was a National Fellow of the Indian Council of Social Science Research. It was during this period that he wrote *Terms of Trade and Class Relations*. This book, which came to be recognised as an outstanding piece of work in political economy, was based on Mitra's rich understanding of economics as ideology and experience. In this monograph, Ashok Mitra sought to explore the relationship between relative prices, income distribution and economic growth. He argued that it is not possible to study the course of economic policy in isolation from the politics of class relations, for, in every country, political biases influence the formulation of economic policy. These biases are not accidental but follow from property relations which govern income distribution. The evolving structure of property, in turn, is determined and shaped by the class character of the State. The manipulation of relative prices between agriculture and industry emerges as a major weapon in this conflicting pursuit of class interests in predominantly agrarian economies attempting to industrialise.

Terms of trade and class relations were, therefore, the theme that ran through the book. But it had three distinct, though closely related, parts. The first part traced the history of ideas about the fundamental role of the terms of exchange between agriculture and industry in the process of economic development: from Adam Smith, David Ricardo and Thomas Malthus through Karl Marx and Rosa Luxemburg to Preobrazhensky and Bukharin. The next part developed an analytical framework: it explored the relationship between relative prices and income distribution to discuss how class forces operating through terms of trade affect the nature of as well as prospects of growth in an underdeveloped economy. The message to emerge was that, in all societies, income distribution determines movements in relative prices, while the latter, in turn, are determined by the exercise of monopoly or monopsony power. The final part, focusing on the political economy of Indian development, put forward a clear hypothesis: the exercise of political authority and State power in India represents an arrangement between the rural oligarchy on the one hand and the industrial bourgeoisie on the other. While the bourgeoisie control the industrial sector and dominate the working class, they also need the rural oligarchy, which can deliver the votes from the countryside and help maintain them in power. This alliance of convenience survives on the basis of mutual trade-offs, for even though political interests often coincide, economic contradictions abound. A principal manifestation of the trade-off principle, Mitra argued, was the steady increase in the relative prices of food and raw materials sold by the surplus farmers. But the terms of trade necessitated by the coalition between the rural oligarchy and the industrial bourgeoisie were corrosive of growth and wholly detrimental to the interests of the poor.

In a world where orthodox economics is increasingly divorced from political realities, this book provided a refreshing contrast from its wider perspective of political economy. It was an explicitly ideological book with a particular view of the world. And it was all the more commendable for that. For ideology is mostly implicit and rarely explicit in academic economics. In the process, it conveyed a basic lesson to the profession of economics. The lasting importance of the book, I believe, was in its moral that 'economic phenomena are determined by political categories and processes: to miss out their interaction is to rob social analysis of its most fundamental content'.

Ashok Mitra spent the academic year 1975–76 as a Visiting Professor in the Institute of Development Studies at the University of

Sussex. He returned to Calcutta thereafter, accepting an appointment as Professor of Economics at the Indian Statistical Institute. It was to be a short interlude in academia.

Mitra was an outspoken critic of the authoritarian regime during the Emergency. It was a difficult period for him, as for many others. When elections were announced, Mitra decided to become a full-time political activist of the Communist Party of India (Marxist), having been an adherent of the communist cause all his life. He was the Minister of Finance, Development and Planning, in the Government of West Bengal for nearly a decade (with a brief interruption) between 1977 and 1987, a period that saw significant changes in the West Bengal countryside. His role in shaping the economic policies of the state government was critical. At the same time, in the national context, he was a leading spokesman for fiscal federalism who emphasised the need for decentralisation and devolution in centre–state financial relations.

The next phase of Ashok Mitra's life began with his resignation as a Cabinet Minister in the Government of West Bengal. In the years that followed he devoted himself to writing extensively in English and Bengali. This was his incarnation as a columnist who wrote with passion about economy, polity and society. His ideological conviction combined with a concern for the poor and a commitment to national development earned him the status of being the moral voice among the literati in the country.

Six years after his resignation as Finance Minister in the Government of West Bengal, Mitra returned to the fold of the Communist Party of India (Marxist). He was elected as a Member of Parliament in the Rajya Sabha as a candidate of the Communist Party of India (Marxist), in August 1993, from West Bengal. In the period since then, he has been an important contributor to the debate on the economy, as an outspoken critic of economic liberalisation, both inside and outside parliament. He has also continued his role as a perceptive and sensitive commentator in the wider context of polity and society – for he always was, and remains, a person with a missionary zeal for establishing an egalitarian society.

Mitra is a rare person with many talents as an academic, administrator, minister, parliamentarian, columnist and *littérateur*. But that is not all. He is also a man of many parts whose interests in life extend much beyond economics and politics. He has a passion for cricket, whether test matches or one-day matches, and loves to write about it in his inimitable style. He is at home among poets and artists. He has written poetry, essays and novels in Bengali. In 1996, he received the *Sahitya Akademi* award for his contribution to Bengali literature, with a citation for his collection of essays *Taal Betaal.*

Ashok Mitra is versatile in his talents. And there is a diversity in his interests. These attributes are reflected in his wide circle of friends and admirers across the spectrum of professions, ideologies and generations. Behind his restless, almost fidgety nature, there is a warmth and affection which has led to close and lifelong friendships. His deep affection for children and close rapport with young people is remarkable for a person who is both shy and intense. In this social dimension of Mitra's life, he owes much to his wonderful wife Gauri, who has kept open house for the past four decades as friends from near and far have dropped in for a chat, for a meal or for a weekend in the Mitra household.

This collection of essays is a tribute to him as an economist. It does not even attempt to span the range of his versatile talents and diverse interests as a human being.

IDEOLOGY:
THE NATIONAL CONTEXT

Unemployment as Failure to Exchange

Prabhat Patnaik

I

Why does involuntary unemployment, in the sense of an excess supply of labour at the prevailing real wage rate, exist? Some economists, in the US in particular, believe of course that it does not. But those who recognise its existence can find three different possible answers to this question in the economic literature, which singly or jointly are supposed to underlie any particular situation of involuntary unemployment. The first of these focuses on a shortage of the means of production, or what Marx called constant capital: the available stock of equipment is insufficient, given its technologically determined labour requirement(s), to employ the total available workforce. It may so happen, in certain exceptional cases, however, that the shortage is not one of equipment in general, but of some basic current input, that is, of equipment in the particular sector producing that input. The first argument states, therefore, that involuntary unemployment cannot be removed because there is not enough equipment, whether in general or in particular critical sectors, to employ everyone who is willing to work at the going real wage. The hallmark of this argument is that, if it holds, no reduction in real wages can possibly increase employment.

The second answer, which is the Keynesian–Kaleckian answer, is well known: it states that idle equipment exists together with involuntary unemployment, but any lowering of unemployment would produce a higher total output for which there would be no commensurate higher demand, because the higher *ex ante* savings out of this higher output would exceed the autonomously given level of real investment. Employment is what it is because it produces a level of output which is just what would be demanded.

The third answer adduces real wage rigidity as the cause of

involuntary unemployment. It covers the neo-classical Pigovian case according to which (eschewing parables about malleable capital) involuntary unemployment can co-exist with idle equipment (of older vintages involving lower labour productivity) because employing the jobless would be profitable only if they could be paid less than the prevailing real wages (whether or not those already employed are also paid less than the prevailing real wages in such a case is, strictly speaking, immaterial), but for some reason this is not possible. The reason may be the resistance of the unemployed to becoming underpaid employees when wage-discrimination is practised (which does not mean that unemployment is 'voluntary'), or the resistance of those already employed to a real wage cut where there is no wage discrimination, or the resistance of the already employed even when there is wage discrimination, to the creation of underpaid jobs, for fear that it would 'spoil' the market, or, putting the matter in general terms, the necessity on the part of the employers to pay 'efficiency wages'.

This third answer, however, is not confined to the neo-classical case. It also covers the case of disproportionality referred to as the 'wage goods' shortage: even assuming in other words that there are no 'marginal' vintages of equipment, that equipment is homogeneous within the wage goods sector as well as within the non-wage goods sector but cannot be shifted from one to the other, employment may be limited by the fact that the wage goods sector is disproportionately small at the prevailing downward inflexible real wages, notwithstanding the existence of idle equipment in the non-wage goods sector. What is central to this third explanation, and what distinguishes it from the first, is the fact that a lowering of real wages in this case would increase employment – in other words, it postulates employment as a diminishing function of real wages.

Keynes, too, subscribed to such an employment function, although it is not necessary for the Keynesian answer. But while subscribing to such a function, Keynes held that real wages could only be lowered through a rise in the level of investment or in the marginal propensity to consume.

The purpose of this chapter is to argue that a very important category of unemployment is not covered by any of these three explanations which invoke, respectively, insufficient equipment, insufficient demand, and rigidity of real wages. While this category of unemployment is relevant, especially in the context of the underdeveloped countries, it can be established as a general category, in other words without specifically taking into account the characteristics of an underdeveloped country. This is the approach of the next section.

II

To understand this category of unemployment, we have to recognise a fourth possible explanation of involuntary unemployment which is *sui generis*: even assuming that investment is not autonomous – that is, all savings are invested – even assuming that idle means of production co-exist with unemployment, even assuming that the unemployed are willing to work at whatever real wages are offered to them and that those already employed are unconcerned about the wages offered to the unemployed, in short, even assuming that none of the three above explanations hold, unemployment may nevertheless exist because a reduction in unemployment, while it increases output, does not commensurately increase the demand for the particular kind of output produced by the hitherto unemployed.

Central to this fourth explanation is the proposition that the outputs produced by the different pieces of equipment are not homogeneous, at any rate as far as the buyers are concerned, and that the mere assumption of flexibility in the relative prices between these heterogeneous outputs is not enough to bring about an increase in employment or capacity utilisation. The idea of heterogeneous outputs will, of course, be readily accepted: an Indian car is different from a Japanese car, and handloom cloth is different from cloth produced on an automatic loom, but the usual belief is that if the relative prices between the two varieties of cars or the two varieties of cloth are flexible, then an equilibrium will exist where both will be demanded, and, unless one of the three explanations mentioned in section I holds, there will be no involuntary unemployment. It is this last belief, in the presumed efficacy of price flexibility, which the fourth explanation challenges; there are, in short, a range of real-life situations of unemployment not explained by the three standard explanations, which represent equilibrium configurations even on the assumption of flexible prices.

To see this, let us assume that there are two economies with two different types of equipment. A unit of equipment of each type requires a certain amount of labour (not necessarily the same for both) to operate it. With the corresponding amount of labour, a unit of equipment of each type can produce either β units of itself or β units of a consumption good, that is, the output-capital ratio is β in both sectors. The two different consumption goods, however, although catering to roughly similar requirements, are not identical in the eyes of the buyers: the capitalists of both sectors, even if we assume (temporarily) that they invest exclusively within their respective sectors, wish invariably to consume the commodity turned out by equipment 1; the workers on equipment 2 consume only the commodity they produce, while the workers on equipment 1, in the aggregate, consume the two goods in a ratio which depends upon their relative price. In each sector, let us assume (for the moment) that the wage rate is a fixed magnitude denominated in terms of the commodity produced; all wages are consumed, while a fixed, but equal, proportion of profits in the two sectors is saved and invested.

It is easy to see that, in equilibrium, equipment of the first type can never remain unutilised. No matter what the relative price between the two sectors' outputs may be, whatever is produced in the first sector would be demanded. Whatever accrues to the capitalists out of this sector's output would be spent on this output itself; and whatever accrues to the workers would partly be spent on this output and partly exchanged against the output of sector 2 whose capitalists would consume whatever sector 1 output is given to them in such exchange. In other words, since the profits in this sector are either consumed or invested, using this product itself, and since consumption by sector 2 capitalists of this product is equal to the excess of sector 1 workers' wage bill in this product over what they consume of it, it follows that sector 1 equilibrium must be a full-capacity equilibrium, in which case its output in real terms must be $K_1 . \beta$, employment $K_1 . l_1$, and wage-bill $K_1 . l_1 . w_1$ where K_1, l_1 and w_1 denote respectively the equipment stock, the employment per unit of equipment, and the product wage rate in sector 1.

The case of sector 2, however, is altogether different. Here, out of what accrues to them, what the sector 2 capitalists do not sell to sector 1 workers, they do not themselves consume, since by assumption they do not consume their own product. This does not mean that full-capacity production in equilibrium is impossible in sector 2; it only means that it is not inevitable. To see what the equilibrium output in sector 2 would be, let us for a moment assume that sector 2 capitalists collude to act as a profit-maximising monopolist. Denoting this sector's output by 0_2, price in terms of the sector 1 product by p, product wage rate by w_2, employment per unit of equipment by l_2, and saving propensity out of profit by s, we can say that sector 2 capitalists maximise

$$p.s.0_2 (1 - w_2 . l_2 / \beta) + p. (1-s).0_2 (1 - w_2 . l_2/\beta)$$

where $(1-s).0_2 . (1 - w_2 . l_2 / \beta) = D (p : K_1 . l_1 . w_1)$, the term $D (.)$ denoting the demand function by sector 1 workers for sector 2's product.

This can be written alternatively as:

$$p. D (p ; K_1 . l_1 . w_1) / (1-s)$$

whose derivative with respect to price reaches zero when the price elasticity of demand for the product is unity. Now, the point at which this happens may be such that full capacity output is less than demand, or it may be such that full capacity output is larger. If we denote by (D^*, p^*) the point on the demand curve (for givens $K_1 . l_1 . w_1$) where its elasticity is equal to unity, then the equilibrium output of sector 2 would be

$$0_2 = \text{min.} [D^* / (1-s) (1 - w_2 . l_2 / \beta) ; K_2 . \beta]$$

Equilibrium output, in other words, would be either the profit-maximising output or the full-capacity output, whichever is smaller. If the demand for sector 2's product becomes inelastic below a certain price, then lowering its price further becomes unprofitable: the relative price between the two products becomes fixed, and unemployment and unutilised capacity can well exist at the level of demand corresponding to this price. In other words, unemployment in sector 2 can exist because any increase in output would not lead to larger profit-realisation in the form of the commodity which the capitalists in that sector wish to obtain.

What we have here is a multiplier of a very different sort from the Keynesian multiplier. In sector 2 the level of output is determined by a kind of foreign trade multiplier. But this foreign trade multiplier operates not because the terms of trade, or the relative price, is fixed for autonomous reasons, but because the profit-maximising behaviour of the capitalists itself fixes the relative price and hence the amount of 'exports'. It may be objected, of course, that in looking at the profit maximising behaviour of the capitalists we have assumed that they behave like a monopolist. But if the demand for their product becomes inelastic at a certain price, then even if the capitalists did not behave like a monopolist to start with, there would be a strong inducement for them to collude and become a collective monopolist instead of undercutting one another in a manner which, from their point of view, is counterproductive.

When such unemployment exists, it is clear that a reduction in wage rate in sector 2 cannot possibly alleviate it, since it would leave D^* and p^* unchanged; on the contrary, by raising the share of profits in sector 2, it would have the effect of increasing the 'import intensity' of that sector and hence of lowering the level of employment. In other words, for sector 2, a lowering of the wage rate would leave the 'exports' to sector 1 unchanged, but lower the value of the foreign trade multiplier, resulting in lower output and more unemployment.

The effect of a reduction in the wage rate in sector 1 on employment in sector 2, however, is less clear. Such a reduction would mean a shift in the position of the demand curve for sector 2's product. Whether or not this raises employment in sector 2 would depend upon whether the point on the new demand curve corresponding to unit elasticity of demand is to the right of the similar point on the old demand curve. Exactly the same conclusion holds in the case where investment in sector 1 is taken to be autonomous rather than merely being equal to savings, that is, if income distribution in sector 1 is assumed to follow a Kaldorian rather than a Kaleckian rule. Stimulating investment in sector 1 may or may not stimulate employment in sector 2.

Finally, let us drop the assumption made until now that each sector invests its savings exclusively within itself. It is more plausible to assume that sector 2 capitalists would be interested in investing in sector 1 rather than in their own sector if demand inelasticity is an established fact. In such a case employment and output in sector 2 will be even lower than what would have resulted if they had invested in their own sector, because D^* will remain unchanged while the value of the foreign trade multiplier will shrink. Sector 2's output in this case will not be $D^* / (1-s) (1 - w_2 .l_2 /\beta)$, but $D^* / (1-w_2 l_2 / \beta)$ which is distinctly lower; employment will accordingly also be lower.

III

The claim that what we have been talking about constitutes a novel variant of involuntary unemployment can very legitimately be disputed. In a general sense, after all, unemployment of the sort we are considering arises because of a deficiency of demand for the product of sector 2 (or, more appropriately, of economy 2), so that its genesis is ultimately traceable to Keynes–Kalecki, notwithstanding the obvious formal difference between an excess of *ex ante* savings and an excess of *ex ante* demand for imports which cannot be paid for. What is more, even if we are rigid about distinguishing between the Keynesian and the foreign trade multipliers, the latter sort of multiplier has in any case been invoked to explain involuntary unemployment by Kaldor;[1] what is the point, then, in presenting what at first sight appears to be a rehash of Kaldor as a novel idea?

The reason for emphasising the novelty of the concept being presented here is not 'salesmanship'; it has to do with the fact that involuntary unemployment of the sort discussed here, if it exists, is exceedingly difficult, alas, to overcome; far more difficult, indeed, than either Keynesian unemployment or the trade-related unemployment discussed by Kaldor. Emphasising the *sui generis* nature of this unemployment, which in my view characterises underdeveloped countries, is essential therefore in ridding ourselves of facile notions about ways of overcoming underdevelopment, and for coming to terms with the real complexities of the task.

Overcoming Keynesian unemployment requires essentially a 'budgetary trick'.[2] True, as the NAIRU literature has argued more recently, and as Joan Robinson suggested long ago through her concept of the 'inflationary barrier', the use of this budgetary trick may give rise to accelerating inflation; but that only underscores the fact that State intervention in demand management cannot reduce involuntary unemployment below a certain level, which may itself be quite high, in a capitalist economy.[3] It does not negate the proposition that the way to overcome Keynesian unemployment is essentially through a budgetary trick.

It is also true that in a world characterised by many nation States, there exist constraints upon each state with regard to the extent to which it can intervene in demand management without causing balance of payments problems, constraints arising from the fact that the current balance may turn negative as demand expands, and also from the fact that finance capital may flow out, whether because of the negative current balance or in independent anticipation of a declining currency. But this, too, does not negate the fact that Keynesian unemployment can be overcome with the use of a 'budgetary trick'. What the point about the current balance turning negative shows is that the budgetary trick can work only up to a point but no further. And the point about financial fluidity underscores the constraints upon the nation state; it does not deny that a budgetary trick, if it could be used, is all that is required for overcoming Keynesian unemployment.

The possibility of a negative current balance is the point of departure for Kaldor, who also talked of unemployment arising because of a failure to exchange. But in his world, there are manufactured goods and primary products, and the terms of trade between the two are fixed, because, in the manufacturing sector, wages are fixed (in terms of primary products) and there is mark-up pricing. Unemployment on account of insufficient exports can therefore exist in the manufacturing sector. The present argument is entirely different from this: it is concerned with buyers' preference for one kind of manufactured good over another, which is why primary products do not figure in the argument, both sectors being taken to be vertically integrated, and demand conditions assume importance in the determination of relative price.

One aspect of the difference between the two arguments should be noted. In the Kaldorian world, a reduction in real wages increases employment (which is why I have not listed the Kaldorian explanation of unemployment separately from the three explanations given in section I above), while in the world of the present chapter, a reduction in real wages reduces employment. A reduction in real wages is not so difficult to effect in an underdeveloped country; if unemployment in such an economy was of the Kaldorian kind, then overcoming it would not pose such a big problem. But if it has to do with buyers' preferences, then changing these preferences is surely an exceedingly complex job; and denying the exercise of these preferences merely through controls turns out to be singularly ineffective in the long run. It is because of this basic complexity in the task of overcoming this type of unemployment that it deserves *sui generis* treatment.

IV

It should be clear by now why this kind of unemployment has not figured in the economic literature, The implicit assumption all along has been that the demand for sector 2 products, and hence for both products, remains elastic with respect to changes in their relative price until full capacity use. In other words, unlike here, where we have made rigid assumptions (such as the assumption that all capitalists consume only sector 1 products, workers in sector 2 consume only sector 2 products) and then raised the possibility that the demand for 2's product may at a certain point become price inelastic, the usual belief has been that if two products meet roughly the same kind of requirement, then there must be significant substitutability between them as far as all consumers are concerned, so that demand for either good must be elastic with respect to variations in relative price. After all, in the end, if the relative price of one of the commodities approaches zero, why should anyone consume the other commodity at all? It follows, then, that variations in the relative price should be perfectly adequate to ensure full employment all around, unless one of the three considerations mentioned earlier intervenes to prevent it.

The problem with this view, and indeed with many of the extant theories of structural change, such as Schumpeter's, which treat price as a determinant of the extent to which goods and services are substituted for one another, is the following: people typically consume commodities not in isolation but in clusters. A person living in a predominantly glass-fronted house for instance requires curtains, burglar-proofing, a temperature-regulating system, and so on. In short, a whole bundle of commodities, more-or-less complementary to one another, are consumed together, and constitute what can be called a 'lifestyle'. Within each bundle or cluster, one commodity may be substituted by another, which also happens to go with the other commodities in the cluster, depending on the relative price; but price variations would not induce the substitution of one commodity by another if the latter, while fulfilling the same functional role, is incompatible with the other commodities in the cluster. In a society in which the use of dish-washing machines is widely prevalent, for example, relative price variations may result in the substitution of one brand of china for another, but no amount of reduction in the price of brass plates would induce consumers to shift from china to brass. Likewise, the choice between 'clusters', that is, between 'lifestyles', is not a function of the relative prices of alternative lifestyles the way consumer theory usually depicts such choices to be. The desire for a transition from one lifestyle to another is culturally determined; and when a transition has occurred it is usually irreversible in the event of a cheapening of the earlier lifestyle. It is this which makes the demand for a whole range of commodities, belonging to a 'cluster' or a 'lifestyle', becoming progressively outmoded for complex cultural reasons, price inelastic over a certain range.

It may of course be argued that this point about the irreversibility of lifestyles, or the incompatibility of certain commodities with certain lifestyles, is being exaggerated and that over a sufficiently long period relative prices do make a perceptible difference to consumer choice, even between commodities belonging to apparently different lifestyles. But even if this were true for the long run, the fact of short- and medium-term price inelasticity of demand for a number of commodities would be quite enough, in their case, to serve as an explanation of an endogenously determined floor to the relative price variation, and as an explanation of unemployment. And in such a case, if relative prices do not fall below a certain level, the question of the difference that would have been made in the long run had they fallen sufficiently becomes an irrelevant one.

What is necessary for the argument here, moreover, is not that for every commodity belonging to a lifestyle that is becoming progressively outmoded, demand should be price inelastic (adaptations of particular commodities surely do occur, as indeed does a revival of interest in 'older' or 'traditional' commodities), but that this should be so for a certain number of them. This is what characterises the context of the underdeveloped countries in particular; it is to capture their predicament in a stark manner that the somewhat rigid assumption of section II have been made. Let us now turn to the specific case of the underdeveloped countries.

V

The experience of the colonial period meant historically in the underdeveloped world a sharp disjunction between the pattern of consumption and the pattern of production, leading to what has been called a process of deindustrialisation.[4] To be sure, the shift in consumption in favour of imported goods was occasioned by a considerable cheapening of machine-made goods as a result of the Industrial Revolution; but even where the local artisans cut into their subsistence to remain competitive, the secular shift away from their products towards imported goods continued, forcing many of them to become general labourers in search of casual employment, which was relatively scarce, or to continue as underemployed artisans. This was the genesis of the modern problem of unemployment in the underdeveloped countries.

The obstacle to a removal or reduction of mass unemployment today in these countries can scarcely be located in an absolute shortage of equipment; the unemployed can surely be absorbed in activities requiring little equipment, or at best simple equipment, which can itself be produced within a relatively short period of time. The shortage of wage goods, in particular of agricultural commodities, appears at first sight to be a more formidable obstacle. But even if this is an immediate constraint in many countries, it does not follow that this constraint cannot be overcome gradually with agricultural supplies adjusting over time to increased demand as the unemployed are progressively absorbed into employment.[5] Indeed it has been argued in the context of particular countries that the constraint upon the growth of agricultural production itself arises on the demand side, in the sense that an acceleration in its growth would, in the existing situation, result in over-production.[6]

The real obstacle to a reduction in unemployment lies not in an agricultural wage-goods shortage, but in the fact that such a reduction, even if accompanied by increased supplies of agricultural wage-goods, would give rise to increased outputs of a kind for which there would be no commensurate increase in demand: the additional surplus income accruing to the agricultural capitalists and rich peasants on account of larger agricultural production would generate demand for commodities which are different from what the hitherto unemployed can produce and which are not obtainable in exchange for the latter. A deliberate policy of unemployment reduction in such circumstances would lead, therefore, to a piling up of unsold goods on the one hand, and the creation of excess demand elsewhere which would eventually spill over into an external trade deficit. This, incidentally, would also happen even when agricultural wage-goods production does not increase commensurately, but rural real wages can be pushed down with impunity through a profit inflation (unless the higher profits can be taxed away). In short, the argument advanced in the previous sections represents a stylisation of what is perhaps a crucial constraint upon employment expansion in underdeveloped countries.

VI

The theoretical discussion in section II considered only a single-period situation. In this section we shall discuss what may happen to unemployment over a sequence of periods. Since the single-period output of sector 2 is determined by the foreign trade multiplier, as long as the value of this multiplier remains unchanged through time the rate of growth of output in sector 2 depends entirely on the rate of growth of its exports (if trade is to remain balanced). The latter, in turn, depends on the rate of growth of output of sector 1 and the changes, if any, in the amount of sector 2 product demanded per unit of sector 1 output.

Moreover, in addition to the labour demand caused through growth in sector 2 itself, there may also be net immigration from sector 2 to sector 1 which would also affect unemployment in sector 2. The crux of the matter in other words is the following: what happens to unemployment in sector 2 is determined entirely by impulses emanating from sector 1.

Let us assume that the economy where sector 1 is located controls immigration in order to match the growth of its total work-force with the growth of labour demand within it. Then, if labour productivities remain unchanged everywhere and if the demand per unit output in each sector for the other sector's product remains unchanged, then unemployment in sector 2 would disappear over time, provided that the rate of growth of output in sector 1 (which I assume always exceeds that of its own workforce) is higher than the workforce growth in the economy with sector 2.

These, however, are stringent assumptions. Process and product innovations in both the sectors, and particularly in sector 1, would be raising labour productivity. And this, *ceteris paribus*, makes the absorption of the unemployed workforce of sector 2 difficult. The problem is compounded if, while sector 2 capitalists continue to prefer the sector 1 product, the demand per unit of product-wage of sector 1 workers for sector 2's product declines over time as they move to newer 'lifestyles' with rising incomes. In such a case, even assuming that the share of the workers remains unchanged in both the sectors, the growth of exports from sector 2 will be less than the growth of output in sector 1, so that the growth rates of the two sectors would diverge. It follows, then, that sector 2, which I take to be synonymous with the underdeveloped countries, may well turn out to be a permanent abode of substantial and non-vanishing labour reserves. The problem of unemployment in underdeveloped countries would not exist if the entire income generated by employing the unemployed was spent exclusively on the goods they produce, but since the local capitalists shun these goods while the developed country consumers have little use for them, unemployment would persist.

From the foregoing it may well be thought that if the underdeveloped countries changed their production structure to produce the goods catering to the new 'lifestyles' which are being imported (for example, if, in terms of our model, the production of sector 1 goods was implanted in sector 2), then their labour reserves could be absorbed and unemployment eliminated. This, however, is not necessarily true. The new 'lifestyles' represent an emulation of what prevails in the West. Embedded in the cultural factors that determine the transition to a new lifestyle is a strong element of cultural hegemony of the West. The desire among the affluent sections in these societies is not just for a new cluster of commodities, but a cluster which is exactly the same as prevails in the West. What prevails in the West, however, is not static but keeps changing through process and product innovations that, incidentally, also have the effect of raising labour productivity.

Within the underdeveloped country, then, the choice becomes limited to two alternatives. Either the structure of production is allowed to change, to adjust to the desire of the affluent for ever-new lifestyles, in keeping with the changing lifestyles in the developed world, in which case the syndrome of a continuous labour productivity increase in one segment of the economy (together with a continuous increase either in the wage-rate in this segment or in the share of surplus going into luxury consumption) becomes replicated domestically in the same way that it has manifested itself internationally, or the production structure remains frozen after the initial introduction of a range of new goods in an effort to make the transition to a new lifestyle a one-shot affair, until, at any rate, the labour reserves have been absorbed; but, in such a case, illicit imports of newer Western-style goods keep filtering into the economy and the country becomes trapped in the 'foreign-trade multiplier' syndrome mentioned above. The fate that had overtaken artisan production now befalls modern industrial production and relative price movements are ineffectual in preventing this, for the reasons discussed above. Either way, however, the problem of unemployment is likely to remain.

VII

If the foregoing argument is correct, then it follows that favourable conditions for the elimination of mass unemployment and poverty in underdeveloped countries can exist in only one of two alternative scenarios: the first is where the country in question can become a receptacle for the spatial diffusion of metropolitan capitalism, where metropolitan capital flows in substantial amounts to produce not only for the local market but, more importantly, for the metropolitan market itself – that is, the country becomes integrated with the metropolitan countries not just as a market but as a centre of production, so that for all practical purposes it becomes an extension of the metropolis itself. The alternative scenario is where the domestic pattern of demand is adjusted to the domestic pattern of production, through a change not only in the latter but in the former too; that is, together with a change in the pattern of production, an attempt is made (and it need by no means be made in an authoritarian manner) to change the pattern of wants as well, in a direction different from that which emulation of metropolitan lifestyles dictates.

One step in the latter direction would have to be a change in the distribution of incomes, and, hence, by implication, of assets, in a more egalitarian direction. But this would by no means be enough; what would also be necessary is a change in the conception of what constitutes a use value.

The traditional advocacy of import substitution, based on the assumption of price- and income-inelasticity of metropolitan demand for primary products, took the domestic pattern of demand for manufactures as an unchanging given, and argued merely for a change in the domestic production structure. The fact that the demand pattern, of the affluent at any rate, would keep changing in emulation of changing lifestyles in metropolitan countries never figured in this conception, which was a major flaw. There was of course 'inefficiency' engendered in the process of import-substituting industrialisation (although such 'inefficiency' has to be more precisely defined than is usually the case in the literature), but a good part of the crisis of such industrialisation, which is often explained by the hold-all concept of 'inefficiency', sprang from a disjunction between the pattern of production and the changing pattern of demand in emulation of metropolitan lifestyles.

To argue for a change in the pattern of demand away from the direction dictated by metropolitan lifestyles is not to doom the underdeveloped countries to a perennial state of what has been called 'a homespun vegetarian paradise'. It is to underscore the necessity for an independent trajectory of innovations, an independent definition, in keeping with the need to maintain full employment, of what an improvement in lifestyle means. To be sure, this is not easy and raises several basic questions, but where the first scenario of metropolitan capital-led growth, appears impossible (which I believe to be the case for large countries like India and China),[7] even leaving aside all questions of desirability, there may not be a choice.[8]

NOTES

1. Nicholas Kaldor, 'What is Wrong with Economic Theory?' reprinted in his *Further Essays on Economic Theory*, London, 1978.
2. This term is taken from Michal Kalecki, 'The Difference between Crucial Economic Problems of the Developed and Underdeveloped Non-Socialist Economies', in *Essays on Planning and Economic Development*, Warsaw (PWN), 1968.
3. Implicit in this assertion is the assumption, which I find altogether plausible, that if unemployment falls below the so-called NAIRU, then accelerating inflation results, while if unemployment rises above the so-called NAIRU, then inflation does not go on decelerating down to negative rates. In other words, there exists a ratchet effect which prevents price reductions, so that every level of the unemployment rate above the so-called NAIRU is also, in a manner of speaking, a NAIRU. This was precisely Joan Robinson's idea underlying the 'inflationary barrier'.
4. For a discussion of this process in the Indian context see A.K. Bagchi, 'Deindustrialisation in India in the Nineteenth Century', *Journal of Development Studies*, January 1976.
5. Putting it in a different way, the shortage-of-agricultural-wage-goods argument would be a valid explanation if this shortage was rooted in deeply structural factors, such as land relations, which were not easily amenable to change. And this is exactly what Kalecki had argued in his 'Problems of Financing Economic Development in a Mixed Economy' reprinted in *Essays on the Economic Growth of the Socialist and the Mixed Economy*, Cambridge, 1972. But notwithstanding the necessity of land reforms, which I underscore for an altogether different reason below, the fact remains that agricultural output is augmentable through larger investment, especially larger public investment. And ensuring larger public investment for wage-goods production, at the very least by diverting such investment from elsewhere, should not have been a problem if wage goods were the real bottleneck. In the other words, if wage-goods shortage is what accounted for the prevailing unemployment, then the removal of this unemployment would have been as easier task than it has actually turned out to be.
6. In the Indian context, for instance, this has been argued by Lance Taylor in his 'Macro-Constraints on India's Economic Growth', *Indian Economic Review*, Vol. XXIII, No. 2 (1988).

7. I have argued in a forthcoming book *Accumulation and Stability under Capitalism* (Oxford) that the social stability of metropolitan capitalism is rooted precisely in the international dualism which it is able to enforce. Spatial diffusion of metropolitan capitalism, in other words, may encompass a few small countries, a process which does not substantially alter this dualism, but would never lead to the absorption of the huge labour reserves of India and China.

8. It is noteworthy that the two most outstanding leaders to have come from India and China this century, namely Mao and Gandhi, have, each in his own way, underscored the need for changing the pattern of demand away from the direction of merely emulating metropolitan lifestyles, as a part of development strategy itself.

2

The Political Economy of Consumer Subsidies in the USSR

Nirmal Kumar Chandra

A common thread running through all strands of socialism is the concern for as decent a living standard for the toiling masses as possible within the limitations of an existing society, capitalist or socialist. One corollary is the attempt to make the basic 'means of subsistence' affordable to one and all, whether in the USSR, or in social democratic western and northern Europe. Control, even in times of peace, over the prices of food items, rent, utilities, etc. has been clamped over short or long stretches of time in all these countries. In the USSR it was carried to an excess over the decades, which shook the very foundations of the planned economy, leading to its ultimate collapse. This paper seeks to develop this theme.

We begin by looking at the fragmentary writings of Engels and Marx on the pricing of the means of subsistence during the transitional phase to communism after the proletariat have seized power. Next, different facets of the food subsidy in the USSR are explored. In the third section a briefer exercise along the same lines is carried out for housing and public transport. In the concluding part we bring out the systemic implications of the consumer subsidies.

I

At the beginning of the Plan era, one of the foremost Soviet economists, Strumilin (1929, p. 26) noted that the 'collectivised part' of the wages, namely, social insurance, workers' welfare fund, etc. already constituted 12–15 per cent of the wages (in cash or kind) received by an individual worker, and that 'the tendency towards socialisation of wages must inexorably get stronger over time.' Thirty years later, Strumilin (1959, p. 261) quoted approvingly from Khrushchev's report at the XXI Congress of the CPSU:

Full satisfaction of the needs of the whole Soviet people in food, housing, clothing – necessary and within rational limits, is possible in the not-too-distant future ... As for adults, ... their subsistence needs are not unlimited. An individual cannot, for instance, ask for more bread and other foods than his organism needs. There are also definite limits to the use of clothing and housing. ... [Here] we have in mind, not capricious fellows aspiring after luxuries, but mature and cultured persons with healthy requirements ... [In future] state outlays [on these heads] will increase. The closer we approach communism, society will care more and more about each person from his birth to the ripe old age.

Although China and her followers elsewhere castigated Khrushchev for trying to usher in 'goulash communism', practically no socialist of any description controverted the latter's contention that essential consumer goods and services should be increasingly distributed, not according to wages earned, but according to some 'norms' almost free of cost to the citizens.

Commenting on Proudhon's proposal that workers should enjoy rent-free housing even under capitalism, Engels (1872, p. 521) in his famous pamphlet on the housing question, pointed out that apart from ground rent, house rent has several cost components like interest on the building capital, including the builder's profit, costs of regular repairs and maintenance, and annual depreciation on the building capital. When

the working people remain the collective owners of the houses, factories and instruments of labour ... [they] will hardly permit their use, at least during the transitional period, by individuals and associations without compensation for the cost. Just as the abolition of private property in land is not the abolition of ground rent but its transfer, although in a modified form, to society. The actual seizure of all the instruments of labour by the working people, therefore, does not at all exclude the retention of rent relation.

But Engels (1872, p. 572) went on: 'To speculate on how a future society might organise the distribution of food and dwellings leads directly to *utopia* ... Even the transitional measures will everywhere have to be in accordance with the relations existing at the moment.' In his *Critique of the Gotha Programme*, Marx (1875, pp. 85–7) wrote that in 'the first phase of communist society', i.e. just after the proletarian seizure of power, 'the individual producer receives back from society – after deductions have been made – exactly what he gives to it.' Among the deductions is *'that which is intended for the common satisfaction of needs*, such as schools, health services, etc. From the outset this part ... grows as the new society develops.' Only 'in a higher phase of communist society ... [can] society inscribe on its banners: From each according to his ability, to each according to his needs!'

Several observations can now be made. (1) What the Soviets called 'social wages' do coincide with the items falling under Marx's 'common satisfaction of needs' and hence the disproportionate increase in social wages, from 12–15 per cent in the late 1920s as seen above, to almost one-third in 1990 (Aslund 1991, p. 188), is in tune with Marx's expectation. (2) Food, clothing and housing are undoubtedly means of subsistence; but neither Engels nor Marx suggested that the State should cover an increasing part of the costs during the transitional phase. On house rent, Engels was quite explicit that it should not fall below the sum of cost components, including possibly a part of the ground rent; and the same might be true for food. (3) The Soviets, it appears, conflated the basic means of subsistence with goods or services of 'common satisfaction of needs' which are analogous to 'public goods' of contemporary economists, and hence provided for increasing subsidies. (4) It is possible that in the higher phase of communism, people will become rational in their consumption and most means of subsistence could be provided gratis. But to expect that kind of rationality of the Soviet population in the late 1950s or 1980s was unrealistic, to say the least, for large chunks of society had been suffering from material privation, and more so because of the international demonstration effect. Sooner or later, explosive consumerism in the West may reach a *cul-de-sac* as many Western scientists and politicians have warned, and vindicate in the end Gandhi and Mao as well as Khrushchev; meanwhile, the Soviet Union has disappeared.

II

Before entering the issue of food subsidies, it is worth looking at the consumption standards. Table 2.1 gives comparative data on the *per capita* intake of calories and proteins for selected countries and regions over three decades, that is, the triennial averages of 1961–63 and 1988–90. Throughout the period, there have been high levels of calories and proteins consumed by the Soviets and the Poles comparable to those in USA, France or West Germany and well

Consumer Subsidies
above those in Japan, not to speak of the NICs like South Korea and Brazil, among others. The proportion of calories coming from animal sources was, however, low in the 1960s for the USSR and Poland *vis-à-vis* the West, and the gap was made good by 1988–90 although the distance between the former and Japan and the NICs has remained quite substantial. If the quantities as well as the percentage share of animal foods are taken as the rough index of 'satisfaction', then the Poles and the Soviets were nearly as well-fed as the Westerners, and much better off than those in Japan or the NICs.

Actually, the quality of food in the USSR as against that in the West is not adequately reflected in the figures of Table 2.1. According to the joint study by the Soviet Goskomstat and the German Federal Statistical Bureau (Anon., 1992) on comparative final consumption levels and patterns in these two countries, taking into account the qualities (evaluated from techno-economic data or directly by experts) of 403 pairs of comparable commodities, it was found that in 1988 Soviet per capita food consumption in 'real' terms amounted to just 45.3 per cent of the West German level; for the aggregate consumption of goods and services the ratio was 28.3 per cent. An earlier CIA study, also correcting for quality differences, was more favourable to the USSR. Per capita Soviet consumption in the aggregate was 34.4 per cent of the US level in 1976, while that of food was 53.4 per cent (Schroeder 1983, pp. 316–17).

TABLE 2.1
CONSUMPTION OF CALORIES AND PROTEINS PER CAPITA PER DAY IN
SELECTED COUNTRIES, 1961–90

| | Calories consumed | | | | Proteins consumed | | | |
| | Total (kcal) | | % Animal source | | Total (gms) | | %Animal source | |
	1961–63	1988–90	1961–63	1988–90	1961–63	1988–90	1961–63	1988–90
World	2287	2697	15.7	15.7	62.6	70.9	31.8	35.0
USA	3067	3642	37.5	30.4	97.7	109.9	66.5	64.7
France	3288	3593	32.4	38.5	101.0	112.9	55.0	64.7
W. Germany	2944	3472	35.0	36.0	80.5	100.9	59.0	62.8
Poland**	3220	3499	28.8	34.5	94.9	108.7	45.4	56.0
Europe*	3088	3452	28.1	32.5	88.0	102.1	47.5	57.2
USSR	3146	3380	21.8	28.1	97.6	107.3	39.1	53.2
Japan	2513	2921	10.5	21.1	73.6	95.1	34.0	55.7
S. Korea	1956	2826	3.8	13.2	50.6	77.3	12.6	33.1
Brazil	2490	3062	12.8	18.2	63.2	80.2	26.7	39.8
Mexico	2320	2730	13.7	15.7	57.2	61.4	31.3	41.2
China	1658	2641	4.0	10.8	42.9	64.2	8.6	20.1
India	1991	2229	5.6	6.9	51.4	55.4	11.7	15.0
Indonesia	1816	2605	2.8	3.3	37.1	56.3	12.9	15.3

* without USSR   ** 1979–81, not 1988–90

Source: FAO Production Yearbook 1992, Rome, 1992.

One may consider in this context the 1991 per capita GDP of the same countries according to the purchasing power parties calculated by the World Bank in Table 2.2. For the USSR and Poland, there was a sharp deterioration in 1991, and hence the earlier year of 1987 is shown; further, for the USSR the data for Russia is used as a proxy, though the level for individual former republics varied widely from 11.9 per cent of the US level in case of Tajikistan to 45.2 per cent for Estonia. It can be seen that the Soviet per capita income in real terms was much higher than low-income NICs like Indonesia, China, and India, or middle-income Brazil, comparable to Mexico's, but lower than that of South Korea and far below that of Japan. From all this one may infer that, *compared to their real income levels, the consumption of 'expensive' foods like meat and milk in the USSR and East Europe was far too high.* This was possible because of the abnormally low prices.

TABLE 2.2

INDEX OF PER CAPITA GDP AT PURCHASING POWER PARITIES IN SELECTED COUNTRIES, 1991

USA	100	Brazil	23.7
France	83.3	Mexico	32.4
W. Germany	89.3	S. Korea	37.6
Japan	87.6	China	7.6
USSR*	35.2	Indonesia	12.3
Poland**	24.8	India	5.2

* Russia in 1987   ** 1987

Source: World Development Report 1993, World Bank, Washington, 1993, pp.296–7.

One may now look at the course of food prices. From 1928 to 1940, the Soviet index of food prices at State shops rose tenfold (Chapman 1963, p. 81). From 1940 to 1960 there was another 47 per cent rise; in the next two decades the total increase was under 7 per cent. Between 1960 and 1989 the overall percentage increases were 30.6 for bread, 76.5 for potatoes, 6.1 for macaroni, 27.6 for butter, nil for vegetable fats, 44.9 for meat and poultry, and −8.2 for sugar (Narkhoz 1983, p. 472; Narkhoz 1989, p. 131). Hanson (1968, p. 55) made an interesting comparison between retail food prices in the UK and the USSR in 1965, that is before the UK joined the Common Market, and owing to unrestricted imports from any sources, prices were among the lowest in Western countries; in that year the weighted average food prices (other than prices of beverages and tobacco) in the USSR was 2.2 times that in the UK. For 1976 Schroeder (1983, p. 316) put the purchasing power parity of similar food items at 90 kopecks/$, or about the same as the official exchange rate. It implied that the overall food price was roughly the same in the two countries; as is well known, food was much cheaper in the USA in 1976 than in Western Europe. *It follows that the extraordinary stability in Soviet food prices is a post-1965 phenomenon for which there are few parallels anywhere.*

In parentheses, it may be observed that post-communist Russia, despite the hyperinflation that set in after prices were unfrozen on the advice of expensive American consultants at the end of 1991, has not surmounted the problem. Food cost much more in New York than in Moscow, if roubles are converted into dollars at the Moscow Auction Rate; the New York–Moscow price ratios on 9 March 1993 were 25.9 for bread, 21.6 for potatoes, 4.8 for beef, 9.4 for milk, 1.6 butter, 5.3 for vegetable fats, etc. (*Argumenty i fakty*, 1993/11). If the Auction Rate undervalued the rouble by a factor of, say, four, most food products were still cheaper in Moscow.

While prices remained stable, the 'prime cost' (*sebestoimost'*) at the collective farms for most food products increased very sharply between 1965 and 1989: by 92 per cent for grains, 211 per cent for potatoes, 115 per cent for milk, 170 per cent for beef, 99 per cent for pork, and 24 per cent for egg; costs at state farms rose in tandem. No wonder that state subsidies had to be multiplied; in billion roubles these amounted to 28.8 in 1982, and 55.0 in 1989. There was also a special subsidy in the form of differential procurement prices for some regions/crops totalling 32.2 billion roubles in 1989 (Cook 1992, pp. 198–201). The total subsidies, direct and indirect, increased more than threefold in the span of seven years.

The importance of the subsidies comes out in sharper relief when these are set against the GNP and the budget deficit. The first ratio rose from 4.2 per cent in 1982 to 7.2 per cent in 1985 and 9.4 per cent in 1989, while for the same years the second ratio stood at 135 per cent, 315 per cent and 95 per cent. (Calculated from Cook 1992, p. 201; Aslund 1991, p. 192.) For the earlier years, we have not seen comparable data. From the estimates of Birman (1981, p. 209), the budget deficit was a small part (2.3 per cent) of the budget revenue until the early 1970s, and became significant since 1975 when the proportion exceeded 8.3 per cent; moreover, Birman did not go into the question of subsidies. Although such subsidies should have begun in the early 1970s, they took on an explosive character somewhere around the late 1970s.

There is another side to the story. The State made enormous investments in agriculture, including industries supplying inputs like machinery or fertilisers to that sector; in total investments the share of agriculture rose from 18.4 per cent in 1961–65 to 23.9 per cent in

1971–75, 24.3 per cent in 1981–85 and 23.2 per cent in 1986–90 (Cook 1992, p. 194). Apart from food subsidies, the State heavily subsidised inputs supplied to the collective and State farms. From the viewpoint of the national exchequer, the huge investments failed to yield positive returns. Paradoxically, agricultural output rose at a moderate rate over the period, which itself exacerbated the fiscal crisis. In other words, agriculture was like a bottomless pit that sucked in during 25 years investible resources, approximating 5 per cent of the GNP each year, and a further 10 per cent by way of annual subsidies in the late 1980s. It is extremely doubtful whether any economy, however well managed it might be in all other spheres, could withstand such a haemorrhage of resources over such a long period of time.

Lastly, food subsidies which encouraged abnormally high levels of consumption, also aggravated the shortage of hard currencies. Most food imports came from developed market economies, while Soviet exports to these regions remained virtually stagnant, fluctuating between 19 and 30 billion US dollars during 1980–88. The annual average value of exports in 1983–88 from developed market economies to the USSR stood at $22.7 billion; food items accounted for 19.1 per cent of the total, and cereals alone constituted 14.8 per cent of the former (*International Trade Statistics Yearbook 1988*, vol. I, United Nations, New York, 1989).

At this stage, it is worth quoting at some length from a recent OECD (1994, p. 155) publication. 'In the early 1970s, the Soviet leadership decided to increase the production and consumption of livestock goods, as an overt way of increasing the population's material standard of living. Receiving a disproportionate share of national investment and resources, the sector responded from 1970 to 1990 by increasing production of meat by 63 per cent, milk 32 per cent, and eggs 100 per cent ... [E]vidence indicates that by the late 1980s the per capita consumption of meat in the former Soviet Union was almost twice as high as in countries that had generally the same levels of per capita GNP. Per capita consumption of meat had risen to levels equal to that in many West European countries, such as Great Britain or Finland. The need for increased feed to support a growing livestock sector was the main catalyst behind the large Soviet imports of grains and soyabean products of the past two decades. (Before 1970 the USSR was a slight net grain exporter.) The common criticism of the Soviet economy that it was incapable of even feeding itself was off the mark; imports were being used to support an artificially high level of livestock production and consumption.'

Returning to food imports, one must admit that the absolute size of food import ($4.3 billion) was by no means excessive, but the burden was quite heavy in view of the small size of Soviet export to these countries, consisting largely of fuels. Simultaneously, the Soviet leaders stepped up their import of Western technology and equipment without being able to sell significant quantities of the updated products or other manufactures in the West. The net result was a one-sided dependence as with a large number of developing countries, culminating in a rising stock of convertible currency debts that the Soviets could barely service. Thus food subsidies contributed in no small measure to the deepening foreign exchange crisis and the ultimate collapse of the system.

III

Let me turn to housing where shortages have been chronic all through the decades. Over the past few decades, the waiting period for those in the queue for an allotment has been typically 8–10 years. It is not that no investments were made. On the contrary, from 1955 until 1975 well over 11 million apartments were built during each Five Year Plan, and another 16 million were built in 1976–83, that is a total of over 60 million in 1955–83; the average size tended to rise from 43 m² initially to 52 m² in the early 1980s. In 1983, for instance, only Japan had a higher rate of construction at 97 apartments per 10,000 population against 75 for the USSR; the rates for other countries were 30 in Britain, 43 in the USA, 60 in West Germany, and 67 in France (Narkhoz 1983, pp. 87, 419). According to Schroeder (1992, p. 93), 'urban public housing now has most of the usual amenities [like running water, modern sanitation, central heating] and the situation improved during the 1980s … [But] most rural private housing lacks all amenities.' Further, it is interesting that in urban areas the percentage share of private construction in the total fell drastically from 25.1 in 1955–60 to 10.8 in 1966–70, and 7.6 in 1981–83. (Narkhoz 1983, p. 418). Clearly, individuals were less and less able or willing to own houses.

House rent in the USSR had remained unchanged since 1928 at about 0.13 rouble/m²; the State was spending of late more than three times as much in repair and maintenance (Narkhoz 1983, pp. 87, 422; Lane 1985, p. 58; Rao 1993). As a result, the share of rent and utilities in family expenditure in Chapman's (1963, p. 70) estimate went down from 6.2 per cent in 1928 to 2.4 per cent in 1937. From Birman's (1981, pp. 236, 240, 276) calculation of the disposable income of the population outside the collective farms, it appears that their outlay on house rent and municipal services was 3.0 per cent of income in 1965 and 2.8 per cent in 1975. Hanson (1968, p. 73) found that while the average Soviet family in 1965 spent 5 per cent of its total expenditure on rent, fuel and power, the figure was as much as 27 per cent for low-income British families that should have had a comparable 'real income'. In 1976 the same ratio came to 5.3 per cent for the USSR, against an average of 12.7 per cent in Italy, 14.6 per cent in Japan, and over 17 per cent in the UK and the USA (Schroeder 1983, p. 321). Another estimate showed that an average worker needed to work 12 hours to pay for his apartment in Moscow in 1982, compared to 28 and 51 hours respectively for the worker in London and Washington (Lane 1985, p. 60). Actually, the situation was more favourable for the Soviets; the above calculations ignored the 'second' or 'shadow' economy for which data became available in subsequent years; the latter fetched upwards of one-third of the 'legitimate' income in the late 1970s in different urban centres of the USSR (Grossman 1987).

State investments in housing amounted to approximately 15 per cent of the aggregate investments from 1961 to 1983 (Narkhoz 1983, p. 358–9). On annual maintenance alone, the State subsidy stood at about 1 per cent of the GNP. There was no question of recovering other costs enumerated by Engels. As with agriculture, more houses of a better quality for the population should have been a cause for celebration all round, but in reality added to the woes of the fisc. Thus housing was another bottomless pit.

Apart from food and housing, passenger transportation was also a big drain on the budget. In 1982 the Moscow worker needed no more than three minutes of his labour time to pay for a bus journey of three kilometres, while his counterparts in London and Washington required 11 and seven minutes respectively (Lane 1985, p. 69). True, 'rational' policy-makers in various countries subsidise urban transport to avoid various kinds of negative externalities from alternative modes. But should there not be any limit? Should long-distance journeys by bus, train or air be as heavily subsidised as intra-city transport, as in the USSR? It is worth emphasising that most modern forms of public transport are highly capital intensive.

IV

There are several broader implications of subsidised food, housing, public transport, and so forth. First, if a large proportion of the annual investments, say, 33–40 per cent, go into these sectors, is it not almost inevitable that investments elsewhere for technological upgrading, research and development, and so on, will suffer as a result? Further, since subsidies arise due to the gap between fixed prices and rising costs, especially labour costs, in an economy with increasing real wages, the subsidies will necessarily increase over time. In this situation the proportion of national income available for investment, *ceteris paribus*, will diminish. The assumption that 'other things would remain unchanged' is not valid as we shall shortly see. Moreover, if one consider the defence burden of the USSR, estimated variously at 15–30 per cent of the GNP in the late 1980s (Aslund 1991, p. 181), both the factors just mentioned acquire an added significance.

Thirdly, excessive subsidies cannot but create shortages; the greater the subsidy element in the retail price, the more acute is the shortage. Thanks to low food costs and rents, and rising incomes, the Soviet consumers shifted as fast as they could, though rather prematurely by international standards, towards meat, milk and such expensive items, and yet their savings increased. As a proportion of disposable income, the savings rate shot up from 5.8 per cent in 1985, to over 12 per cent in 1990; the cumulative stock leaped from 24.3 billion roubles in 1985 to 80.5 in 1990 (IMF *et al.* 1990, p. 49). Although comparable data are not available for earlier years, the trend started in the late 1960s. This growing 'liquidity overhang' with the population disrupted the 'planning system' with centrally fixed prices, and created excess demand across the board. And it was this excess demand, along with other known deficiencies like overcentralised allocation of resources, the faulty 'success indicator' of *val* (gross output) for firms, that led to the technological stagnation in most industries. The manager of every factory as well as his superiors knew that whatever was produced would somehow be sold or wasted (at the cost of the State), and hence no one was compelled to make continuous improvements to provide greater satisfaction to the consumer.

On the other hand, underpricing leads to wasteful consumption, as all textbooks in economics predict. Since the 1960s, apartment buildings in the urban USSR often had 'bread baskets' into which residents would dump unwanted bread that cost virtually nothing. As for housing, overall statistics show that per capita floor area was generally the highest for households with one or more old persons living by themselves, while young married couples had to wait 8–10 years to obtain an apartment. Under Soviet conditions the old people never moved from a larger apartment to a smaller one, once their grown up sons and daughters left home. Hence the maxim of 'need-based' housing could never be fulfilled. Acute shortage and wastage co-existed side-by-side over the decades.

Nearly 60 years ago a leading Soviet economist, Novozhilov

(1926), developed an interesting dynamic model; it showed how pricing of consumer goods at prime cost (without allowing for profit) widens the gap between demand and supply with inflationary consequences, causes a growing disparity between the actual and the real distribution of incomes when some consumers have, for example, a privileged access to goods, or a scramble for producer goods among the enterprises – all leading to a slowdown in economic growth. Another contemporary writer, Shaposnikov (1925), put it succinctly: 'the politics of lowering prices [in a period of shortage] raises consumer demand artificially, and hampers the development of the productive forces of our industry. ... In essence, [it] strongly subserves *current* at the cost of *future* consumption, or *private* at the cost of *productive* consumption.' (Emphasis in the original.) Yet the then policy-makers actually lowered prices in the midst of shortages, which along with many other factors undermined the very foundations of the market-friendly NEP regime. Although the market was relegated to a back seat in the subsequent Plan era, consumer prices increased manifold since 1929, vindicating in a curious way the Novozhilov–Shaposnikov stand!

The post-war planners in the USSR and East Europe were alive to the dangers of excessive consumer subsidies. Indeed, attempts were made in East Germany and Poland through the 1950s until the late 1970s to drastically raise critical food prices. Instantaneous popular resistance forced the governments to retreat. *In the USSR no serious efforts were ever made as the 'correct lessons' were drawn from the events elsewhere in East Europe.* As for house rent, none of these governments even mooted any scheme to enhance it.

Instead of facing the challenge, the *nomenklatura* took full advantage of these subsidies to get better quality foods at shops and restaurants from which the *hoi polloi* were barred; of course, they never had to live with shortages as supplies were especially earmarked for them. The same was true for housing. They received the more luxurious homes and even paid 'penal rates' (actually, ridiculously low) for additional (that is above the per capita 'norm') housing space (Bergson 1989, p. 62).

In conclusion, our hypothesis is that the endemic shortages in the Soviet economy had different roots in different periods. These were caused by reckless target-setting for heavy industries during the First Plan, 1928–32; these deficiencies were rectified in the Second Plan which was relatively crisis-free until the war clouds darkened the horizon by 1938. From the late 1950s onwards there was no evidence of growth mania in the USSR or East Europe, but an altogether *new type of crisis* surfaced by the end of the 1970s, namely the time bomb of consumer subsidies.

But the metaphor should not be carried too far. A single time bomb may not destroy an entire edifice; if other elements in the system functioned well, rising consumer subsidies alone could not bring about the collapse of the Soviet system. Students of 'socialist economics' have unravelled many crucial factors behind the malfunctioning of the system; I do not underestimate their importance. But we believe that many of these are organically linked to the subsidy question, which has not been sufficiently underlined in the existing literature.

On the other hand, our examination of the writings of Marx and Engels on the 'transitional phase' do not provide a justification for the Soviet practice. The crassly self-seeking successors of Khrushchev found subsidies exceedingly convenient from their personal point of view; in any case, doing away with subsidies was considered by them as too risky. It is this degeneration of the *nomenklatura* or of the bureaucracy, as Trotsky suggested long ago, or of the Party Headquarter as Mao put it, that was probably the proximate cause of the collapse of the system. The rot could have been stemmed if a socialist democracy had been in place. But that is the subject for another essay.

NOTE

I have benefitted from the comments of Amit Bhaduri and Michael Ellman on earlier drafts of this paper.

REFERENCES

Anon. (1992), 'Sravnenie zhiznennogo urovnya naseleniya SSSR i FRG 1988 g.', *Vestnik statistiki*, no. 2.

Aslund, A. (1991), *Gorbachev's Struggle for Economic Reform*, Pinter Publishers, London.

Bergson, A. (1989), *Planning and Performance in Socialist Economies: The USSR and Europe*, Unwin Hyman, Boston.

Birman, I. (1981), *Secret Incomes of the Soviet State Budget*, Martinus Nijhoff Publishers, The Hague.

Chapman, J.G. (1963), *Real Wages in Soviet Russia since 1928*, Harvard University Press, Cambridge, MA.

Cook, E.C. (1992), 'Agriculture's Role in the Soviet Economic Crisis', in Ellman and Kantorovich (eds).

Ellman, M. and V. Kantorovich (eds) (1992), *The Disintegration of the Soviet Economic System*, Routledge, London.

Engels, F. (1872), 'The Housing Question', in K. Marx and F. Engels, *Selected Works*, vol. I, Moscow, 1954.

Hanson, P. (1968), *The Consumer in the Soviet Economy*, Macmillan, London.

IMF *et al.* (1990), *The Economy of the USSR: Summary and Recommendations,* International Monetary Fund, International Bank of Reconstruction and Development, Organisation for Economic Co-operation and Development, and European Bank for Reconstruction and Development, Washington.

Marx, K. (1875), 'Critique of the Gotha Programme', in *Marx–Engels Collect Works*, vol. 24, Moscow, 1989.

Narkhoz, *Narodnoe khozyaistvo SSSR,* Moscow, annual.

Novozhilov, V. (1926), 'Nedostatok tovarov', *Vestnik finansov*, no. 2.

Schroeder, G.E. (1983), 'Consumption', in A. Bergson and H. S. Levine (eds), *The Soviet Economy Towards the Year 2000*, George Allen & Unwin, London.

Schroeder, G.E. (1992), 'Soviet Consumption in the 1980s: A Tale of Woe', in Ellman and Kantorovich (eds).

Shaposnikov, N.N. (1925), 'Promyshlennaya kon'yunktura i politika tsen', *Vestnik promyshlennosti, torgovli i transporta*, no. 1.

Strumilin, S.G. (1929), 'Planovye notatki na 1929/30 g.', *Planovoe khozyaistvo*, no.9, reprinted in Strumilin (1959).

Strumilin, S.G. (1959), 'Semiletnyi plan na 1959-65 gg.', in his *Ocherki sotsialisticheskoi ekonomiki SSSR (1929-1959 gg.)*, Moscow, 1959.

3

The Planning Principle:
An Unresolved Debate

C.P. Chandrasekhar

Discussions induced by the collapse of the erstwhile socialist regimes in eastern Europe tend to focus on one ostensible 'lesson' from that experience, namely, that central planning based on command economy structures does not deliver adequate results either in terms of growth or in terms of innovative efficiency. For example, Bardhan and Roemer (1992) argue: 'What the Eastern European experience has shown is that a system of pervasive state control of firms, plus the absence of markets, does not work.' This perception leads to the conclusion that countries seeking a more egalitarian and socially rational economic order should not opt for a planned system where 'major economic decisions (such as would be entrepreneurial decisions in a capitalist economy) are taken by some central government body, and embodied in a general complex of decisions, or conspectus, co-ordinated *ex ante* for a definite planning period' (Dobb, 1969). Instead, implicitly positing the 'planning principle' and the market as alternative mechanisms for organising production, it is argued that countries seeking an alternative to capitalism should adopt some variant of 'market socialism'.

The common feature in all variants is a significant role for decentralised market-mediated decisions in determining both the allocation of resources and the dynamics of the system. However, definitions differ on questions such as the nature of ownership or on the need for institutional structures conducive to entrepreneurship. Thus, one definition (Bardhan and Roemer, 1992) allows for public or state ownership of the means of production, while doing away with the command/administrative allocation of resources and commodities and the phenomenon of 'non-competitive, non-democratic politics'. The idea is to approximate competitive markets, while using State ownership and political democracy to ensure that the disposal of the surplus is decided by the democratic process.[1]

The challenge for this revisionist view, therefore, is to shape 'socialist' markets in a fashion where they maintain their 'capitalist' dynamism, but combine it with equity and sustainability. Markets are the best bet so long as they are rendered 'people-friendly' by combining them with participatory institutional mechanisms, the argument goes (UNDP, 1993). Since this requires the redistribution of assets, incomes and opportunities, a degree of intervention by the State is seen as essential.[2]

Thus, while making the case for embracing markets on the premise that markets and planning are alternative economic mechanisms, the revisionist argument ends up with the ostensibly benign view that the collapse of socialism paves the way for a pragmatic blend of the best elements of two systems. This contrasts with what has been termed the 'abstract logic' of the Marxist approach to the problem of socialism's economic rationality, which 'stripped of particularisms, shows perhaps more clearly than otherwise the incompatibility of the market with the scheme of a rational socialist economy' (Brus and Laski, 1989).

This question of the compatibility of markets and socialism is the point of departure for this chapter. It examines different episodes in the relatively long history of the effort to work out a 'pragmatic partnership' between 'capitalist' efficiency and 'socialist' compassion, to show how that effort undermines the original case for planning, viz. the need to overcome the anarchy characteristic of market-based systems. This implies that an alternative to the 'turn to markets' response to the failure of socialism as it actually exists needs to be worked out.

Such an alternative must be based on a critique of the planning principle, which is different from that implicit in the currently dominant desire to embrace markets. While attempting to outline such a critique, the paper focuses on the assumptions needed in theory for the success of a mechanism involving centralised investment co-ordination, even in systems characterised by complete State ownership. To the extent that such assumptions are not warranted by material reality, the 'costs' of centralisation may overwhelm its expected benefits, especially in the intensive phase of growth when productivity increases are crucial. There is, therefore, a case for a decentralised structure under socialism, which provides appropriate incentives and adequately disciplines decision-makers. The challenge for socialism is the fashioning of institutions that both ensure such a decentralised structure without just 'replicating' or imitating the market, and also allow social objectives and concerns to dominate the dynamics of the system. Since State ownership *per se*, which can be combined with user rights of different kinds, does not ensure such a structure, the issue of the feasibility of socialism would remain on the agenda so long as the institutional framework which provides such an alternative to decentralisation through the market is not worked out.

THE CASE FOR PLANNING

To those acquainted with the socialist calculation debate, the case made by the 'market socialists' that markets and planning should work in tandem suffers from some obvious inadequacies. The old debate had made it clear that within the socialist tradition there existed two rather differing conceptions of the need for, and hence the character of, a planned system.

The first conception of economic planning emerged out of a *critique of capitalism*, which focused on the anarchy associated with the atomistic decision making characteristic of systems based on private property. In such systems, the level and allocation of investment becomes determined by the 'guesses or expectations of a large number of independent decision-takers (entrepreneurs), in the long run "revised" by *ex post* movements of market prices' (Dobb, 1960). Since the investment in fixed capital that results is not by definition reversible, decision errors are costly in individual and social terms. And such errors are bound to occur since private investment decisions must be based on estimates of prices that would prevail over the lifetime of the project. In the circumstances, existing prices cannot be a guide to future prices, as the atomistic, individual investment decisions made on the basis of the prevailing prices together influence subsequent movement in prices. Without an anchor, there is no reason to believe that expectations would actually be realised, leading to over-investment, unutilised capacity and closure. Hence a system that seeks to supersede the anarchy of capitalism must co-ordinate investment and arrive at *ex ante* decisions on the total volume of investment, its allocation to sectors, and particular projects and the technical forms in which it would be embodied.

The benefits from such co-ordination were twofold. First, by overcoming the 'secondary uncertainty' inherent in a regime where investment was based on atomistic decisions, it reduced the waste and unemployment characteristic of capitalism. Second, by ensuring the incorporation of appropriate inter-temporal judgements in the choice of the investment ratio, the allocation of investment and the technical forms in which it was embodied, it permitted a process of maximising growth subject to the consumption requirements set by social and political conditions.

The second conception of a planned system was developed in the course of a *defence of 'socialism'* against the argument that in the absence of markets and prices for resources, including produced means of production, it lacks in practice a feasible mechanism that could allocate resources efficiently. That argument was formulated by Von Mises (1935) and Hayek (1935) as a response to Barone's suggestion that the central planner could, like the Walrasian auctioneer, solve a system of equations involving an equivalent number of unknowns to arrive at a set of prices that would clear all markets. Lange's defence of socialism against the Mises-Hayek critique presumed that investment and production decisions would be 'decentralised', but would be undertaken by plant- and industry-level managers according to accounting rules specified by the central planning board, taking a list of prices put out by the board as parameters. The accounting rules themselves were similar to, if not identical with, those adopted 'naturally' by profit maximising agents in a competitive market with free entry and exit. If, as a result of such decisions, the quantities supplied and demanded of any commodity at the notified prices do not tally, the central planning board would adjust its prices upwards or downwards and move the system towards an equilibrium. Acting in this manner, as a 'price setter' and an agency that ensures the adherence to accounting principles handed down from above, Lange argued, the central planning board could ensure that a socialist system replicates the allocative equilibrium typical of a competitive market.

IMPLICATIONS OF THE DEFENCE

This defence implicitly accepted the notion that price signals generated by perfectly functioning markets were the most efficient allocators of resources to meet ends specified by consumer preferences. Naturally, therefore, it was concerned with the extent to which the socialist economic mechanism could approximate those prices by imitating such markets. Besides the fact that the debate ignored even conventional scepticism about the efficiency of 'as-perfect-as-possible' real world markets where information is incomplete and trading occurs sequentially (Hahn 1989), it gave the argument away by addressing the question of whether an interventionist regime could approximate the automatic equilibrium generated by the market. As Dobb argued, the comparison was between an 'ideal-type' which costlessly arrived at an equilibrium, and a cumbersome, interventionist regime that attempted to approximate that equilibrium. And in the process of winning the debate that socialism can actually ensure the approximation of 'equilibrium prices' the unsatisfactory and inappropriate comparison undermined the real strength of the planning principle in the classical tradition, which was its ability to co-ordinate investment decisions within a regime where only the markets for labour and consumption goods were relatively free.

Lange went on to suggest that, not being wedded to the principle of private ownership, the State could start with a more acceptable distribution of endowments. Further, the central planning board could ensure that the prices chosen are more comprehensive and take account of externalities, that adjustment proceeds faster and that monopolistic price-fixing policies are not used. That is, the socialist economy can not only replicate a competitive market, but it can also ensure that endowments are more equally redistributed, that externalities are taken into account and that monopolistic restrictions on trade that result in inefficiency are kept under control. Markets in this system could not only be closer to perfection in their working, but could also be more 'people friendly'.[3]

BLENDING MARKETS AND THE PLANNING PRINCIPLE

The obvious blend of markets and planning in Lange's model of socialism is ensured through the separation of the structure of decision-making (which is decentralised) and the hierarchical structure of objectives on which those decisions are made. Societal, macro scale objectives dominate the latter, so that 'lower-rank objectives become the means for attaining higher-level ones, and the criteria for rational behaviour of the subsystems (sectors, branches, enterprises) are subordinated to the system as a whole' (Brus and Laski, 1989). The presumption is that decentralised decision-makers would not deviate in terms of behaviour from what is centrally ordained, even if such behaviour is not the most rational seen solely from their 'decentralised' perspective.

There are three aspects of this argument that drew criticism. First, by implicitly doing away with the plan–market dichotomy, the argument made the case for socialism purely an egalitarian one. And this it did by accepting the terrain of a critique of socialism which compared it with an 'ideal-type', namely, the competitive market, which automatically ensures an equilibrium behind people's backs. As compared with that, a socialist market required a cumbersome interventionist trial-and-error process, that was less attractive on 'efficiency' grounds, even if it were more egalitarian. Second, the dichotomy was discarded essentially by doing away with the planning principle, involving investment co-ordination. Planning essentially involved the creation of an agency that served as a 'price-setting body', which imposed known accounting rules and policed the system. Finally, the dichotomy was discarded at the expense of importing into the system the likelihood of the instability and the unemployment characteristic of the system that planning was expected to replace. That likelihood arises the moment we allow decentralised investment decisions to respond to decentralised signals. While most of those signals are 'prices' specified as part of an exercise aimed at equating economy-wide supply to demand, the interest rate cannot be seen as the price that equates the demand for capital with the supply of a given stock of capital, and its resulting marginal productivity. Capital, being a produced means of production, is not given exogenously but is an internally 'accumulated' stock. This process of accumulation through investment generates its own additional demand for capital. That is, any increase or decrease in the 'supply of capital' simultaneously increases or decreases the 'demand' for it. It should be clear that if investment creates its own draught in this manner, the system tends to be characterised by 'knife-edge'-like properties that can lead to persisting inflation or unemployment.

This tendency of a Lange-type system to replicate the instability characteristic of capitalism is not surprising. What is surprising, however, is the fact that the collapse of the erstwhile socialist regimes in the wake of a rather long period of successful development in economic terms, has resulted in a return to arguments that fall back on a conception of an efficiently functioning system implicit in the Lange formulation. The argument seems to be as follows. In practice, after all, dominantly market-based systems have performed better than those based on the planning principle. And even though those actually functioning markets have little to do with 'perfectly competitive' representations of them, we can assume that their actual performance must just be a deviation from the ideal rather than a negation of that ideal. Hence, while striving to retain elements of egalitarianism, erstwhile socialist regimes must transit to ones that allow for the dynamism and efficiency that markets provide.

MARKET SOCIALISM: THE REVISED CASE

A more rational discourse must, of course, go beyond reasoning that discards more than half a century of theorising, to accept actual markets as being adequate approximations of an ideal which can be replicated 'in a world of fully informed and well-motivated agents'. After all, the so-called 'revolution' currently under way in neo-classical microeconomic theory rests on the 'abandonment of the simple world of Walrasian general equilibrium in favour of a richer world of imperfect information, incomplete markets, unenforceable contracts, costly transactions, and strategic interaction' (Bowles and Gintis, 1993). This was bound to affect the argument in favour of a transition towards market-based systems in the erstwhile socialist countries as well. One influential case for market socialism, which has gradually evolved into an argument for markets without socialism, stems from Janos Kornai's (1982) analysis of the debilitating weakness of socialist economies. Starting from the idea that unlike capitalist economies that were 'demand-constrained', socialist economies were 'supply-constrained', Kornai went on to suggest that these 'shortage economies' were characterised by a host of inefficiencies including the prevalence of unemployed resources. There were two ideas that were central to Kornai's reasoning: first, that shortage is a result of the 'soft budget constraints' that characterise socialism; and second, that in shortage economies, shortage and slack co-exist, with both being symptoms of the same malaise. With access to credit from the State or subsidies to cover losses, firms, unlike households, are characterised by an insatiable hunger to maximise production and investment. Inasmuch as this runs up against real constraints in the form of restrictions on access to capital goods, intermediates and components, firms are characterised by a tendency to resort to large-scale hoarding that intensifies shortage and makes it an essential feature of the system. Faced with intensified shortage, firms are forced to accept high downtime rates, use poor quality or more expensive inputs, and ignore both quality and cost. But the system muddles on since producers are protected by the 'sellers' market' that shortage engenders and the soft budget constraint that the system supports.

The investment and production hunger that this situation drives helps propel the system so long as unutilised reserves of labour and other resources exist. The system is characterised, therefore, by the ability to mop up such reserves, or what Kornai terms 'external efficiency'. On the other hand, in terms of a whole host of efficiency parameters varying from input-use coefficients to quality and cost, the system is internally inefficient. Sooner or later available labour reserves are exhausted, bringing to the fore the canker of internal inefficiency that saps the system. But, organisationally, there is little in the system to make the financial risks associated with investment and production significant. Hence, the problem persists, leading to a deepening of the economic crisis.

It should be clear that, in this framework, the persistence of shortage is due to the fact that inflation and the government's response to it can have no corrective role, so long as the institutional framework that allows for 'soft budget constraints' remains.[4] Hence within the framework of Kornai's analysis, institutional changes that impose 'hard budget constraints' on firms are the only mechanisms of overcoming the essential weakness of shortage economies. The implication of a hard budget constraint is that firms making losses would not be supported by the government and would have to go bankrupt if not turned around. But the process of ensuring that a firm makes profits or of turning around a loss-making firm requires a substantial degree of autonomy for the enterprise managers, with respect to investment, output and pricing decisions. Thus, Kornai's framework provides a theoretical case for reforming centrally planned systems in a specific direction, namely, that which leads to a situation where autonomous publicly owned enterprises enter into exchange relations with one another on the market guided by the profit motive (Patnaik, 1988).

The deviation from Lange is obvious, since this framework does not concentrate on the parametric role of prices in a 'competitive market' and the need to replicate that role under socialism by enforcing centrally defined 'competitive behaviour' on decentralised agents. Rather it accepts the real world with its features of imperfect information, non-compatible incentives and non-price transaction mechanisms, but still seeks to approximate the 'decentralised' capitalist equilibrium which is considered more 'internally efficient' than that generated by centralised systems of decision-making. That is, there is no distinction here between centrally determined objectives and decentralised functioning. The intention is to remove any central influence on, or support for, decentralised decision-makers.

This is because the principal aim of reform is to 'invisibly' discipline firm managers so that they behave as profit maximisers faced with hard budget constraints. The idea ostensibly is to leave ownership in the hands of the populace, or the State which holds assets on their behalf, while removing management and control of day-to-day functioning out of the State's orbit. This is partly because such ownership is considered conducive to egalitarianism without loss of production efficiency, when firms are autonomous.[5] On the other hand, unlike in the Lange-type mechanism, rather than relying on the ability of the central planning board to enforce a predetermined pattern of behaviour on managers, which the latter may not have adequate reason to accept or the former to enforce, the new system seeks automatic mechanisms to realise its goal.

Market socialism is reduced to a version of socialist commodity production.

In fact, recent contributions have focused on this aspect of the issue, arguing that 'socialist managers' faced with soft-budget constraints are characterised by agency problems similar to corporate capitalism with separation of ownership and control. 'Just as in a socialist firm which although owned by everybody is really owned by nobody (because nobody takes responsibility), so a capitalist firm owned by thousands or even millions of investors may have difficulty in ensuring responsibility.' This is because 'the large body of shareholders, the collective principal in this case, may have a difficult monitoring problem at hand, as the individual investor has neither the ability nor the full incentive to monitor' (Bardhan and Roemer, 1992).

Under capitalism this agency problem is dealt with by disciplining managers through two routes: the managerial labour market and the capital market, which continuously assesses corporate performance. While market socialism may, through appropriate institutional reform, replicate a managerial labour market, the lack of ownership makes the task of reproducing the capital market more difficult. One way is to give citizens vouchers that constitute a claim on the capital stock of an enterprise, which can be traded. This, of course, amounts to giving up the only characteristic of 'market socialism' that could justify, if at all, the socialist tag. The other route, argue Bardhan and Roemer (1992), is to replicate the Japanese *keiretsu* type organisation where a main bank provides a nucleus to a corporate financial grouping and monitors individual enterprises within the group on behalf of the others. But if the main bank derives a substantial part of its resources from the State, what is to prevent it from behaving like an agent with a soft budget constraint? Nothing ultimately, making the whole exercise redundant.

Further, it should be clear that this form of 'market socialism', even if it manages to discipline managers, provides enterprises with a substantial degree of autonomy in the determination of prices, production and investment. In fact, the whole intent of the exercise of defining such a form of socialism is to work out an arrangement where, unlike the Lange mechanism where the central planning board prescribes the mode of determination of prices, enterprises have a high degree of autonomy in this regard. Two effects are inevitable under such an arrangement. First, a high degree of instability for reasons delineated earlier. And second, a tendency towards inflation since enterprises which have a monopoly or an oligopolistic position in what is by definition a 'supply-constrained' system, would raise prices to bid up their share in surpluses (Patnaik, 1988). In this conflict over the division of the surplus the system becomes trapped in an inflationary spiral, unless it is subjected to the disciplining force of 'international competition' as has happened in many East European countries.

NON-MARKET MONITORING

What accounts for the fact that a framework which leads to instability, inflation and balance of payments crises is embraced by even the most insightful of critics of the erstwhile socialist economies? Our discussion points to a fundamental reason, namely that, as in the case of Lange's defence of socialism, they start with the premise that there can be no mechanism of non-market monitoring of economic systems because the question of who is to monitor the monitor is unresolvable. Hence, an 'invisible', 'behind-the-back' agent in the form of a disciplining market has to be found. The social loss involved in such a system of monitoring is seen as less than one in which all-powerful non-market monitors manipulate the economy. The difficulty here, as in the Lange-type formulation, is the assumption that even in a world of asymmetric information and unequal asset-holding, the market actually serves as an impersonal monitor. Once it is accepted a range of features of actual markets (information control, advertising, manipulation of monopolistic power) does away with arms-length transactions and subverts their role as impersonal monitors, logically, at least, we are back with the problem of who is to serve as regulator and who is to monitor the regulator. That is, just as Lange's defence of socialism incorporated an implicit critique of the 'planning principle' based on the allocative virtues of an ideal market that cannot exist, these critics develop their case on the assumption that markets can serve as impersonal and objective monitors, when in practice they cannot.

THE OTHER BEGINNING

However, the fact that these variants of 'market socialism' offer an inadequate alternative mechanism to the 'centralised planning principle' does not obviate the need to modify the latter. Since the failing of the former appears to be the inadequacy of their critique of the planning principle itself, it is useful to focus on an alternative critique. The point of departure of that critique is the set of presumptions on which the planning principle, which has at its core a centralised system of investment co-ordination, is based. Those presumptions originate in discussions on the plan-market dichotomy that were central to Marx's understanding of the anarchy of the social division of labour under capitalism as compared with the despotic functioning of the capitalist workshop. Marx held that 'the *a priori* system on which the division of labour within the workshop is regularly carried out, becomes in the division of labour within society, an *a posteriori*, nature-imposed necessity, controlling the lawless caprice of the producers' (Marx, 1959). This difference, according to him, was the fall-out of little else than the property, and therefore social, relations characteristic of capitalism. He argued that:

> The same bourgeois mind which praises the division of labour within the workshop, life-long annexation of labour to a partial operation, and his complete subjection to capital, as being an organisation of labour that increases productiveness – that same bourgeois mind denounces with equal vigour every conscious attempt to socially control and regulate the process of production as an inroad upon such sacred things as the rights of property, freedom and unrestricted play for the best of the individual capitalist. It is very characteristic that the enthusiastic apologists of the factory system have nothing more damning to urge against a general organisation of the labour and society, than it would turn all society into one immense factory.

Implicit in this line of reasoning was the perspective that the productivity enhancing *a priori* order of the factory was case enough to do away with the caprice of the market in order to optimise use of resources and accelerate growth and the only reason this did not occur was private asset holding itself. That is, once private property and the atomism it results in is done away with, the organisation of society would naturally move towards one similar to the *a priori* organisation of the factory. This strand of reasoning in Marx and its subsequent elaboration, contributed in no small measure to the near exclusive emphasis on the benefits of co-ordinated investment decision-making in the literature on planning. With hindsight there appear to be two factors that supported this tendency. First, the evidence discussed in detail even by Marx which suggested that the integration of science and production gives rise to concentration and large-scale production. These tendencies were seen as rendering the continuous socialisation of production inevitable, culminating in a social order that parallels the factory. Second, the 'productivist', catching-up syndome that international inequality generated, which was justified by the slack in market-based systems suggested by the factory–society parallel.

There are three contentious issues here. First, the notion that society can be democratically organised as one large factory ignores the implications of the despotic character of technology within the capitalist factory, analysed in great detail by Marx. That is, it ignores the fact that there could be unusual difficulties encountered when a set of technologies that are predicated on the existence of inequalities, which validate the hierarchical structures of knowledge-diffusion and decision-making internal to those technologies, are sought to be imposed on a more democratic and egalitarian social and economic order. The non-existence of such inequalities (epitomised by the dole queue), makes the realisation of the work discipline required for the efficient functioning of such technologies difficult to achieve. On the other hand, the hierarchical nature of organisation implicit in central planning and in the dominance of despotic technologies provide a basis for the excessive bureaucratisation that erodes the flexibility needed to manage complex systems.

Second, the factory–society parallel does not recognise the inevitably contradictory relationship between such despotic technologies and an anarchic market. On the one hand, the benefits of scale economies associated with many such technologies and the high transaction costs associated with dealing at arms length with suppliers and markets, warrant a shift of the firm–market boundary in favour of centralised structures, as evidence by the process of growth of transnational firms, On the other hand, the utilisation of the threat of closure and the unemployment characteristic of anarchic markets, to ensure both capitalist and worker discipline, requires that production is 'organised' with a substantial degree of market mediated relationships.

Third, the emphasis on the factory–society parallel also encouraged the neglect of the fact that the 'technological success' of market-based systems was partly explained by their ability to use resources released because of inadequate demand from the poor for even basic necessities for sustaining a trajectory of product and accompanying process innovations that cashed in on created markets among the upper income groups. To the extent that the 'catching up' slogan implies an imitation of such product profiles in egalitarian systems, it was inherently contradictory. The success of such systems in creating egalitarian societies which provided the basics of cheap food, shelter, clothing, education and culture to the population as a whole meant that resources were spread thinly per capita. That is, even with a high share of income devoted to accumulation, it was unlikely that the profile of products and technologies available in inegalitarian systems could be replicated.

This in itself posed a problem in a world with socialism in few countries, because the media revolution exposed people all over to product profiles that widened the gap between 'desired' and actual consumption patterns. But the problem was aggravated by the fact that, despite long years of sacrifice of consumption in aggregate and *per capita* terms, the rate of increase in consumption in many planned societies over time was limited. The need to catch up militarily and otherwise meant that a high share of output was devoted to investment. But the full benefits of this diversion were not realised. Not only were there obvious instances of inefficient use of resources, but there was also enough evidence to suggest that, in a whole range of 'essential' civilian technologies, the pace of innovation was far slower than elsewhere. The resulting loss of dynamism was, of course, not as visible so long as there existed unutilised labour resources that could be mobilised and put to work at the margin, even if in low productivity environments. But as they were depleted, the above constraints became more visible and binding. Not having an alternative within the 'productivist' thinking captured by the catching up slogan, governments in these countries succumbed to the pressure to accommodate demands for more open regimes that provide access to product profiles available elsewhere in the world. And once they chose that consumption profile, they soon realised that they had no option but that of replicating, even if unsuccessfully, the development path in the capitalist world as well.

Thus the need for a departure from the excessive centralisation that such thinking generated is obvious. But the alternative terrain is not easily defined. Two things have normally been taken as given in theoretical representations of even centrally planned systems: (i) the system should be characterised by free choice of occupation and a market for labour, so that differences in wages between different types of work and locations are the factor ensuring adequate labour supply to less preferable areas; and consequently (ii) the retail market for consumer goods must also be free so that income (and consumption) inequalities actually serve as incentives to attract labour in the direction that it should go. This is because differences in money incomes would lose much of their force as incentives if their recipients are not free to spend them as they please and are free to adjust their patterns of consumption to their individual tastes. It is within such a framework that the efficacy of degrees of centralised decision-making can be assessed. Given such a framework, we could argue that the logical case for co-ordinated investment decision-making notwithstanding, there were a number of strong and questionable assumptions about the area of control of the State which were implicit in a regime where the planning principle was in command.

First, it was assumed that, despite the demands on the surpluses available to the system made by the need to build defence capabilities and ensure basic needs for all, the State could ensure correspondence between the real and financial realms, in a context where labour and consumption goods markets were, on the surface, 'free'. If wage differentials between occupations, necessary to ensure an appropriate allocation of the labour force, were to be meaningful, those money incomes had to be translatable into real purchases based on preferences. With a substantial share of investment pre-empted by the requirements specified earlier, this could prove difficult unless the prices of 'non-essentials' were completely flexible to wipe out any excess demands resulting from supply shortages. But as part of the policy of inflation control it was ensured that, even in the case of non-essentials, it was not prices that were flexible but availability, resulting in suppressed markets (with shortages and queues) and a monetary overhang. In practice, equilibrium was difficult to ensure, creating a gap between consumption aspirations and actualities.

Second, while co-ordinated investment decision-making had an element of logical elegance in theory, its operation required information access and an iterative process of communicating that information that was near perfect. Inasmuch as that chain of communication was constituted of agents with incentives that were not always compatible, there was little that the purely formal organisational structure of the system could do to ensure the near-perfect transmission of relatively correct information. The adverse fall-out of that incompatibility would be all the greater if central decisions are perceived as being arbitrary and based on inadequate information, as interested agents could distort the reverse flow of information. Needless to say, in an interdependent system which is sought to be operated taut through *a priori* planning, any error arising from these problems would transmit itself across the system in ways that are not always predictable.

Third, while primary uncertainty of the kind created by, say, the possibility of wars or natural calamities is an inevitable constraint on growth, there are other less rigidly binding constraints that uncertainties about the likely evolution of consumer preferences and product and process innovations create. Since socialism was a system in which investment in research and development, and in capacity, was co-ordinated and planned *a priori* over a relatively long period, these kinds of uncertainties were implicitly being treated as predictable. The unexpected innovative dynamism of capitalism after the Second World War and the inability of socialist regimes to insulate their populations from the 'needs' generated by that dynamism, rendered this assumption of the predictability of trends in consumer preferences and technological requirements wrong. The area of control of the State was far less here as well.

Finally, all of this proved even more of a problem when, faced with difficulties, many of these regimes opted for a degree of interdependence and reduced insularity *vis-à-vis* the external, non-socialist world. Not only did they find it extremely difficult to compete in international markets to earn the foreign exchange needed to finance enhanced imports, but they were soon subject to the difficulties created by the fluidity of international finance, whose confidence in the economy in part determined the extent of growth and investment that could be sustained. That is, as these economies responded to the problem of limitations on the area of control of the State by opting for a degree of 'liberalisation', they undermined that area of control even further.

There is one implication that could be read from these propositions. Command economy structures tend to fail not only because of the constraints set by the economic and military 'encirclement' by capitalism, but also because they are based on assumptions about the area of control of the State that are not warranted in practice. That is, just as there exists a non-monotonic relation between size or the area of operation of the firm and the efficiency of its operation, there exists a contradictory relation between the efficiency gains of co-ordinated investment decision making and the effort to expand excessively the area of control of a central decision-making authority.

This in itself provides a basis for a system that is more flexible or is run in a manner that makes it less taut than command economy structures. Both theory and experience with socialism in practice suggest that the assumption of the possibility of an omniscient state underlying the 'planning principle' is extreme. Once we do away with that assumption, however, we are left without an alternative structure of functioning institutions, in societies with social ownership. That is, even if we postulate a socialist economy as a planned economy, until we have specified the precise categories of decisions that are centrally planned, the institutions that would make decentralised decisions, and the fall-out of central decisions for the operational functioning of lower units of command, we have not fully specified the system. We are also still left with the problem that the extent and organisational form of decentralisation needs to be defined so as to avoid importing in full the instability and waste of capitalism. That is, we must not only move into a mode of reasoning which neither explicitly nor implicitly counterposes centralised and decentralised economic mechanisms, but also dilute the view that 'no clear-cut logically defined frontier can be drawn between the province of centralised and of decentralised decisions', and that 'only experience can decide the expedient extent of the one and the other' (Dobb, 1969).

NOTES

Detailed comments on an earlier draft of this chapter by Deepak Nayyar are gratefully acknowledged.

1. A more inclusive definition, with characteristics that are not necessarily consistent, is provided by Ortuno-Ortin, Roemer and Silvestre (1993), which takes market socialism 'to be a system of economic organisation in which (1) the state has the authority to influence the pattern and levels of investment across sectors; (2a) most, if not all resources are distributed via markets; (2b) citizens, in particular, earn income from labour that is traded on markets; (3a) firms are publicly owned, which means that profits are distributed to members of the population in proportions that are politically determined; and (3b) firms maximise profits.'

2. One cannot help but note the similarity with the notion that while markets beginning with a given distribution of endowments ensure 'efficient' equilibria, distributional objectives are best ensured through (interventionist) lump-sum taxes and transfers.

3. The assumption was, of course, that planners were 'efficiency-maximising politicians' who were by definition interested in income and asset redistribution, in internalising externalities and in encouraging competition rather than monopoly. This assumption was not borne out by experience in the erstwhile socialist societies.

4. 'The main characteristic features of this system . . . chronic shortage, strong expansion drive, quantity drive, unrestrainable investment spirit – can also be observed when the price level is stable. But they would also persist if the price level began to change and a slow or accelerating inflation evolved.' (Kornai, 1982.))

5. To quote Bardhan and Roemer (1992), 'the whole purpose of designing blueprints for market socialism that can achieve production efficiency roughly similar to that of capitalism, instead of rushing for the 'real thing', is our conviction that such a system would have a more egalitarian income distribution, and would be more sensitive to social needs, such as education, health care and environmental protection. Under market socialism the social dividend, the surplus after payment of wages, interest and taxes in large firms can be redistributed in the form of private consumption for workers or social consumption and investment, We do not believe that entrepreneurial functions require, for their elicitation, the large drain on the social surplus that corporate capitalists usually exact, nor that inherited wealth serves a useful social purpose.'

REFERENCES

Bardhan, Pranab and John E. Roemer (1992), 'Market Socialism: A Case for Rejuvenation', *Journal of Economic Perspectives*, Vol. 6, No. 3, Summer.

Bowles, Samuel and Herbert Gintis (1993), 'Post-Walrasian political economy', in Bowles *et al.* (1993).

Bowles, Samuel, Herbert Gintis and Bo Gustafsson, eds (1993). *Markets and Democracy: Participation, Accountability and Efficiency*, Cambridge: Cambridge University Press.

Brus, Wlodzmierz and Kazimierz Laski (1989), *From Marx to the Market: Socialism in Search of an Economic System*, Oxford: Clarendon Press.

Dobb, Maurice (1960), *An Essay on Growth and Planning*, New York: Monthly Review Press.

Dobb, Maurice (1969), *Welfare Economics and the Economics of Socialism: Towards a Commonsense Critique*, Cambridge: Cambridge University Press.

Hahn, Frank (1989), *Equilibrium and Macroeconomics*, Delhi: Disha Publications.

Hayek, Friedrich A. (1935), *Collectivist Economic Planning: Critical Studies on the Possibilities of Socialism*, London: Routledge.

Kornai, János (1982), *Growth, Shortage and Efficiency*, Oxford: Basil Blackwell.

Marx, Karl (1959 reprint), *Capital, Vol. I*, Moscow: Progress Publishers.

Mises, Ludwig von (1920), 'Economic Calculation in the Socialist Commonwealth', in Hayek (1935).

Ortuno-Ortin, Ignacio, John E. Roemer and Joaquim SIlvestre (1993), 'Investment Planning in Market Socialism', in Bowles *et al.* 1993.

Patnaik, Prabhat (1988), 'Efficiency, Planning and Reforms in Socialist Economies: Some Theoretical Comments', *Social Scientist*, No. 185, October.

Shleifer, Andrew and Robert W. Vishny (1994), 'The Politics of Market Socialism', *Journal of Economic Perspectives*, Vol. 8, No. 2, Spring.

United Nations Development Programme (1993), *Human Development Report 1993*, Oxford University Press: New York.

4

Markets: Evolution, Limits and Relationship to Governance

Arun Ghosh

The role of the market in stimulating economic growth – through the optimisation of production – is a subject which has, of late, given rise to considerable debate. There has also been some confusion – perhaps with justification – between the proposition that markets are an essential feature of the capitalist system, and the assertion that markets (and untrammelled consumer choice) are essential elements of a free society. Liberal thinkers have, in fact, tended to identify the market economy with not only a capitalist society but also a democratic polity. This chapter proposes to examine the logic of both assertions. It is true that, historically, socialist economies (such as have existed in Eastern Europe and elsewhere) have experimented with the organisation of the economy without a market system. It is also true that, historically, markets have thrived in countries which have a capitalist system, and often political democracy. But democracy is not a necessary condition for the functioning of a market system; in fact, the existence of highly autocratic regimes has helped in the development of a flourishing market economy. Nor is it essential for a democratic country to have a 'free market'; indeed, as will be argued later, a truly democratic country *cannot* have a totally free market; and it is also possible to envisage an essentially socialist economy – at least one with a socialistic pattern of distribution – with a functioning market system for a considerable part of the social product. Markets do have an important role in mediating between production and consumption of goods and services. But neither the manner of organisation of production (that is, the capitalist or socialist modes), nor of the distribution of the social product need necessarily be dictated by the norms of (or mediated through) what has come to be described as a 'market economy'.

ORIGIN OF MARKETS

J.R. Hicks[1] has given the best history of the evolution of markets, and has traced the origins of large-scale exchange on a commercial basis. A brief narration of the process, extracted from Hicks, is given here primarily to question a part of the basic premises in that otherwise excellent analysis. Hicks states:

> We have been so accustomed, ever since Adam Smith, to the association of division of labour with market development that it comes with something of a shock when we realise that this was not its origin. The first development of skill is independent of the market ... This alternative description of the non-market economy as a Revenue Economy, in which a surplus of food and other necessaries is extracted from cultivators, and used to provide sustenance for public servants is the final point ... It is a genuine form of economic organisation, which is to be contrasted with the market form ... (Hicks, pp. 23–4).
> ... it is specialisation upon trade which is the beginning of the new world; not the preliminary stages of trading without specialisation. ... How does the trader – the specialised trader – come upon the scene? He cannot trade unless he has something to trade with ... It is tempting to conclude that he ... must have begun by being a pirate or a brigand ... (Hicks, pp. 25–6).

Hicks, however, discounts this possibility. He also discounts the possibility of large specialised traders emerging from the exchange of goods for social gatherings (such as a religious festival). Hicks' explanation of the origin of commerce is the appointment by the King of a steward for revenue collection; and the extension of the duties of the steward to carrying gifts (for the purpose of exchange of gifts between kings). These stewards – who would have kept part of the revenue collection – would have started indulging in trade. However, the explanation can at best be only partial; namely, *who started trading.* The rationale of early trade between the Phoenicians, the Egyptians, the Chinese, the Indians – including the trade in spices and silks and linen, in 'cedarwood, sandalwood and sweet white wine' – would not have been connected primarily with tribute to be paid to emperors. The tribute had to be paid (by the traders) for the facility of being allowed to engage in trade in the new territory. Hicks' explanation of the transition from *petit commerce* to *grand commerce* does not quite explain the emergence of specialised traders.

One must agree with Hicks in regard to the distinction to be drawn between 'the pure trader, who buys to re-sell, to re-sell what is physically the same as what he had bought, and the artisan or "producer" who works on the things he has bought, so as to re-sell them in a different form ...' This is a correct distinction. But then, Hicks goes on to say, that 'It is a technological, not an economic distinction' (Hicks, p. 28). Therein lies the questionable part of his reasoning. The evolution of markets as we see them today – in fact, the very development of the capitalist system through the accumulation of capital – owes its origin to the emergence of specialised trade. The emergence of widespread exchange gives rise to the rapid accumulation of capital. The extraction of 'surplus' from labour predates capitalism, and is a characteristic of feudal societies also. Exchange by the trader is what Karl Marx described as the M–C–M circuit, and not the C–M–C circuit wherein producers participate to exchange 'use-values'. Hicks is, of course, aware of this interpretation, and he has categorically stated that he is 'following the modern view (of Menger and Pareto), not that which Marx took from Adam Smith' (Hicks, p. 29). We would return to this issue later. (For a fuller discussion of this subject, see C.T. Kurien.)[2]

Hicks has drawn attention to the 'political structures' that facilitate the growth of trade; *regulation* to ensure an orderly system of exchanges in a market place; protection of 'property' (by way of wares brought for sale in the market) and 'protection of contract'. The latter calls for legal (or quasi-legal) institutions. At a certain conjuncture in history, as Hicks puts it, it became possible for the mercantile law, which the Greeks had established, to penetrate into Roman law, which then provided the legal framework for the growth of trade in Europe. Hicks also goes on to propound the principle that 'so long as the trade is voluntary, it must confer an All-round Advantage', to the seller, the merchant and the buyer. 'A less profitable trade might have been less inclined to grow; but a profitable trade would grow, simply by the re-investment of profits.' Despite the possibility of 'diminishing returns' which could form an 'obstacle to trade expansion', Hicks feels that 'In trade, as in industry, there are genuine "increasing returns" tendencies ... [arising from] what Marshall called "external economies"' (Hicks, pp. 44–7).

One must point out two major historical violations of Hicks' views. Hicks refers to the fact that 'the merchants of seventeenth century Osaka were even able to proceed to the most sophisticated mercantile dealings, such as the establishment of futures markets ...' (Hicks, p. 37). That they were able to do so reflects the structure of

Japanese society and the characteristics of the mercantile community in Japan, and not simply the political-cum-legal institutions in Japan of that era. Even today, in the unorganised money market in India, deals worth millions are finalised by word of mouth, and the tradition survives – in the community of traders who know each other – because of mutual trust and of a certain business ethic of a people who believe that promises must be honoured. The formal legal contract becomes necessary only when the trader ventures into new territory. And the legal structures work only where there is a a *strong* government, which can ensure the implementation of a contract, however unfair. The growth of trade was thus facilitated by the existence of *strong* governments. But then, none of these essential *requirements* of the growth of a market economy fully explains the rationale of the evolution of a pure trading class. One does not have to believe in socialist ideology to accept the historicity of the evolution of the capitalist system. The displacement of small farmers following the enclosure movement in England, and the growth of colonial markets exploited by a class of pure traders – gave rise to the accumulation of capital. The Industrial Revolution opened up the possibility of division of labour which gave a spurt to the possibility of more rapid capital accumulation. For the evolution of the capitalist process from the 'guild system' in Europe, one must necessarily pass on from the C–M–C exchange circuit to the M–C–M exchange circuit (in Marxian terminology) which ensures the accumulation of capital and the beginning of a purely capitalistic form of production. For the beginning of the capitalistic form of production, we must go back to the commencement of pure commerce – facilitated by the colonies – and the Industrial Revolution which brought about the increasing division of labour (with increasing specialisation of production). The distinction is not merely technological, it is economic. The *accumulation* of capital followed the proliferation of exchange activity by the pure trader.

Hicks has accepted the connection between mercantile expansion and colonisation. He also admits that 'it would be absurd to pretend that those who are dispossessed by colonies of settlement are likely, even in the very long run, to be benefited (by the growth of trade)' (Hicks, p. 52). This may not be a case of people entering into trade 'voluntarily' – *pace* the example given by Hicks of 'penetrations by the market into primary production ... This is indeed what seems to have happened with the very early (seventh to six century BC) export of wheat from the Greek colonies in Sicily' (Hicks, pp. 53–4). The theory of 'All-round Advantage' from trade which is voluntary, is questionable on two further counts.

Historically, trade appears to have expanded in the early days of capitalism wholly on the basis of colonial exploitation, which is a case of unfair exchange. Secondly, and more importantly, exchange between parties with widely divergent resource power is likely to end up with all the gains from exchange ending up with the party with better command over resources. Absence of holding power on the part of the weaker party is the economic rationale; there are other factors including social dominance, powers of persecution, and others, which go with socio-political authority. The brief point is that capitalist exchange is, in a sense, unfair exchange in most cases, starting with the extraction of 'surplus' from labour by the capitalist, to the making of oligopolistic profits in the market for products. That is frequently also true of the division of the gains from international trade (see, Alfred Marshall).[3]

Hicks goes on to say that

> The extension of trade does not necessarily imply more goods; its main function is not to increase the quantity of goods produced, but to reshuffle them so that they are made more useful. The variety of goods available is increased, with all the widening of life that entails. This is a gain which 'quantitative economic theory' which works with index-numbers of real income, is ill-filled to measure, or even to describe (Hicks, p. 56).

One cannot quarrel with the above statement, except that one could question whether the more proliferation of the same variety of consumer goods, with different brand names – involving considerable waste of social capital – necessarily improves the quality of life. Even at the cost of a slight digression, it may be pertinent to quote in this context from a recent issue of the London *Economist* (24 October 1992).[4]

> Every year the world's motor industry spends at least $20 billion developing new cars, and perhaps half as much again revamping last year's models. All this can be money down the drain. Ford spent more than $1 billion redesigning the European version of its Escort model, only to have the car replanned after its launch in 1990. It has now been spruced up again, at considerable cost. (see p.82.)

Since the credentials of the London *Economist*, as a champion of the free market economy, are never in doubt, the sheer waste of reshuffling the product mix, and the doubtful gain in consumer welfare or 'the widening of life' resulting from annual changes in the styling of vehicles, to give only one example, are issues that would need to be studied carefully in reviewing the theory of the market economy.

In a more recent work of his, *A Market Theory of Money*,[5] Hicks has attempted to formalise the theory of 'price formation in competitive markets'; and, in that context, Hicks has sought to explain the functioning of the market system not only for commodities – some of them perishable – which is somewhat distinct from the functioning of the market for manufactures; the function of speculation (and the role of what we now call a 'futures market') and of stockholding for stabilising market prices; the functioning of the labour market; and finally, the nature and characteristics of the market for money and capital. This essay is *not* a review of Hicks' thought, and reference to his most recent work is a little redundant in the present context because there is little that is path-breaking in Hicks' analysis of different markets. A brief word on two points, however, appears to be necessary: first, Hicks' oblique criticism of Keynesian 'full employment' which, under present conditions, is likely to lead to greater employment of those who constitute a *fluid* labour market rather than of those who expect to have 'established' or *solid* employment (to use Hicks' terminology); and secondly, the omission (by Hicks) of the role of international finance capital in recent years – in the form of the Eurodollar/Eurocurrency market following the emergence of a large volume of petrodollars since the mid-1970s – which renders the neoclassical explanation of economic events much like a shadow play (without real characters) because of the sharply divergent rates of growth of world trade and of international finance capital.

One may wonder why so much space has been devoted to summarising what is at best one economist's – although doubtless an eminent one's – view of the evolution of the market system. The reasons are twofold. First, Hicks' is the only authentic description available – other than that of Karl Marx – of the gradual evolution of the exchange economy we see in the developed countries of the world today. Second, although Hicks' view – according to his own description – is premised on the Pareto-efficient version of the market equilibrium concept, Hicks has not failed to observe the obvious cases of unequal exchange (with the colonies) which had helped to foster the growth of the capitalist system in the Western part of the world. What we would suggest in the succeeding sections of this essay is that reliance on an 'unbridled' market economy, especially in the context of a very unequal distribution of resource power, can only lead to the accentuation of the process of unfair exchange that has characterised the development of the capitalist system, and that in a democratic polity, market signals need to be subordinated to meet the basic 'needs' of society, in a manner verging on the principles of a socialist society.

Polanyi's analysis of the market system

Perhaps even more space ought to be given to Karl Polanyi's analysis[6] of the evolution of the market system, and, more particularly, of its impact. However, we need to only briefly give the salient points of Polanyi's analysis, because much of Polanyi's approach is reflected in the problems and limitations of the 'market system', as discussed in subsequent pages. In fact, Polanyi's is a more severe indictment of the present market economy system. It is a trenchant criticism of the 'wrong' premises on which the entire classical theory of Adam Smith and Ricardo is built; and Polanyi takes a historical/sociological view of the total destruction of cultures and of whole societies because of the imposition of a 'global market economy'-based pattern of demand and supply on traditional societies, which disrupts traditional modes of production and age-old norms of equitable distribution. The primacy of the legal 'contract', as opposed to unwritten (but widely observed) codes of conduct within traditional societies, has sought to 'commoditise' both labour and nature to the degradation of human values and devastation of the ecology. Polanyi feels that the emergence of both fascistic and communistic regimes in Europe may be ascribed to the ravages wrought by the market economy, particularly in the inter-war period.

'Man's economy', says Polanyi, 'is submerged in his social relationships' (Polanyi, p. 47). He cites the example of the Melanesian people in the Trobriand Islands whose life was guided by two principles of behaviour, '*reciprocity* and *redistribution*' (Polanyi, p. 47) before the advent of the market economy ravaged them and left them destitute. Polanyi adds that 'it should by no means be inferred that socio-economic principles of this type are restricted to primitive procedures or small communities; that a guilders and marketless economy must necessarily be simple' (Polanyi, p. 49). In a capitalist economy, 'the control of the economic system by the market is of overwhelming consequence to the whole organization of society' (Polanyi, p. 57). Polanyi adds:

> the reasons are simple. Markets are not institutions functioning mainly within an economy, but without. ... The dominating feature of this doctrine is the origin of trade in an external sphere unrelated to the internal organization of economy. (Polanyi, p. 58.)

Polanyi questions the basis of the economic argument for self-regulating markets in 'fictitious commodities', namely, labour, land and money. 'A market economy is an economic system controlled, regulated, and directed by markets alone' (Polanyi, p. 68). Polanyi explains further:

> Commodities are here empirically defined as objects produced for sale on the market; markets, again, are empirically defined as actual contacts between buyers and sellers. ... The crucial point is this: labour, land, and money are essential elements of industry; they also must be organized in markets ... But labour, land, and money are obviously *not* commodities ... Nevertheless, ... with the help of this fiction ... they are being actually bought and sold on the market ... (Polanyi, p. 72.)

Polanyi goes on to trace the development of the market system and the logic of its defence by classical economists, even as sectional interests led to 'protectionism' (in the matter of agricultural produce in England). 'The spread of the market was thus both advanced and obstructed by the action of class forces. ... All this should warn us against relying too much on the economic interests of given classes in the explanation of history' (Polanyi, p. 155).

Polanyi goes on to say:

> America has been adduced by economic liberals as conclusive proof of the ability of a market economy to survive ... The explanation, of course, is simple; it is free labour, land, and money. Up to the 1860s, the frontier was open and free land lasted; up to the Great War, the supply of low standard labour flowed freely ... (Polanyi, p. 201).

When these conditions are exhausted, and they were exhausted in Europe much earlier than in the USA, we have the development of 'the seeming paradox of imperialism — the economically inexplicable and therefore allegedly irrational refusal of countries to trade together indiscriminately, and their aiming instead at the acquisition of overseas and exotic markets' (Polanyi, p. 214).

Polanyi concludes:

> *The congenital weakness of nineteenth century was not that it was industrial but that it was a market society.* ... Yet the shifting of industrial civilization onto a new non-marketing basis seems to many a task too desperate to contemplate. (Polanyi, p. 250.)

Polanyi's solution is a moral/ethical one: 'The problem of freedom arises on two different levels: the institutional and the moral or religious' (Polanyi, p. 254). We do not need to dwell on the Polanyi thesis on this issue, for our own enquiry is on the 'limitations' of the market system, and the possibility of combining some degree of 'freedom of choice' for consumers with the greater freedoms associated with the release of the latent energies of all human beings in a system which would avoid some of the major problems of the present market economy.

We pass on, then, to an examination of the neoclassical view of the market economy.

THE NEOCLASSICAL VIEW OF THE MARKET ECONOMY

We take a quantum jump from the distinctive explanation of Hicks and Polanyi of the evolution of markets to the basic precepts and assumptions of a market economy, as expounded by economic analysts of the neoclassical mould.

The neoclassical theory of the market economy may be said to owe its origin to Leon Walras,[7] who first expounded the concept of a 'general equilibrium'. The theory has been refined by many economists, and later given a mathematical formulation by Koopmans[8] and further by Arrow.[9] Walras believed that, under conditions of free competition between buyers and sellers, not only is the production of goods (and services) optimal, but that the market process would lead to the *simultaneous determination of both product prices and factor prices in an optimal equilibrium.* In other words, the compensation to labour (by way of wages), to capital (by way of interest) and to entrepreneurs (by way of profit) would be moderated for all production sectors through the interaction of demand and supply. The argument for a free market economy basically rests on this formulation of the general equilibrium system.

Of course, modern neoclassicists recognise that there are a number of simplifying assumptions here which do not obtain in real life. The theory rests on the perfect mobility of labour and capital, and assumes the existence of perfect competition. It does not allow for 'indivisibilities' in regard to certain types of investment, and discounts the problem of 'externalities'. These are problems which are well recognised by neoclassicists. Frank Hahn[10] states, for instance, that

> General equilibrium … answers a purely logical question: can a
> decentralised economy of rational and greedy agents whose

actions are guided only by prices be coherent? ... We know that under certain postulates the answer to this question is 'yes'. The answer does not entail the conclusion that, even given the postulates, actual economies are always in a coherent state ...

The central consequence of missing markets is that the Arrow-Debreu economy is transformed into a sequence economy. That is, in general, there will be trade at every date–event pair. ...

The most notorious difficulty with rational expectations arises from a multiplicity of rational expectations equilibria ...

... My conclusion is that in any case we shall have to have a theory of sequence of short runs if we are to have a viable long-run equilibrium theory ... (Hahn, pp. 93–4, 112–13).

What the above boils down to is that 'general equilibrium' is an elusive concept which (a) generally does not obtain in real life, and (b) can only be seen as the goal towards which a series of short period equilibria *may* tend to gravitate. The word *may* is to be underscored in the above statement. If long-period equilibrium is, then, elusive, and we keep having a shifting short-term balance between demand and supply (between each pair of buyers and sellers) in an imperfect market, can we really claim that the allocation of resources under this system is optimal? In this background, two basic issues arise. First, all neoclassical writers (who generally hail from Western Europe/North America) tend to generalise on the basis of the economic systems prevailing in their countries, where some semblance of 'competition' (however imperfect) does exist. Second, *all* neoclassical writers tend to underplay the importance of 'resource power' as a key factor in market decisions and transactions. In fact, since the inequality in resource power is increasing rapidly, it is surprising that this crude fact of life tends to be ignored by otherwise very competent experts on economic motivations.

Thus, what is not recognised by modern economic theory is, first, that the *unequal resource power* of different agents of production makes for an unfair distribution of the social product among different agents of production (inconsistent with Walrasian equilibrium); and, second, that a basic problem with the capitalist system is that it helps to accentuate the problems created by the initial unequal distribution of resource power. A free-market economy rests on the premise of private ownership of the means of production, a concomitant of a capitalist economy. While capitalism doubtless makes for progress (through productivity increases) there are certain innate features of the capitalist system – for example, the tendency towards the development of oligopolistic production, and other restraints (arising from the increasing concentration of production, partly due even to technological changes), and the insufficiency of demand (as Rosa Luxemburg had pointed out quite early) – all of which make for a tendency for labour to be displaced by machinery. In fact, capitalist progress must displace labour by machinery; and the capitalist system has not found a way to transform the gains of productivity into a steady reduction in working hours or reduction in workers' drudgery. It is thus that capitalism invariably tends gradually to displace labour (the only exception being where a capitalist country can pass on this cost to some other country – historically, a colonial country). Again, historically, capitalism has not found a way to 'bump along the path of full employment', as Hicks[11] had once deemed possible. It is thus that, with periodic cycles of the inadequacy of effective demand, and the fear of inflation under conditions of full employment, the economy has a tendency to lapse into a sub-optimal equilibrium. This is familiar ground for those versed in Keynesian theory, although one must add that Keynes[12] was concerned with the short-term cyclical problem of excess capacity (with unemployment and inadequacy of effective demand) in a capitalist economy whereas the issue we are considering is the longer-term tendency in a capitalist economy – arising from its tendency to displace labour by machinery – to settle down to a lower level of employment and output than is feasible. This is a 'structural' weakness of the capitalist system under free market conditions – that is, in the absence of State intervention. A Pareto-efficient equilibrium does not have to be an equilibrium at an optimum level of employment of all factors and, therefore, at an optimum level of output.

Modern neoclassicists (Arrow and Debreu; Arrow and Hahn) make an important assumption in this context. They assume the existence of 'public goods'. Indeed, one should really go back to Adam Smith[13] for this concept, as well as for a pattern of wage payment which is equitable (and which, therefore, would not be consistent with the Walrasian equilibrium wage payment). On this issue, Smith opines that

> What improves the circumstances of the greater part can never be regarded as an inconvenience to the whole. No society can surely be flourishing and happy, of which the far greater numbers are poor and miserable. It is but equity besides, that they who feed, clothe, and lodge the whole body of people, should have such a share of the produce of their own labour as to be themselves tolerably well-fed, clothed and lodged. (Smith, Vol. I, p. 70)

Smith makes no reference to 'market-determined' wage payments in the above context. Furthermore, among the duties or responsibilities of the 'Sovereign' (or the State) outlined by Adam Smith there is – apart from defence, the administration of law and justice, and of educating the populace – the important one

> of erecting and maintaining those public institutions and public works [which], though they may be in the highest degree advantageous to a great society, are, however, of such nature that the profit could never repay the expenses to any individual or small number of individuals, and which it therefore cannot be expected that an individual or small number of individuals should erect or maintain. (Smith, Vol. II, pp. 210–11.)

Thus, there is a crucial role for the State in a capitalist economy, and that pertains to the provision of social and economic infrastructure – the former by way of education and the latter by way of economic infrastructure like, say, roads and communications, even as per Adam Smith. Such heavy investment, low profitability facilities are necessary to facilitate the proper functioning and operations of diverse private agents of production. Incidentally, these ideas find scant reflection in Adam Smith's *Theory of Moral Sentiments*[14] although he does propound the view that 'the wise and virtuous man is at all times willing that his own private interest should be sacrificed to the public interest of his own particular order or society' (Smith, p. 235). In fact, we tend to forget that Adam Smith's 'invisible hand' is heavily guided by 'moral sentiments'.

From the provision of social and economic infrastructure to the provision of social security – in the event of involuntary unemployment – is but a short step taken by most capitalist societies of the West (following Keynes), but that leads us on to the 'limitations' of a free-market economy.

LIMITS TO THE 'MARKET ECONOMY'

It is necessary, in this context, to reiterate not only the problem of 'externalities' (which can be tackled by the provision, by the State, of social and economic infrastructure) but also the innate tendency of the capitalist system (as discussed earlier) to displace labour. In fact, as indicated earlier, the market system has an innate tendency to accentuate the inequalities of income and wealth. And, while most modern societies have found ways to moderate such tendencies (through progressive direct taxation, and through the supply of public goods), the point to note is that the market system, left to itself, is the cause of serious aberrations in the orderly functioning of the economy. In fact, the historical evidence is that, for the capitalist system to function without inflation, the disciplining factor of a permanent reserve army of unemployed labour is necessary, the only exception being during the 1950s and the 1960s when the uninterrupted progress of the capitalist world was possible because of the steady decline in the prices of primary commodities and the abundant availability of cheap oil. To the extent that the success of capitalism depends on the existence of a 'reserve' of unemployed labour, it cannot be said that the 'equilibrium' brought about under the market system represents the optimal use of all resources available in the economy (see, in this connection, Prabhat Patnaik).[15] Indeed, this problem – namely, the tendency of the market system, if not checked, to increase the inequalities in the distribution of the gains of productivity – is a problem which the most advanced developed countries of the West have not been able to resolve. A 'market economy' has found no way to equitably distribute the social product among all citizens; we started with the thesis that, as a result of the unequal resource power of different agents of production, the distribution of the social product is never in accord with a Pareto-optimal Walrasian equilibrium. We also find that with technological progress, capitalism tends to displace labour which causes a further dent in the distribution of the social product insofar as the working class is concerned. All developed countries of the world today (as of 1992) are afflicted by involuntary unemployment of some 6 to 10 per cent of their workforce.

One needs, of course, to remember that, even prior to the evolution of the market system, there existed a highly skewed distribution of resource power. This made for unequal bargaining power; and the evolution of capitalism – with its free market theology – led to the accentuation of an already skewed distribution of income. In that sense, free competition (of the Adam Smith variety) does not exist in real life; what we see is an unequal exchange between different economic agents in any society. It is for this reason that all Western societies have, since the Second World War, followed different variants of a 'Welfare State'. The concept of a Welfare State goes far beyond the type of State intervention envisaged by Adam Smith. To quote from Kurien in this context: 'Far too often the hand of the state is made invisible by describing its economic role as social responsibility lying outside the role of economics' (Kurien, p. 149). Indeed, to put it very succinctly as one author (Heilbroner)[16] has done: 'Remove the regime of capital and the State would remain, although it might change dramatically, remove the State and the regime of capital would not last a day' (Heilbroner, p. 105).

This leads one to the issue that needs to be faced: the nature of the market system is inextricably linked to the nature of the State. It was noted earlier that the market system calls for a number of institutions for its functioning. The nature of these institutions depends crucially on the nature of the State. The market system therefore inevitably reflects the nature of the State in which it functions; and the regulatory principles – for the functioning of the market – reflect the power equations within the State. As a result, the institutions created by the State are likely to reflect the extant coalitions/compromises within different interest groups within the State. Inevitably, the institutions that are likely to be built by such a State would leave an indelible imprint on the functioning of the economic system generally and of the market system in particular.

There are other limits to the application of the 'market principle' in ordering production activity. Of course, certain functions of the State – like, say, the judicial functions – must necessarily remain outside the realm of market forces. But increasingly, even in the purely economic sphere, there are areas where State intervention is inescapable. The issue of ecological balance and environmental pollution control is one such. Left to themselves, market forces would lead to an immense deterioration of the quality of life through unbridled environmental pollution and the destruction of the ecology. This also leads on to a judgment that must be made by every society as to the heritage to be left behind for succeeding generations. Conservation of non-renewable resources – together with improvement of the ecology – would fall under this category of issues on which a judgment has to be exercised by society, in regard to present versus future consumption, where the 'future' is not that of the present generation but of the generations to come.

Finally, one must record the 'wastes' of competition that we see today through the proliferation of the diversity of consumer goods available. Reference has already been made earlier to investments made, because of competitive conditions, in continually redesigning automotive vehicles. One may add numerous other examples, in particular in the cosmetics industry, where competitive advertisements and changes in packaging constitute the cutting edge explaining the success of some brands over others. There is also the worrisome feature of spurious drugs being marketed with impunity in most developing countries, essentially through the power of advertisements, and an ineffective control mechanism to ward off this menace. Just as markets cannot be left free to deal with, say, drugs, the latest trends in regard to 'intellectual property rights', say in the area of microbiology, point to a catharsis of values in the capitalist world of today, in defiance of Adam Smith's 'moral sentiments'.

How frightening the extant regime of the world market system can be would become obvious from another quotation – a rather long one this time – from the same issue of the London *Economist*, under the caption 'Mapping Mankind':

> Genetic engineering is an attractive subject for those who like to have something to worry about. It seems to reduce life from a mystical essence to a lowly commodity. One of the ways this change comes about, in as much as it does, is through the patent process. The idea of patents being granted on genes – the blueprints of life which are being identified in ever greater numbers ... makes lots of people uneasy, especially when the genes concerned are human genes. Luckily, *their discomfort has not prevailed; the world has listened politely, looked at its dividend payments, and carried on regardless.* It is now standard practice to issue patents to companies which have invested time, money and effort in locating and purifying human genes. Those genes then make it easier to produce, sometimes life-saving, proteins. All in all, patents have become crucial to the biotechnology business. [emphasis added] (*Economist*, 24 October 1992, p. 16).

The above illustrates vividly, first, the unequal pattern of competition under the extant philosophy of the capitalist system in the developed world; and secondly, the mythical nature of 'freedom' under the guise of a competitive market economy, where the (developed) world merely looks at 'the dividend payments', and carries on with its *restrictions* imposed by intellectual property rights coupled with freedom of markets.

To conclude this section, every society has to decide what goods/services should be commoditised and produced through the interaction of demand and supply in the market, and what goods/services cannot (or should not) be commoditised, for the welfare of society. The real issue is, therefore, how effectively markets can be used for determining the allocation of resources, within the context and framework of any given society, its objective conditions, and its specific developmental priorities.

MARKETS AND SOCIALISM

Historically, the socialist countries between the years 1917-90 have generally attempted to work out an economic system without the intervention of the market. However, as Oscar Lange[17] has shown, it is possible for a socialist State to plan in such a manner as to make the production system correspond to what would have been produced under an 'ideal' market system. The difference between the organisation of production under the capitalist and socialist economies has been vividly brought out recently by Kurien. To summarise part of his exposition on this issue, under capitalism:

> goods are produced, not in response to the needs of the consumers, but to the differential intensity of the purchasing power of buyers. In a socialist economy, on the other hand, production responds to social needs ... [which] can be shown most clearly with reference to the manner in which socialist economies have been responding to the social need for education and health facilities, recalling that even at rather low levels of resource availability and production, all socialist economies have set aside resources to meet these social needs. (Kurien, p. 167.)

However, whether one has a computerised analogue for market decisions or a functioning market system, raises complex issues.

There are two views in regard to the possibility of introduction of even a *limited* market economy under socialism. Prabhat Patnaik has argued strongly that 'a distinction must be drawn between the market as a social phenomenon, and the market as a computer analogue' (Patnaik, p. 23). In fact, he goes on to say that 'the market as a social phenomenon functions quite differently under capitalist conditions from what the computer analogue view of the market would suggest' (Patnaik, p. 24); and he goes on to expound how the introduction of even a limited market under socialism would introduce the same aberrations and dichotomies as under capitalism. Patnaik's solution is the build up of 'democratic and meaningfully participatory institutions as far as the working class is concerned'.

Kurien, in his exposition of a post-capitalist economy, is prepared to make some compromises in regard to the egalitarian principle.

> [A] post-capitalist economy must be an *inclusive* one; it must give the actual producers – the labourers – the decisive say in matters

relating to production and the settlement of claims; it must not
have the exploitation of workers as one of its systemic features.
(Kurien, p. 160.)

And yet, Kurien emphasises that 'a post-capitalist economy does not
aim at bringing about equality of claims ... differences will exist, the
broad principle being "to each according to his/her work"' (Kurien,
p. 204). One must observe a logical flaw here: the definition of
'work', including mental work, is such that either one goes by the
principle of demand and supply or one goes by the egalitarian
principle of 'from each according to his capacity, to each according
to his need'. And since Kurien also suggests the democratisation of
the polity and participatory character of decision making, it appears
that Kurien's compromise is essentially by way of a transition from
a capitalist society to a truly socialist society.

In the above context, it would be appropriate to add a few
comments from Amartya Sen:[18]

> ... the role of the market mechanism in socialist countries must be
> seen as an important instrumental question. The incentive
> advantage mechanism, in addition to its informational economy,
> are sometimes contrasted with the disincentives of socialist
> economic organisation. That contrast ... is deeply misleading,
> since a socialist economy is free to use or not use the market
> mechanism consistently with public ownership.
>
> The question of incentives was extensively discussed by Marx
> himself in his *Critique of the Gotha Programme*, leading to his
> famous defence of wage payments in line with productivities. In
> fact, the formal exploration of the incentive structure and the
> efficiency of the market mechanism owes a great deal to the
> pioneering writings of socialist economists, including among
> others Oscar Lange and Abba Lerner ...
>
> As it happens, the formal economic literature on the market
> mechanism has also brought out the limitations of that instrument
> when it comes to the allocation of 'public goods' and of
> commodities yielding large 'externalities' ... (Sen, pp. 4–5).

We have discussed this issue earlier. In the present context, it is only
pertinent to emphasise that marketisation of a part of the social
product could well be inconsistent with a socialist pattern of
economic organisation, as Prabhat Patnaik has argued.

What emerges? Is it possible to foresee, first, the ordering of
production in terms of market demand *for a part of the social product*,
and second, competition among State enterprises, in order to ensure

that there is no let up in the effort to secure increased productivity, and greater efficiency? Instead of seeking an unequivocal or categorical answer, let us see what this implies for India which is only beginning to see the evolution of a capitalist production system.

The two most important aspects of socialism are: first, its 'inclusiveness' (as Kurien describes it, which implies the provisioning of the basic material needs of all members of the society), as against the 'exclusive' nature of a capitalist economy wherein 'only owners of commodities can be participants' in the distribution of the social product; and secondly, the 'participatory' character of all decisions – including the crucial decisions regarding the distribution of the available goods (and services) and the pattern of settling claims of different members of society on the available social product. As Kurien observes, 'these decisions must be arrived at through the maximum possible participation of the community at large.'

Is a combination of socialism and limited market operations feasible? We must, in this context, recognise two characteristics of a 'market economy'. First, a market economy essentially rests on the existence of private property, for 'market signals' work through the lure of profits. Second, once we accept the existence of property relations, we must accept the fact that the market system would inevitably lead to inequalities of income distribution, and of wealth. In the event, how does one envisage socialism with even a partly functioning market system? Should we content ourselves with working out the outlines of a system which is as near the socialist ideal as one may reasonably hope to achieve, through appropriate State interventions in both production activity and the distribution of the social product?

Let us take the example of India. In the Indian situation, the existence of a large number of peasants – most of them with extremely small holdings – ensures the existence of private property unless the system is changed totally, as was the case with China in 1949. That is not a feasible proposition. For a very large part of the workforce, therefore, we have a system of private property, where *the problem today is the protection of the interest of the producers rather than the reverse.* In fact, the number of small and marginal farmers is so large that one has to think of ways to make them viable, through 'joint farming' or through 'pooled investments', assisted by State-level investments to improve the productivity of land (by, for instance, improving irrigation and drainage, and the moisture retention capacity of the soil in 'dry' areas), and diverse other innovative ways. We also have a large number of 'tiny' manufacturers, some of them of a cottage-industry type, like, say, the handloom industry. They may need protection for a period until their looms and skills can be upgraded. As long as we are somehow able to work out a production system which gives all these small producers a reasonable income, we have the basis of a functioning market system. But, then, are the small producers condemned to remain small (and in need of support) for ever? Under competitive conditions, some of them would be eliminated and some would grow larger. One does not know, except that technological advances – the Third Industrial Revolution by way of microbiology, of chips and computerised manufacture, of decentralised, renewable energy sources – have now made it possible to think of *efficient* small scale (even household) production, provided the required level of knowledge and skills can be disseminated among all and sundry. In practice, one needs to experiment. One point is clear: effective intervention is necessary to shape the market so that the forces of production are directed towards increased human welfare.

This brings us to the nature of the State, or the nature of governance, for, as we have seen, even the market system is patterned by the nature of the State. The failure of centralised socialist states warns us of the danger of the rule of 'bureaucracy' in the absence of a market system. An unbridled market system, as we have seen, is not acceptable; in fact the international tendency is now to impose the laws of the strong on the weak (*pace*, the recent proposals for the one-sided reform of the GATT). What we need therefore is a *participatory* democracy, so that the organisation of production and the distribution of the social product can be organised in the interest of the entire populace. In fact, if the State is benevolent, the market system can also be guided and made benevolent. To the extent that we are able to induct the Third Industrial Revolution and upgrade the education and skills of the workforce, decentralisation not only of governance but also of economic decision-making may help; but certain rules of the game need to be laid down in regard to providing for the minimum consumption needs of all citizens, and the extent and range of market choice, avoiding the wastes of capitalism. There is no set or universal panacea for human development. Nor is the process of dialectical development predictable. We must constantly experiment so as to combine the advantages of technology, of capitalist production, with socialist distribution. This appears, on the face of it, contradictory; so we must endeavour to reach as near a perfect equilibrium between the two opposite principles of a 'partly capitalist form of production', and 'by and large a socialist pattern of distribution of the social product' as is possible. Kurien accepts that 'a post capitalist economy cannot be converted into a purely logical or theoretical system'. The essence is to (a) provide healthy competition and yet avoid the wastes of competition, (b) lay down certain parameters in regard to the minimum material needs of the population for which provision must be made, and (c) determine a socially acceptable system for settling the manner of distribution of the social product. As Kurien puts it: '"the economy" is a structure of human relationships embedded in and mentally carved out from a larger network of social relationships' (Kurien, p. 206). In this conclusion, Kurien comes close to Patnaik's formulation, wherein institutional structures and participatory decision making are emphasised.

One point is clear. In a genuine democracy, there is need for strong intervention by the State to *moderate* the influence of the market, both for the production of goods and services and for the distribution of the social product.

CONCLUDING REMARKS

In the history of the human race – extending over some 50,000 years or more – the capitalist form of production has a history of considerably less than 300 years. A brief experiment at socialist production – extending over some 70 years in the USSR and some 40 years in Eastern Europe and China – has run into problems, and is being dismantled in the USSR and other countries of Eastern Europe, and modified in China. Meanwhile, capitalism itself has undergone diverse changes in different countries. In the Scandinavian countries we have an extremely modified version, verging on social democracy. On the other hand, in the OECD countries the belief in the 'market economy' has been transformed into the concept of 'market access' for developed countries, with different rules of the game for different countries at different levels of development. Meanwhile, there are problems within the developed countries themselves. The world of 'free markets' is in a flux.

In a perceptive article entitled 'Markets and States: Against Minimalism', Paul Streeten[19] has, *inter alia*, stated:

> Perhaps the most serious problems arise, as Michael Lipton has reminded us, not from market failure but from success, not from government failure but from government success. If it were just a matter of correcting failures, the task would be relatively easy. But

> if the signals propagated by the market are based on a very
> unequal distribution of land, other assets, and income, it is market
> success in responding to these signals that causes trouble.
> (Streeten, p. 20.)

It is this, namely the widely divergent resource power among different agents of production, that nullifies Adam Smith's 'invisible hand', that negates the Walrasian concept of 'general equilibrium'.

One can conclude this essay with an apt quotation from the late Sukhamoy Chakravarty: 'Markets are a very good servant, but a very bad master.' In other words, society has to *use* the market system to its best advantage; society should not allow the market system to run wild and to start dominating production relations and threatening the very fabric of social relations.

In conclusion, one has to remember, that 'markets' essentially reflect the nature and characteristics of the organisation of the polity and the character of the government in a country. A truly democratic country would know how to tame and regulate the market system so that it does not become an instrument of exploitation of man by man.

REFERENCES

1. John Hicks. *A Theory of Economic History*, Oxford University Press, Oxford, 1909.
2. C.T. Kurien. *The Economy: An Interpretative Analysis*, Sage Publications, New Delhi, 1992.
3. Alfred Marshall. 'The Pure Theory of Foreign Trade (1879)', in J.K. Whittaker, *The Early Writings of Alfred Marshall*, London, 1975.
4. *The Economist.* London, 24 October 1992.
5. John Hicks. *A Market Theory of Money*, Clarendon Press, Oxford, 1989.
6. Karl Polanyi. *The Great Transformation* (1944), Octagon Books, New York, 1975.
7. Leon Walras. *Elements of Pure Economics* (1874) (translated by William Jaffe), Homewood and Unwin, London, 1954.
8. T.C Koopmans. *Three Essays in the State of Economic Science*, McGraw Hill, New York, 1957.
9. Kenneth Arrow and F.H. Hahn. *General Competitive Analysis*, North Holland Publishing Co., Amsterdam, 1971.
10. Frank Hahn. 'General Equilibrium in an Imperfect World: Imperfect Markets', in Kenneth Arrow (ed.), *Issues in Contemporary Economics*, Vol. I, Macmillan in association with the International Economic Association, 1990.
11. J.R. Hicks. *A Contribution to the Theory of the Trade Cycle*, Clarendon Press, Oxford, 1950.
12. J.M. Keynes. *The General Theory of Employment, Interest and Money* (1936), Macmillan, London, 1967.
13. Adam Smith. *An Inquiry into the Nature and Causes of the Wealth of Nations* (1776), Everyman's Library, Ernest Rhys (ed.) (1910), reprinted with an Introduction by Seligman, London, 1931.
14. Adam Smith. *The Theory of Moral Sentiments*, D.D. Raphael and A.L. Macfie (eds), Liberty Classics, Indianapolis, 1982.
15. Prabhat Patnaik. *Economics and Egalitarianism*, Oxford University Press, Delhi, 1991.
16. Robert Heilbroner. *Behind the Veil of Economics*, W.W. Norton, New York, 1978.
17. Oscar Lange. 'On the Economic Theory of Socialism', in Lippincott (ed.), *On the Economic Theory of Socialism*, McGraw Hill, New York, 1964.

18. Amartya Sen. 'Socialism, Markets and Democracy', Presidential Address at the Annual Conference of the Indian Economic Association, Trivandrum, Dec. 1990 (mimeographed).
19. Paul Streeten. 'Markets and States: Against Minimalism', in *Political Economy Journal of India*, Centre for Indian Development Studies, Chandigarh, July–Dec. 1992.

IDEOLOGY:
THE INTERNATIONAL CONTEXT

5

Some Lessons from the Two Economic Systems

Amit Bhaduri

I. INTRODUCTION

In the interplay of continuity with change, which is the essence of history, it is far too easy to err on either side. Major historical events appear to be a complete break from the past for those who view history as punctuated mostly by the discrete changes of revolutions and counter-revolutions. But the same historical events may appear to others as the continuation of the past, with perhaps only temporary disturbances. Either view, pushed to the extreme, becomes misleading in judging the significance of major historical events.

By any standard, we are living in eventful times. The collapse of so many socialist countries (and ideological defeat of socialism in others which still pretend to be socialist) within the short span of a few years must be recognised as one of the most dramatic events in the recorded political history of mankind. Probably there exists no parallel to such sweeping changes of political regimes in so many countries, in so short a time, virtually without bloodshed and serious outside intervention. Ironically, if ever a system collapsed under the weight of its own 'inner contradictions', it is the socialist, not the capitalist system!

However, the deeper significance of these events and their implications are bound to be missed if we take an over-simplified view of history. Historical processes are neither a simple continuation of the past nor a sudden break from it. Thus, the critics of socialism, who now rejoice over its collapse, tend to believe that capitalism is being restored in these countries, after the temporary aberration of a few decades of socialism. In other words, capitalist development is the thread of continuity in history, which the socialist experiments tried to circumvent only temporarily. Or, as a current east European joke would have it: 'socialism is the longest route from capitalism to capitalism'.

Dogmatic defence of socialism is an over-simplification of the opposite type. The recent events are seen mostly as 'counter-revolutions' which are undoing the gains of the previous socialist revolutions. It is an over-simplification which hardly goes beyond political posturing; but more importantly, it misleads. A 'counter-revolution' suggests a sudden and discontinuous change – perhaps conspiratorial, perhaps an accidental failure of the leadership – which might not have happened otherwise. This is simply false, because it ignores the cumulative effect of several internal weaknesses of the socialist system, which built up gradually over time to undermine it completely. It is this 'systemic failure' of the socialist countries, despite their many early achievements, which this paper intends to analyse from a macroeconomic point of view.

II. THE MODEL OF 'SOCIALIST ACCUMULATION'

It is a matter of an accounting identity, and is therefore totally non-controversial, to decompose statistically per capita income (GDP) into its three main components: (a) *participation ratio*, the ratio of active to total population; (b) *occupational distribution* of labour, especially between the relatively low (labour-) productivity agricultural and high productivity non-agricultural sectors, and especially organised industry and services; and, (c) *labour productivity* in individual sectors.[1] It follows that together they constitute the three basic sources of economic growth and every historical pattern of economic development, whether largely left to the market forces or consciously driven by the State, has to tap these three sources of growth for the rise in per capita income and output over time.[2] Growth patterns may differ but they cannot escape this arithmetic.

Almost all the socialist countries, with perhaps the singular exception of former Czechoslovakia, showed a satisfactory, high rate of economic growth in their early years – for about a decade – immediately after the establishment of the socialist regime. The high rate of economic growth was especially marked in the Asian socialist countries like China and the former North Vietnam. It may be safely inferred, as some commentators have pointed out, that the main source of this growth was a State-propelled model of accumulation which relied almost entirely on raising the participation ratio and intersectoral labour transfer from lower productivity traditional agriculture to industry. The rise in the participation ratio did not only come from adopting a conscious full-employment policy. It was also due to a significant rise in the participation of women in the labour force. Both China and North

Vietnam pushed this strategy to its extreme, but with a basic difference from their East European or Soviet counterpart. Unlike in the Soviet Union and East Europe, they largely provided employment and reallocated labour *within* the agricultural sector. Thus, labour was employed on irrigation, land improvement, construction work etc., mostly in agriculture, as members of communes or cooperatives. They were mostly paid through a fairly complex rationing system of 'work points', often graded according to the nature of the work performed. Macroeconomically, the system boiled down to providing 'full-employment' through a *redistribution* of consumption goods from the already employed to the previously unemployed, who were now being drawn into the labour force.[3] The 'savings' to finance the investment or capital formation (mostly in agriculture and related construction) came largely *not* from an increase in immediately consumable output but from redistribution, which depressed the real wage rate *per worker*. Analytically, it constituted a change in the *composition* of output in favour of investment, as the content of the growth process failed to raise per capita consumption in any significant way. In this respect, 'socialist accumulation' was distinctly different from 'capitalist accumulation'; it was redistribution, rather than rapid expansion of consumable output which was relied upon, to finance the process of agricultural development, particularly in North Vietnam and in China in the early phases.

This essential characteristic of relying on the redistribution of consumption through a tight rationing system for financing development was also present in the State-sponsored industrialisation process in all socialist countries. The Soviet Union was the model. However, there is a common misconception which arose probably from the heat of the debate between Bukharin and Preobraensky over inter-sectoral terms of trade and, the ruthless collectivisation under Stalin (who got rid of both the debaters physically, in succession, as 'right' and 'left' deviationists). The debate was concerned with the mechanism by which 'agricultural surplus' is to be provided for industrialisation, on the implicit assumption (not made by Bukharin) that agriculture would 'finance' industrialisation. In actual fact, recent analysis of data, at least by some authors, suggests that industry largely 'financed itself'. But it did not happen in a way that Burkharin had wanted, that is by engaging peasants in voluntary exchange of agricultural products for industrial goods at reasonably attractive 'terms of trade' for the peasants. Instead of offering such price incentives to the peasants to raise food production, much of Soviet industrialisation was financed by depressing the real wage rate *per industrial worker*.[4] The poor production performance of collectivised agriculture coupled with a forced industrialisation drive tended over time to accentuate this tendency of depressing real wages. With some variations on this basic theme, 'socialist accumulation' therefore came to be characterised by a mixture of full employment or high participation ratio with depressed real wages, a marked feature even today of many CIS countries. On hindsight, it is easy to see that this mixture is sustainable over time only by denying workers the right to strike for higher wages and related trade union activities. Ironically, just as today's developing countries that wish to attract multinational investment for 'capitalist accumulation' have to keep real wage low and labour 'disciplined', socialist accumulation with full employment became possible only under similar conditions.

There was, however, an even deeper macroeconomic problem which undermined the system in the longer run. Socialist accumulation was 'supply determined', rather than 'demand determined'. Its proponents tended to confuse this with the virtues of full employment, but the reality was somewhat different. In so far as industrial investments are concerned, it meant that the 'acceleration principle' the positive link between increased demand (or, more generally, capacity utilisation) and investment ceased to operate; or rather, it operated in *the reverse.* The volume and pattern of investment were decided by the central planners, which through the multiplier mechanism created a corresponding level and pattern of demand (at any given real wage). However, virtually no feedback mechanism was allowed for that level and pattern of demand to influence investment through the accelerator. Despite all its ruthless bias against the poor, the market mechanism has been capable of fostering growth with periodic fluctuations, precisely because there exists a strong *interaction* between demand generation through investment (the 'multiplier') and investment generation through demand (the 'accelerator').[5] 'Socialist accumulation' reduced itself to a bureaucratically determined investment programme, irrespective of the level and pattern of demand. Thus, rationing became a permanent feature of this system, not simply because a high level of investment had to be financed through depressing real wages (as mentioned earlier) but also because the bureaucratically determined supply composition of output bore almost no relation to the composition of demand. As a Polish economic statistician, working on the real wage time-series data for the 1970s and 80s, summed up in 1989: 'the problem is not only low and falling real wage, but many of the important items which constitute the real wage basket are simply not available at almost any price'.[6] Real wage ceased to represent the purchasing power over the *relevant* range of goods for most workers in the socialist countries, as the divergence between the supply and the demand pattern increased over time. The system, in other words, faced a double squeeze: real wage restraint was severe to finance investment accumulation and, at the same time, wage goods were absent or hopelessly scarce because of a bureaucracy-driven investment programme. A peculiar paradox increasingly plagued the socialist economies. Despite apparent full employment, they became characterised by horrible scarcity. In contrast, the capitalist economies, despite significant unemployment over business cycles produced too much in relation to market demand!

III. WHY THE MODEL FAILED

One might try to sum up the socialist economic experiment with accumulation. In its early phase, it was undoubtedly successful in generating a process of *extensive growth,* which depended on raising the participation ratio as well as inter-sectoral labour transfer (less in China and Vietnam) from agriculture to industry. That pattern of extensive growth was 'financed' mostly through *redistribution* from the already employed to the unemployed, who joined the labour force under the process of extensive growth. This was a mixed blessing even in the early phase. It meant the achievement of *full employment,* but at the cost of *depressed real wage per worker* as the composition of output consistent with the extensive growth had to be biased against immediate consumables. But this growth process became more or less stuck at its early extensive growth phase for two reasons. The two obvious sources of economic growth – higher participation ratio and inter-industry labour transfer – began to dry up, as these economies used up available labour and industrialised to a significant extent. The strategy now needed to be changed from extensive to intensive growth, which relied more on growth in labour productivity in individual sectors. This did not happen, however. Even the most elementary macroeconomic mechanism of creating mutual feedback between the level and pattern of investment on the one hand and the level and pattern of demand on the other, was not in place. In analogy with the Keynesian separation between investment and saving decision, the socialist economies saw a growing *separation* between bureaucratic central planners allocating investments and ordinary consumers generating the pattern of demand. Keynes taught us that the fluctuations in income and employment in a capitalist economy are caused by that separation between investment and savings decisions. Experience of socialist planning sadly showed something worse: the separation between bureaucratic investments and demand by ordinary consumers not only leads to a persistent pressure to keep down real wages, but it also creates an acute scarcity of essential goods entering the wage basket. It is simple-minded dogmatism to believe that 'Western consumerism' through modern telecommunication undermined the system. Scarcity of even essential goods was increasingly becoming acute, as the mismatch between bureaucratically determined supply and consumer demand grew worse over time. The system did not correct itself and ultimately paid the price.

The interesting political question is why the system failed to correct itself. The problem is often misunderstood, both by the sympathisers and by the critics of socialism. It is often posed as a problem of the State versus the Market and, the associated incentive structure, e.g. 'rent seeking' versus 'private profitability', that are supposed to operate as the prime movers of the two respective systems. This debate is mostly vacuous without a more careful analysis of both the nature of the State and the structure of the market as an institution. The crux of the matter is simple: reasonably self-regulating markets cannot be in place without assigning a proper regulatory role to the State.[7] But, on the other hand, unless the institution of the State itself has a built-in self-correcting mechanism, it would tend to abuse its regulatory role.

The sympathisers of socialism have all along been right in pointing out the 'anarchy' of the market place and the failures of the price mechanism. Its distributive ruthlessness against the poor is often unacceptable. Moreover, it may generate faulty signals regarding private and social profitability. But this well-founded scepticism about blind reliance on the market does not, in any way, justify reliance on the State without analysing the nature of the State. It is in this latter respect that socialist thinking erred fundamentally. Its root can be traced back at least to Lenin's purposive over-simplification of the problem.[8]

The view that the State represents the interest of a well-defined class and, the Communist Party as the 'vanguard' of that proletariat class would represent unerringly the interest of the working class turned out to be incorrect in two fundamental ways. First, the Marxist view of capitalist development was historically flawed, in so far as the industrial workers even in advanced capitalist countries never attained a numerical majority.[9] Either the State had to inflate artificially the 'working class' (e.g. Stalinist collectivisation of agriculture) or drift away from the interests of the working class towards the amorphous majority composed of several social groups, as recognised by European social democrats. In this respect, the problem which large, organised trade unions face today in Western capitalism is probably not so different from the problem faced by the 'working class' oriented socialist States earlier. Second, and more fundamentally, the idea that the communist party, *by definition,* invariably represented the interest of its chosen class (or classes) almost becomes a metaphysical 'doctrine of infallibility' (like the principle of the Pope's infallibility). The communist State becomes devoid of any significant self-correcting mechanism, as the Leninist formulation encourages one to equate the 'Party' with the society at large, in the mistaken belief that the former acts always as a barometer of the mood of the latter. Serious mistakes in the process of socialist accumulation could perhaps be corrected, but the 'incentive structure' generated by socialist theory and practice does not encourage correction. Without any independent self-correcting economic or political mechanism, extraneous to the Party structure – either in the form of a reasonably functioning market mechanism or in the form of a political democracy of countervailing centres of power – the socialist experiment of creating a 'better society' could not have succeeded. It failed not because it made mistakes, but because doctrinaire rigidity ruled out serious attempts at correction. That no social system – no matter, how good it looks in theory – can survive long without a strong built-in political and economic mechanism for self-correction, may be the most important lesson we should learn from the failure of doctrinaire socialism.

NOTES

1. Let P = population, L = active labour force and X/L = labour productivity x, with subscripts a, i and s denoting agriculture, industry and services respectively. Then, by definition,

$$(X/P) \equiv (L/P) \ [(X_a/L_a).(L_a/L)+(X_i/L_i).\ (L_i/L)+(X_s/L_s)(L_s/L)]$$

as indicated in the text.
2. One sector models, e.g. R.M. Solow's 'Technical change and the aggregate production function', *Review of Economics and Statistics,* 1957, Vol. 39, pp. 312–20, attributed an absurdly high figure (87 per cent) as the contribution of technical progress to American growth, primarily because it was incapable of incorporating structural changes, especially in the occupation structure. Just as our habit of thought is conditioned by our language, similarly the questions we can ask are conditioned by the 'model' we choose!
3. This was forcefully argued by R.F. Kahn in 'The challenge of economic development' in his, *Selected Essays in Employment and Growth,* Cambridge, Cambridge University Press, 1972.
4. See M. Ellman, 'Did agricultural surplus provide the resources for the increase in investment in the USSR during the First Five Year Plan?' *Economic Journal,* December 1975, Vol. 85. Note, however, that a decline in real wage per worker does not

necessarily imply lower earning *per family,* if the participation rate increases, with more than one family member, on average, employed gainfully.

5. Most formal models of endogenously generated cycles and/or growth rely on various specifications of the interaction between the 'multiplier' and the 'accelerator' mechanism.

6. Private communication with the Polish economist, W. Sadowski in Warsaw, 1989.

7. The revised orthodoxy of the World Bank would have us believe that 'the State should do things it can do best', e.g. education, health and (perhaps) some economic infrastructure, but it should keep away from industrial production. The simplicity of this view is almost touching! There is no reason to believe that the State (or the government) which cannot run (say) an electric bulb factory would be able to run an efficient or worthwhile education system. Again, the crux of the problem is an understanding of the nature of a particular State or government.

8. Especially in V.I. Lenin's *State and Revolution,* New York, International Publishers, 1943.

9. See A. Przeworski, *Capitalism and Social Democracy,* Cambridge, Cambridge University Press, 1985:

    > . . . from 1890 to 1980 the proletariat continued to be minority of the electorate. In Belgium, the first European country to have built substantial industry, the proportion of workers did break the magic number of the majority when it reached 50.1 per cent in 1912. Since then it has declined systematically, down to 19.1 per cent in 1971. In Denmark, the proportion of workers in the electorate never exceeded 29 per cent. In Finland, it never surpassed 24 per cent. In France, the proportion declined from 39.4 per cent in 1893 to 24.8 in 1968. In Germany, workers increased as a proportion of the electorate from 25.5 per cent in 1871 to 36.9 in 1903 and since then have constituted about one-third of the electorate. In Norway, workers constituted 33 per cent of the electorate in 1894 and their proportion peaked in 1900 at 34.1 per cent. In Sweden, the proportion of workers in the electorate grew from 28.9 per cent in 1908 to 40.4 per cent in 1952; then it declined to 38.5 in 1964. (pp. 23–4)

6

International Trade and Factor Mobility: Economic Theory and Political Reality

Deepak Nayyar

This chapter attempts to explore the relationship between international trade and international factor movements in the sphere of economics and situate it in the realm of politics. It argues that the explicit prescriptions and the implicit neglect of economic theory both conform to the compulsions of political reality. The hypothesis is borne out by the developments in the theory of international trade, when juxtaposed with the evolution of the free trade doctrine in the political arena during the nineteenth and twentieth centuries.

The structure of the discussion is as follows. Section I traces the origins of the free-trade doctrine in classical political economy to set out the fundamental propositions of orthodox trade theory which provide the basis for the prescription that free trade would lead to both efficiency and equity. Section II endeavours to analyse the relationship between international trade and factor mobility in the abstract world of economic theory. However, it considers not only international trade in goods and international capital movements, which have been the subject of attention, but also international trade in services and international labour movements, which have been the object of neglect. Section III situates this economic theorising in the wider context of the political realities which have shaped the sequence of developments in the international trading system over 200 years. The discussion concludes by focusing on the present conjuncture to highlight the asymmetrical treatment of international trade and factor mobility.

I. FREE TRADE DOCTRINE

The analytical foundations of the orthodox theory of international trade, as it now exists, were laid in the era of classical political economy by Adam Smith, David Ricardo and John Stuart Mill.

Smith (1776) enunciated the principle of absolute advantage to demonstrate that there were gains from trade by extending his concept of the division of labour between men to a division of labour between countries. Ricardo (1812) formulated the theory of comparative advantage to develop an explicit argument against protection and an implicit argument for free trade. The concerns of Smith and Ricardo did not lie in abstract economic principles. Their economics was rooted in politics. Indeed, their intellectual pursuits were motivated by a strong desire to challenge the political dominance of mercantilist ideology. At the same time, their economic thinking endeavoured to provide a rationale, and to analyse the conditions, for a transition to nascent capitalism.

Thus, in the limited sphere of trade, the Ricardian formulation of comparative advantage was not simply about the pattern of trade or the gains from trade, as contemporary text books would have us believe. It was as much, if not more, about the impact of international trade on income distribution, capital accumulation and economic growth. The repeal of the Corn Laws and the adoption of free trade was advocated by Ricardo in the belief that it would redistribute incomes away from the reactionary landed gentry, who would at worst not save and would at best invest in agriculture, which promised diminishing returns, in favour of a progressive industrial capitalist class, who would earn more profits (given a lower corn wage) through cheap imports of wheat, and invest in manufacturing which promised increasing returns. The moral of the story was that, consequent upon the removal of restrictions on trade, an increase in profits would lead to an increase in the rate of accumulation which in turn would lead to a growth in employment, income and wealth. Economics and politics were closely interwoven in this world, for the redistribution of incomes from rents to profits was bound to be associated with a redistribution of political power from landlords to capitalists.

Subsequent economic theorising about international trade began to separate the economics from the politics. This process started with Alfred Marshall and Francis Edgeworth in the late nineteenth century. It was taken to its logical conclusion by Eli Heckscher, Bertil Ohlin and Paul Samuelson during the first half of the twentieth century. In retrospect, it would seem that economics, so divorced from politics, slowly but surely acquired a life of its own. The selectivity in the choice of problems and the abstraction in the choice of assumptions made this difficult task much simpler. These choices shaped a corpus of thought where elegant models based on restrictive assumptions reached strong conclusions. Orthodox trade theory, which began life in this mode, soon came to don the mantle of mainstream economics. In this milieu, seeking a different set of answers, let alone asking a different set of questions, was perceived as unorthodox. The intersection of economics and politics in the sphere of trade was of course set aside, as a model-fetishism captured the imagination.

The neo-classical paradigm as it emerged emphasised the gains from trade. The economic logic underlying the proposition was indeed simple. In the most elementary sense, there are gains to be derived from trade if it is cheaper, in terms of domestic resources used, for an economy to import a good than to produce it at home, and pay for it by exporting another. The gains are attributable in part to international exchange when costs or prices differ among countries before trade is introduced, and in part to international specialisation in production after trade commences. In a world where countries enter into international trade on a voluntary basis, each partner must derive some benefit to be in the game. The very existence of trade, then, becomes proof of its mutual benefit, irrespective of how the gains from trade are distributed between countries. It is clear, however, that the formal exposition of the gains from trade proposition was no more than an analytical contribution to economic theory. Its message was already widely accepted, as the mercantilist view about asymmetry in the gains from trade – exports were beneficial but imports were not – had been discredited much earlier in the mid-nineteenth century.

There were two other propositions which emerged from the theory of international trade in this phase and provided the basis for dramatic policy prescription: the free trade argument and the factor-price equalisation theorem. The free trade argument, formalised in the normative dimension of orthodox theory, served an explicit prescriptive purpose in stating that free trade is efficient. The factor-price equalisation theorem, set out in the positive dimension of orthodox theory, carried an implicit prescriptive significance in suggesting that free trade is also equitable. Let me elaborate.

In terms of the orthodoxy, the economic logic of the gains from trade proposition combined with the assumption of perfect competition establishes that free trade would be optimal. The reasoning is straightforward in a two-commodity model. Perfect competition ensures an equalisation of the domestic price ratio with the marginal rate of substitution in domestic production. Free trade ensures an equalisation of the domestic price ratio and the international price ratio. Thus it is argued that free trade will enable the economy to operate with technical efficiency in production in terms of resource allocation. Given well-behaved utility functions, free trade, which equalises domestic and international prices, would also enable the economy to optimise consumption through trade, by equalising the marginal rate of substitution in consumption and the international price ratio, in terms of utility maximisation. The neat conclusion derived from such theorising was that free trade ensures efficiency.[1]

The factor-price equalisation theorem emerged as a corollary of the Heckscher–Ohlin formulation of comparative advantage. Samuelson (1948) set up a model in which there are two countries (America and Europe), two commodities (food and cloth) and two factors (land and labour). It is assumed that there is free trade in goods and that there is no factor mobility between the countries. The factor endowments are such that America has a higher ratio of land to labour than Europe and the production conditions are such that food requires a higher ratio of land to labour than cloth. Production functions, which differ between commodities, are identical across countries, and are characterised by constant returns and diminishing marginal productivity. There is perfect competition in both commodity markets and factor markets. These assumptions about production conditions ensure a unique relationship between the factor-price ratio and the commodity-price ratio. In this world, free trade equalises commodity prices. As long as both countries continue to produce both commodities, the marginal productivities of the factors must be the same in both. Thus, if complete specialisation is ruled out, commodity-price equalisation necessarily leads to factor-price equalisation.[2] The abstraction in the assumptions of the model represents substantive departures from reality but yields a powerful conclusion to suggest that, even in a world where international factor movements are not possible, free trade would ensure equity through an equalisation of factor prices across countries.

It is clear that the free trade argument and the factor-price equalisation theorem were not simply about abstract principles. Their prescriptive significance, whether explicit or implicit, is obvious. The economic theory may have been separated from political reality but it was not divorced from it. Indeed, the ideology of free trade, which ran into acute difficulties during the period from the Great Depression to the Second World War, served not only the economic interests but also the political interests of Britain and the United States during the first half of the twentieth century.[3]

II. ECONOMIC THEORY

The theoretical literature on international economics, mostly in the neo-classical tradition, has grown at a phenomenal pace during the second half of the twentieth century, yet it has not made a significant contribution to our understanding of the relationship between international trade and factor mobility. The orthodox theory of international trade, both positive and normative, even in the 1990s, is mostly about the movement of goods and not very much about the movement of capital or labour across national boundaries. Insofar as it is concerned with international factor movements, the focus is on capital mobility so that labour mobility is, at best, a corollary.

The Heckscher–Ohlin–Samuelson formulation of comparative advantage, which seeks to explain the pattern of trade between countries in terms of differences in factor endowments, suggests that international trade in goods and international factor movements are substitutes for each other. The underlying logic is straightforward. In the conventional two-country, two-commodity, two-factor model, export of the labour intensive good by the labour-abundant country constitutes an implicit export of labour, while export of the capital intensive good by the capital abundant country constitutes an implicit export of capital. If, instead of goods, it is factors of production that move across countries, from where they are relatively abundant to where they are relatively scarce, the basis for trade in goods would narrow and vanish over time. Indeed, the factor-price equalisation theorem discussed above, which assumes free trade in commodities but no mobility of factors, suggests that international trade in goods and international factor movements are perfect substitutes for each other.[4] In such a world, the movement of capital from rich to poor countries and the movement of labour from poor to rich countries should erode the basis for trade but strengthen the tendency towards an equalisation of factor prices.

This proposition was validated by the earliest theoretical analysis of the relationship between international trade and capital mobility.[5] Given the assumptions of the Heckscher–Ohlin framework, Mundell (1957) examines the consequences of a tariff on imports of the capital intensive good in the labour abundant country which raises the real wage of capital, the scarce factor. Capital mobility would then progressively reduce commodity trade. The model suggests that impediments to trade stimulate factor mobility, but it is plausible to reverse the causation and argue that factor mobility dampens trade flows.

The conclusion is not surprising. International trade in goods, and movement of factors, would tend to be substitutes for each other if differences in factor endowments are the basis for trade. However, if international trade is attributable to other structural differences between economies, it is possible that trade in goods and movement of factors between countries may complement each other rather than acting as substitutes for each other.

Subsequent theoretical developments did move in this direction. Kemp (1966) and Jones (1967) dropped the assumption of identical production functions, or technologies, across countries but retained the Heckscher–Ohlin framework to examine the impact of capital mobility on international trade, where countries are simultaneously engaged in cross-border trade and investment. In this Ricardian setting, their conclusion is that international capital movements may complement, rather than substitute for, trade in goods. In the same mode, it was argued that if technologies differ between countries, the possibility of international capital movements may enlarge and not diminish the volume of trade.[6]

Attempts to explain the observed pattern of trade between countries with similar, or dissimilar, factor endowments developed theoretical understanding further. The technological gap theories of trade sought to focus on differences in technology between countries as a source of trade.[7] The product cycle theories of trade sought to focus on differences in wages between countries as a source of trade.[8] The synthesis of the two approaches, which emphasised scale economies and product differentiation in the analysis, came to the conclusion that international trade and international investment complement each other. Thus, in a world where there are differences in technology and differences in wages between countries, international trade stimulates cross-border investment just as international investment enhances cross-border trade flows.

The complementarity between trade and investment in these models provides an explanation for the phenomenal, simultaneous, expansion of international trade in goods and international capital movements during the past three decades. The theory followed the reality, insofar as it was difficult to explain the changing patterns of trade and the increasing capital mobility observed in the world economy in terms of the Heckscher–Ohlin–Samuelson formulations.

In sharp contrast, the theoretical literature on the relationship between international trade and international labour movements has remained sparse. The theorising on factor movements and national advantage, where capital mobility is the theorem and labour mobility is the corollary, addresses two basic questions. First, is there a difference between private and social costs or benefits or do the interests of migrant labour and labour-exporting countries coincide?[9] Second, what is the distribution of gains between labour-exporting and labour-importing countries?[10] There is, however, no analysis of the relationship between migration and trade, just as there is no examination of the factors underlying international labour movements. Simple extensions of intra-national rural–urban migration models, set out in terms of differences in wages and employment probabilities, are obviously inadequate.[11] It is not surprising, then, that the determinants of the timing, the duration, and the volume of international labour movements remain unexplored.

It is not as if there is a basis for this neglect either in theory or in reality. The treatise by Ohlin (1933), which provides the analytical foundations of orthodox trade theory, discusses not only international trade in commodities but also international factor movements, whether capital or labour. Indeed, Ohlin recognised the relationship between labour mobility and trade flows in citing the example of French Huguenots who moved to Germany and Holland during the seventeenth century to set up textile production, which squeezed French textile exports. Later history provides an altogether different example. The abolition of slavery in the British Empire led to the migration of people from India as indentured labour for mines and plantations in south-east Asia, southern Africa and the Caribbean during the nineteenth century, which, together with the movement of capital from Britain, stimulated international trade flows that were based on natural resources or climatic conditions.[12] The twentieth century has also witnessed a movement of labour from surplus labour countries to labour-scarce countries, which may have been stimulated by colonial or post-colonial ties embedded in language or culture, and the dimensions are by no means insignificant. Thus, historical experience suggests that there is a relationship between international trade and international migration, whether as substitutes or as complements.

An important question arises. Why is there such a mismatch, or asymmetry, between theoretical constructs and historical experience? In my judgment, it has much to do with the observed reality in the world economy during the second half of the twentieth century. There has been a rapid liberalisation of trade in goods associated with a progressive dismantling of restrictions on the movement of capital across borders. But, as boundaries between nation states have become sharper, restrictions on the movement of labour have not only continued but have intensified. Thus, economists have tended to assume that international labour movements are determined primarily by non-economic factors. Economic theory has therefore sought to analyse the consequences of the observed labour mobility on international trade, but has not attempted to analyse the causes of labour mobility. It is no surprise that the interactive causation between international trade and international migration, which may run in both directions, remains unexplored.

Given the complexity of historical experience, it is obviously difficult to generalise and to theorise. A complete or systematic analysis is, in any case, beyond the scope of this chapter. Nevertheless, in the context of the contemporary world, it is plausible to hypothesise as follows. International trade in goods and international capital movements broadly complement each other, for reasons explored in the theoretical literature, particularly differences in technologies and wages between countries. The internationalisation of production combined with the integration of international capital markets, which is reflected in an increase in the share of world trade in world output and an increase in the share of intra-firm trade in world trade, has reinforced this process. In contrast, international trade in goods and international labour movements are now mostly substitutes for each other, because, given immigration laws and consular practices, capital-abundant countries which are relatively labour-scarce prefer to export capital and employ cheap labour abroad, or simply import goods that embody the cheap labour, rather than import labour. In either case, labour is embodied in goods and moved across national boundaries, thus acting as a substitute for direct labour imports. But this is not possible with international transactions in services, where the service must be provided directly by its producer.

The emerging complementarity between international trade in services and international labour movement must be recognised, although it has received almost no attention in orthodox trade theory. Trade in services is a phenomenon that has gathered momentum over the past decade, but it is in its early stages despite the internationalisation of production and because of the lack of integration in international labour markets. The labour mobility associated with international trade in services takes the form of temporary migration. The guest-workers in western Europe, the seasonal import of Mexican labour in the United States, the export of workers from south Asia and north Africa to the oil-exporting countries of the Middle East, and the more recent import of workers by labour-scarce countries in east Asia, are, at least in part, an illustration of the complementarity between labour mobility and services transactions across national boundaries.

At an analytical level, trade in services can be defined as international transactions in services between the residents of one country and the residents of another country irrespective of where the transaction takes place. International trade in services, so defined, can be divided into four categories: those in which the producer moves to the consumer, those in which the consumer moves to the producer, those in which either the producer or the consumer moves to the other, and those in which neither the producer nor the consumer move to each other.[13] In the last category, where a service can be disembodied from the producer and transported to the consumer in much the same way as a good, international trade in services is no different from international trade in goods. The first three categories, however, derive from the characteristics of services as distinct from goods. For one, the production of a service and its consumption are simultaneous and, as a rule, services cannot be stored. For another, the producer and the consumer must interact with each other for which physical proximity is essential if the international service transaction is to take place. Therefore, unlike goods or disembodied services which can be shipped or transported from one country to another, most services have to be executed and delivered on the spot. It follows that cross-border movements of capital and labour are not just complements to, but constitute an integral part of, international trade in services.

Labour mobility is essential for trade in services whenever the producer must move to the consumer to deliver the service. The temporary migration of unskilled, semi-skilled or skilled workers in manual or clerical occupations, from poor countries to rich countries, may be necessary to deliver labour-intensive services. The temporary migration of persons with professional expertise, technical qualifications or managerial talents, from rich countries to poor countries, may be necessary to deliver capital-intensive or technology-intensive services. In either case, the temporary movement of labour across national boundaries represents a situation where the producer of a service moves to its consumer. Elsewhere, I have argued that production and consumption of the service are then both located in the importing country.[14] The service is provided by a non-resident producer to a resident consumer, for which the former receives payment and returns him after a specified duration. The payment, presumably made out of the income of the consumer, may or may not cross borders in its entirety after the transaction, but the producer crosses national boundaries before and after. The movement of non-resident producers in such international transactions is characterised by a specificity of purpose and a limited duration. In situations where a non-resident producer becomes a resident foreigner, so that the duration is unlimited, transactions with resident consumers are no longer trade because the relocation of production on a quasi-permanent basis, or in perpetuity, becomes a substitute for trade in services. In theory, it follows that the moment a non-resident producer ceases to be non-resident and becomes resident, trade ends and migration or investment begins. In practice, of course, it is far more difficult to make a clear distinction between international trade in services and international migration or international investment, simply because trade and factor movements are closely intertwined in the realm of services.

III. POLITICAL REALITY

The preceding discussion suggests that the contours of economic theory in the sphere of international trade, in emphasis as much as in neglect, were shaped by politics, which was more transparent in classical economics than it is in neo-classical economics. It is also clear that economic ideas about trade have not shaped political reality. However, economic interests, whether perceived or real, have exercised an important influence on the political objectives of nation states in the world economy. The experience of the past 200 years provides ample confirmation.

Economic theorising about trade has always considered a world in which countries at similar levels of development are equal partners, thus ruling out the use of political power to foster economic interests. This abstraction simply does not conform to reality. It never did, as Joan Robinson (1974) wrote, even in Ricardo's world. In a now famous example, Portugal was to gain as much from exporting wine as England from exporting cloth. This was not quite true even in terms of economics. Once we introduce capital accumulation into the picture, it is clear that free trade promised growth for England and stagnation for Portugal, for investment in cloth would be associated with increasing returns whereas investment in wine would be associated with diminishing returns. But that is not all. In the realm of politics

> Portugal was dependent on British naval support, and it was for this reason that she was obliged to accept conditions of trade which wiped out her production of textiles and inhibited industrial development, so as to make her more dependent than ever. (Robinson, 1974, p. 1.)

The consequences of imperialism in trade are brought home by another historical example which also illustrates flexibility in the use of the free trade doctrine over time and space.[15] To begin with the British cotton textile industry in Lancashire grew up under protection from superior Indian imports. When it became competitive, free trade was imposed on India. A century later,

Indian textiles were once more able to undersell Lancashire. In response, the British turned to protection again, this time through the multi-fibre agreement.

It is clear why free trade was in the interest of countries which were the pioneers in industrialisation. Their economic strength was perhaps a source of their political, even military, power which enabled them to impose free trade on the rest of the world. For this reason, the ideology of free trade went well with British imperialist expansion until the early twentieth century and with American political hegemony thereafter. The imposition of free trade on the underdeveloped world was simple enough because much of Asia, Africa and Latin America was colonised either *de jure* or *de facto*. It was, however, difficult to impose on countries at similar levels of development, such as Germany and Japan, which were latecomers not only to industrialisation but also to colonial empires. The exclusion of such rivals from sources of raw materials and from promising markets contributed to the tensions that led to the two world wars.[16] The 1930s witnessed a different form of economic conflict between the advanced capitalist nations, attributable to similar causes, as countries resorted to import controls, competitive devaluations and so on to protect their own levels of income and employment at the expense of the outside world.

The lessons that emerged from this experience of economic chaos and political conflict were not lost on the architects of the international trading system that was created, with the GATT as its centrepiece, in the late 1940s. Its basic foundation was the principle of non-discrimination embodied in the 'most-favoured-nation' clause. The virtues of unilateral free trade were recognised in theory but were not accepted in practice. It was agreed that trade barriers would be made transparent by a conversion into tariffs which, in turn, would be progressively reduced through negotiations. Thus, universal free trade was perceived as the ultimate objective, but the conceived transition path was characterised by an implicit reciprocity principle that was almost mercantilist. The contractual framework of the GATT meant that countries would negotiate market access and tariff reductions on a reciprocal basis, through bargaining among major trading partners, and this was to be multilateralised through the GATT system. Clearly, the countries of Western Europe seeking to reconstruct after the war, and conscious of American dominance, were not willing to accept free trade at that juncture.

The acceptance came soon. The next 25 years witnessed trade liberalisation among the major industrialised countries at a rapid pace. The *modus operandi* was successive rounds of multilateral trade negotiations, under the GATT umbrella, which brought tariffs in the industrialised countries to levels that were almost negligible. This process was facilitated in politics by American hegemony and in economics by rapid growth associated with full employment. The influence of these factors began to wane in the mid-1970s, and there was a turn of the tide as the industrialised world resorted to increasing protectionism over the 20 years that followed. Large segments of world trade such as agriculture and textiles were excluded from GATT discipline. Non-tariff barriers proliferated: some misused GATT rules (anti-dumping or countervailing duties), others circumvented GATT rules (grey-area measures like voluntary export restraints and orderly marketing arrangements), while a few were not even in the realm of trade (laws about standards or health regulations). The outcome was a steady erosion of the principle of non-discrimination. The surge of trade liberalisation and the rise of protectionism in the second half of the twentieth century were both attributable to the pursuit of national economic interests by countries which had the requisite political power. In the first phase, the industrialised world led by the United States wanted free trade and had the political hegemony to achieve it. In the second phase, as growth slowed down, and as recession persisted and unemployment mounted in the industrialised economies, the United States and the European Community both turned to protectionism as a means of preserving their economic interests; the East Asian countries, led by Japan, wanted free trade but did not have the political strength to impose it on others.

The Uruguay Round of multilateral trade negotiations was launched in an attempt to resolve the crisis in the international trading system, but was different from the earlier rounds in a fundamental sense. It was not concerned with conventional tariff reductions for trade liberalisation. At one level, in the realm of traditional GATT issues, it was about the implementation of existing rules in the multilateral trading system, which have been eroded, circumvented or flouted in the recent past. At another level, *à propos* new issues, it was about the formulation of new rules in vital spheres of international economic transactions, many of which have thus far been a matter for bilateral negotiations. It is necessary but not sufficient to recognise why and how the Uruguay Round was different from the earlier rounds of multilateral trade negotiations. The differences are much wider and deeper than its enlarged scope. GATT-type rules and principles, with provision for dispute settlement, compensation and retaliation are sought to be extended beyond trade in goods to international flows of capital, technology, information, services and personnel. The quest for international regimes of discipline on trade-related investment measures, trade-related intellectual property rights and trade in services is closely intertwined with the interests of transnational corporations who are capital exporters, technology leaders and service providers in the world economy. For them, these new issues represent the final frontier in their global reach to organise production and trade on a world scale without any fetters.[17] The interests of transnational corporations were perhaps an important factor underlying the political impetus to conclude the negotiations, with compromises wherever necessary to resolve the issues of conflict among the major industrialised countries.

The conclusion of the Uruguay Round is going to change the rules of the game for international trade as the twentieth century draws to a close. The new international regime of discipline will provide for a progressive dismantling of barriers to international trade in goods and international capital movements. This will be associated with a strict regime for the protection of intellectual property rights but there is nothing to facilitate international labour movements. It is striking that the principle of non-discrimination embodied in the most-favoured-nation clause, which is being extended beyond the limited sphere of trade in goods,would still not govern labour mobility so that immigration laws can, as always, continue to practise discrimination by country-of-origin. The proposed multilateral framework for trade in services also caters to the interests of rich countries which have a revealed comparative advantage in capital-intensive or technology-intensive services, but makes little allowance for labour-intensive services in which poor countries have a potential comparative advantage. The movement of labour from developing countries to deliver services in the markets of industrialised countries is a matter for bilateral, sector-by-sector negotiations, where immigration laws and consular practices would remain the dominant constraints.

It would seem that the institutional framework for globalisation, which has been shaped by political reality, is characterised by a striking asymmetry. National boundaries should not matter for trade flows and capital flows but should be clearly demarcated for technology flows and labour flows. This asymmetry implies that developing countries would provide access to their markets without a corresponding access to technology and would accept capital mobility without a corresponding provision for labour mobility. It should come as no surprise that orthodox economic theory would conform to this reality by suggesting that free trade combined with capital mobility is both efficient and equitable, insofar as the import of goods that embody cheap labour together with the export of capital that employs cheap labour is a substitute for labour mobility. The opposite question, as to why the same objectives of efficiency and equity cannot be attained by international labour mobility, will simply not be asked by conventional economics because it is a mark of orthodoxy not to ask politically inconvenient questions.

NOTES

I would like to thank Amit Bhaduri for helpful discussion and useful comments.

1. There were, however, two critical assumptions underlying this persuasive prescription: first, that market prices reflected social costs and, second, that a country's trade in a good was not large enough to influence world prices. If these assumptions do not hold, free trade cannot ensure an efficient outcome. This was recognised a century earlier by Mill (1848). Market failure provided the basis of the infant industry argument just as monopoly power provided the basis of the optimum tariff argument. Modern neo-classical economics accepts these as reasons that justify departures from free trade but reduces the validity of such arguments to a demanding set of conditions. See, for example, Corden (1974) who provides a meticulous analysis of the conditions under which the infant industry argument and the optimum tariff argument constitute valid arguments for protection.
2. For a systematic and rigorous exposition, see also Samuelson (1949).
3. For an interesting analysis of the interplay between ideology, interests and institutions in the context of the political debate about free trade, both in Britain and in the United States, see Bhagwati (1988).
4. Cf. Samuelson (1948) and (1949).
5. See, for example, Mundell (1957).
6. See Purvis (1972).
7. The seminal contribution came from Posner (1961). This was developed further by Hufbauer (1966).
8. See, in particular, Vernon (1966) and Hirsch (1967).
9. This issue is discussed by several authors. See Grubel and Scott (1966), Johnson (1967) and Berry and Soligo (1969).
10. For a discussion of this issue, see Ramaswami (1968) and Bhagwati (1979).
11. The most frequent cited model of rural–urban migration within surplus labour economies is that of Todaro (1969).
12. This phase of international labour migration from India is examined, at some length, by Tinker (1974).
13. For a detailed discussion on problems of definition and the distinction between different categories of trade in services, see Nayyar (1988).
14. Cf. Nayyar (1989). The following discussion in this paragraph draws on earlier work of the author cited here.
15. This example, too, is drawn from Robinson (1974).
16. For a lucid discussion on economic conflicts during this period, see Diaz-Alejandro and Helleiner (1982).
17. It is worth noting that the Uruguay Round agenda did not extend to short-term capital movements across national boundaries, which are an integral part of international financial transactions and international currency markets.

REFERENCES

Berry, R.A. and Soligo, R. (1969), 'Some Welfare Effects of International Migration', *Journal of Political Economy*, pp. 778–94.

Bhagwati, J. (1979), 'International Factor Movements and National Advantage', *Indian Economic Review,* pp. 73–100.
Bhagwati, J. (1988), *Protectionism,* Cambridge MA: The MIT Press.
Corden, W.M. (1974), *Trade Policy and Economic Welfare,* Oxford: Clarendon Press.
Diaz-Alejandro, C.F. and Helleiner, G.K. (1982), *Handmaiden in Distress: World Trade in the 1980s,* Ottawa: North-South Institute.
Grubel, H.G. and Scott, A.D. (1966), 'The International Flow of Human Capital', *American Economic Review,* pp. 268–74.
Hirsch, S. (1967), *Location of Industry and International Competitiveness,* Oxford: Clarendon Press.
Hufbauer, G.C. (1966), *Synthetic Materials and the Theory of International Trade,* London: Duckworth.
Johnson, H.G. (1967), 'Some Aspects of the Brain Drain', *Pakistan Development Review,* pp. 379–411.
Jones, R.W. (1967), 'International Capital Movements and the Theory of Tariffs and Trade', *Quarterly Journal of Economics,* pp. 1–38.
Kemp, M.C. (1966), 'The Gain from International Trade and Investment: A Neo-Heckscher–Ohlin Approach', *American Economic Review,* pp. 788–809.
Mill, J.S. (1848), *Principles of Political Economy,* with an introduction by W.J. Ashley, London: Longman.
Mundell, R.A. (1957), 'International Trade and Factor Mobility', *American Economic Review,* pp. 321–35.
Nayyar, D. (1988), 'The Political Economy of International Trade in Services', *Cambridge Journal of Economics,* pp. 279–98.
Nayyar, D. (1989), 'Towards a Possible Multilateral Framework for Trade in Services: Issues and Concepts' in UNCTAD, *Technology, Trade Policy and the Uruguay Round,* New York: United Nations.
Ohlin, B. (1933), *Inter-regional and International Trade,* Cambridge: Harvard University Press.
Posner, M.V. (1961), 'International Trade and Technical Change', *Oxford Economic Papers,* pp. 323–41.
Purvis, D.D. (1972), 'Technology, Trade and Factor Mobility', *Economic Journal,* pp. 991–9.
Ramaswami, V.K. (1968), 'International Factor Movements and the National Advantage', *Economica,* pp. 309–10.
Ricardo, D. (1812), *The Principles of Political Economy and Taxation,* with an introduction by Donald Winch, London: Dent, 1973.
Robinson, J. (1974), *Reflections on the Theory of International Trade,* Manchester: The University Press.
Samuelson, P.A. (1948), 'International Trade and the Equalisation of Factor Prices', *Economic Journal,* pp. 163–84.
Samuelson, P. (1949), 'International Factor-Price Equalisation Once Again', *Economic Journal,* pp. 181–97.
Smith, A. (1776), *The Wealth of Nations,* with an introduction by Andrew Skinner, Harmondsworth: Pelican Books, 1970.
Tinker, H. (1974), *A New System of Slavery: The Export of Indian Labour Overseas: 1830–1920,* London: Oxford University Press.
Todaro, M.P. (1969), 'A Model of Labour Migration and Urban Unemployment in Less Developed Countries', *American Economic Review,* pp. 138–48.
Vernon, R. (1966), 'International Trade and International Investment in the Product Cycle', *Quarterly Journal of Economics,* pp. 190–207.

7

Local and Global Monopolies and the Prospects of Global Democracy

Amiya Kumar Bagchi

1. CONTRASTING TRADITIONS IN THE ANALYSIS OF MONOPOLIES AND LANDLORD POWER

The neo-classical economics that ruled academic establishments from the late nineteenth century to the end of the 1920s refused to consider monopoly or oligopoly as a regular feature of the capitalist economy. What is often considered to be the greatest achievement of the marginalist revolution, that is, the Walrasian theory of general equilibrium, explicitly assumed that all individual economic agents were price takers. Although A.A. Cournot, J. Bertrand and F.Y. Edgeworth built rigorous mathematical models of the behaviour of monopolies and duopolies, they continued to be treated as special cases until the Sraffa–Chamberlin–Robinson revolution put forward the claim that the behaviour of monopolistic, oligopolistic or imperfectly competitive firms should be treated as the norm, and pure competition as a polar case of idealisation. This, however, did not happen for a long time. Perhaps the best proof of that non-acceptance is that John Maynard Keynes, when he formulated his general theory of employment, while breathing the atmosphere of the Sraffa–Robinson revolution in the theory of competition, still assumed that firms were price takers in product markets. Indeed, the 'neo-classical synthesis' that ruled the roost as Keynesian economics in post-Second World War academia had the purely competitive behaviour of firms embedded in its foundational structure. (For a short introduction to the varieties of macro-economics that have evolved since Keynes, see Bagchi, 1994a.)

In contrast to this tradition, there has been a strong current in Marxian political economy, which takes price-making behaviour by large firms as the standard pattern in a modern capitalist economy. A clinching example of the strength of this tradition is that Michal

Kalecki, while independently formulating a theory of involuntary unemployment under capitalism, assumed that a typical firm enjoyed a degree of monopoly power and fixed its prices on a cost-plus basis.That the tradition derives directly from Marx is shown by the latter's formulation of the laws of centralisation and concentration of capital under industrial capitalism.

While these laws – and the general perspective that capitalism evolves through a process of competition and building up of monopoly power working simultaneously – originated with Marx, there is another aspect of monopoly power under capitalism which was signalled by the masters of classical political economy to whom Marx repeatedly acknowledged his debt. This aspect is the monopoly control of land by landowners. For a long time after capitalism had come into being, land remained the most valuable means of production under the control of the capitalists. David Ricardo and many of his associates viewed the power of landlords to increase their share of the national income through various stratagems and, most importantly, through the curbing of competition in the grain market with the help of laws against the free import of corn, as a serious impediment to the accumulation of capital and hence to economic progress.

Following in this tradition, but modifying it to put the concentration of land in a few hands as an enemy of progress, Marx pointed to the exaction of ground rent by private landowners as an impediment to the mobility of capital between different sectors and localities in search of the highest rates of profit, and hence to capitalist competition, increases in productivity and accumulation of capital (Marx, 1894, Chapters XXXVII to XLVII).

For various reasons which I need not go into here, the general run of academic economists bypassed, if they did not actively suppress, the classical political economy heritage of analysis of shares of income along the lines of social classes. They also seemed to be oblivious of the problematic of long-term economic change at least until the Second World War. Schumpeter was a major exception to this collective amnesia, but Schumpeter was greatly influenced throughout his life by the Marxian problematic even as he strove strenuously to fight the spectre of socialism portended by proclaimed followers of Marx.

Among the professed Marxists, the contributions of V.I. Lenin, Rudolf Hilferding and, later on, Kalecki, Paul Baran and Paul Sweezy may be singled out for the attention they paid to the role of capitalism in giving rise to monopolistic organisations, the influence of monopolies on patterns of capitalist growth, and on inter-capitalist competition and conflicts, and on the other side, for emphasising the role of landlord power in slowing down capitalist transformation. Among the major theorists named above, Lenin combined all the strands to produce theories of uneven development. The Baran–Sweezy theories of hegemony of monopoly capital at one pole and continued underdevelopment at the other can be regarded as having been derived from Lenin's theories of uneven development and imperialism. (There are, of course, differences of opinion about how 'pure-blooded' the theories of underdevelopment are in the genealogical tree of the Marxist-Leninist canon: see, in this connection, Palma, 1978).

Lenin analysed the development of capitalism in a rather backward country, namely Tsarist Russia, and showed how private ownership of land was both hindering and advancing that development. He combined that study with an analysis of how new organisational forms were evolving in the most advanced areas of capitalism to give rise to new patterns of competition and new bases of monopoly power and thus involving the whole world in horrendous crises of uneven development. I will not try to engage in any such exercise in the present essay. What I will try to do to here is to recall briefly that continual striving for supernormal profits or monopoly rents has been a characteristic feature even in the pioneer capitalist countries of the world, and that the 'dissipation' of rents earned by landlords has been the result of further growth of capitalist competition in that singular case, but the abolition of landlord power has been the necessary condition of both sustained capitalist growth and bourgeois democracy in the world after the French Revolution. I will also argue that the analysis of 'rent-seeking' behaviour in the 'new political economy' churned out by the adherents of the Chicago–Virginia school can be embedded in a broader analysis of macroeconomic conjunctures and configurations of social classes in order to derive lessons for conducting struggles for democracy on a global scale. In carrying out such an analysis we can draw on the Marxist tradition as well as a considerable amount of modern work which demonstrates how monopolistic positions are generated and reproduced by the forces of competition for markets, command over finance, and technology. (For summaries of this work and a guide to the literature, see Tirole, 1989, especially Chapters 6–10).

Within the genre of the new political economy, Gordon Tullock (1967) has been credited with a systematic discussion of rent-seeking behaviour in the context of public regulation. But the term 'rent-seeking' was used for analytical purposes for the first time by Krueger (1974). Krueger confined her attention to the development of 'a simple model of competitive rent seeking for the important case when rents originate from quantitative restrictions upon international trade' (Krueger, 1974, p. 291). Krueger's examples of licit and illicit gains arising from the use and manipulation of the import licences were derived almost exclusively from the case of India. Most of the further applications of this type of reasoning have been made in the context of the so-called restricted foreign trade regimes occurring in less-developed countries before the recent spate of IMF–World Bank-inspired structural adjustment policies swept away most of the restrictions on foreign trade.

The analysis of rent-seeking by the committed ideologues of the Chicago–Virginia school concentrates very largely on government regulation, and many of the adherents neglect the possibility of 'fruitful' or socially useful dissipation of rents or, conversely, of the utilisation of rents for purposes of accumulation and infant technology protection (see, in this connection, Tirole, 1989, pp. 76–8). But even when attention is turned to the study of rent-seeking outside the domain of government regulation, the analysis remains largely microeconomic in nature and takes little account of the influence of private economic power on the patterns of social relations. Moreover, most of the rent-seeking literature assumes supply-constrained rather than demand-constrained behaviour on the part of economic agents. By contrast, for example, Baran and Sweezy (1966), in their analysis of the behaviour of capitalism under the hegemony of monopoly capital, assumed that the dominant capitalist economy – the US economy of their time – was operating under a regime of deficient demand. Lenin (1917) recognised the role of both inter-capitalist struggle for markets and, conversely, of acquiring resources for accumulation, in generating conflicts that could not be resolved peacefully, or more generally, without altering the rules of the capitalist game. In the rest of this chapter I shall use the phrase 'rent-seeking' without the implication that the analysis of rent-seeking by the practitioners of 'the new political economy' can be assimilated in an unadulterated fashion to the rival Marx–Hilferding–Lenin–Baran–Sweezy tradition of monopoly capital in its panoply of contradictions and global spread.

2. VARIETIES OF RENT-SEEKING

Our discussion above suggests that there is no reason to confine the domain of rent-seeking behaviour to a single country or to look for the genesis of rents only in the regulatory behaviour of governments (as it is done, for example, in the chapter on rent-seeking in Mueller (1981), or in the entry on rent-seeking in the *New Palgrave*

(Tullock, 1987)). Historically, rents have been sought by:

(a) landlords,
(b) merchants looking for extraordinary profits,
(c) companies which were granted special charters by European powers for trading abroad,
(d) colonial governments,
(e) individuals or companies which obtained special privileges because of government regulatory measures, including tariffs and quotas restricting foreign trade,
(f) companies or entities utilising their initial advantages in marketing, finances, new technologies, privileged access to markets or raw materials to obtain above-normal profits.

Among these entities, group (a) was a special target of attack by David Ricardo, James Mill and John Stuart Mill. Some of Karl Marx's most vitriolic prose was reserved for Thomas Robert Malthus, whom Marx regarded as a reactionary spokesman for landlord interests. Henry George, Leon Walras, and Lenin all regarded landlordism as a major constraint on capitalist development (for a summary of Lenin's views on rural classes and the nature of land reforms needed to promote capitalist development, see Bagchi, 1982, Chapter 6). One of the most fascinating stories in history is how landlord power consolidated itself in Britain, then gradually merged with the political power of the bourgeoisie in trade, finance and industry, and liquidated itself by the end of the nineteenth century. We shall briefly sketch this story in a later section, partly because recent work helps us understand how political power at the command of those seeking rent from land allowed them to consolidate their power and how, eventually, structural changes in the economy led to the euthanasia of this particular set of rent-seekers. One problem with the 'restricted foreign trade regime' style of analysis of rent-seeking is that it is not rich enough to throw light on the dynamics of historical change of any but the most restricted kind.

Now we turn back to rent-seekers among merchants, financiers and industrialists.

3. RENT-SEEKING BY MERCHANTS, FINANCIERS AND INDUSTRIALISTS

The early history of modern capitalism, especially in respect of long-distance trade and trans-oceanic trade, is replete with rent-seeking by merchants. The most conspicuous examples of this were, of course, the European companies which were granted special charters by their governments to trade with distant parts of the world. The spoils of the Dutch and British East India companies, the Baltic companies, the Africa companies, the slave trade carried on between Africa and the Americas, and numerous such enterprises for trading with and plundering foreigners, aided the process of primitive accumulation in Europe. These enterprises and the colonies founded by these pioneers laid the foundation of the 'unequal exchange' relations that have characterised the trade between Europe, North America and the rest of the world for the last 400 years (for succinct accounts of this aspect of primitive accumulation see Marx, 1867, Chapters 31 and 33 and Dobb, 1963, Chapter 5; for analyses of the phenomenon of unequal exchange, see Bharadwaj, 1985, and Chandra, 1986).

These monopoly companies were global rent-seekers, and there were no instruments they did not use in seeking global rents. They engaged in piracy on the open seas, raided and burned ports and cities, massacred the population of whole regions, and confiscated crops and valuables of the people they brought under their sway; their directors and functionaries also repeatedly sought to influence the policies of their home governments. Many of these companies ceased to engage in commerce while their owners led an exalted life as colonial overlords and receivers of rent and tribute from millions of peasants and artisans.

Paradoxically enough, in their drive to maximise total rents, colonial governments could appear as champions of the local peasantry. Thus in British India, the advocates of the *raiyatwari* settlement wanted no *zamindars* to share in the rents to be extracted from the peasants. Their drive to maximise rents was often accompanied by an ideology of egalitarianism as far as the colonial society was concerned, but with a firm determination that all State power should be concentrated in the hands of a few foreigners (Mill, 1818, Volume VI; Thackeray, 1806; Stein, 1989). The publicists and politicians in the early days of colonial India often gave matter-of-fact accounts of the tribute extracted from the dependency but, in the later period, the ideology of the White Man's Burden, or the civilising mission of the colonial power, led official spokesmen to deny the reality of the tribute (Mill, 1826; Barber, 1975, Chapters 8 and 10). So vehement opponents of rent-seeking by 'natives' such as James and John Stuart Mill turned out to be supporters of maximisation of rents by the colonial rulers. (Failure to appreciate this colonial–metropolitan duality and duplicity has misled many later commentators, who have put forward Mill, the father or Mill, the son as a champion of democracy or peasant farming. See, for example, Platteau, 1983; Majeed, 1990.) The monopolisation of rents by a single authority may well be less wasteful of resources than competition for the sharing of rents (Tullock, 1980). But it makes a difference as to whether the monopolist is a foreign government intent on remitting as much of the rent as possible or a local despotism intent on increasing investment at home, or, in the alternative case, whether the competitors for rents are local capitalists or landlords who invest most of their profits locally or at least spend most of their incomes on domestic goods, or whether they are foreign capitalists keen to repatriate most of their profits to their home countries or other foreign countries.

Apart from these global merchants in commodities, arms and political power, there were also local merchants speculating in times of famine, exercising legally constituted monopoly powers or cornering essential goods through rings and cartels. There were money-lenders who had the custom of whole villagers under their monopolistic control. There were bankers and financiers who financed local landlords, princes and emperors. Some of them ceased to be bankers and emerged as revenue collectors, revenue farmers and potentates controlling large territories. The whole of the eighteenth century and much of the period of colonial rule in India is a history of such transformations. In these ages, the State and private interests co-existed as joint rent-maximisers, and there was often little distinction between the interests of the rent-earners and those of the State.

In this early period of the emergence of capitalists as industrialists, individual industrialists could seldom become controllers of a particular branch of manufacture. Economies of scale were quickly exhausted, product differentiation could not establish monopoly power on a national scale, and the arts of advertising had not developed enough to endow particular products with the aura of magic. Even in those days, however, some manufacturers or artisans could utilise their skills to create special niches for themselves. Moreover, in countries which had established systems for protection of inventions through patents, some clever inventors could create rents for themselves by defending their patents against alleged infringements. Watt's steam engines, for example, were considered uneconomical by many mine-owners and manufacturers because of their high price so long as his patents were valid. The firm of Boulton and Watt won a large sum as arrears of money due for patent infringement in its action against Jonathan Hornblower in 1799, only a year before the patent monopoly of 25 years granted to Watt's basic invention by an Act of Parliament was due to expire (Ewing, 1888, p. 414; Von Tunzelmann, 1978, pp. 77–8).

In later times, as economies of scale became much more pronounced, especially in process technologies, and as technical invention and changes in consumer tastes brought forth new products, product differentiation, advertising and advantages in transport and communication often allowed many local monopolies to come up. With the progress of the industrial revolution, research and development in industry were also characterised by economies of scale. Although there are doubts as to whether large firms are uniformly, or even on average, better at research and development than small firms, the former can generally reap the advantages of research and development – whether carried out by themselves or by others – better than the small firms, and can thus add to their monopoly power (Scherer, 1984). Moreover, the growth of the financial power of large manufacturers, and the backing by independent financiers, led to movements for horizontal and vertical mergers of firms. These national cartels could then become formidable players in the international game. The various anti-trust measures passed by the US Congress in the late nineteenth century were meant to address the problem of private monopoly power and barriers against new competition erected by the actual and potential monopolistic or oligopolistic firms. However, there was no organisation to extend the Sherman Act internationally. While law-enforcing authorities in the US – or the other advanced capitalist countries – took a dim view of restrictive practices at home, they had neither the power nor the willingness to enforce any norms of competitive behaviour abroad. Oligopolistic or monopoly firms based in G7 countries have become the most powerful rent-seeking entities in the world today, and we will turn our attention to that rather neglected aspect of rent-seeking behaviour in a later section. Just now we will briefly look at the transformations in rent-seeking that took place in Britain, the first industrial nation in world history.

4. TRANSFORMATION OF A RENT-SEEKING SOCIETY: THE BRITISH EXPERIENCE

As the first country to make a full transition from feudalism to capitalism, and also as the first country to have passed through the industrial revolution, Britain has been studied as an exemplar by the admirers and critics of capitalism and democracy from Montesquieu and Voltaire to Karl Marx, Joseph Schumpeter, Maurice Dobb and Barrington Moore. In *Capital,* Volume 1 (Marx, 1867, Chapters 26–33), and in numerous other writings, Marx analysed the course of British economic and social policy since the decline of serfdom and feudalism in England. He clearly perceived that serfdom had already declined in England by the fourteenth century and that, during the next two centuries in a series of civil wars and spoliation of church lands, the feudal tenures were superseded by the estates of noblemen and substantial landlords. Many peasants were driven from the land and a class of propertyless labourers grew up, mostly in the countryside. Along with feudal dues, feudal claims of peasants to the land were also abolished (in fact, although not always in law). Marx noted another wave of expropriation of the peasants, starting in the late seventeenth century with the Settlement of 1688, during the period which has been characterised as that of the consolidation of the Whig oligarchy. This time around, a series of Parliamentary enclosures were used by the landlords and their friends or clients in Parliament to achieve the purpose of privatising common lands and expropriating many of the peasants. H.J. Habakkuk put forward the proposition that the degree of concentration of land in England, which was already large by the end of the seventeenth century, increased further during the next 60 years or so (Habakkuk, 1940). This Marx–Habakkuk hypothesis has largely been confirmed by later research (Cooper, 1967; Thompson, 1969; Stone and Fawtier Stone, 1984; and Beckett, 1984).

Robert Allen (1992) has recently focused his analysis sharply on the formation of a class of landowners and capitalist farmers at one pole and a class of small peasants and agricultural labourers at the other pole during the five centuries of evolution of capitalist agriculture in England. He has put forward the proposition that we should distinguish between two agricultural revolutions in English history – the yeomen's and the much more famous landlords' (Allen, 1992, p. 13). In the enclosures and conversion of arable land to pasture that occurred between 1450 and 1525, as many as one-tenth of the villages in the English Midlands (the area studied intensively by Allen) were destroyed; but the process alarmed the Crown, which proceeded to protect the remaining open-field villages, and thus the yeoman appeared as a major player in the English countryside. The free peasants or yeomen were, however, impoverished, sold up or enclosed out during the eighteenth century which saw the consolidation of the great estate in England.

In fact, Allen's conclusions are not as original as they sound, and Allen recognises this. He was anticipated by Marx, Habakkuk, Dobb (1963, p. 125) and Cooper (1967), among others. However, Allen introduces a relatively new theme into the debate. He challenges the view that the rise of the great landowner was in some sense necessary or functional from the point of view of acceleration of economic growth in general or agricultural development in particular. Some work on English and Scottish husbandry had already shown that independent peasants were as capable as capitalist tenant farmers (of great landlords) of responding profitably to the demands of the market, increasing productivity, extruding a surplus population for employment in non-agricultural sectors and providing a growing home-market for new industries or old industries operated with new technologies or organisations (Carter, 1979; Gregson, 1989). Similar work in the US and France has also shown the persistence of peasant farming in the era of capitalist industrialisation in those countries (Friedmann, 1978; Heywood, 1981; and Meyring 1983).

It would appear, then, that the enormous increase in rents obtained by the big landlords in eighteenth-century England could not be justified in terms of capitalist growth, and since much of this increase was obtained through explicit political acts, the first industrialising country turns out also to be a rent-seeking society. Rent-seeking by the British upper classes during the eighteenth century, and the first half of the nineteenth century as well, extended beyond the ground rent earned by the great landowners. Most of the peers of the land were ennobled because they possessed appropriately large incomes and sufficient wealth, measured in acres of land. But when a person who had been ennobled did not have sufficient income or wealth, the Crown or Parliament gave him a large enough income or made a suitably generous grant for him to be able to afford his position as a duke, earl or viscount as the case might be (Beckett, 1986, Chapters 2 and 3). The position of the landed aristocracy was deliberately maintained and admission to its ranks or its impoverishment deliberately restricted through systems of primogeniture, entail and strict settlement of property at the time of marriage. Although entail was frowned upon, the other devices were kept more or less inviolate despite the arguments of would-be reformers such as Jeremy Bentham and James Mill (Halevy, 1960, Part II, Chapter I; Beckett, 1986, Chapter 3).

The ruling classes of England in the eighteenth century comprised not only great or small landlords, but also bankers, top lawyers, career politicians and holders of offices of profit under the Crown and the Parliament. The surprising part of the picture was that few industrialists made the grade in terms of wealth or status during the classic period of the Industrial Revolution (that is, from 1760 to 1830). The wealthiest men in Britain before 1850 were virtually all landlords, and they had mostly inherited their estates, although some might have added to the family inheritance as they grew in wealth or political power. But a sizeable proportion of the top income-earners were

neither landowners in the strict sense, nor manufacturers nor
merchants, but were engaged in activities which would now be
classified as in the professional, public administrative and defence
occupational categories, including especially Anglican clerics,
lawyers and judges, government bureaucrats and the policemen.
Nearly 10 per cent of all British half-millionaires deceased in the
early nineteenth century, and as many as 23 per cent of those
leaving more than £150,000 but less than £500,000 during the
years 1809-29 were engaged in such activities. (Rubinstein, 1983,
p. 266.)

The Old Corruption, that is, the generation of income and power
through links with the Crown and Parliament, declined as far as the
internal affairs of England were concerned. But while it lasted, the
oligarchy of the landlords, the Old Corruption, and the economic
power of the rising commercial, industrial and financial bourgeoisie
co-existed with a growing proletariat, many segments of which
experienced impoverishment during the years 1770–1820. While
there is some controversy about the exact period when the real
wages of the workers began to rise on a sustained basis, most new
work has substantiated the Phelps Brown–Hopkins–Hobsbawm
hypothesis of impoverishment of many sections of workers in
industry during the classic period of the Industrial Revolution
(Phelps Brown and Hopkins, 1956; Hobsbawm, 1957; Lindert and
Williamson, 1983; and Williamson, 1989). In particular, agricultural
workers in the less dynamic regions, artisans in traditional
occupations and even in new trades concentrated in towns without
sanitation or public water supplies suffered a decline in real incomes
and an increase in mortality (see, for example, Amstrong, 1980).
Reform in administration and in the electoral college led to a rapid
decline in incomes derived from political sinecures and patronage,
but landlords continued to remain on the top of the heap until the
coming of the agricultural depression of the last quarter of the
nineteenth century. But, by then, many landlords had shifted to
assets other than agricultural land, and some of them had become
owners of enormously valuable real estate in London or other
thriving cities or towns.

The British economy during the industrial revolution phase, and
in the nineteen century, continued to be characterised by a low
degree of mobility of labour between stagnant and growing regions
and, even more surprisingly, by low mobility of capital between
sectors. In the later part of the nineteenth century, too much capital
was locked up in agriculture, and too little was invested in industry.
It is also probably true that too much capital went into bonds floated

by various foreign governments and into portfolio investments in foreign companies and not enough into home investment, as judged by prospective rates of return (Kennedy, 1987, Chapter 5). One reason for this was that foreign – and especially colonial or British Indian government – bonds and railway securities yielded higher rates of return than British government paper (consols) and other first class home securities. The yields of British Indian securities or comparable paper from other dependent (non-white) colonies remained higher because they were transacted in narrow, segmented markets and many of the companies in which the investments were made operated local monopolies, often backed by the power of the local colonial government (for evidence on rates of return in home and foreign investments see Edelstein, 1982; for evidence and analysis of segmentation of money and capital markets in Britain, see Kennedy, 1987, Chapters 5 and 6).

'Rent-seeking' in the areas of land ownership and government patronage declined in Victorian Britain, and industrial capitalism remained by and large competitive for most of the nineteenth century. But the upper strata of British society earned rents through various channels by virtue of their control of the political and economic commanding heights of the dependent colonies. The white-settled colonies were given dominion status by the 1860s or 1870s, and were largely self-governing, so the opportunities for British citizens to obtain tributes or rents from them were rather restricted. The case was quite different for India, Ceylon (Sri Lanka) and other non-white colonies. From many of them a tribute accrued to the British economy in the shape of an unrequited export surplus, of which the main component was the so-called 'home charges' for defraying the expenses of the London-based administrative and coercive apparatus. Out of this tribute, and also in addition to it (as far as incomes earned and spent by British citizens in the dependent colonies were concerned), individual members of the upper classes earned above-average incomes as governors, secretaries of government departments, collectors or administrators of districts, and officers of the army stationed in the colonies or paid for by the colonial governments. The so-called exchange banks, which were formally organised in a cartel, had a virtual monopoly of India's foreign exchange business. The Bank of England earned a tidy sum by managing the debt of the government of India, which was mostly in sterling in the nineteenth century, and would not give up the management of the sterling debt of British India when the Imperial Bank of India, constituted in 1921 through the merger of the three presidency banks, became banker to the government of India. The various technical services organised by the colonial governments only appointed Europeans to their senior positions, and were slow in admitting colonial subjects even after they acquired the requisite certification. The certification process itself involved raising barriers to entry and increasing the rent element in the earnings of the more successful professionals (Reader, 1966; Rubinstein, 1986, pp. 34–6). Thus there was a considerable amount of rent-seeking and rent-earning outside agriculture, even in the age of free trade in Britain.

In the era of the rise of monopoly capital based in industry and finance – that is, between the 1870s and the First World War – the British economy did not give rise to cartels and monopolies to the same extent as the German or the US economies did. However, the movement for 'centralisation and concentration of capital', prefigured already in Marx's writings, also affected the British economy. Indeed, building on the foundation of the British Empire and the centrality of the London money market in the financial transactions covering the whole world, merchant banks and the new breed of joint stock banks evolved into global rent-seekers. Not only Baring Brothers (which collapsed in 1891), N.M. Rothschild and Co., Samuel Montagu & Co., Hambros and other merchant banks, but Lloyds Bank, Barclays Bank, Midland Bank, the Chartered Bank of India, Australia and China, and the Hong Kong and Shanghai Banking Corporation used the power of their London bases, and manipulated government policies in the dependent colonies and semi-dependent governments allied with the British to seek secure and above-normal returns in all countries within the general sphere of British influence (see Jones, Bostock, Gernstein and Nichol, 1986, and King, King and King, 1988, Part II). By the 1930s they were, of course, challenged in many third countries by the financial and economic power of the US, and were driven out from most of central Europe by the rising Nazi power. The Soviet revolution destroyed one of their most profitable sectors of operation. Rent-seeking on a global scale is often hampered by competition from other rent-seekers and by unforeseen political developments. But that does not deter surviving rent-seekers from new ventures, nor does it prevent new entrants from engaging in the same, or a related, range of activities promising rents from different sources.

5. RENT-SEEKING THROUGH PRIVATE MONOPOLIES AND ITS GLOBALISATION

Monopolies have been organised by private firms with or without explicit government sanction, and with or without the help of government regulation.[1] Even when no single firm was able to dominate a whole field, a small group of firms have been able to carve it up among themselves under explicit or implicit market-sharing arrangements, rules of price or quantity leadership, and so on. The propensity of private traders or manufacturers to collude, often against the public interest, had been commented upon by Adam Smith. Formal analysis of price and output behaviour by a monopoly firm, or under a duopoly, started with Cournot in the 1830s but the further development of the theory – with the exception of a few theorists in the interim – had to wait till the Sraffa – Chamberlin–Robinson revolution in the theories of imperfect and oligopolistic competition in the 1920s and 1930s. As often happened in the area of economic life, policies to curb monopolistic pursuit of rents at the cost of the public good preceded, by several decades, the rigorous theoretical analysis of monopolistic behaviour. The Sherman Act of 1890 was passed by the US Congress in order to tackle the challenges posed by the new trusts and cartels being set up by the leading industrialists and bankers of the time.

I cannot, of course, hope even to sketch the developments in the analysis of the nature and sustenance of non-competitive behaviour, or its ramifications in the international arena. But the enormous flood of literature utilising ever-new technical tools often loses sight of the legitimate concern for the impact of private monopoly. Private monopoly has serious implications for economic development and for the prospects of democracy or authoritarianism in society. I will simply refer to some typical studies in the orthodox literature on market structure and indicate how they can be used to make a richer analysis of less-developed countries caught in the web of local oligarchies and international economic and political domination by the G7 club.

Three major strands in the literature since the 1950s may be distinguished for our purpose. The first is the analysis of welfare costs imposed by the rent-seeking monopolies or oligopolistic enterprises. The second is an analysis of the bases for monopoly, or the barriers to new competition, to use the title of the book which set a research programme in this area (Bain, 1956). The third is an empirical analysis of the monopoly rents or super-profits realised by the monopoly firms or oligopolistic enterprises.

Ideological changes, and changes in economists' tools and paradigms, have played their role in this area as in other fields of economic research. For example, a dominant trend in the Chicago school in the beginning was its general distrust of monopoly and anti-competitive behaviour. Stigler (1951) is a succinct statement of the Chicago school's case against monopoly. There was, however, the powerful voice of Schumpeter (1947, especially Chapters VII and VIII) who argued that monopolistic firms were the major engines of growth of modern capitalism and that monopolistic practices were very often devices to bring down uncertainty to acceptable limits and to generate the profits needed for technical innovation and growth. In Schumpeter's words, 'the large-scale establishment or unit of control', 'has come to be the most powerful engine of economic progress', and of long-run expansion not only in spite of, but to a considerable extent through, a strategy of concentration, 'which looks so restrictive when viewed in the individual case'. 'In this respect, perfect competition is not only impossible but inferior, and has no title to being set up as a model of ideal efficiency' (Schumpeter, 1947, p. 106). To the voice of Schumpeter was added that of John Kenneth Galbraith who argued in his *American Capitalism* (Galbraith, 1952) that American capitalism 'worked' despite the caveats of its critics and that large size permitted firms to mobilise resources and plan for growth without having to look over their shoulder for every dime dropped on the street.

However, it is probably true to say that the majority of the economics profession remained worried about monopoly and monopolistic practices (see, for example, Mansfield, 1964 and Mason, 1964). Galbraith himself coupled his defence of big business in the US with the argument that it could not misbehave too flagrantly because its power was 'countervailed' by that of consumers and workers organised in trade unions. Eminent lawyers remained convinced that 'the rule of law' had to be enforced through special legislation of the kind embodied in the Sherman Act and that large corporations could not be left to police their own behaviour (see, for example, Chayes, 1964).

But an article by Arnold Harberger (1954) of Chicago, purporting to prove that the deadweight loss caused by monopoly was of a small order of magnitude, seemed to convince at least a section of economists that the welfare loss caused by private monopoly behaviour could after all be neglected for most purposes. Typical of this strand of thinking was the argument of the conservative legal theorist Richard Posner (1975) who concluded that we should worry about the social costs of public regulation rather than of private monopoly power. The rent-seeking analysis of Tullock was later applied by other economists who took into account the resources used by monopolists to create or maintain their monopolistic or oligopolistic control. On that showing, the deadweight loss caused by private monopoly or oligopoly turned out to be several times larger than had been found by Harberger.

Whereas the latter had found the welfare loss of the US from private monopoly power to be only 0.1 per cent of GNP, Cowling and Mueller (1978) found it to be between 4 and 13 per cent of the gross product produced by the group of US corporations included in the study. For the UK a similar calculation showed the welfare loss to be above 7 per cent of the gross product of the corporations covered by the study. This conclusion has not remained unchallenged (Littlechild, 1981), but if one assumes collusion among the players in the oligopolistic industries studied by Cowling and Mueller, the results remain virtually unscathed (Cowling and Mueller, 1981). Masson and Shaanan (1984) found that while the potential monopoly loss was 11.6 per cent of the value of output of the concerned industries, oligopolistic competition brought it down to 2.9 per cent – which was again much higher than the 0.1 per cent found by Harberger (1954). They also underlined the importance of competition or contestability.

A second major area of study opened up by the pioneering work of Bain (1956) was taking stock of the various barriers to competition utilised by monopolistic or oligopolistic firms to keep out potential entrants. Bain distinguished between four types of barriers limiting new competition in an existing industry, namely (1) strong economies of scale, forbidding the survival of all but a few firms in a profitable condition, (2) product differentiation leading to strong brand attachment or customer loyalty towards the products of existing firms, (3) the control of strategic raw materials or critical patent rights or other firm-specific assets and 'know-how' and (4) the need for large volumes of capital to set up business (Bain, 1956, Chapters 3–6; Mann, 1966). In addition to the so-called *innocent* barriers to entry, there can also be strategic barriers in which incumbent firms manipulate variables under their control in order to deter the entry of new firms (Salop, 1979). Some of the variables that were suggested as measures of deterrence were limit pricing by the incumbent firms (this was put forward by Bain and Sylos Labini and formulated as a model by Modigliani, 1958), patent wars (Salop, 1979), credible commitment to engage in price or quantity wars through the maintenance of excess capacity (Dixit, 1980), advertising wars and so on. Some strategies proved vulnerable when two-stage or three-stage games between actual or potential oligopolists were analysed (see, for example, Tirole, 1989, Chapters 5–10; Kreps, 1990, Chapters 13 and 14). There can be an 'equilibrium configuration' of oligopolistic firms emerging out of such strategic interactions. But the equilibrium configurations themselves depend on the acceptance of certain rules by the parties, including certain norms laid down by the legal apparatus or regulating agencies. There is also the possibility that, under certain conditions, anti-trust measures may themselves be used by firms to facilitate anti-competitive practices. In order to guard against this possibility, the regulatory agencies may have to monitor the *conduct* of potential monopolists not only in the domain of price-quantity behaviour, but also in the areas of investment, patenting and so on. (A recent survey of the literature on anti-competitive behaviour is provided by Ordover and Saloner, 1989.) (When no holds are barred in the use of all available strategies, we witness the emergence of such phenomena as the Medellin cartel of Colombia or the drug lords of the Golden Triangle, spanning the frontiers of Myanmar, Thailand and Laos.)

The empirical verification of the existence of monopolistic or oligopolistic market structures has spawned a vast literature. Controversies abound in this area since the specification of the theoretical models differs from author to author as do the statistical tests used to verify the particular theories. The number of models of oligopolistic behaviour has really proliferated since the entry of advanced game-theory techniques to trace out the paths of the control variables. For the older vintages of models of monopolistic or oligopolistic behaviour, Mann (1966) found, for major US industries, positive evidence of the association of very high barriers to entry with higher-than-average profit rates, and a combination of high or very high barriers to entry and high seller concentration (meaning a concentration ratio above 70 per cent for the top eight firms) with above-normal profit rates. In another important contribution, Comanor and Wilson (1967) found that for the US economy

> inter-industry variation of profit rates [could] be explained quite
> well by a model incorporating the rate of growth of demand,
> some measure of advertising intensity, and variables reflecting the
> importance of concentration and technical barriers to entry (Ibid,
> p. 304)

In later studies, the relationship between profit rates and seller concentration or barriers to entry was found to be more clouded. This was partly because models became more sophisticated, leading to doubts about the exact relationship between *ex ante* predictions and *ex post* results (were prices found to be lower than would yield maximum collective profit because actual competition forced the prices to those levels or were they deliberately kept low as a threat to potential entrants?), but also because financial deregulation and securitisation of portfolios led to a more rapid revaluation of assets in security markets to reflect actual profit rates and because the rapid development of conglomerate structures led to the obscuring of industry-specific monopoly power. Economy-wide monopoly power would now be the proper subject of study, but such studies are still rather thin on the ground and tend to be undertaken by sociologists and political scientists rather than by economists wielding the honed tools of cooperative, or non-cooperative game theory.

In spite of all these problems, Richard Schmalensee (1989) in his survey paper found support for several stylised facts which are broadly covered by the Sylos Labini paradigm:

> In cross-section comparisons involving markets in the same industry seller concentration is positively related to price. (Ibid., p. 988.)

> The profitability of industry leaders in U. S. manufacturing may be positively related to concentration; the profitability of firms with small market shares is not. (Ibid., p. 983.)

> Rank correlations of manufacturing industries' concentration levels between industrialized nations are very high. Among large industrialized nations concentration levels do not decline much with increases in the size of the economy. (Ibid., p. 992.) [This, of course, links up more with Marx and Schumpeter's dynamic theories than with the static theory of the Bain–Sylos Labini– Modigliani variety but is not inconsistent with the latter.]

> Levels of seller concentration are positively related to estimates of the market share of a plant of minimum efficient scale. (Ibid., p. 992.)

> Advertising intensity is negatively related to entry in manufacturing industries. (Ibid., p. 998.)

In a companion survey of empirical studies of industries with market power, Bresnahan (1989) comes to three major conclusions:

> Conclusion A: There is a great deal of market power, in the sense of price–cost margins, in some concentrated industries. (Ibid., p. 1052.)

> Conclusion B: One significant cause of high price–cost margin is anti-competitive conduct. (Ibid., p. 1053.) [The problem with some of the studies on the effect of market power on profitability was that they used the profit rate rather than profit margins and thus were tangled up with problems of valuation of capital by the

stock market or outside it. The use of price–cost margins in the Lerner–Kalecki tradition of measurement of monopoly power sidetracks the valuation problem.]

Conclusion C: Only a very little has been learned from the new methods about the relationship between market power and market structure. (Ibid., p. 1053.)

The import of the last conclusion is not that the new methods are to be discarded by economists, but that analysis of power exercised by monopolies and policies to meet such rent-seeking, welfare-damaging or growth-depressing activities cannot be suspended indefinitely while theorists and econometricians are busy honing their tools. That monopolies and monopolistic behaviour can be sustained in surprising situations is illustrated by the case of the production and sale of pure salt in the UK in recent times. There are just two dominant producers producing and selling around 97 per cent of the total amount of salt consumed in the UK. The first is British Salt, a subsidiary of Stavely Industries, an engineering and contracting group, and the second is ICI Weston Point, a part of the ICI conglomerate (MMC, 1986; Rees, 1993). The Monopolies and Merger Commission (MMC) of the UK investigated this case of duopoly and rejected the claims of the two firms that they did not collude in fixing their prices and outputs. The MMC concluded that the firms 'had severely restrained price competition' (MMC, 1986, para. 9. 10, as quoted by Rees, 1993, p. 834). The two producers maintained high levels of excess capacity, and changed their prices almost simultaneously. In a careful application of Nash equilibrium models developed by Abreu and Lambson (for references, see Rees, 1993, pp. 847–8), Rees found the allocation of outputs not to be consistent with a purely competitive outcome under which one of the firms would shut down production. Nor was it consistent with joint profit maximisation since that would require side payments by the firms and this was prohibited by the anti-monopoly norms enforced by the MMC.

As we said earlier, we have not tried to summarise the work on monopoly, concentration and monopolistic behaviour in the advanced capitalist countries. Our purpose in providing this sketch is threefold. First, this sketch is sufficient to indicate that there is a good deal of privately induced monopoly (rather than induced by public regulation or restrictions on foreign trade) even in economies which are supposed to be at the opposite pole of LDC economies characterised by restricted foreign trade regimes. Second, it is necessary not only to investigate more intensively similar rent-seeking behaviour patterns in LDCs but also to lay bare the history of collaboration between rent-seeking by the ruling classes of advanced capitalist countries and the more traditional rent-seekers – such as landlords and usurers – in LDCs, and to continually monitor the political ramifications of such collaboration or collusion. Third, the global rent-seekers from the advanced capitalist countries, namely, the transnational non-financial corporations (TNCs, for short) and transnational banks (TNBs, for short), are now poised for a new breakthrough in global dominance. This fact is generally obscured by the microtheoretic or country-specific approaches to the analysis of rent-seeking behaviour. A closer analysis of the behaviour of these global giants is needed in order to evolve a consensus about the kind of rule of law they have to be governed by for the sake of global prosperity, a minimal degree of global democracy, and in the worst-case scenarios, for global survival.

6. COLLABORATION AND CONFLICT BETWEEN LOCAL AND GLOBAL RENT-SEEKERS

In the nineteenth century, the British ruling classes looking for markets proved to be friends of the liberators of Latin America from Spanish and Portuguese rule. The *criollo* élites welcomed the British connection because of the promise it opened up for more profitable trade with the external world. The landlords controlling grain crops and livestock hoped to profit through expanded exports with North America and Europe. These trades were often routed through exchanges in London, Manchester or Glasgow, and were financed by trade credits extended by British banks. The newly emerging governments also became borrowers on an extensive scale in the London money market (for a brief history of some of these developments, see Bagchi, 1982 and references cited therein).

The ruling classes of Latin America, almost to the last *caudillo*, accepted the tenets of *laissez faire* and liberalism but not of democracy. In the name of freedom of contract, much of the remaining communal organisations and property holdings of Amerindians were broken up and local power-brokers profited greatly from the forcible or distress sales of Amerindian lands. The British capitalists did not have to openly engage in gun-boat diplomacy except on rare occasions, because the local rent-seeking landlords saw their interests as being congruent with those of the rent-seeking British traders, mine-owners or financiers. The Chilean civil war of 1891 was sparked off by a conflict between the followers of President Balmaceda who wanted industrialisation and national control of the Chilean nitrate mines and other members of the trading and landed oligarchy who were more interested in low wages for workers and a smooth, collaborative relationship with foreign, mainly British, interests. The nationalists were overthrown symbolically by a revolt in the navy, and Chilean nitrate mines became almost exclusively the property of foreign owners.

In the 1930s rifts opened up in the smooth plateau of landlord–foreign capital *entente* in Latin American governments when the latter began to follow policies of import restriction and promotion of a (rather limited) range of manufactures. The dominance of British capital in Latin America was finally ended only for its place to be taken by US capital (for case studies of operation of US capital in Latin America up to the 1960s, see Bernstein, 1966). During the next few years many of the conflicts were not simply along lines of seekers of self-reliance under the leadership of national bourgeoisie and the foreign rent-seekers, but between adherents of different foreign powers – such as the US, Germany or Britain – seeking to acquire what they considered to be legitimate hegemonic power, or resisting the loss of such power. In Central America, of course, the US had long acquired hegemony – mostly for the benefit of giant agribusinesses such as the United Fruit Company, and US Marines had been freely used to keep the US peace there. When there were genuine popular movements against the ruling oligarchy and foreign interests, as in Guatemala, Mexico, Cuba, Chile or Nicaragua, the US sought either to quell the popular regimes militarily or subvert them through covert operations of various kinds (Bagchi, 1982, Chapter 3).

These conflicts over shares and the *modus operandi* of rent-seeking have occurred as frequently under regimes of free trade as under regimes of restricted foreign trade. Unlike the case of the US, few LDCs ever enacted any laws to curb the growth of monopolies or to check the restrictive practices among them. India passed the Monopolies and Restrictive Trade Practices Act only in 1969, and its effective operation was always diluted by the official ambivalence towards the objectives of the Act (Chandra, 1977). By the 1980s, explicit moves were made to successively blunt the striking power of the Act, and by the beginning of the 1990s, with the enforcement of structural adjustment and liberalisation policies, the Act had become virtually a dead letter. In most ex-colonial LDCs many of the monopolies were affiliates of the TNCs based in the metropolis and anti-monopoly moves were often interpreted as xenophobic gestures, likely to endanger the prospects of foreign investment. That was one of the reasons deterring governments from encoding or enforcing anti-monopoly legislation. Any literature that concentrates on local rent-seeking under restricted foreign trade regimes to the exclusion of all the moves in the game of global economic and political domination by the G7 countries and their allies is likely to be seriously misleading for the reasons spelled out above.

7. THE TRIPLE GRID OF RENT-SEEKING POWER AND THE PROBLEM OF GLOBAL DEMOCRACY

In an earlier article (Bagchi, 1993) I explored the implications of rent-seeking by landlords, money-lenders and traders for the operation of democracy where a multi-party system is in operation. In most countries which are governed by local oligarchies with implicit support of a dominant foreign power or foreign capital in general, authoritarianism rather than democracy has been the usual regime. This is true of Zaire under Mobutu as well as of Côte d'Ivoire under Houphouet-Boigny or Indonesia under Suharto. In the 1980s the economic dislocation of most LDCs has further increased the importance of foreign support for keeping a regime in place. In some cases, such as those of Somalia, Sierra Leone, or Liberia, a government has virtually ceased to exist. There is now a new academic interest in the relationship of development and democracy (see, for example, Dunn, 1992; Held, 1993; Rudebeck, 1992). While, generally speaking, authors working directly in or on LDCs are aware of the minimum economic sustainability conditions for the emergence or maintenance of democracy in a real sense (see, for example, Bangura, 1992; Mandaza, 1987) only a few academic authors working within the paradigm of the Westminster model of democracy stress the interaction between the power of foreign capitalists, aid-giving agencies and local oligarchs in determining the regime of a particular country (see, in this connection Callaghy, 1986, and Hawthorn, 1993).[2]

By the time Lenin wrote his *Imperialism* (Lenin, 1917), the emergence of large transnational cartels dominating whole industries and influencing policies of domestic governments was a fact of life (ibid., Chapter V). However, the sustained growth of TNCs with plants or branches in many countries is a phenomenon which came into prominence in the post-Second World War world. It is interesting that a Marxist economist, Stephen Hymer, put forward the first coherent theory – which is still debated – of the emergence of the multinational or transnational corporation (Hymer, 1960). Since then the emergence of the TNCs has been theorised from the vantage points of both the theory of international trade and the theory of industrial organisation (see, for example, Caves, 1982; Ethier, 1986; Helpman, 1985 and Krugman, 1989). It took a long time for economists to recognise that with the increasing importance of trade in manufactures, a major or even a predominant part of international trade was taking place under highly imperfect conditions of competition. It also took theorists quite some time to recognise that much of this trade was taking place between branches and subsidiaries of large TNCs. Among economic theorists in general, the recognition is yet to emerge that the rise to dominance of TNCs requires a political theory – a theory which might be an updating of Lenin's theory of imperialism (see, for example, Bagchi, 1986 and other essays collected in Patnaik, 1986).

Raymond Vernon (1971) may have been premature in his judgement that TNCs had already put sovereignty at bay by 1971. There were intervening years when OPEC and the resistance of Third World countries seemed to keep TNCs in check. But in the eighties most of the Third World was involved in a debt crisis, and TNBs spearheaded the global rent-seeking brigade. They had embroiled most LDC governments in their debt trap. After pushing loans to many entities which had often only a nominal domicile in LDCs, they then held the LDC governments to ransom, since neither other TNBs, nor the two major watchdogs of world capitalism, viz. the IMF and the World Bank, would extend even any bridging loans to the LDC governments if the demand of the TNBs were not satisfied. The structural adjustment policies imposed by the twin Yakshas of Washington further sapped the resistance of Third World élites, many of whom belonged to local rent-seeking groups collaborating with global rent-seeking TNCs and TNBs. By the end of 1993, the TNCs had obtained their charter of rights in the form of the GATT draft treaty signed on 15 December 1993 by 117 states (Bagchi, 1994). Under this treaty, and the provisions of its trade-related investment measures (TRIMs), little distinction can be made between home and foreign companies for policy purposes. Under the TRIPs provisions, the power of the existing patent holders in the G7 countries has been made absolute and extended to many areas such as patenting of life forms, and actual flora and fauna existing in nature that were disallowed under the patent laws of most countries. Much of the debate about the relative importance of large corporations and small firms (as surveyed, for example, by Kamien and Schwartz, 1982 and Scherer, 1984) has been rendered irrelevant, because incumbent large TNCs will have an overwhelming advantage under the new GATT treaty.

Under the structural adjustment and economic liberalisation

policies, new forms of rent-seeking behaviour have sprouted or old forms have been revived under government and IMF-World Bank patronage. For example, in India, the government has guaranteed a return of 16 per cent to foreign enterprises investing in the power sector, and the profits are to be repatriated at a fixed rate of exchange (Rs. 32 to the US dollar) whatever the current rate of exchange of the Indian rupee. Thus, not content with the rents generated through private monopolies, TNCs have found new vantage points for rent-seeking under a régime which ostensibly wants to abolish rent-seeking in public enterprises, or through the utilisation of government regulation (see in this connection Ghosh, 1994). Global rent-seeking and the global order of domination by TNCs are analytically connected like Siamese twins.

The struggle for democracy in LDCs today will have to be waged against the authoritarian dominance of three blocs of power, that is, the local rent-seeking élites, the G7 governments trying to cure their economic ills by passing on the recessionary impulses and the ecological damage caused by their policies to the LDCs, and the TNCs seeking to monopolise trade, production and assets. The increasingly unrestricted mobility of capital combined with the compulsion of most LDC governments to settle their external debt obligations to rent-seeking TNBs, TNCs, and their watchdogs, has meant that a larger and larger proportion of the assets of the LDCs is passing into private hands, and an increasingly large fraction of those assets is gravitating towards the TNBs and TNCs. According to the estimates made in 1993, one-third of the private sector assets of the world at that time were controlled by the TNCs (UN, 1993, p. 1). More than 37 per cent of the 37,000 TNC had headquarters in the developed capitalist countries and accounted for an even larger percentage of the stock of foreign direct investment (FDI) in the world. Most of the FDI was going to either the developed countries or to a few East Asian and South East Asian countries. For most of the LDCs, FDI meant transfers of existing assets to TNCs with little growth to show for the so-called investment, since the net inflows from developed countries to LDCs had been strongly negative during the 1980s and continued in the same fashion into the 1990s. The pressures for controlling the transfer of resources through transfer pricing (Vaitsos, 1974) or through other channels had been thoroughly neutralised by the onslaught of the global recession and the ideological and economic bludgeoning practised by the G7 countries, ably assisted by the IMF and the World Bank.

It is obvious, however, that there can be no real democracy in the LDCs if the major players in the game – in this case the TNCs as well as local rent-seeking élites – remain outside the purview of the rule of law. Most LDC governments have proved unable or unwilling to deal with the damage caused by the irresponsible power of TNCs (witness the continued agony caused by the gas disaster at the Bhopal plant of Union Carbide and the utter failure of the government of India to hold the real culprits to account). In the closing years of the century, believers in democracy must try to impose certain norms of behaviour on TNCs or give up the pretence that ordinary people can be empowered to have any control over their own lives.

NOTES

I am indebted to an anonymous referee for searching comments on an earlier version of this chapter.

1. In a rejoinder to an earlier paper (Bagchi, 1993) on 'rent-seeking behaviour', Karnik (1993) alleged that I had ignored the explicit reference to monopolies in Mueller (1989, Chapter 13). However, Mueller's chapter almost exclusively discussed monopoly rents earned explicitly with the help of various restrictions or regulations enforced by the government. Tullock (1980) has shown how private strategic behaviour may prevent monopoly rents from being dissipated through the forces of competition. But most of the recent policy literature on rent-seeking is almost entirely concerned with rent-seeking in a single economy with the help of government regulations and has not analysed the pursuit of monopoly rents primarily through the use of private economic (and political) power. Nor has the analysis been extended internationally to take account of the power of transnational corporations. Finally, the current literature on rent-seeking is very much in the domain of political economy. But the new political economy, by calling into question virtually the whole gamut of policies of public regulation, has sought to narrow the scope of political engagement and also of analysis directed at illuminating the interconnection between private economic power and political behaviour (cf. Bagchi, 1993 and references cited there).
2. For a brief summary of political and economic issues involved in the discourse on democracy and development, see Bagchi, 1995.

REFERENCES

Allen, R.C. 1992. *Enclosure and the Yeoman: the Agricultural Development of the South Midlands 1450–1850,* Oxford, Clarendon Press.

Armstrong, W.A. 1981. 'The trend of mortality in Carlisle between the 1780s and the 1840s: A demographic contribution to the standard of living debate', *Economic History Review,* 34(1), February, pp. 94–114.

Bagchi, A.K. 1982. *The Political Economy of Underdevelopment,* Cambridge, Cambridge University Press.

Bagchi, A.K. 1986. 'Towards a correct reading of Lenin's theory of imperialism', in Patnaik (ed.), 1985, pp. 27–55.

Bagchi, A.K. '"Rent-seeking", new political economy and the negation of politics', *Economic and Political Weekly,* XXVIII (34), 21 August, pp. 1729–36.

Bagchi, A.K. 1994. 'Some charter of rights: GATT (Sutherland) treaty', *Frontline* (Madras), 11(7), 26 March–8 April, pp. 119–23.

Bagchi, A.K. 1994a. 'Macroeconomics', in A.K. Bagchi (ed.), 'Teaching Economics in Developing and Other Countries', *Journal of Development Planning,* No. 24, New York, United Nations, pp. 19–88.

Bagchi, A.K. 1995. 'Democracy and development: history, aspirations and reality', editorial introduction to Bagchi (ed.), *Democracy and Development,* Macmillan, London, on behalf of the International Economic Association.

Bain, J.S. 1956. *Barriers to New Competition,* Cambridge, MA, Harvard University Press.

Bangura, Y. 1992. 'Authoritarian rule and democracy in Africa: a theoretical discourse', in Rudebeck (ed.), 1992, pp. 69–104.

Baran, P.K. and P.M. Sweezy. 1966. *Monopoly Capital,* New York, Monthly Review Press.

Barber, W.J. 1975. *British Economic Thought and India, 1600–1850: a study in the history of development economics,* Oxford, Clarendon Press.

Beckett, J.V. 1984. 'The pattern of landownership in England and Wales, 1660–1880', *Economic History Review,* 2nd Series, 37(1), February, pp. 1–24.

Beckett, J.V. 1986. *The Aristocracy in England,* Oxford, Blackwell.

Bernstein, M.D. (ed.). 1966. *Foreign Investment in Latin America: Cases and Attitudes,* New York, A.A. Knopf.

Bharadwaj, K. 1986. 'A note on Emmanuel's "Unequal Exchange"', in Patnaik (ed.), 1986, pp. 353–74.

Bresnahan, T.F. 1989. 'Empirical studies of industries with market power', in Schmalensee and Willig (eds), 1989, pp. 1011–57.

Callaghy, T.M. 1986. 'Politics and vision in Africa: the interplay of domination, equality and liberty', in P. Chabal (ed.): *Political Domination in Africa: Reflections on the limits of Power,* Cambridge, Cambridge University Press, pp. 30–51.

Carter, I. 1979. *Farm Life in Northeast Scotland, 1840–1914,* Edinburgh, John Donald.

Caves, R.E. 1982. *Multinational Enterprise and Economic Organization,* Cambridge, Cambridge University Press.

Chandra, N.K. 1977. 'Monopoly legislation and policy in India', *Economic and Political Weekly,* Special Number, August: reprinted in Chandra, 1988, pp. 304–38.

Chandra, N.K. 1986. 'Theories of unequal exchange: a critique of Emmanuel and Amin', *Economic and Political Weekly,* 26 July; reprinted in Chandra, 1988, pp. 128–54.

Chandra, N.K. 1988. *The Retarded Economies: Foreign Domination and Class Relations in India and other Emerging Nations,* Bombay, Oxford University Press.

Chayes, A. 1964. 'The modern corporation and the rule of law', in Mason (ed.), 1964, pp. 25–45.

Comanor, W.S. and T.A. Wilson. 1967. 'Advertising market structure and performance', *Review of Economics and Statistics,* November, reprinted in Needham (ed.), 1970, pp. 278–310.

Cooper, J.P. 1967. 'The social distribution of land and men in England, 1436–1700', *Economic History Review,* Second Series, Vol. XX, pp. 419–40.

Cowling, K. and D.C. Mueller. 1978. 'The social costs of monopoly', *Economic Journal,* Vol. 88, December, pp. 727–48.

Cowling, K. and D. C. Mueller. 1981. 'The social costs of monopoly power revisited', *Economic Journal,* Vol. 91, September, pp. 721–5.

Dixit, A. 1980. 'The role of investment in entry-deterence', *Economic Journal,* Vol. 90, March, pp. 95–106.

Dixit, A. 1984. 'International trade policy for oligopolistic industries', *Economic Journal,* Vol. 94, Supplement, pp. 1–16.

Dobb, M. 1963. *Studies in the Development of Capitalism,* revised edition, London, Routledge & Kegan Paul.

Dunn, J. (ed.). 1991. *Democracy: The Unfinished Journey, 508 BC to AD 1993,* Cambridge, Cambridge University Press.

Eatwell, J., M. Milgate and P. Newman (eds). 1987. *The New Palgrave Dictionary of Economics,* Vols 1–4, London, Macmillan.

Edelstein, M. 1982. *Overseas Investment in the Age of High Imperialism: The United Kingdom 1850–1914,* London, Methuen.

Ethier, W.J. 1986. 'The multinational firm', *Quarterly Journal of Economics,* November; reprinted in Grossman (eds), 1992, pp. 303–24.

Ewing, J. A. 1888. 'James Watt', in *Encyclopaedia Britannica,* ninth edition, Vol. XXIV, Edinburgh, Adam and Charles Black, pp. 412–14.

Firminger, W.K. (ed.) 1918. *The Fifth Report from the Select Committee of the House of Commons on the Affairs of the East India Company dated 28th July 1812,* Vol. III, Calcutta, R. Cambray & Co.

Friedmann, H. 1978. 'World market, state and family farm: Social bases of household production in the era of wage labour', *Comparative Studies in Society and History,* 20(4).

Galbraith, J.K. 1952. *American Capitalism,* Boston, Houghton Mifflin.

Ghosh, A. 1994. '"Rent seeking" and economic reform', *Economic and Political Weekly,* XXIX (1 2), 18 January, pp. 13–15.

Gregson, N. 1989. 'Tawney revisited: custom and the emergence of capitalist class relations in north-east Cumbria', *Economic History Review,* Second Series, 42(1), February, pp. 18–42.

Grossman, G.M. (ed.). 1992. *Imperfect Competition and International Trade,* Cambridge, MA, MIT Press.

Habakkuk, H.J. 1940. 'English land ownership 1680–1700', *Economic History Review,* 1st series, Vol. 10, pp. 2–17.

Halevy, E. 1960. *England in 1815,* second (revised edition), translated from the French by E.I. Watkin and D.A. Barbour, New York, Barnes & Noble.

Harberger, A. 1954. 'Monopoly and resource allocation', *American Economic Review,* Vol. 44, May, pp. 73–87.

Hawthorn, G. 1993. 'Sub-Saharan Africa', in Held (ed.), 1993, pp. 330–54.

Held, D. (ed.). 1993. *Prospects for Democracy: North, South, East, West,* Cambridge, Polity Press.

Helpman, E. 1985. 'Multinational corporations and trade structure', *Review of Economic Studies,* July; reprinted in Grossman (ed.), 1992, pp. 285–302.

Heywood, C. 1981. 'The role of the French peasantry in French industrialization 1815–80', *Economic History Review,* Second Series, 34(3), August, pp. 359–76.

Hobsbawm, E.J. 1957. 'The British standard of living, 1790–1850', *Economic History Review,* Second Series, Vol. 10, pp. 46–68.

Hymer, S. 1960. *The International Operation of National Firms: a Study of Direct Foreign Investment,* Ph.D. dissertation, Massachusetts Institute of Technology; published by MIT Press, 1976.

Jones, G., F. Bostock, G. Gernstein and J. Nichol. 1986. *Banking and Empire in Iran: the History of the British Bank of the Middle East,* Vol. I, Cambridge, Cambridge University Press.

Kamien, M.I. and N.L. Schwartz. 1982. *Innovation and Market Structure,* Cambridge, Cambridge University Press.

Karnik, A. 1983. 'On "rent-seeking"', *Economic and Political Weekly,* XXVIII (44), 30 October, p. 2420.

Katrak, H. 1977. 'Multi-national monopolies and commercial policy', *Oxford Economic Papers,* Vol. 29, pp. 283–91.

Katrak, H. 'Multinational monopolies and regulation', *Oxford Economic Papers,* Vol. 32, pp. 453–6.

Kennedy, W.P. 1987. *Industrial Structure, Capital Markets and the Origins of British Industrial Decline,* Cambridge, Cambridge University Press.

King, F.H.H., D.J.S. King and C.E. King. 1988. *The Hong Kong Bank in the Period of Imperialism and War, 1895–1914,* Cambridge, Cambridge University Press.

Kreps, D.M. 1990. *A Course in Micro-economic Theory,* Englewood Cliffs, NJ, Prentice-Hall.

Krueger, A. 1974. 'The political economy of the rent-seeking society', *American Economic Review,* 64(3), June, pp. 291–303.

Krugman, P. 1989. 'Industrial organization and international trade', in Schmalensee and Willig (eds), 1989, Vol. 2, pp. 1179–223.

Lenin, V.I. (1917). *Imperialism, the Highest Stage of Capitalism: a popular outline,* Petrograd; translated from the Russian and reprinted in Lenin, *Collected Works,* Vol. 22, Moscow, Progress Publishers, 1964, pp. 185–304.

Lindert, P.H. and J.G. Williamson. (1983). 'English workers' living standards during the Industrial Revolution: a new look', *Economic History Review,* 2nd Series, 36(1), February, reprinted in Mokyr, 1985, pp. 177–205.

Littlechild, S.C. 1981. 'Misleading calculations of the social costs of monopoly power', *Economic Journal,* Vol. 91, June, pp. 348–63.

Majeed, J. 1990. 'James Mill's "The History of British India", and utilitarianism as a rhetoric of reform', *Modern Asian Studies,* 24(2), pp. 209–24.

Mandaza, I. (ed.). 1987. *Zimbabwe: the Political Economy of Transition 1980–1986,* Harare, Zongwe Press.

Mann, H.M. (1966). 'Seller concentration, barriers to entry, and rates of return in thirty industries, 1950–1960', *Review of Economics and Statistics,* August; reprinted in Needham (ed.), 1970, pp. 214–34.

Mansfield, E. (ed.). 1964. *Monopoly Power and Economic Performance,* New York, W.W. Norton.

Marx, K. (1867). *Capital: a Critique of Political Economy,* Vol. I: translated from the German by B. Fowkes, Harmondsworth, Middlesex, Penguin Books, 1976.

Marx, K. (1894). *Capital: a Critique of Political Economy,* Vol. III: translated from the German edition, edited by F. Engels; Moscow, Progress Publishers, 1966.

Mason, E.S. (ed.). 1964. *The Corporation in Modern Society,* Cambridge, MA, Harvard University Press.

Masson, R.T. and J. Shaanan. 1984. 'Social costs of oligopoly and the value of competition', *Economic Journal,* Vol. 94, September, pp. 520–35.

Meyring, A.C. 1983. 'Did capitalism lead to the decline of the peasantry? The case of the French Combraille', *Journal of Economic History,* 43(1), March, pp. 121–28.

MMC. 1986. 'Monopolies and Merger Commission': *A Report on the Supply of White Salt in the United Kingdom by Producers of such Salt,* London, HMSO.

Mill, James. 1817. *The History of British India,* Vols. I–VI, 5th edition, with notes and continuation (Vols I–VI), by H.H. Wilson, London, James Madden, Piper, Stephenson and Spence, 1858.

Mill, James. 1826. 'Colonies', *Encyclopaedia Britannica,* Edinburgh, Adam and Charles Black.

Modigliani, F. (1958). 'New developments on the oligopoly front', *Journal of Political Economy,* June; reprinted in Needham (ed.) 1970, pp. 194–213.

Mokyr, J. (ed.). 1985. *The Economics of the Industrial Revolution,* London, Allen & Unwin.

Mueller, D.C. 1989. *Public Choice II: a Revised Edition of Public Choice,* Cambridge, Cambridge University Press.

Needham, D. (ed.). 1970. *Economics of Industrial Organization,* New York, Holt, Reinhart & Winston.

Ordoner, J.A. and G. Saloner. 1989. 'Predation, monopolization and antitrust' in Schmalensee and Willig (eds), Vol. 1, pp. 537–96.

Palma, J. G. 1978. 'Dependency : a formal theory of underdevelopment or a methodology for the analysis of concrete situations of underdevelopment?' *World Development,* Vol. 6, pp. 881–924.

Patnaik, P. (ed.). 1986. *Lenin and Imperialism: an appraisal of theories and contemporary reality,* Hyderabad (India), Orient Longman.

Penrose, E. 1987. 'Multinational corporations', in Eatwell, Milgate and Newman (eds), 1987, Vol. 3, pp. 562–4.

Phelps Brown, E.H. and S.V. Hopkins. 1956. 'Seven centuries of the prices of consumable compared with builders' wage-rates', *Economica,* NS, Vol. 23, pp. 296–314.

Platteau J.P. 1983. 'Classical economics and agrarian reform in underdeveloped areas: the radical views of the two Mills', *Journal of Development Studies,* 19(4), pp. 435–60.

Posner, R.A. 1975. 'The social costs of monopoly and regulation', *Journal of Political Economy,* Vol. 83, August, pp. 807–27.

Reader, W.J. 1966. *Professional Men: the Rise of the Professional Classes in the Nineteenth Century England,* London.

Rees, R. 1993. 'Collusive equilibrium in the Great Salt Duopoly', *Economic Journal,* Vol. 103, July, pp. 833–48.

Rubinstein, W.D. (1983). 'The end of "Old Corruption" in Britain, 1780–1860', *Past and Present,* No. 101, November; reprinted in Rubinstein, 1987, pp. 265–303.

Rubinstein, W.D. 1987. *Elites, and the Wealthy in Modern British History,* Brighton, Sussex (UK), Harvester Press.

Rudebeck, L. (ed.). 1992. *When Democracy Makes Sense: Studies in the democratic potential of Third World popular movements,* Uppsala (Sweden), AKUT, Uppsala University.

Salop, S. 1974. 'Strategic entry deterrence', *American Economic Review,* Vol. 69, May, pp. 335–8.

Scherer, F.M. 1984. *Innovation and Growth: Schumpeterian Perspective,* Cambridge, MA, MIT Press.

Schmalensee, R. 1989. 'Interindustry studies of structure and performance', in Schmalensee and Willig (eds), 1989, Vol. 2, pp. 952–1009.

Schmalensee, R. and R. Willig, (eds). 1989. *Handbook of Industrial Organization,* Vols 1 and 2, Amsterdam, Holland.

Schumpeter, J.A. (1947). *Capitalism, Socialism and Democracy,* second edition, London, Allen & Unwin, 1966.

Stein, B. 1989. *Thomas Munro: the Origins of the Colonial State and His Vision of Empire,* Delhi, Oxford University Press.

Stigler, G.J. (1951). 'The case against big business', *Fortune,* May; reprinted in Mansfield (ed.), 1964, pp. 3–12.

Stone, L. and J.C. Fawtier Stone. 1984. *An Open Elite? England 1540–1880,* Oxford, Clarendon Press.

Thackeray, W. (1806). 'Memoir of Mr. Thackeray, in favour of Ryotwar Permanent Settlement, being Extract from Fort St. George Consultations, 29th April 1806', in Firminger (ed.), 1918, pp. 455–65.

Thompson, F.M.L. 1969. 'Landownership and economic growth in England in the eighteenth century' in E.L. Jones and S.J. Woolf (eds): *Agrarian Change and Economic Development,* London, Methuen, pp. 41–60.

Tirole, J. 1989. *The Theory of Industrial Organization,* Cambridge, MA, MIT Press.

Tullock, G. 1967. 'The welfare cost of tariffs, monopolies and theft', *Western Economic Journal,* Vol. 5, pp. 224–32.

Tullock, G. 1980. 'Efficient rent-seeking', in J.M. Buchanan, R.D. Tollison and G. Tullock (eds): *Towards a Theory of the Rent-Seeking Society,* College Station (USA), Texas, A & M Press.

Tullock, G. 1987. 'Rent-seeking' in Eatwell, Milgate and Newman (eds), 1987, Vol. 4, pp. 147–9.

UN. 1993. *World Investment Report 1993: Transnational Corporations and Integrated International Production,* New York, United Nations.

Vaitsos, C.V. 1974. *Intercountry Income Distribution and Transnational Enterprises,* Oxford, Oxford University Press.

Vernon, R. 1971. *Sovereignty at Bay: the Multinational Spread of US Enterprises,* Harmondsworth, Middlesex, Penguin Books.

Von Tunzelmann, G.N. 1978. *Steam Power and British Industrialization to 1860,* Oxford, Clarendon Press.

Williamson, J.G. 1989. 'The constraints on industrialisation: Some lessons from the First Industrial Revolution', in J.G. Williamson and V.R. Pachamukhi (eds), *The Balance between Industry and Agriculture in Economic Development,* London, Macmillan, pp. 85–105.

EXPERIENCE:
THE INDIAN CONTEXT

8

Terms of Trade and Demand Patterns

N. Krishnaji and T.N. Krishnan

This paper examines the impact of food and non-food prices, in absolute and relative terms, on the changing patterns of consumption in India. Contextually, the reference here is to the observed shift in demand, during the last two decades or so, away from inferior cereals and food grains, and to demand factors that might have played a role in boosting industrial growth during the early 1980s.

The analysis is carried out with the help of a model Ashok Mitra formulated earlier for explaining the deceleration in industrial growth during the late 1960s and early 1970s – a period when the terms of trade moved in favour of agriculture. With changes since then, whether the terms of trade have influenced industrial recovery during the 1980s thus becomes an interesting question.

1. INTRODUCTION

Ashok Mitra (1979) divides the Indian population, for analytical purposes, into four classes based on two dichotomies. In the rural areas the dichotomy is between (1) labourers and small peasants – 'net buyers' of food grain and (2) surplus-producing large landowners and traders. In urban India it is between (3) workers in industry and those in professions with fixed incomes, and (4) the bourgeoisie in industry and trade.

When analysing the Indian political economy it is possible to think of other types of division into classes, but what interests us here is the manner in which Ashok Mitra uses this framework to discuss the role of relative prices in the determination of the structure of demand, especially the demand for manufactures. Briefly, Ashok Mitra's argument set forth in the context runs as follows.

When the price terms of trade (TOT) move in favour of agriculture the rural income distribution worsens because of the concentration of the marketed surplus in the hands of the rural rich. On the other hand, despite the adverse movement in the TOT for them, the industrialists are able to maintain their profits by squeezing the workers, or by 'marking up' prices. This ability is derived from a political alliance between the industrial class and the rural rich. In general, wages, both in agriculture and industry, lag behind prices entailing a fall in real wage incomes. The story is similar in respect of the real incomes of small farmers and fixed salary-earners in the urban domain. The most important consequence (for the structure of demand) is that the poorer sections of the population 'are compelled to make a larger monetary outlay on food grains if they want to maintain their level of intake; simultaneously, they have to pay higher prices for a whole range of industrial goods'. Thus will a shrinkage in the demand for manufactures come about.

The model has been subjected to much critical review, with reference to its 'politics' and its empirical validity on the economic plane (see, for example, Vaidyanathan, 1992, for a discussion of the data). However, it is possible to analyse the changing demand patterns in terms of what has been stated at the end of the last paragraph. This possibility arises from the undeniable fact that, for the poorer classes as well as for some sections of the middle classes, food constitutes a major item of consumption. It seems reasonable to infer that what determines the demand for industrial goods – at least for these classes – is the residual income, that part remaining after food expenses are met.

2. THE NATURE OF THE FOOD GRAIN ECONOMY

Expenditure on food grains constitutes between 40 and 70 per cent of total expenditure in Indian family budgets. Poor families spend two-thirds or more of their incomes on food grains. Still, their daily calorie intake falls below the norm recommended by the Indian Council of Medical Research. The food grain consumption of the bottom 30 per cent in the population is 20 to 30 per cent lower than the mean consumption for the population as a whole which itself has been hovering about the average norm during the last three decades (Krishnan, 1992).

During the period 1960–90, per capita food grain output has shown only a marginal increase. And, per capita *availability* (which takes into account imports, exports and changes in stocks) for 12 out of the 19 years between 1971 and 1990 was below that of 1971. The per capita availability of food grains has remained more or less steady, largely due to the rise in wheat output. In fact, per capita availability of 'inferior cereals' like jowar, bajra, etc., consumed largely by the poor, has steadily declined over this period, from 44 kilograms per annum in 1971 to 30 kilograms in 1989.

Another aspect of the food grain economy is a widening of the regional disparity in production. There has been a continuous increase in the inter-state coefficient of variation in the per capita output of food grains from the mid-1960s; it rose from about 40 per cent in 1966 to 84 per cent in 1988–89. This has happened because the wheat revolution led to a dramatic increase in the per capita output in Punjab, Haryana and Western Uttar Pradesh, while grain production in almost all other states declined in per capita terms irrespective of the gains in yields per hectare (Krishnaji, 1988; Krishnan, 1992).

As regards the consumption of food grains, per capita cereal consumption has more-or-less remained constant during this period. The widening disparity in production does not seem to have affected the levels of consumption in different parts of the country. The coefficient of variation in per capita cereal consumption has even marginally declined in the 1970s and 1980s and the disparity in consumption is only half as much as the disparity in production. There is no doubt that the public distribution system has played an important role in keeping the inter-regional inequalities in consumption within bounds.

The differences in food grain consumption among the regions of India depend not only on the spatial spread in production but also on the amounts of grain transported over long distances. Such transportation involves substantial storage and transport costs and adds to the total cost of distribution of grain. Consumer behaviour in respect of food grains shows three distinct characteristics. Firstly, at the household level, it indicates a high and positive income (and expenditure) elasticity of demand for food grains. Secondly, time series data point to a very low (generally close to zero) income elasticity at the aggregated all-India level. Thirdly, as between states, levels of per capita consumption of food grains do not appear to be positively related to per capita state incomes; for some years, this association is strongly negative (Krishnan, 1992).

An analysis of the determinants of the consumption of food grains at the state level indicates that it is principally determined by the level of per capita production of food grains in each state. Such a relationship was noticed earlier in a study for the year 1961–62 (United Nations, 1975), but analysis of data which have become available since for the later years shows that this relationship has not altered in the least (Krishnan, 1992). This suggests that inter-state transfers are not wholly governed by differentials in demand conditions. Speculatively, we have suggested earlier that this market failure might be associated with the lack of adequate movement of grain into rural areas across state boundaries. (On the other hand, high urban incomes presumably attract grain from everywhere.)

Another critical factor is the change in consumption brought about by the changes in the composition of the grain output. The significant decline in the per capita production and, hence, in the availability of inferior cereals meant that poorer classes had to buy rice or wheat at higher prices to meet their requirements. This meant that, given their low incomes, they could buy only smaller quantities of grain. An analysis of the National Sample Survey (NSS) consumption data for the bottom 30 per cent of the rural population confirms these conjectures. For this class, the quantity of grain consumed has declined between 1960 and 1989 while the expenditure on food grains at constant prices has risen, possibly because of the shift in consumption from the lower-priced to the higher-priced grain (see in this context Radhakrishna and Ravi, 1990).

Another significant finding is that there is a considerable variation in food grain prices among the states. This cannot easily be explained by the differences in the composition of the consumption basket or in income levels. It has presumably more to do with how much grain is available from domestic or local production. As suggested earlier, the markets for inter-state transfers are not 'perfect'.

Given these characteristics of the food grain economy, we may ask how a shift in the terms of trade would affect the demand for food and the products of industry. A shift in terms of trade in favour of agriculture alters the income distribution between the producers and consumers of food grains. It also shifts the income distribution in favour of food-surplus states and against food-deficit states. Real incomes of producers rise while those of consumers decline. Since the demand for commodities is a function of real income, there will be an increase in the demand for all commodities by agricultural producers whereas the demand for all commodities, including that for food grains, will decline in the case of non-producers of food grains. The aggregate demand for food, as well as manufactures, will be determined by the net effect of these two opposing tendencies. Similarly, movements in the terms of trade against agriculture work in different ways for the different classes.

3. THE STRUCTURE OF DEMAND

The outcome in aggregate depends not only on how the poor spend their incomes but also on how the rich do. It has been correctly argued that a worsening distribution in income along with overall income growth in real terms may only change the composition of demand (in favour of non-wage goods): the aggregate demand for the products of industry need not necessarily decline. The data required for closely scrutinising actual changes, for example data on the relevant distributions of income, are not available. Therefore, it is possible only to assess the net effects (the end effects) of changes in relative prices and of income growth: it is difficult to measure the impact of changes in the distribution of income.

In the last section we discussed the determinants of inter-state variations in food intake. Generally, demand studies, whether based on time series or on household cross-sections, yield low price elasticities and fairly high income elasticities (which, however, decline with rising income) for cereals and food grains. Moreover, studies of both pre- and post-Mitra-model vintage exhibit an inverse relationship between the prices of cereals (and food grain) and the consumption of manufactured goods (Krishnan, 1966; Murty and Radhakrishna, 1982). Another interesting fact is that the NSS data yield a positive expenditure elasticity even in the highest per capita expenditure group: this may be a reflection of the superior qualities of grain consumed by the rich. Therefore there is some advantage in looking at expenditures, apart from consumption, in terms of quantities.

The data on private consumption expenditure in the *National Accounts Statistics* (NAS) may be divided into four groups as follows:

(A) cereals and cereal substitutes (item 1.1.1. in NAS);
(B) all other food, beverages and tobacco (item 1 excluding 1.1.1.);
(C) clothing, footwear, rent, taxes, fuel, power, furniture, household equipment, etc. (covering items 2, 3 and 4);
(D) medical expenses, education, transport, etc., covering all other items of consumption (items 5 to 8).

While (D) refers to expenditure on services, (C) includes mostly manufactured articles, including consumer durables. Other items, such as rent and taxes in (C), constitute a very small part of the total. We are using here the NAS data on the above variables in respect of expenditures in current and constant (1970–71) prices. This enables us to derive the implicit price indices (deflators) for the four groups. We also have the data on disposable incomes in current prices. The period covered is 1960–61 to 1984–85. (For the data see Tables 8.6 and 8.7.)

It is well known that from the mid-1970s the TOT have started moving against agriculture, reversing the earlier trend dating from the mid-1960s in favour of agriculture. Accordingly it is necessary to look at the two periods, 1960–61 to 1974–75 and 1975–76 to 1984–85 separately. During the first period, the prices of A, B, C and D derived as the implicit deflators in the NAS expenditure data, increased respectively at the rates of 8.17, 8.00, 4.50 and 5.33 per cent per annum – in other words the prices of food articles rose faster than those of non-food items. In contrast, during the second period, these rates were 5.89, 8.05, 7.95 and 8.87 respectively. The corresponding trend rates of increase in relative prices are given in Table 8.1. It should be noted that these prices are not appropriate for analysing *à la* Mitra the impact of the TOT on changes in distribution; for that purpose producer prices are needed. (In any case, as said before, we do not have data on rural income distributions.) The relative price structure set out in Table 8.1 is, however, relevant to the determination of the demand patterns.

TABLE 8.1
TREND RATES OF GROWTH IN RELATIVE PRICES
(per cent per annum)

	1960–74	1975–84	1960–84
1. Cereals relative to (/) non-food	3.32	−2.50	−0.14
2. Non-cereal food/non-food	3.15	−0.34	1.03
3. All food/non-food	3.22	−1.10	0.58

Notee: These rates are estimated by trend equations of the form $ln\ Y = a + bt$. All the rates are significant at the one per cent level. The price data on which this table is based are in Table 10.7.

It is clear that, with cereal prices moving at slower rates during 1975–84, relatively larger proportions of income would have become available for the consumption of non-cereal food as well as for manufactured articles in that period.

The trend rates of growth in per capita consumption expenditure in real terms (1970–71 prices) in respect of the different commodity groups are given in Table 8.2, along with the rates for disposable income (in money terms) and prices of all commodities and services. Incomes rose faster than prices by about 1.2 per cent per annum during 1960–74, but more impressively by about 2.3 per cent thereafter. Thus, if we go by the logic of the Mitra model, for the period since 1975, conditions for a faster growth in non-cereal consumption were present both in terms of relatively low cereal prices and an unusually – for the Indian economy – high rate of real income growth.

TABLE 8.2
RATES OF GROWTH IN INCOME AND CONSUMPTION (per cent per annum)

Item		1960–74	1975–84	1960–84
Disposable income per capita in current prices		8.26	10.04	8.69
All prices		7.05	7.75	7.04
Per capita expenditure in 1970–71 prices				
Commodities in group	A	0.31	0.47	0.31
	B	0.01	2.12	0.53
	C	2.16	2.99	2.45
	D	2.85	3.72	2.76

Note: These are trend rates estimated from NAS data as explained in the note to Table 10.1. The rates for A for 1960–74 and 1960–84 (both 0.31) are insignificant at the five per cent level. All the others are significant at the one per cent level.

It can be seen that growth rates in the per capita consumption of manufactured goods and services (groups C and D respectively) were higher in 1975–84 than in the earlier decade-and-a-half. Also, more prominently, while the per capita consumption of non-cereal food virtually stagnated during 1960–74, it grew at an impressive rate of 2.12 per cent per annum thereafter.

To analyse the impact of relative price movements on the structure of demand we consider the following models:

(M1): Each of x_a, x_b, x_c, and x_d (per capita real expenditure on items in A, B, C and D respectively) is a linear function of all the corresponding prices $(p_a, p_b, p_c$ and $p_d)$ and per capita disposable income in current prices (Y).

(M2): The same as M1, all the variables measured in logarithms.

(M3): With all variables in logarithms, x_b, x_c, and x_d (non-cereal expenditures) are functions of p_b, p_c and p_d, and Y_R the residual income (per capita disposable income minus the expenditure on cereals in current prices).

While M1 and M2 are the usual forms, M3 is in accordance with the Mitra model. Each of these is estimated along with an alternative version with two additional variables: D a dummy with values 1 for 1975–84 and 0 otherwise – and D*Y (or D*Y_R as the case may be) to account for possible changes in demand behaviour in the second period. Table 8.3 gives the adjusted R-square values for the different models.

TABLE 8.3
ADJUSTED R-SQUARE VALUES

| | Without dummies | | | | With dummies | | | |
	x_a	x_b	x_c	x_d	x_a	x_b	x_c	x_d
M1	0.08	0.84	0.93	0.96	0.14	0.86	0.96	0.98
M2	0.39	0.75	0.97	0.98	0.32	0.88	0.97	0.98
M3		0.69	0.98	0.99		0.84	0.98	0.99

Let us first consider the demand for cereals (group A). Demand functions of different forms (estimated through regressions), involving all the price variables and income, yield an income elasticity greater than unity and insignificant price elasticities. However, the fits are poor, with the adjusted R-square values ranging between 0.08 and 0.39. This is partly because the consumption of cereals has virtually stagnated during the period we are analysing and the year-to-year fluctuations that are present are related more to levels of production than to price movements. The correlation coefficient between the per capita real expenditure on cereals and the per capita production of cereals is as high as 0.875. All this is broadly consistent with the argument developed in the last section.

Turning now to non-cereal expenditure, it can be seen from Table 8.3 that model M3 performs slightly better than M1 and M2 in respect of x_c and x_d (manufactured goods and services respectively), while the unrestricted forms M1 and M2 provide a better explanation for x_b – non-cereal food. Since, however, our purpose here is to see whether the data are consistent with the Mitra type of hypothesis, and not to establish it beyond doubt, we work with M3 in what follows.

In both the estimated versions of M3 – with and without dummies – there is multicollinearity arising from the highly correlated price series. Accordingly, we have re-estimated the equations retaining the significant (at five per cent) variables and those close to significance at the ten per cent level. The results are given in Table 8.4.

TABLE 8.4
ESTIMATED LOG-LINEAR REGRESSIONS

Variable	Constant	D	p_b	p_c	p_d	Y_R	D^*Y_R	Adj R-Sq.	DW
x_b	4.82	−0.75	−0.37			0.37	0.10	0.82	2.33
x_c	2.98		−0.26	−0.28		0.67		0.98	1.62
x_d	2.46		−0.15		−0.50	0.80		0.99	1.09

Note: Except for the last two colums, the tabulated values are the respective coefficients in the log-linear model M3 explained in the text. The value for p_b in x_d (−0.15) is significant at the ten per cent level. All other values are significant at the five per cent level. DW in the last column refers to the Durbin–Watson statistics. Blanks in the table indicate that the corresponding variables were dropped. The total number of observations is 25 (1960–61 to 1984–85).

We note first that the dummy variables seeking to capture structural changes in demand (after the mid-1970s) are significant only in respect of x_b – the demand for non-cereal food. Thus the income and price elasticities of the demand for non-cereal food are different for the two periods. Next let us note that since the residual income $Y_R = Y - p_a{}^* x_a$, if the coefficient of log Y_R is positive (as in fact it is for all the three variables, the logarithms of x_b, x_c and x_d), it would imply a negative elasticity with respect to p_a – cereal price. If, in any equation, the coefficient of log Y_R is beta, it is easy to verify that the elasticity with respect to Y (e_Y) is given by beta/(1–p), where p is the proportion of cereal expenditure (in nominal terms) in the disposable income, and the elasticity with respect to p_a is given by (beta e_Y). All these elasticities, estimated at means, on the basis of the regressions in Table 8.4 are set out in Table 8.5.

TABLE 8.5
ELASTICITIES OF DEMAND

Elasticities with respect to

Commodity group	Period	p_a	p_b	p_c	p_d	Y
B	1960–74	−0.17	−0.37			0.50
B	1975–84	−0.11	−0.37			0.58
C	1960–84	−0.20	−0.26	−0.28		0.87
D	1960–84	−0.24	−0.15		−0.50	1.04

Note: For both C and D, the dummies are insignificant and therefore no distinction is made between the two time periods.

The elasticity of demand for non-cereal items with respect to cereal prices is negative, and ranges in absolute value between 0.11 and 0.24. (In our formulation, that is in model 3, this elasticity is restricted to be negative. But, as noted before, there are many studies demonstrating the negative impact of the increases in cereal, and food grain prices on the growth of the demand for 'other things'.)

What is remarkable, however, is that the demand elasticities of C and D (non-food) with respect to the price of non-cereal food are also negative. This suggests that while cereals are posited here as a priority item, other food is probably next in the hierarchy of consumer goods.

4. CONCLUDING REMARKS

Our analysis supports the view that in the Indian economy there is in operation what may be described as a food constraint on growth.

About a third of the population is not able to eat enough by any norm. For perhaps another third or more, the income elasticities of food expenditure tend to be high as a result of both quantitative and qualitative preferences. The markets for manufactures are thus constrained by low levels of residual incomes left over after food needs are met.

In principle the constraint can be relieved through a sustained growth in the incomes of the poor. That, however, is a distant prospect. A medium-term goal must therefore be an improvement in the level of food grain production in the regions that have experienced a steady fall in per capita production during the last two decades. Indeed, since we have thus far invested in technology and improvements in productivity in only a few regions and states, a radical shift in policies in favour of the hitherto neglected regions is called for. Since food consumption at the state level appears to be determined largely by how much is locally produced, boosting domestic production is the only choice in the absence of strategies for improving employment and incomes of the poor in non-farm activites.

The public distribution (PDS) has of course helped in keeping inter-state inequalities in food consumption within tolerable limits, through the supply of grain and, indirectly, through the control of food price inflation. However, the rural poor in many states still have no access to the PDS. The control of food-price inflation, however, seems to have played a part in the industrial recovery of the 1980s, although, of course, several other factors are also responsible for the recovery.

REFERENCES

Krishnaji, N. 1988. 'Foodgrain Stocks and Prices', in Amiya Kumar Bagchi (ed.), *Economy, Society and Polity,* Calcutta, OUP.
Krishnan, T.N. 1964. 'Demand for Mill-Cloth in India – A Study of the Interrelationship between Industry and Agriculture', *Artha Vijnana,* Vol. 6, No. 4.
Krishnan, T.N. 1992. 'Population, Poverty and Employment in India', *Economic and Political Weekly,* Vol. 27, No. 46.
Mitra, Ashok. 1979. *Terms of Trade and Class Relations,* Calcutta, Rupa & Co.
Murty, K.N. and R. Radhakrishna. 1982. 'Agricultural Prices, Income Distribution and Demand Patterns in a Low Income Country', in R.E. Kalman and J. Martinez (eds), *Computer Applications in Food Production and Agricultural Engineering,* Amsterdam.
Radhakrishna, R. and C. Ravi. 1990. *Food Demand Projections for India,* Hyderabad, Centre for Economic and Social Studies.
Vaidyanathan, A. 1992. 'Demand for Manufactures in India', mimeo, Madras Institute of Development Studies.
United Nations. 1975. *Poverty, Unemployment and Development Policy: A Case Study of Selected Issues with Reference to Kerala.*

TABLE 8.6
PER CAPITA INCOME AND EXPENDITURE:
ALL INDIA

Year	ydisp	x_a	x_b	x_c	x_d
1960	293.0	146.7	206.8	76.5	58.5
1961	302.0	145.3	204.3	76.8	60.0
1962	310.0	138.1	207.6	78.1	61.6
1963	345.0	140.8	199.5	82.3	64.5
1964	403.0	153.4	211.3	86.7	67.0
1965	408.0	130.6	206.9	84.6	69.4
1966	466.0	132.2	200.9	88.8	70.5
1967	543.0	152.0	204.9	89.1	73.1
1968	542.0	156.1	200.2	91.3	74.7
1969	584.0	156.4	207.8	89.0	77.6
1970	611.0	159.0	218.0	94.8	79.7
1971	636.0	152.5	216.3	101.5	83.9
1972	692.0	142.7	204.2	100.9	83.5
1973	848.0	147.7	198.8	100.7	86.1
1974	967.0	141.0	202.8	100.4	82.8
1975	991.0	156.0	207.7	103.7	84.8
1976	1035.0	134.0	201.5	110.9	89.0
1977	1158.0	159.4	209.5	115.5	92.6
1978	1219.0	157.7	213.8	120.7	96.8
1979	1305.0	135.0	203.5	116.8	99.3
1980	1546.5	160.5	226.6	117.2	100.8
1981	1721.0	153.3	233.4	123.3	103.4
1982	1860.9	145.1	230.3	136.0	109.5
1983	2183.2	164.3	240.3	137.3	114.8
1984	2349.9	151.6	243.5	137.7	122.5

Note: Year 1960 refers to 1960–61, etc.; *ydisp* stands for per capita disposable income (Rs.) in *current* prices; x_a etc., stand for per capita expenditure (Rs.) in 1970–71 prices for commodity group A etc., as defined in the text. The data are from *National Accounts Statistics*.

TABLE 8.7
IMPLICIT PRICE INDICES
1970–71=100

Year	p_a	p_b	p_c	p_d
1960	52.7	51.5	71.1	64.1
1961	52.9	52.8	75.3	67.5
1962	53.2	55.2	76.1	69.6
1963	59.8	60.7	79.2	72.9
1964	68.5	66.2	84.0	77.8
1965	80.2	70.6	89.4	80.1
1966	93.6	85.0	94.7	86.5
1967	106.6	98.2	98.1	93.0
1968	100.0	93.2	102.1	94.5
1969	104.6	99.1	105.5	97.3
1970	100.0	100.0	100.0	100.0
1971	104.4	103.2	107.3	104.9
1972	118.1	119.7	113.7	111.4
1973	139.1	150.5	129.6	123.6
1974	193.9	164.2	149.5	156.5
1975	159.8	156.1	156.8	164.1
1976	158.6	163.9	162.7	170.8
1977	153.4	180.2	176.7	177.3
1978	155.8	185.4	191.1	184.6
1979	175.7	207.8	217.2	205.2
1980	184.0	233.8	235.5	236.3
1981	203.6	250.3	254.2	276.0
1982	226.1	256.0	269.6	294.9
1983	252.6	292.8	284.0	319.6
1984	240.2	319.5	310.9	332.7

Note: These correspond to the commodity groups A etc., defined in the text and are obtained from the expenditure data in current and constant (1970–71) prices in *National Accounts Statistics*.

9

Targeting Internal Public Borrowing

Iqbal S. Gulati

With the focus of current fiscal policy in India on reducing the fiscal deficit, a term that stands for net public borrowing, it is only appropriate that questions relating to public borrowing are fully discussed. This paper can be taken as a contribution to such a discussion.

SUSTAINABILITY, THE FOREMOST QUESTION

Let us start by noting the sort of issues that can be, and are being, raised in this context, especially by those arguing for a sharp reduction in internal public borrowing.[1] One major argument being advanced already is that the size of public debt has by now reached a level in India which is unsustainable because of the annual interest burden it entails. But this itself raises several questions. Do we take into account gross or net interest liabilities? Is the burden of interest outflow rightly assessed relative to gross domestic product (GDP) or current government revenues? Will the burden not become lighter if either denominator, GDP or current revenues, were to expand and expand faster than interest outflow?

The matter of sustainability of public debt cannot be determined without being clear about what one has in mind, hence the importance of clarifying the context in which doubts regarding the sustainability of the present level of public debt in India are being raised.

PRINCIPAL CHARACTERISTICS OF INDIAN PUBLIC DEBT

We begin with what could be said to be the principal relevant characteristics of public debt in India. Firstly, public debt in India has grown rather rapidly in recent years. The combined debt of the central and state governments had already reached the level of 50 per cent of GDP in 1980–81. During the 1980s, it grew at the rate of 18 per cent per annum as against the GDP growth rate of 14 per cent (both in current prices). As a result, the ratio of public debt to GDP, increased further. It went up from 50 per cent in 1980–81 to 75 per cent in 1990–91.[2] Thus an additional 2.5 per cent of GDP was added to the Indian public debt every year during the 1980s. Secondly, the public debt in India largely consists of internal debt; only one-sixth of this debt was owed externally (see Table 9.1). Even during the 1980s when both internal and external public debt in India increased rather quickly the internal debt increased even faster. Between 1980–81 and 1990–91, the increase in the internal public debt was almost six times (5.84) as against the external public debt of almost five times (4.92).[3] Thirdly, only one-tenth of the combined debt of the central and state governments is accounted for by the latter. But this is so not because the state governments in India do not borrow much but because they borrow very largely from the central government. Over 70 per cent of the states' outstanding debt is owed to the centre.

TABLE 9.1

TOTAL OUTSTANDING PUBLIC DEBT IN INDIA: ITS BROAD DISTRIBUTION IN 1990–91

		Per cent
Of central government		89.9
	External	17.0[b]
	Internal	72.7
Of state government		10.3[c]
	Internal	10.3
Total		100.0[a]
	External	17.0
	Internal	83.0

Notes:
a   The combined outstanding debt of the central and state governments is estimated at Rs.3900 billion at the close of 1990–91.
b. External debt is calculated at the year-end exchange rate for the purposes of our estimates.
c. In estimating the outstandidng debt of the state governments, the portion they owe to the centre is excluded.

Source: Principally, *Economic Survey, 1992–93.*

Let us also be clear that the growth in the country's public external debt, although slower than that of the internal public debt of the country, is by no means a matter of lesser concern. Indeed, the matter of all external debt, its magnitude and growth, should, in our considered judgement, be of the utmost concern, given the pressures servicing of external debt creates for the country's balance of payments. In this context, it is also relevant to take note that although the public debt component of the country's external debt has been on the decline lately (it was as high as 70 per cent in 1980–81 and came down to 55 per cent in 1992–93) it is nevertheless quite substantial even now. At the same time, let it be noted that one reason why the public debt component of the external debt came down in the recent past was that external funds were raised by, or through, government-owned companies or corporations. To the extent this happened, the decline in the public debt component of the external debt was not real and the problems of servicing this debt continued to arise largely on account of its public debt component.

The point remains, however, that increasingly the servicing of the internal public debt has posed serious questions and it is on this component of public debt that our paper concentrates. In fact, our focus is even narrower in that we shall concentrate on the central government's internal debt. As pointed out above, it currently accounts for the bulk, 87.5 per cent, of the combined internal debt of the central and state governments.[4]

RISING INTEREST OBLIGATIONS

While the central government's outstanding internal debt, as a proportion of GDP, rose from 35.6 per cent in 1980–81, to 53.3 per cent in 1990–91, gross interest payments on internal debt more than doubled, as they rose from 1.7 per cent to 3.7 per cent of GDP. Other measures of growth in the gross interest liabilities show a similarly dramatic increase. As we have shown elsewhere,[5] as a proportion of the central government's total expenditure, these payments showed an escalation from 10.5 per cent to 18.7 per cent during the same period; as a proportion of the revenue account expenditure from 15.4 per cent to 26.1 per cent; as a proportion of revenue receipts from 18.1 per cent to 34.6 per cent and as a proportion of tax revenues from 24.6 per cent to 45.7 per cent. Each of these measures has a story of its own to tell, depending upon the denominator used for the purpose. The first two measures relating gross interest payments to total and revenue account expenditure tell us that a substantially higher proportion of the central government's expenditure was accounted for by interest payments on internal debt in 1990–91 than in 1980–81. When we relate gross interest payments to revenue account receipts and tax revenues, not only are the proportions substantially higher but the increase in these proportions over the period is also quite substantial. This has a major implication in the sense that it reflects not only on the growth of the interest liabilities of the government but also on that of government revenues.

DECLINING RECOVERY RATIO

Assessing the burden of public debt in terms of gross interest obligations, without taking into account the returns on investments financed out of funds raised by public borrowing could, however, be questioned. All funds borrowed by a government need not be, and are not actually, deployed in investments, physical or financial. Still, the portion so deployed, particularly that made in financial investments, yields returns, and does so directly, in the form of interest receipts, dividends and profits. In 1980–81 as much as 84.3 per cent of the interest paid on the central government's total public debt was recovered as interest receipts, dividends and profits.[6] Compared to that, the amount recovered in 1990–91 added up to 44.5 per cent. For 1992–93, the corresponding percentage works out to a slightly higher figure of 50 per cent, which is still considerably lower than the recovery ratio in 1980–81. Thus, while the central government's debt mounted and its gross interest obligations increased correspondingly, its recoveries declined, relatively speaking, with the result that the burden fell, with even greater force on the general budget.

The spurt in net interest outflow, that is, after netting for receipts on account of interest, dividends and profits, has been quite phenomenal over the period 1980–81 to 1990–91. Between 1980–81 and 1990–91, the net interest outflow, as a proportion of GDP, increased from 0.9 per cent to 2.5 per cent; as a proportion of the central government's current account receipts, from 9.5 per cent to 23.4 per cent; and as a proportion of the central government's tax revenues from 12.9 per cent to 30.9 per cent. Relative to the central government's total expenditure, the net interest outflow registered an increase from 5.4 per cent to 12.8 per cent.[7]

With direct receipts of the central government's exchequer from public investments registering niggardly increases – measured as a proportion of GDP, the increase was marginal, from 1.6 per cent in

1980–81 to 1.8 per cent in 1990–91 – the government has been constrained to meet a larger and larger proportion of its net interest outflow from the general budget.

TARDY REVENUE MOBILISATION

Of course, it can be argued, and quite justifiably so, that to view the matter of the burden of public debt in terms of the declining recovery ratio, or the burden of net outflow on the general budget, as was done in the preceding paragraphs, would still be to take too narrow a view. Deployment of funds raised by a government for purposes which are not directly remunerative in the sense of yielding interest, dividends or profits, could nevertheless be quite productive for the economy as a whole, in the sense of improving its efficiency of production or adding to its productive capacity through improved economic or social infrastructure. In that case, could one not legitimately expect the public investments to reflect themselves in higher growth of national income and correspondingly in better revenue receipts, especially tax receipts, of the government?

Let us see how the situation unfolded in reality. Between 1980–81 and 1990–91, the central government's revenue receipts, as a proportion of GDP, increased from 9.4 per cent to 10.7 per cent (+ 1.3 per cent) and tax receipts from 6.9 per cent to 8.1 per cent (+ 1.2 per cent). During the same period, annual growth registered in GDP was of the order of 5.5 per cent in real terms, whereas net borrowing (including borrowing from RBI) of the central government increased from 6.6 per cent to 8.6 per cent (+ 2.0 per cent). Gross interest obligations increased from 1.9 per cent to 3.7 per cent (+ 1.8 per cent) of GDP over the period. Obviously, the increase in the central government's revenue receipts, as well as in its tax receipts, has been far below the increase in its gross interest obligations even though the growth in GDP during the period was by no standard insubstantial. So while the productive impact of a large proportion of public expenditure cannot be ruled out, the fact cannot be overlooked that it has failed to reflect itself in sufficiently enhanced revenues for the central government.

To have a fuller idea of how the government's revenue mobilisation efforts lagged behind increased government spending, it should be added that, as against the increase in revenue receipts of the central government from 9.4 per cent to 10.7 per cent (+ 1.3 per cent) of GDP, the increase registered by revenue expenditure was from 10.9 per cent to 14.2 per cent (+ 3.3 per cent) of GDP. This meant that almost three-fifths of the increase in revenue expenditure were left uncovered. Not surprisingly, therefore, the revenue deficit was as high as 3.5 per cent of GDP in 1990–91 compared to 1.5 per cent in 1980–81.

The increasing ratios of net outgo on account of interest payments to the government's current revenues and tax revenues, both of which, as noted above, rose significantly during the 1980s, tell us more than that the recovery ratio declined during the period. On the other hand, the burden of servicing the internal debt increased, in the sense of the proportion of the government's current receipts required to be set apart for meeting the net outflow on account of interest payments. This came about partly because of the decline in the recovery ratio, that is in the ratio of interest and related receipts of the government to its gross interest obligations. As we noted already, this ratio came down sharply from close to 85 per cent to well below 50 per cent in the course of one decade. At the same time, it was also the very tardy expansion in government revenues, particularly tax revenues, that was responsible for the net outflow registering the sort of sharp increase observed above as a proportion of government revenues.[8]

SUSTAINABILITY AND REVENUE EFFORT

In addressing the question of the sustainability of public debt, posed at the very outset, it is the ratio of the net interest outflow to the government's total current receipts that becomes of critical importance. If direct returns from government investments do not expand as public debt mounts and if, at the same time, government revenues do not expand sufficiently, the higher relative burden of the net outflow, relative to total government expenditure, can mean either reduced non-interest government spending or larger fiscal deficits, or of course, a combination of both. To the extent that a government relies on fiscal deficit, a sort of vicious circle can come into motion with higher deficits leading to larger borrowing which causes still higher deficits because of the larger net outflow. It must be recognised that the villain of the piece is not just inadequate recovery in the form of interest, dividend and profits but also insufficient revenue mobilisation. Sustainability or otherwise of internal public debt, it must be emphasised, depends *not* on the magnitude of the net interest outflow of a government taken in isolation but on the increase in such outflow relative to the increase in the government revenues.

However, there still remains a question regarding the courses of action open when the burden of public debt can be said to become unsustainable in the sense that the outflow on account of interest payments rises quickly in proportion to the total current revenues of a government and reaches levels which are considered high. The higher the proportion of a government's current revenues to be earmarked for meeting its interest liabilities, the lower is the proportion available for meeting its other expenditures. These are expenditures, which the government is not contractually obliged to incur, but they may still be very necessary. Quite a substantial part may be necessary for the government to meet its obligations on the basis of the social compact with its people or to sustain the country's economic growth. Therefore, to seek to reduce the burden of public debt by reducing the government's non-interest expenditures may well amount to reneging on its obligations under its social compact or harming economic growth. Instead, the government should be exploring ways and means of mobilising additional current revenues. Larger·tax revenues will reduce the government's deficit on its revenue account, as well as its fiscal deficit. Moreover, larger recoveries in the form of interest receipts, dividends and profits will reduce the net outgo on account of interest on public debt. True, in the end, the government may have to borrow less, given the level of its total expenditures. Such restraint in public borrowing will, however, have been achieved by following a route that will have forced the government neither to renege on its social compact obligations nor to have forsworn the major role it has in sustaining economic growth in a country, such as India, at its present stage of development. These considerations cannot be overlooked when there is recognition all round that the government must continue to play a substantial role, given the present stage of India's development, in further building the socio-economic infrastructure required to sustain a high rate of economic growth and to attain a higher level of social well-being.

DEBT BURDEN AND ECONOMIC GROWTH

It will be appropriate at this point to refer to the 1944 paper written by E.D. Domar.[9] This paper was, no doubt, written in the context of the post-Second World War fiscal situation in the US but it is, in our judgement, eminently relevant to the current discussion in India on fiscal policy. In this paper, Domar demonstrates that 'the problem of the debt burden is essentially a problem of achieving a growing national income'. With a growing national income, Domar shows, the taxation required to finance the interest liabilities of a government on its public debt will not impose a particularly unbearable burden on the economy. In fact, he shows that 'the greater is the rate of growth of income, the lower will be the tax rate (required to meet the interest charges on public debt), even though a more rapidly rising income results in a larger absolute magnitude of the debt'[10] (parenthesis added). In other words, the revenue effort required to service public debt will be less if the economy grows fast.

What is necessary to ensure the sustainability of public debt, according to Domar, is that government expenditures are productive in the sense of contributing to economic growth. He is careful, however, to warn that government expenditures did not have to be productive in the narrow sense that 'the assets constructed make a direct contribution to the federal treasury or are self-financing'. He deliberately avoids the term 'investment expenditures' in this context because 'it is too closely associated with steel and concrete'. On the other hand, he would consider expenditure on public health as productive 'if healthier people are more productive'. The same holds true, according to Domar, 'for expenditures on education, research, flood control, resource development, and so on'. 'National income', Domar asserts, 'would be able to advance at a higher rate if governmental expenditures were productive in our sense'.[11]

A few points can be said to emerge from Domar's analysis of the problem of public debt. Firstly, in order to shoulder the burden of public debt, as reflected in the annual interest liabilities it entails, a government has to raise additional taxation. Secondly, the required additional tax revenue as a proportion of national income, is inversely related to the rate of growth of national income. Thirdly, the rate of growth of national income could be higher the more productively the government deploys its expenditures.

Thus, to ensure that the burden of public debt does not become unsustainable, the thing for policy makers to do, according to Domar, would *not* be to stop or reduce public borrowing but to review the existing allocations of governmental expenditures and make sure that the maximum possible proportion of these expenditures is incurred in areas, and in a manner, that contributes optimally to the growth of national income. Then, with national income growing fast, indeed faster than before if reallocations are done correctly, it will be possible to keep the burden of taxation required to finance the interest outgo from the budget low. The sort of situation currently being faced by India, with the increasing proportion of the government's current account receipts having to be earmarked for interest payments, can then be avoided. Of course, the required quantum of tax effort will still have to be made.

TARGETING BORROWING MISPLACED

By targeting the fiscal deficit, defined as the excess of total government expenditure over government current account receipts, recent fiscal policy has sought to focus attention on containing public borrowing since the excess referred to is, by definition, financed through borrowing. Strictly speaking, when the proponents of the concept speak of the fiscal deficit, no distinction is drawn, between covering the fiscal deficit through external public borrowing and covering it through internal public borrowing. We assume for our purposes, however, that the fiscal deficit, whatever its magnitude, is covered through internal public borrowing. So, to target fiscal deficit reduction means, under our assumption, targeting reduced internal borrowing by government.

Internal borrowing by government is targeted regardless not only of whether it takes the form of borrowing from households, or from banks or from the Reserve Bank of India but also what the funds raised in public borrowing could have been used for by the government.[12] In fact, going by the position taken in the latest Economic Survey, it would appear that the government would like to go much further than containing current net borrowing and effect a reduction in the outstanding government debt.[13] Since any positive net borrowing would imply an increase in the absolute level of outstanding public debt, to achieve a reduction in the outstanding debt, net public borrowing would indeed have to become negative at some stage.

It must, however, be recognised that to emphasise the reduction in internal public borrowing in order to reduce the fiscal deficit amounts to shifting the accent of fiscal policy from the mobilisation of current revenues and the productive deployment of government expenditure to blanket reduction of government spending. Of course, one cannot rule out the possibility that a stage arrives when it may not be necessary to raise further the level of total government spending as a proportion of GDP and it may be advisable to effect a reduction in that level. The question is whether that stage has arrived already. Has a proper assessment been made of the role of government spending of various types? For instance, has the limit been reached already for the role of government in the expansion and/or improvement of the country's socio-economic infrastructure? Here, one should add that distinguishing between revenue account and capital account government spending may not be as helpful as distinguishing between the purposes for which government spending, be it on revenue or capital account, is to be incurred. For that matter, even the distinction, currently in fashion, between plan and non-plan spending is not very useful because a good part of non-plan spending is meant for the maintenance and running of the socio-economic infrastructure on which rests the whole edifice of the country's current economic growth. This should not, however, be construed as approval of all types of non-plan government spending at their present levels including, for example, spending on defence and internal security.

CONCLUSION

The aphorism that only a poor workman blames his tools is very pertinent here because the basic mistake being made in appraising the burden of the internal public debt derives from confusing the tool with the workmanship. What the government uses this tool for – in other words, the expenditures that public borrowing is used to finance and what such spending results in – is part of the government's fiscal workmanship. In forswearing further public borrowing,[14] fiscal policy is wrongly focusing on the tool instead of the workmanship.

As we have seen, during the 1980s, while the internal debt in India was allowed to pile up, revenue effort did not keep pace with it despite fairly good economic growth. While recovery ratio declined substantially, the increase registered during the decade in the government's current revenues as a proportion of GDP was far, far below the increase in interest obligations. Whether it was because the tax effort was tardy or because increasingly government funds were being deployed unproductively are questions which need to be addressed rather than whether public borrowing, as the instrument of fiscal policy, has to be forsworn, partially or wholly.

NOTES

The reason I have chosen this particular subject for my contribution to this volume is that it is Ashok Mitra who, knowing my strong reservations on the focus of the current fiscal policy in India, as agreed to with the IMF, has kept urging me to put down my thoughts on the subject.

I found the comments and suggestions of the referee to be extremely useful and I hereby acknowledge them.

1. See, in particular, Chelliah (1992). He has emerged as the high priest of the current stance in fiscal policy in favour of reduced public borrowing, as advocated by the IMF.
2. The calculations are made after converting the outstanding external public debt at the exchange rate prevailing at the end of the financial year and adding them to outstanding internal liabilities. As the Economic Survey 1992–93 (p. 22) observes, 'it is more appropriate to convert them (i.e. external liabilities of the government) at current end-of the year exchange rates to reflect the burden of the debt fully.'

3. Thanks to the sharp devaluation of the rupee since July 1991, the more recent figures have a different story to tell. The increase between 1980–81 and 1992–93 (RE) of the internal public debt works out to 7.35 times as against 8.31 times for the external public debt (see *Economic Survey, 1992–93*, pp. 15 and 118). One has to be a little cautious here. What is referred to here as public external debt appears to be too narrowly defined and is understood to exclude the external debt of even fully owned government commercial undertakings, though almost all of it carries explicit public guarantees. The increase in the overall external debt by 10.42 times over the same period was much higher. Here, our assumption is that the figures put out for both public and overall external debt are broadly correct, at least in regard to change over the period. But note has to be taken of the existence of disparities between various estimates of the magnitude and growth of the country's overall external debt. Moreover, these disparities are, partly at least, traceable to differences in the estimation of public external debt (Ghosh 1993).

4. In working out this figure, we have excluded the debt owed by the state governments to the central government. This avoids double counting. It is well to bear in mind, however, that the states' debt to the central government is almost 2.5 times the debt they owe currently to others, including banks and financial institutions.

5. See Gulati (1993). The author draws heavily upon this article for the present paper.

6. While interest payments are shown separately in the official documents for internal and external debt, interest receipts, dividends and profits are not so shown. The practice followed so far in the official documents is to publish figures of total net outflow on account of interest payments. But in netting for receipts, account is not taken of the government's receipts as dividends and profits and to that extent the net outflow on account of interest payments has tended to be overstated.

7. These figures are different from those given in the Economic Survey, 1992–93 (p. 26). Our net outflow figures, which include dividends and profits in addition to interest receipts, show the increase over the period to be of the order of 2.4 times, substantial no doubt, but far short of the fourfold spurt referred to in the *Economic Survey*. See Gulati (1993).

8. While direct returns from government investments figure in the numerator, the indirect returns, assuming that they are reflected in the expansion of tax revenues and therefore of total revenue receipts, will figure in the denominator while working out the relative burden of the net outflow relative to the government revenue receipts. Expansion in tax revenues may come about either because national income itself grows fast or because given the rate of increase in national income the ratio of tax revenues to national income rises. Of course, both factors should operate simultaneously, assuming an elasticity of above unity. To finance an increasingly higher net outflow on account of interest, the expansion in tax revenues would have to be even higher.

9. See Domar (1957).

10. Following Domar, the required tax rate to meet the interest charges on public debt would approximate to:

$$\frac{\alpha}{r} \quad \times \quad i$$

where α is the fraction of national income being borrowed by government, r is the rate of growth of national income and i is the real rate of interest. Thus, assuming $\alpha = 6$ per cent, $r = 5$ per cent and $i = 2$ per cent, the required tax rate would work out as 2.4 per cent. With only r changing to 8 per cent, the required tax rate will work out as 1.5 per cent. Given Domar's definition of taxable income, his required tax rate is none other than the ratio of tax revenue to national income.

11. The view taken in the *Economic Survey, 1992–93* (p. 20) in regard to the efficiency of government expenditure is totally opposite to Domar's. 'In an efficient system', the Survey observes, interest payments by the government 'would have been covered by returns on productive capital expenditure and investment financed by debt.' Adjudged thus, the government's plan spending is found to be severely wanting and therefore comes in for severe strictures when the *Survey* notes that 'instead of providing such a cover, plan expenditure has been characterised by low returns from investments and inefficiency'.

12. The present writer has sought to bring out the implications of this particular shift in fiscal policy's focus requiring a blanket reduction in fiscal deficit. See Gulati (1991); also Mody (1991) and Rakshit (1991).

13. See *Economic Survey 1992–93,* p. 28, for the clearest statement so far of the government's goal to effect a 'reduction of debt' and how it could be achieved. In principle, the *Survey* observes, a reduction in the government's outstanding liabilities is possible through 'either a primary surplus or from the proceeds of asset sales'. The *Survey* goes on to elaborate that 'the effectiveness of the latter (that is, debt reduction with the proceeds of asset sales) can be increased by retiring high interest debt or disinvestment of the equity of selected issues which were making losses' (parenthesis added). Chelliah (1992) is even more forthright when he calls for the 'liquidation of a substantial part of the existing stock of internal debt', without which, according to him, 'it would not be possible to eliminate the revenue deficit within even the next five years' and 'the volume of government investment will have to be kept too low, affecting growth and welfare'. He fails to note however that the course he is advocating is bound to affect government investment immediately.

14. After noting that 'interest payments net of interest received increased by nearly four times, from 3.6 per cent to 13.9 per cent' of total government expenditure between 1980–81 and 1991–92 (RE), the *Economic Survey 1992–93* speaks of the fiscal correction measures taken to reduce the level of borrowings and expresses the hope that within a few years the reduced level of borrowings will have 'a perceptible impact on the heavy interest burden of the government'. What the Survey fails to address are the factors underlying the phenomenal increase in the net outflow on account of interest payments, particularly as a proportion of the revenue receipts of the government. Not surprisingly, therefore, the main focus of the so-called fiscal correction measures seems to be directed at the reduction in borrowings.

REFERENCES

Chelliah, R.J. (1992), 'Growth of Indian Public Debt', in Bimal Jalan, *The Indian Economy, Problems and Prospects,* Viking.

Domar, Evsey D. (1957), 'Burden of the Debt and the National Income', in his *Essays in the Theory of Economic Growth,* Oxford University Press.

Ghosh, Arun (1993), 'India's External Debt in Relation to BOP Prospects', *Economic and Political Weekly,* 6 February.

Government of India (1993), *Economic Survey 1992–93,* Ministry of Finance, Economic Division.

Gulati, I.S. (1991), 'Reducing the Fiscal Deficit', *Economic and Political Weekly,* 20 July.

Gulati, I.S. (1993), 'Tackling the Growing Burden of Public Debt', *Economic and Political Weekly,* 1 May.

Mody, R.J. (1991), 'On Defining the Fiscal Deficit', *Economic and Political Weekly,* 21 September.

Rakshit, Mihir (1991), 'The Macroeconomic Adjustment Programme: A Critique', *Economic and Political Weekly,* 24 August.

10

The State and the Poor

Pramit Chaudhuri

I

Much has been written on the actual and potential effects on poverty of changes in economic and social policy. Some of it has focused on the effects of structural adjustment policies and some on endemic and acute manifestations of hunger in society (Cornia *et al.* 1987; Dreze and Sen, 1989). This chapter attempts to outline State action towards the alleviation of poverty rather than to evaluate any particular set of policies. Much of what I have to say is of a general nature, although examples are drawn most commonly from India. In this essay, 'poor' is meant to refer to those suffering from absolute poverty, although I occasionally deal with policies aimed at benefiting low income groups, some of whom may not be 'poor' in this strict sense.

The success or failure of State policy towards the poor has to be assessed in terms of the objectives the State sets itself. The obligations it accepts towards the poor depend partly on its views about the nature and causes of poverty and partly on the perceived limits to its own powers. Neither of these need reflect a social consensus and what the State should do to alleviate poverty has always been an area of contention. The structure of the essay is as follows: Section II attempts to put the Indian state's perception of poverty into an historical context; Section III provides a more detailed characterisation of poverty, while Section IV discusses the relationships between the various characteristics of poverty and policy measures that the state can adopt that are pro-poor. The concluding section argues for a broader approach to the problem of poverty alleviation. I am not primarily concerned in this essay with aspects of famine policy as it affects the poor (Sen, 1981).

II

No state, autocratic, democratic or theocratic, can be wholly impervious to the presence of poverty and hunger in society. Most, however, have found it easier to offer a rationalisation of such presence rather than a remedy. The government of British India in the nineteenth century held that poverty in India reflected the country's low GDP and that, in a normal year, it did not give rise to mass hunger and starvation. Incomes could only rise at a natural rate appropriate to a poor country and governments could do little to hasten the process. If and when famine struck, the government had a duty to intervene and save lives at the least possible cost. The most significant difference between colonial and post-colonial attitudes to poverty lay in the fact that the latter believed, at least in theory, that poverty was a social and economic fact that was mutable and which governments had a duty to try to ameliorate.

Anti-poverty policies in India have gone through various phases, with some subtle and not-so-subtle changes in direction and emphasis. The main strands of anti-poverty policy can, however, be clearly identified. Somewhat paradoxically, the objectives of a policy towards poverty have come to be defined more narrowly over time, just as our theoretical perceptions of what constitutes poverty, and thus what the poor need in order not to be poor, have opened out and deepened. In part, this may simply underline the fact that politics is the art of the possible. It is also a sign of the inability to explore the structural roots of poverty in south Asian society and the unwillingness to acknowledge the degree of marginalisation and social disenfranchisement that characterises poverty.

The poverty objectives of the earlier planning exercises were largely 'growth mediated' (Dreze and Sen, 1989). Poverty was seen to reflect a low level of per capita income and capital accumulation. A faster rate of growth was seen as the major instrument with which to attack poverty (India, 1974). The diagnosis was not very different from that of the Raj; what was different was the State's willingness to deal with the malady. There is, however, more to poverty at the personal or household level than the shared citizenship of a poor nation. A failure of entitlements at these levels reflects in a large measure the particular 'structural' aspects of poverty that lie in a denial of access to a share in productive resources and productive activities in the shape of both physical and human capital. Since 'being denied' implies the presence of someone who denies, it is difficult to conceive of an anti-poverty policy that is not 'redistributive' in a dynamic sense. However, the State put a rather static interpretation on 'redistribution' that has persisted to this day, and not only in India (World Bank, 1990).

Thus defined, redistributive policies could be fairly easily ruled out as either politically unfeasible or economically unnecessary, the latter argument having been revived recently in the context of the 'green revolution' (Singh, 1990). Nowhere, perhaps, was this change in focus more noticeable than in the context of land reform, given the emphasis on agrarian problems and the very detailed investigation of the structural causes of agrarian distress that the Indian National Congress had undertaken in the 1930s (UP Congress, 1931).

The Directive Principles of the Indian constitution provide an early statement of social policy. As a general objective, they sought to promote 'a just social order for the promotion of welfare' of the people. They also made some specific commitments, marking out important areas of policy intervention. More important, in doing so they offered a particular view of what was seen to constitute relative and absolute deprivation in society. A living wage, equal pay for equal work, increased levels of nutrition and health make interesting reading. More significant are equal rights for men and women, the abolition of child labour and free and compulsory education for all children under the age of 14 years by 1961 (Banerjee and Chatterji, 1957). There was also a recognition of some fundamental areas of social discrimination, only one of which, 'untouchability', was pursued with any administrative vigour.

Over the years, the most noticeable change in anti-poverty policy has been a more targeted approach towards various special groups and regions. Some of these fall into the category of growth-mediated policies as they are attempts to provide sources of sustainable livelihood for some of the poor. Others, such as school meals programmes, are clearly 'support-mediated' (Dreze and Sen, 1989). My purpose here is neither to catalogue nor to evaluate these policies and programmes. It is to point out that the shift amounts on the one hand to an admission of failure of the fundamental strategy and, on the other, to circumscribe the obligations of the State towards the poor. For the selectivity of these forms of intervention, in terms of groups or regions, acknowledges the fact that the State does not possess the resources or the capacity to help the majority of the poor or even the 'poorest' into the mainstream of economic growth. (On special programmes see, for example, Paul and Subramanian, 1983; Rath, 1985.)

III

Both colonial and post-colonial governments sought to explain poverty at the personal or household level in terms of the material poverty of the nation, emphasising the low level of development of powers of production rather than exploring the particularities of relations of production, as Marxist terminology might express it. They differed in the extent to which they believed that the State could and should actively seek to promote economic growth but. shared the belief that poverty was largely a matter of low levels of income, which growth could raise. However, both theory and experience suggest that poverty has many facets and an anti-poverty strategy might need different instruments to address these. We need, therefore, to explore the nature of poverty in a wider context before we can discuss the range of policy choices that are available to the State for reducing poverty. The perception of the State may, moreover, differ from a wider social perception, which in turn will influence its choice of policy. There is, of course, no social consensus on what poverty is but I believe that many will agree that the following are some of the major characteristics of poverty.

To begin with, it is worth remembering that the characteristics of poverty are those that we attribute to the poor. If society listens to the poor, it hardly ever records what the poor think of as poverty. If it did, it is highly unlikely that the poor would blame their poverty primarily on the poverty or underdevelopment of their country. Yet, this is how mass poverty, absolute poverty, is most readily explained.

There are, of course, good reasons for doing so. The majority of the poor are to be found in the less-developed countries (LDCs). According to the World Development Report 1990, 633 million 'extremely poor' people (with per capita incomes below US $275 per year at 1995 PPP dollars) and another 483 million 'poor' (per capita income below US $370 at 1995 PPP dollars) people lived in LDCs. Of these, 520 and 180 million respectively were to be found in South Asia and sub-Saharan Africa. In these countries, roughly 1 in 3 people were characterised as 'extremely poor' and almost every other person as 'poor' (World Bank, 1990, p. 29). While there is no precise agreement on norms, and therefore on actual numbers, it is unlikely that alternative nutrition-based definitions will produce figures that differ by more than approximately plus or minus 10 per cent.

While the poor are mostly to be found in poor countries, there is no simple relationship between levels of GNP per capita and the extent of poverty in poor countries. This is so whether we use a nutritionally determined poverty level or broader indicators of welfare such as life expectancy or the infant mortality rate (Dreze and Sen, 1989). It is so, whether we compare per capita GDP to a headcount index of poverty, or per capita calorie availability to extent of malnutrition (Sen, 1983; Reutlinger and Selowsky, 1976). It is well known that some countries have managed to achieve high rates of growth of GNP with a reduction in poverty while in others rapid growth has not reduced poverty; compare South Korea with Brazil. All this is unsurprising and merely underlines the importance of the distribution of income and wealth, and of public policy as determinants of poverty and hunger in society. The regional distribution of poverty serves to complicate the picture further, for no uniform pattern emerges. Thus, the poor in China are mostly concentrated in resource-poor regions in the west and south-west. There is no such pattern in India, where significant numbers can be found to be living in poverty in some of the wealthier states (World Bank, 1985; Vaidyanathan, 1988).

The most commonly observed characteristic of poverty is endemic hunger or food insecurity, commonly measured in terms of a calorie norm and levels of expenditure on food required to meet that norm. This is how we intuitively think of poverty. Even people who argue for a lower level of calorie intake, say 1900 kcals as opposed to 2300 kcals, would not deny the importance of inadequate or insecure food intake as a prime characteristic of poverty. That we should not be too nutritionally economical in fixing our calorie norms has been cogently argued by Dasgupta and Ray, who drew attention to the welfare and resource costs of such adaptation to the poor (Dasgupta and Ray, 1990). For all these reasons, a low level of food intake by the individual or the household is an important aspect of poverty.

The relationship between food intake and poverty can be seen in a number of ways. Firstly, there is Engel's Law, which records across a very wide range of data sets that the average and marginal expenditure elasticity of expenditure for food is significantly and negatively correlated with levels of expenditure. This rather robust statistic can be 'read' in different ways for policy purposes. It can be used to identify pockets of poverty in society. It is a matter of some dispute whether it can be used to differentiate between the 'poor' or the 'poorest' and other income groups. The argument partly turns on the question of whether there is some observable 'kink' in the expenditure elasticity function for food and, if so, whether the 'kink' occurs at an expenditure level that would make it useful for policy purposes (Anand *et al.*, 1993). What cannot be denied, however, is that poor households have a high share of food expenditure and that any reduction in poverty measured by the real consumption of the poor requires increased food availability for the poor. Engels' Law can be used to evaluate food price policy. It can be used as a reminder of an important social fact, that both the urban and the rural poor are net buyers of food in the market. However, the rural poor do not relate to food only as consumers but also as producers. They not only normally convert a large proportion of their 'entitlements' into food; they also derive, or seek to derive, a large part of those 'entitlements' through participation in food production. I shall return to this point later.

Other important aspects of poverty are low and variable income and asset status, or low 'entitlements' of the poor. Poor landless households can only gain 'entitlements' through an exchange of labour. Dynamically, the persistence of poverty in this regard arises from the following factors: (i) a low overall level of growth; (ii) low employment elasticity of growth; (iii) changes in sectoral composition of growth away from labour-intensive to capital-intensive sectors, for example from agriculture to large-scale industrial production; (iv) labour market imperfections that create conditions of surplus labour and impose a real wage/employment trade-off favourable to labour in organised industrial and financial sectors and in the public sector, which is inimical to the poor; (v) social and institutional constraints to spatial and occupational mobility of labour, such as gender or caste restrictions. Even where employment is available, it can be highly variable and insecure, either on a daily or a seasonal basis. Much of the employment is in low productivity occupations, commanding low real wages, which not only reflects the existence of unemployed and under-employed labour but also a low level of skills and human capital formation in this part of the labour force.

Of physical assets that the rural poor possess, land appears to be the commonest. This may reflect reality or our relative ignorance of non-farm rural poverty and the asset position of non-farm rural households (Chadha, 1992). The average size of holdings of poor or marginal small peasant households is by definition below 'subsistence'. We know little about the average quality of their landholdings although there is a presumption in the literature that it tends to be inferior land. In this respect the controversy about the proportion of irrigated land in small holdings is irrelevant because there we are mostly talking about non-poor small cultivators. We do know that much of the 'surplus' land that has been distributed to marginal peasants or the landless in India is of poor quality. A necessary but not sufficient condition for these households to lift themselves out of the reach of poverty is clearly to increase the size of their productive land holdings.

This is not a sufficient condition because the poor may lack access to credit or non-labour inputs, such as better quality seeds or fertilizers, to make effective use of land. They may also suffer from constraints such as a lack of access to superior technology. Common property resources (CPRs) are a land-based resource to which the poor need access but where access is being made progressively more difficult for the poor. These may consist of common land or wasteland necessary for grazing cattle; land where natural fodder or fuel wood can be collected 'free' (in other words not for cash but with considerable energy and time expenditure, especially by female labour, which is normally ignored for national accounting purposes see Pyatt, 1990). They may include ponds and water channels for drawing water not otherwise available or available only at a far greater distance. It is common in semi-arid areas both of Africa and south Asia for women and children to have to walk long distances to collect daily supplies of water. A most valuable form of supplementary nutrition for the poor, and not only in famines, is wild fruits, berries, roots, fish, molluscs and so forth, which might be available as common property resources. A most important form of CPR is, of course, forests, often the sole source of livelihood for some groups of the poor. It is true that, to an extent, continuous exclusion from CPR is a reflection of growing population density. However, exclusion of the poor from forest resources has been actively pursued by the State for a long time (Jodha, 1986; Guha, 1991).

Physical capital is not the only form of capital that the poor lack. Recently, attention has been directed to human resource development and the low level of human capital formation as a cause of deprivation and poverty (World Bank, 1990; UNDP, 1992). Lack of access to education and health facilities is a great barrier to human capital formation in poor households, in turn leading to low levels of skills, employment, productivity and income and thus a perpetuation of endemic poverty.

High rates of return, both social and private, of primary education have been recorded across a wide sample of countries (Psacharopoulos, 1988; for an earlier Indian study, see Blaug *et al.*, 1969). Arguably, this is a major cause of poverty for the urban poor, herding them into low wage occupations. The linkage between human capital and poverty is not only income related but operates through a range of socioeconomic variables; for example, a negative correlation between levels of female literacy and fertility rates can be observed in many less-developed countries. If we chose a wider definition of poverty, we could argue that low levels of access to health and education in a sense truly prevents the development of human capabilities (Sen, 1987).

The aspects of poverty that we have discussed so far share a common feature. They all refer in some way to the relationship of the poor to productive resources, either of direct user rights over them or a means of exercising labour 'entitlements'. They can be said to be 'market mediated', forming a part of a wider market nexus. Much poverty that exists in less developed countries is, of course, not of this nature in that it embraces children and female members of households. Not all of this type of poverty is intra-family poverty but much of it is not 'market mediated'.

If poverty is measured, as it most commonly is, in terms of nutritional deficiency, then a major part of the world's 'poor' must be children. The same would be true if we chose to look at mortality rates. We do not have the figures for what proportion of the 'poor' in this sense are children but the proportion must be very high. As we noted earlier, anything between 30 to 50 per cent of the population of south Asia and sub-Saharan Africa can be counted as 'poor'; the rate for all less developed countries is 18 per cent for the 'extremely poor' (World Bank 1990, p. 29). Of the world's population in 1990, 32 per cent were below the age of 14. For south Asia, the rates were 43.8 per cent for Bangladesh, 35.8 per cent for India (24.8 per cent up to 9 years) and 34.8 per cent for Sri Lanka (23.6 per cent up to 9 years); the figure for Pakistan for 1981 was 44.7 per cent. For sub-Saharan Africa, the mean rate was 45 per cent, covering a range from 39 to 47 per cent (UNO, 1992). While the numbers quoted as being in poverty implicitly include large numbers of children, policy debates on poverty all too often exclude them, regarding them as something to be added on at the margin of policy making, to be dealt with by supplementary or special programmes.

This does not mean that the problem of intra-family poverty is the key to the problem of poverty. Children in society are probably more deprived by being born into poor families than through any intra-family bias, not only as children but in terms of their life chances if they are fortunate enough to reach adulthood. The lack of education or health care for such families prevents human resource development, to use up-to-date terminology (UNDP, 1992; UNICEF, 1992). Indeed, the significance of intra-family bias rests partly on the fact that it often occurs in situations *in extremis*. Moreover, it is not clear that certain forms of intra-family bias, say against female children, are common to all less developed countries, being absent not only in sub-Saharan Africa but also in some parts of south Asia (Harriss, 1991).

Gender bias in poverty can operate against women. In labour markets, it takes the form of discrimination in occupational choice or in pay and working conditions. It takes the form of intra-family gender bias, which may or may not be market related; functionalist explanations of gender bias do not command universal support (Agarwal, 1986; Tinker, 1990; Whitehead, 1990).

The last characteristic of poverty that I wish to note is also one of the most intractable. I refer to the institutional aspect of poverty. It is not clear to me whether this forms a sub-set of poverty characteristics or acts as some sort of a locus. The term 'institutional' in this context can have two meanings: the 'rules of the game' or the structure of mediating organisations that operate these rules in society (Bardhan, 1989). At an operational level, the 'rules of the game' may discriminate against the poor through the denial of access, say, to rural credit or to medical treatment. The former may be due to the way in which the rules of eligibility are drawn up; the latter to spatial distance or simply through a denial of information, for the ability to use or manipulate a system depends critically on having information about it to act on. At a more fundamental level, institutional discrimination takes the form of denial of basic human rights, from the kind witnessed in Bhopal to ignorance of one's legal rights, or to the failure of the judicial or the administrative system to protect those rights. This is historically witnessed by the response of colonial courts of law to the problem of rural indebtedness, and currently, for example, by the unwillingness of some State governments to protect the rights and lives of the 'untouchables' in parts of India. Or it may simply be a question of a lack of information, of not knowing how to obtain justice, or of not knowing who to bribe. An important way in which the institutional 'rules of the game' impinge on poverty is through the shaping of expectations of the poor. If the poor are kept ignorant of their rights, they cannot expect to have those rights upheld. The concept of 'empowerment' is close to this range of problems, although a link between it, the formation of expectations and aspirations, and the development of the 'capabilities' of the poor still remains to be forged (Friedman, 1992; Sen, 1987).

IV

In this section, I discuss how State action or inaction relates to the various characteristics of poverty that I have outlined. In doing so, I do not wish to mimimise the difficulties faced by the state in either formulating or implementing anti-poverty policies. These difficulties may be of several kinds. Firstly, many economic and social aspects of poverty are still unknown territory; the existence and universality of certain characteristics and causes of poverty are still vigorously disputed. Among these, for example, are the concept of a nutritional or calorie 'norm', the consequences of breaching such a 'norm', discrimination against women and children, and the effects of nutritional deprivation and morbidity on labour productivity and, thus, on incomes (see Dasgupta and Ray, 1990). Secondly, the State's perception of what are the key areas of intervention and the resource constraints it faces may differ from those of society's or its critics. Lastly, the State's capacity to intervene may be limited, making it difficult to implement policies (Chakravarty, 1987). In spite of these qualifications, I would argue that there is a large element of choice in how the State defines its agenda for public action.

We have identified various characteristics of poverty, such as nutritional deprivation, low income and asset status, child poverty, gender bias and institutional discrimination. What forms of public action are most suited to address each of these? The most influential determinant of poverty policy is the view that equates personal or household poverty with national poverty. Seen in this light, the objective of the State is clear and easy to formulate; it is, to use a Victorian term, the progress of the nation. Here, the State sets a high rate of economic growth as an objective and expects this growth to 'trickle down' the income distribution spectrum. The desired strategy can be spelt out in terms of a number of alternative growth models, amongst the most discussed and influential being the Harrod-Domar, the Fel'dman-Mahalanobis and the Lewis dual economy models and their many variants. These put capital formation centre stage (Chaudhuri, 1989). Such an approach does not call for any specific State action directed towards the poor as a group, except as a short-term palliative, a kind of 'bridging loan' until the investment bears fruit. Indeed, any resource transfer of that kind is seen as inimical to the main objective, expressed in terms of the growth–poverty 'trade off'. The problem with such a strategy, as is well known, is that it has not worked in practice. Furthermore, it is also deficient in not exploring in any depth how any 'trickle down' mechanism might operate. It tends also to overlook an important aspect of structural or long-term poverty, which is the 'marginalisation' of the poor within the economy.

The problem, of course, is that while economic growth is normally a necessary condition for the alleviation of poverty, it is not a sufficient condition. The poverty effects of economic growth depend very much on the kind of growth that occurs, particularly in terms of its employment and sectoral composition. Historically, in the developed countries (DCs), these two factors interacted positively. On the production side, relatively labour-intensive technologies created a demand for labour as industrial output expanded, while the supply of labour was augmented by a relative shift away from agriculture, which in turn allowed for a rise in labour productivity in that sector. Real wages, after an initial period, could rise in both sectors, a tendency reinforced by the fact that a large part of the expanding industrial output took the form of either basic consumer goods or 'wage goods' such as textiles or simple manufactures, or inputs for these and for investment in productive social infrastructure, such as the railways. It is this interaction that allowed economic growth to trickle down through rising labour absorption and real wages.

As is widely acknowledged, this synergistic relationship has broken down in the less-developed countries of our days (Lefeber, 1974). Overall employment elasticity of output is low and appears to be falling (Mundle, 1992). This would require a much higher level of labour absorption within the rural sector, which in turn is threatened by declining labour intensity (Bhalla, 1987). As employment sags, the resulting excess supply of labour tends to keep down real wages (Jose, 1988). An unequal distribution of income tends to make it more profitable for producers to increase the supply of more sophisticated forms of consumer goods and durables which are not those that the poor are likely to consume. In such an environment, there is little opportunity for growth to trickle down. An exception to this is the increase in food grain production brought about by the 'green revolution', which is likely to have benefited the poor as consumers while it has done little to benefit them as producers.

The evidence on this point is admittedly controversial. The consumption effects are clear; there has been a substantial rise in the production of a basic 'wage good', food grain, in south Asia. In India its spread has been regionally uneven. Those states where it has made rapid progress are also those where the incidence of poverty has fallen, partly due to a relatively slow rise in food-grain prices (Minhas *et al.*, 1990). The sensitivity of poverty to changes in food prices is now a well-attested fact. On the production side, the evidence is less clear. A comprehensive review argues that the 'green revolution' technology has become widely diffused over time over a wider range of farm-size groups (Lipton and Longhurst, 1989). Other studies also support this conclusion, especially as regards spatial dispersion (Alagh, 1988). However, there is no evidence that marginal farmers have participated in this to any extent. As regards employment, there do not appear to be strong displacement effects on labour (Pandya, 1994). Real wages also appear to be rising after a long period of stagnation, as recent NSS data suggest. On the other hand, labour intensity is falling and large-scale underemployment still persists in the rural sector. Indeed, the need for special intervention programmes in rural areas is a reminder of the persistent problem of labour absorption in agriculture.

The State therefore has to think in terms of specific policy measures to help the poor, even within the context of 'growth mediated' strategies. This requires the State to try to increase the demand for labour within the economy, labour power being the major potential resource that the poor possess (World Bank, 1990). This can be done in two ways, either by a shift away from industry towards agriculture, where technology is more labour-intensive or within each sector, by choosing more labour-intensive methods of production. The dominant neoclassical view, which is strongly voiced by the World Bank and the IMF, is that all this can be achieved simultaneously by reducing factor and commodity market imperfections, by 'getting prices right'. By allowing real wages to fall and the real interest rates to rise, and the agricultural terms of trade to improve, it is argued that substantial amounts of new employment can be created to make an impact on poverty. In what follows, I shall dwell only on what the State's role in this can be in the context of poverty alleviation.

The impact on poverty of an improvement in the agricultural terms of trade is problematic. The only solid facts that we have are that the poor, both rural and urban, are net buyers of food. A recent study of Pakistan, for example, suggests that a rise in food prices can significantly increase poverty (Malik, 1992). On the supply side, the elasticity of supply of aggregate agricultural output tends to be lower than for its individual crop components (Askari and Cummings, 1976). Supply response is also higher with substantial investment in rural infrastructure, in irrigation, marketing and transport facilities, than with price changes alone. Moreover, with existing inequalities in land distribution and its accompanying result that a large part of the marketable surplus is produced by large farmers, it is by no means clear that a shift in the terms of trade in favour of agriculture will substantially benefit small and poor farmers, unless rural purchasing power rises and incomes and assets are equally distributed. This sets out a rather more active and directed role for the State than price reform.

So far as factor prices are concerned, a rise in real interest rates and a fall in real wages will no doubt tend to increase labour-intensity in production. However, there are several points to be noted. Firstly, the State has little knowledge of the range over which factor substitution is possible within existing technologies. It appears to be an act of faith almost that sufficient additional employment will be created at the *lower end of the wage-skills spectrum* to make a significant impact on poverty. The theories of 'efficiency wages' or 'transaction costs', for example, cast doubt on this view. Secondly, as price incentives work only through competition, the strength of these effects will depend on the extent to which an oligopolistic industrial structure can be made more competitive and open to new entry. Market imperfections do not consist solely of price distortions nor do price distortions arise solely from State intervention.

If institutional change is a necessary condition for price changes to work, or work more effectively, then we find ourselves in a dilemma. How can the State, seen as a highly inefficient producer of goods and services and regulator of markets, be highly efficient in engendering the right types of institutional change?

It has been rightly argued that one way of helping the labouring poor is by 'investing in the poor' (World Bank, 1990). That is, by helping them develop their human capital resources through education and training, thus making them able to compete in the labour market for productive employment. This would be excellent and it is probably one of the most effective ways of helping small producers in the informal sector, particularly the urban informal sector. However, it requires far more from the State than shifting items of the education budget from higher education to primary education or urban to rural education.

Firstly, the time-scale for such a policy to work is a long one and, while the general 'welfare' effects of primary education can be quickly felt (a literate or educated child is closer to fulfilling her or his 'capabilities') its income effects will have to wait for the child to be ready to enter the labour market and profit from it. Secondly, the ability of a poor child to benefit from education is not unrelated to her or his poverty; drop-out rates are significantly higher for poor children. The reason for this may be the opportunity costs of schooling, or poor health leading to frequent illnesses or absences, or low expectations of any positive gain at the end. To benefit from 'investment in the poor', the poor need something to build on (Wiener, 1991). To be fully effective, education, health and income generation for the poor need to be seen as complementary rather than alternative policy measures. 'Growth-mediated' and 'support-mediated' policies need to work hand-in-hand in this area. Thirdly, there are strong social constraints against allowing the poor to benefit from any human capital resources they might accumulate, not least constraints arising from the not-so-poor. These are matters of changing social attitudes so that advocacy for 'investment in the poor' may lead the State into areas of policy intervention not normally favoured by international financial institutions.

We can return now to a more conventional area of policy debate, that of asset redistribution. A large part of the rural and urban poor, especially the former, are not wage labourers but small producers in the farm or non-farm sector. While their poverty indisputably arises out of inadequate asset holdings, it is a matter of dispute whether asset redistribution needs to be seriously considered as a policy measure. It has been recently argued, for example, that as the purpose is to raise farm incomes, the same objective can be reached through an equivalent yield-increasing technology (the 'green revolution') as can be obtained by the transfer of a given amount of land of the previous level of yield (Singh, 1990).

In the document that I have quoted, the World Bank points philosophically to the political constraints on land reform and goes on to develop its policy advice clearly in the belief that land reform is dispensable as a policy measure, although it does not provide any rationale for such a belief (World Bank, 1990). Lipton has recently made the case for the continuing need for a land-reform policy at some length and it is indeed difficult to believe that the State can ignore it, if it believes that a lack of productive assets is a major cause of poverty amongst small cultivators (Lipton, 1992). A difficulty that faces the State in this sphere is the need to mediate between the poor and the not-so-poor. Much of the opposition to land redistribution and tenancy reform may come from small non-poor producers whose relative economic and social position is threatened by such measures and from agricultural labourers facing a lower demand for labour.

Asset redistribution may concern resources other than land, such as water or livestock, where access can be widened and improved through the mediation of credit. In the rural sector, some positive results have been obtained by the Grameen Bank in Bangladesh, for example, by advancing credit to small groups which make a living by selling irrigation water to farmers. In the urban sector, small-scale credit schemes allow women to set up small businesses in sewing, food retailing, and so forth. Evidence from Africa suggests that small informal sector activities, which survive in spite of the State's hostility to them, can be made to thrive with a little additional help and an encouraging policy environment.

Common property resources (CPRs) are usually land-based and include forests, scrub and grazing land. Attention has increasingly been drawn to the destruction of CPRs and its anti-poor impact, exacerbated over the years by the exclusion of the poor from the enjoyment of these resources. At the same time, poverty itself is a cause of degeneration of CPRs, through overgrazing or overutilisation of forest resources. The policy dilemma that CPRs pose is, of course, a classic in environmental economics (Hardin, 1964). A rational policy approach to the conservation of CPRs has to be an essential part of State policy towards an alleviation of poverty, yet it is an extremely difficult area of intervention, partly because the balance between our hard factual knowledge of processes of conservation and destruction, and the strong emotional reponse they understandably generate is not yet quite right. The problem is made more difficult by the fact that sometimes a conflict of interest may exist within groups of the poor or low income households, say, between men and women, in relation to use of resources for subsistence or market-based activities. Yet the State can do a great deal here, not so much through direct management and control as by creating the right policy environment. This ranges from defining and protecting customary rights over common land and other CPRs, to extending legal protection to the poor against abuses of their customary rights and encouragement of small-scale social forestry projects (Jodha, 1986).

CPRs stand on the borderline of those poverty-related issues which are market-mediated and those which are not, a policy space they share with the major characteristic of absolute poverty, hunger, or nutritional deprivation. Some regulations of CPRs can be influenced through market processes, while others cannot. Better income opportunities for the poor will, through Engels' Law, find part of their way into a higher level of food expenditure for poor households, which if food prices are stable, will lead to less hunger. Incidentally, in spite of much that has been written on least-cost diets for the poor, there is little hard evidence that the expenditure elasticity for tinned fish, or biscuits or Coca-Cola is high for poor households in south Asia. However, if there is intra-family bias against children in poor families, there is little that the State can do directly to help the situation. There are layers of social intercourse that are impermeable to State policies.

Policies aiming to raise family incomes to deal with the problem of intra-family food bias are likely to be inefficient, for incomes may have to rise significantly above poverty levels for the income effect itself to rid a poor family of anti-child bias. This is a hypothesis, because there are no empirical studies of the level of household income or expenditure at which intra-family food bias disappears in societies where it can be normally observed. The State can use alternative policies, such as special feeding programmes for children, mostly for pre-school children. I think that a little too much is made of the point that these are subject to 'leakages'; the net welfare gains must still be high, compared to alternative use of these resources, if the 'leakages' are mostly within the poor households (Guhan, 1992). A more important limitation is that fiscal constraints make them wholly inappropriate for tackling a large number of poor children and they become selective in a somewhat arbitrary fashion.

It may be more effective for the State to tackle child poverty indirectly, by concentrating on those goods and services on which the welfare of children depend. These may include clean water, better sanitation, and better health or educational opportunities. Investment in these facilities and improving access of the rural and urban poor to existing facilities may be highly effective ways of improving child welfare. This may come about not only by reducing infant mortality and improving health status but also by improving nutritional status via the health-nutrition synergy. Of course, they will also improve the health status of the adult poor, a characteristic of 'public goods' being their 'non-exclusivity'. Potentially, such a policy may reach a much larger proportion of poor children than special feeding programmes are likely to. If the gains from health policy can be reaped in a relatively short period, the returns in the form of better primary education will take longer to mature but these can be very substantial at the poor/not-so-poor interface.

A very substantial literature exists today on gender bias, so I need to make only a few points. Firstly, the scope for reducing gender bias through market-mediated policies is very much wider for adult females than for children. There are two reasons for this. One is that better employment opportunities directly improve the extra-family status of women. Such a policy needs to include much more than job creation or equal pay legislation. Especially in rural societies, it requires the State correctly to identify the role of women in the productive process, which can be complex (Whitehead, 1990). An important consideration is improved educational and skill development opportunities for women workers, so that they can gain access to higher productivity occupations. The other is that improved economic status may also work to reduce intra-family gender bias, partly through their improved earning position outside the family and partly by making them more aware of their legal rights and more willing to protect them (Tinker, 1990).

Ensuring basic human rights for the poor is a neglected area of State action. Denial of human rights may affect the poor substantially in a number of ways, and protection and enlargement of these rights can increase their welfare significantly. To be operationally useful, much action has to be defined in more precise terms than 'human development' or fulfilment of 'capabilities', although this is the ultimate aim. Examples of such specific actions include arbitrary evictions in the name of slum clearance, harassment by the police or landlords, and denial of opportunities to obtain justice and compensation through the legal and administrative systems. The resource cost of promoting such human rights is unlikely to be as high as for some alternative policy measures. In any case, they are likely to yield a favourable social cost benefit ratio to justify such action. The real constraints are, of course, the political benefits and costs to the State of such action.

This leads me to end this chapter on a somewhat abstract, pessimistic note by dwelling on some deep-rooted problems of effective anti-poverty policy. How does the State know that it has chosen the correct objectives, and that it has pursued them to the proper extent, and what propels the State towards such policies at all? (On the importance of the political attitudes of the State, see Kohli, 1987.) The first issue concerns the problem of alternative perceptions of poverty, for the objectives of an anti-poverty policy are normally articulated by the non-poor for the poor. As Jodha, for example, has argued, the priorities of the poor, in terms of their perceptions of poverty, may be different from those of policy makers or the researchers (Jodha, 1989). A similar point is made by De Waal in the context of famine. However, this aspect of the problem cannot be separated from the concept of 'capabilities' of the poor, for perceptions and priorities are conditioned by normal expectations, which are conditioned by an awareness or lack of awareness of 'capabilities'. To say, that the poor 'accept' the fact of a high infant mortality rate or ill health or economic exploitation does not absolve the State from working to end them. Similarly, the ignorance of the 'poor' of their basic human or legal rights does not justify the State's abuse of them. It is a characteristic of poverty, however, that the potential beneficiaries of anti-poverty can exercise little influence on the State to make it pursue them with vigour, hence the need to talk in terms of 'empowerment' of the poor, to make them both aware of their 'capabilities' and be able to demand their fulfilment (Friedman, 1992). It is difficult, however, to think of the State as working to 'empower' the poor, to participate in the diminution of its own powers that such 'empowerment' requires. To make matters worse, States that have chosen to wither away are not always good news for the poor, as the dissolution of civil power in large parts of sub-Saharan Africa and the recent experience of eastern Europe show.

NOTE

I am grateful to Mamta Murthi, Deepak Nayyar and an anonymous referee for comments on an earlier version of the paper. I alone am responsible for any errors and omissions.

REFERENCES

Agarwal, B. 'Women, Poverty and Agricultural Growth in India', *Journal of Peasant Studies*, Vol. 13, 1986.

Alagh, Y.K. 'Regional Dimensions of Indian Agriculture', in Lucas, F. and Papanek, G. (eds), *The Indian Economy*, Delhi, 1988.

Anand, S., Harris, C. and Linton, O. 'On the Concept of Ultrapoverty' (mimeo), 1993.

Askari, H. and Commings, J.T. *Agricultural Supply Response*, New York, 1976.

Banerjee, A. K., and Chatterji, K. L. *Commentary on the Constitution of India*, Calcutta, 1957.

Bardhan, P. (ed.). *The Economic Theory of Agrarian Institutions*, Oxford, 1989.

Bhalla, S. 'Trends in Employment in Indian Agriculture, Land and Asset Distribution', *Indian Journal of Agricultural Economics*, Vol. 42/4, 1987.

Blaug, M., Layard, R., and Woodhall, M. *The Causes of Graduate Unemployment in India*, London, 1969.

Chadha, G. K. *Non-farm Sector in Rural China*, ILO/ARTEP, New Delhi, 1992.

Chakravarty, S. *Development Planning*, Oxford, 1987.

Chaudhuri, P. *The Economic Theory of Growth*, Hemel Hempstead, 1989.

Chaudhri, D. P. *Education, Innovations and Agricultural Development*, London 1979.

Cornia, G., Jolly, R. and Stewart, F. *Adjustment with a Human Face*, Vol. 1, Oxford, 1987.

Dasgupta, P. *An Enquiry into Well-being and Destitution*, Oxford, 1993.

Dasgupta, P. and Ray. D. 'Adapting to Undernutrition: The Biological Evidence and its Implications', in Dreze and Sen, 1990.

Dreze, J. and Sen, A. *Hunger and Public Action*, Oxford, 1989.

Dreze, J. and Sen, A. (eds). *The Political Economy of Hunger*, Vol. 1, Oxford, 1990.

Friedmann, J. *Empowerment*, Blackwell, Oxford, 1992.

Guha, R. *The Unquiet Woods*, Delhi, 1991.

Guhan, S. 'Social Security in India', in B. Harriss, S. Guhan and R. H. Cassen (eds), *Poverty in India*, Oxford, Bombay, 1992.

Hardin, G. 'The Tragedy of the Commons', *Science*, 1964.

Harriss, B. 'The Intrafamily Distribution of Hunger in South Asia' in Dreze and Sen, 1991.

India. 'Perspective of Development 1961–76' in T. N. Srinivasan and P. K. Bardhan (eds), *Poverty and Income Distribution in India*, Calcutta, 1974.

Jodha, N. S. 'Common Property Resources and Rural Poor in Dry Regions of India', *Economic and Political Weekly*, Vol. XXI, 27, 1986.

Jodha, N. S. 'Social Science Research on Rural Change: Some Gaps', in Bardhan P. (ed.), *Conversations between Economists and Anthropologists*, Oxford, Delhi, 1989.

Jose, A. V. 'Agricultural Wages in India', *Economic and Political Weekly*, Vol. XXIII/26, 1988.

Kohli, A. *The State and the Poor*, Cambridge, 1987.

Lefeber, L. 'On the Paradigm for Economic Development', in A. Mitra (ed.), *Economic Theory and Planning*, Calcutta, 1974.

Lipton, M. 'Land Reform as Unfinished Business' (mimeo), 1992.

Lipton, M. and Longhurst, R. *New Seeds and Poor People*, London, 1989.

Malik, S. *Rural Poverty in Pakistan with Special Reference to Agricultural Price Policy*, unpublished D.Phil. dissertation, University of Sussex, 1992.

Minhas, B. S., Jain, L. R., Kansal, S. M., Saluja, M. R. 'Rural Cost of Living: 1970 to 1983, States and All-India', *Indian Economic Review*, 1990.

Mundle, S. 'The Employment Effects of Stabilisation and Related Policy Changes in India, 1991–92 to 1993–94', in ILO/ARTEP, *Social Dimensions of Structural Adjustment in India*, New Delhi, 1992.

Pandya, K. 'Agrarian Structure, New Technology and Labour Absoprtion in Indian Agriculture – Gujrat', University of Sussex, D.Phil. thesis, unpublished, 1994.

Paul, S. and Subramanian, A. 'Development Programmes for the Poor' in *Economic and Political Weekly*, Vol. XVIII/10, 1983.

Pyatt, F. G. 'The Value of Time', *Income and Wealth*, 1990.

Rath, N. 'Garibi Hatao: Can IRDP do it?', *Economic and Political Weekly*, Vol. XX/6, 1985.

Reutlinger, S. and Selowski, M. *Malnutrition and Poverty*, Johns Hopkins, Baltimore, 1976.

Sen, A. *Poverty and Famines*, Oxford, 1981.

Sen, A. 'Development: Which Way Now?', *Economic Journal*, Vol. 93, 1983.

Sen, A. 'The Standard of Living: Lives and Capabilities', in A. Sen *et al.*, *The Standard of Living*, Cambridge, 1987.

Singh, I. *The Great Ascent*, Johns Hopkins, Baltimore, 1990.

Srinivasan, T. N. 'Malnutrition: Some Measurement and Policy Issues', *Journal of Development Economics*, Vol. 8, 1981.

Tinker, I. (ed.). *Persistent Inequalities*, Oxford, 1990.

UNDP. *Human Development Report 1992*, New York, 1992.

UNICEF. *The State of the Worlds Children 1992*, Oxford, 1992.

UNO. *Demographic Yearbook, 1992*, New York, 1992.

UP Congress. *Agrarian Distress in the United Provinces*, Report of the United Provinces Provincial Congress Committee, Allahabad, 1931.

Vaidyanathan, A. 'Agricultural Development and Rural Poverty', in E. B. Lucas and G. Papanek (eds), *The Indian Economy*, Oxford, 1988.

Waal, A. de. *Famine That Kills*, Oxford, 1989.

Weiner, M. *The Child and the State in India*, Princeton, New Jersey, 1991.

Whitehead, A. 'Rural Women and Food Production in Sub-Saharan Africa', in Dreze and Sen, 1990.

World Bank. *China: Longterm Development Issues and Options*, Washington DC, 1985.

World Bank. *World Development Report 1990*, Washington DC, 1990.

11

The Political Economy of India:
From the Law of Value to
Structuralist Macroeconomics

Ranjit Sau

In the 1960s a distinguished school of thought on the social and economic evolution of India arose. History is defined as *the representation in chronological order of successive changes in the means and relations of production*. This definition has the advantage that it enables history to be seen as something distinct from a series of dated episodes. Pursuing this approach it transpires that India displays a peculiar *zigzag* process. A new stage of production manifests itself in formal change of some sort; when the production is primitive, the change is often religious. India's development has been in its own way more 'civilised' than other countries. The older cults and forms were not demolished by force but were assimilated. Superstition reduced the need for violence. Much more brutality would have been necessary had Indian history developed along the same lines as that of Europe or the Americas. At every stage, in almost every part of the country, a great deal of the superstructure survived, along with the productive and formal mechanism of several previous stages. There always remained some people who could and did cling stubbornly to the older modes (Kosambi, 1970, pp. 10–23).

'Political power in India is concentrated in the hands of the urban bourgeoisie who are currently in alliance with the affluent peasantry' (Mitra, 1967: p. 451). Furthermore, 'in view of the uneven evolution of the Indian economy, dissimilar modes of production exist simultaneously in nearly each sector of productive activity. As the modes vary, so do the production relations among groups associated with each activity' (Mitra, 1977, p. 96).

The following conceptualisation is similar:

> *The South Asian village is ... like a complex molecule among whose parts extreme tensions have been built up.* Although the tensions crisscross

in a manner that maintains equilibrium, it is conceivable that they
might reorganize in a way that would explode the molecule. This
probably would not happen spontaneously, but as a result of a
forceful onslaught from outside. (Myrdal, 1968, pp. 1063–4.)

From these narrations we get an image of the Indian economy
that harbours several modes of production with a *criss-cross* of class
interests. Apparently such a perception promises to shed light on
some major contemporary issues, for example, the economic crisis
of the early 1990s, the subsequent drive for liberalisation, and the
rise of religious fundamentalism since the 1980s. But, as we proceed
to formalise the above paradigm in terms of economic theory in
order to draw inferences, we come across a severe limitation.
Economic theory, it seems, has been meandering in the narrow
confines of a two-class model of capital and labour. As such it has
precious little to say on even a three-class economy, and much less
on the question of *transition* to capitalism. This paper is an attempt
to extend the scope of economic theory in this respect. Rent as a
form of income distribution will be the key to our exploration. To
concretise our ideas we shall use India as an occasional point of
reference, not as a complete case study.

The domestic product of an economy is distributed broadly into
three parts – wage, profit, and rent. The first two have been well
analysed in the literature. The relationship between wage and profit
is a much debated subject since the days of Ricardo. Rent found a
prominent place in classical economics; Ricardo and Marx had
their respective theories on it. It received an honourable mention by
Marshall and Wicksell. Thereafter economics seems to have all but
forgotten about rent.

There is a qualitative difference between a game with two
players and one with three or more. Corresponding to wage, profit,
and rent there are three basic classes. Having abstracted from rent,
modern economic theory has reduced the number of classes from
three to two, and thereby cramped its own analytical power and
relevance. Profit and rent occur in agriculture, industry, trade and
commerce in various forms which are manifested in fragmentation
of classes. The relationship between profit and rent is no less
significant than that between wage and profit. This paper will be
concerned mainly with the former which would provide the theory
for interpreting the political economy of India.

A variety of classes, groups, or strata inhabit the Indian
economy, all deriving their sustenance from wage, profit, or rent in
one form or another. Suppose there are five classes. Taken two at a
time, there are nine possible combinations among them, with as

many separate binary or dyadic relationships. These nine binary class relations are the primitive components of the political economy. It would be a costly oversimplification to force this complex matrix into a scalar of two-classes as is done in modern economic theory. Here, the five main actors in our script of the Indian drama are: (a) landlords, (b) capitalist farmers in agriculture, (c) ordinary capitalists, (d) monopoly capitalists in industry, and (e) the finance capitalists in the stock market. There are other characters – poor peasants and workers – who will appear in supporting roles. This paper gives only the bare sketches of a plot, not the complete manuscript.

While traditional economics has a narrow focus, it is reassuring that a new branch of study, structuralist macroeconomics, has taken shape in the last two decades. It is inspired by Keynes, Kalecki, and Marx. Structuralist macroeconomics explicitly recognises several classes. The first computable general equilibrium (CGE) model of this school is on the Indian economy (Taylor, 1983). The India model has become a benchmark for similar works on other countries like Brazil, Colombia, Egypt, Mexico, Nicaragua, Sri Lanka, and Thailand (Taylor, 1990). In these models there are three, four, or more classes. The structuralist theory thus has the potential to open up a new dimension. The present essay begins in Section 1 with a critical review of the theory and modelling of this genre. We shall observe that, having no distinct theory of income distribution of its own, structuralist macroeconomics is but *ad hoc* and arbitrary.

A central insight gleaned from the law of value can be put as follows: the 'economic surplus', 'surplus product', or 'surplus value', defined as the excess of the national product over wage bill, is a *generic* category, while profit, interest, rent, and so forth are its *particular* forms (Marx 1862–63, p. 503; Marx and Engels, 1965, pp. 192, 198). It is this proposition that forms the core of the philosophy and methodology of this paper. In that light Section 2 analyses the conversion of the surplus into profit and rent in agriculture. As it turns out, the transition from feudalism to capitalism goes through two phases. We also see here the possibility of a reverse movement from agrarian capitalism back to feudalism – somewhat like the 'second serfdom' in the East of the Elbe during the Middle Ages (Dobb 1967, pp. 3, 6).

Section 3 deals with the ordinary profit and super profit in industry. Super profit is a variant of the Marxian or Ricardian rent that we have computed with the method used by Sraffa (1960, pp. 74–8). Our model reveals a complex relationship between the two forms of profits leading to the possibility of cleavages among industrialists – ordinary and monopolist, domestic and foreign.

The next two sections will draw upon our previously published works which are brought together here in summary for the sake of completing the structure of our theory of political economy. Section 4 reports a new model. It concerns the relationship between industry and finance – that is, between productive activities in the factory and transactions of shares in the stock market. The stock market is visualised as a medium to appropriate a portion of the surplus product essentially in the fashion of Ricardian rent. The model imbibes the economics of Ricardo, Marx, and Keynes. Accumulation of capital will necessarily be governed in this model by a first-order non-linear difference equation that has extremely complicated dynamics known as *chaos* in mathematics. This feature of inherent instability in the accumulation process paves the way for an organically defined role for the government which is now called upon to bring some sort of order in the economy. Conceptually it marks the end of the classical stationary State and the 'invisible hand' doctrine of Adam Smith.

All these parts will be combined in Section 5 to form a comprehensive system. A model, we know, is not something to believe in; it is only something to be used. To try the explanatory power of our construct we shall speculate with it on the political economy of India. This exercise is motivated by the belief that, to repeat, the traditional two-class model of the economy cannot capture the essence of a modern economy that has a multiplicity of major contradictions along with a principal one. The task of political economy is to identify the contradictions, to relate them, and to explain the pattern of evolution of the object. Our endeavour, we realise, is no door, but only a little window that, hopefully, opens out upon a complex world.

1. SAM, CGE AND CLOSURES

According to Taylor (1983, p. 3):

> An economy has structure if its institutions and the behaviour of its members make some pattern of resource allocation and evolution substantially more likely than others. Economic analysis is structuralist when it takes these factors as the foundation stone for its theories.

One might think that, of course, every economy has a structure, and that economics, therefore, cannot but be structuralist. But no; that is not always the case, we are told.

Taylor explains: 'North Atlantic or neoclassical professionals do not practise structuralist macroeconomics.' Their standard approach to theory is to postulate a set of interlocking maximisation problems by a number of agents and to ask about the characteristics of the solutions. Institutions are conspicuously lacking in their calculus. Allowable economic actions are curiously circumscribed. For example, markets are almost always postulated to be price-clearing when it is patently obvious that many functioning markets are cleared by quantity adjustments or queues. To put it another way, the real world is non-Walrasian, while the neo-classicals, according to Taylor, persist with their Walrasian illusions.

Identities of national accounts are taken as the starting point of structuralist macroeconomics. A social accounting matrix (SAM) is constructed combining national accounts with the Leontief input-output table. The SAM thus provides a consistent picture of flow-of-funds accounts of the separate institutions, 'agents', or 'actors' in the economy that one may wish to distinguish. The defining characteristic of a SAM is that each row and column reflects a separate account for which expenditures and receipts must balance. The focus is on the nominal flow-of-funds with the rows representing receipt accounts and the columns expenditure accounts. In contrast to the input-output table the SAM is a square matrix, and the corresponding row and column sums are equal. The major usefulness of a SAM is that it brings together the accounts of each of the various economic actors whose behaviour is to be modelled into a consistent framework (Dervis, De Mello and Robinson, 1982, pp. 155–62; Taylor 1983, pp. 58–62, 1990, pp. 35–8).

The circular flow of the economy having been well laid out in a SAM the next step is to record the pattern of behaviour of the actors on the stage. Now is the time to reckon with some of the structural properties such as the tenancy in land, the distribution of income and wealth, the type and degree of specialisation in foreign trade, control of the means of production by the private sector, the State, and the external capital. Agricultural supply is assumed to be inelastic. Industry, however, fixes its price as per the Kalecki formula of mark-up on prime cost, and adjusts to shocks through variation in output. The story hinges on the absolute price level. Relative prices are devoid of any resource-allocating or commodity-substituting rôle, and are best kept out of sight in the green room. As a rule, consumers have a linear expenditure system, and industry a Leontief technology. With occasional exceptions, there is no explicit optimisation by the actors. Apparently structuralist macroeconomics is not unduly anxious to trace its micro-foundation, if there is any.

Finally, all these materials are arranged into a system of simultaneous equations to produce the general equilibrium. To solve a linear system it is usually necessary that the number of equations be equal to the number of unknowns. To meet this requirement we can play with either side – we can change the number either of the equations or of the endogenous variables. This is the celebrated problem of alternative closures (Piggott and Whalley 1985, pp. 412–16). No doubt the outcome depends very much upon the choice of equations and variables.

Structuralist macroeconomics starts with an eminently sensible premise that theory must keep in view the specific structural features of an economy. No one could possibly deny that. Even the neo-classical works on CGE that initially envisaged a pristine Walrasian kingdom are now veering towards accepting various imperfections. CGE models, otherwise neo-classical in letter and spirit, have been built with the SAM, price rigidities, rural–urban wage differential and migration, tariff barriers, tax and subsidy, and the like (Bergman, Jorgenson and Zalai, 1990). Practitioners of structuralist macroeconomics, on the other hand, are increasingly incorporating in their models the vital role of relative prices and returns on assets. There are signs of a convergence of the two apparently opposing camps.

The theoretical basis of structuralist macroeconomics is inadequate. Beyond accounting identities it has no theory of income distribution to claim as its hallmark. Its CGE models, no doubt, allow several classes or groups to receive income, but more as an *ad hoc* exogenous arrangement in the short run than as an organic process. As it ignores the relative prices it loses sight of certain contradictions among classes that are inherent in a commodity economy. This is where perhaps the above-mentioned central insight of the law of value might be useful. It is also strange that probably no one has yet seen any structuralist model for a developed economy like the United States, Germany, or Japan. Is structuralist macroeconomics only for the poor?

2. PROFIT AND RENT IN AGRICULTURE

Whether India's agriculture has or ever had all the essential features of European feudalism still remains a subject of controversy. Here we define feudalism to be a mode of production where landlords lease out land to poor peasants and extract as rent the entire surplus product. By contrast, a capitalist farmer, who may or may not lease in land, operates a farm with hired labour and takes a part of the surplus product as profit. Thus landlords and capitalist farmers become engaged in a tussle over sharing the surplus product (Dutt, 1984).

This simple plot develops through two phases. It can climax into full-fledged agrarian capitalism, or the transition may be aborted mid-way to relapse into feudalism. In this story (Sau, 1988, 1990) there are four classes: landlords, capitalist farmers, poor peasants, and landless labourers. Poor peasants do not own land; they cultivate leased-in land with family labour. We shall compare a poor peasant's farm with a capitalist's farm.

In a poor peasant's farm, x is the gross output, b the labour input and c the material input, all per unit of land, while s is the surplus product, and w the subsistence requirement or necessary product, both per unit of labour.

$$x = c + wb + sb \qquad (1)$$

Rent per unit of land is denoted by e which is equal to the entire surplus product.

$$e = sb = x - (c + wb) \qquad (2)$$

The peasant farm makes no profit. The rent goes to the landlord. The capitalist farm has, per unit of land, gross output x', labour input b', and constant capital c'. The surplus product is s' per unit of labour; and the wage rate is w, the same as the subsistence requirement of a poor peasant.

$$x' = c' + wb' + s'b' \qquad (3)$$

The surplus product in the capitalist farm is split into two: rent e and profit f, both per unit of land.

$$s'b' = e + f \qquad (4)$$

Capital in the capitalist farm has two parts: variable capital or wages advanced by the capitalist, and constant capital or the machinery and other material inputs. The rate of profit r, per unit of capital, is given by

$$r = f/(c' + wb') \qquad (5)$$

Using (2) and (5) to eliminate e and f we get

$$r + 1 = [(x'-x) + (c+wb)]/(c'+wb') \qquad (6)$$

It follows that

$$dr/dw \gtreqless 0, \text{ if } x' - x \lesseqgtr (bc'/b') - c \qquad (7)$$

Typically, a capitalist farm uses, per unit of land, more constant capital and less labour, but gets a higher output than a peasant farm. In other words, $x' > x$, $c' > c$, and $b > b'$.

With (7) we can delineate two phases of capitalism in agriculture, distinguished by the pattern of class contradictions. In phase I, x' is not adequately higher than x, so that the upper inequalities of (7) are satisfied. The wage-profit curve is then upward-sloping. But by (2), we know, the wage-rent curve always slopes down. So in phase I capitalist farmers can have an alliance with poor peasants and landless labourers, all being against the landlords.

In phase II, x' is sufficiently larger than x, and the lower inequalities of (7) hold. The wage–profit curve is downward-sloping. By (6) the profit rate is high; so the landlords themselves may take to capitalist farming. The capitalist transformation will be completed when poor peasants disappear leaving only landless labourers to till the land. Now the contradiction is between capital and labour. Thus the two phases have quite distinct class alignments.

Although the algebra does not indicate any chronology we can set up a reference scenario of transition as follows. In the early stage the economy is in phase I, and then it passes on to phase II. But the actual history of a country may show *zigzags* in terms of this model. After the economy goes through phase I and enters phase II it may so happen that x improves in such a way that, by (6), that profit rate falls. Now capitalist farming ceases to be attractive. The landlord class may reassert its authority, and thereby reverse the process of capitalist development.[1] As narrated by Dobb (1967, pp. 3, 6), during the Middle Ages, indeed, serfdom revisited the East of Elbe after a certain period of time.

3. ORDINARY AND SUPER PROFITS IN INDUSTRY

One of the weakest points of traditional economic theory is that it views the capitalists as a homogeneous class. But in the modern era there are, in fact, sharp cleavages within the ranks of the bourgeoisie. The class interests of 'ordinary' capitalists and monopoly capitalists are often divergent; so may be those of domestic and foreign capitalists. The following model is designed to capture some of the tensions among these appropriators of surplus product. The crux of the conflict lies in the relationship between what is called the 'ordinary profit' and the 'super profit'. The latter is normally a Ricardian differential rent, or the Marxian absolute rent depending upon the context.

Rent can appear in any branch of the economy. Two kinds of rent can be distinguished. The rent ascribed to the scarcity of land is claimed by landlords; it is called ground rent. The rent associated with the scarcity of such things as old machines, some specific raw materials, or new technology usually accrues to the capitalists; it may be termed 'super profit' which is quite separate from 'ordinary profit'. Here the recipient of super profit will be viewed as a monopoly capitalist who makes ordinary profit as well. The capitalist who gets only the ordinary profit is called an ordinary capitalist.

Suppose the economy produces two commodities: machines and cloth, each with two possible 'activities' or technologies. Activities are marked 1, 2, 3 and 4 respectively. There is no joint production. Machines are the output of the first two activities; cloth of the last two. As for input, besides labour and machinery there are four *specific* factors of production indexed 1, 2, 3 and 4. Examples of such factors are: special raw materials, technological know-how, and political concessions. Specific factor j ($j = 1, 2, 3, 4$) is used only in activity j. For the moment, suppose that specific factors 2 and 3 are plentiful, so there is no scarcity rent on them. (Later this assumption will be relaxed.) Specific factors 1 and 4 are scarce; so they enable their owners to extract rent, which is identified as super profit in the present context. It is assumed that the capitalist who operates activity 1 or 4 owns specific factor 1 or 4 respectively.

Production takes one period. There is no fixed capital; even machinery is a circulating capital which is bought at the beginning of the period. Wages are paid at the end. With cloth as the *numeraire*, the price of machinery is p, wage w, and rent q_j ($j = 1, ..., 4$). The uniform rate of ordinary profit is r. Following standard practice, the level of activity is given by assumption, the demand for cloth and machinery being independent of income distribution and price level. With respective input coefficients a, b, and m the price equations corresponding to the four activities are as follows:

$$a_1\, p(1+r) + b_1\, w + m_1\, q_1 = p \tag{8}$$
$$a_2\, p(1+r) + b_2\, w + m_2\, q_2 = p \tag{9}$$
$$a_3\, p(1+r) + b_3\, w + m_3\, q_3 = 1 \tag{10}$$
$$a_4\, p(1+r) + b_4\, w + m_4\, q_4 = 1 \tag{11}$$

By assumption, specific factors 2 and 3 are in abundant supply. So

$$q_2 = q_3 = 0 \tag{12}$$

We consider the state of the economy where activities 2 and 3 are in operation, while others may or may not be activated depending upon whether or not the rent on the corresponding specific factor is positive.

Take w as exogenous. Given (12) we can solve (9) and (10) for r and p. It is easy to show that w and r vary inversely. This proves the universal contradiction between wage rate and ordinary profit rate, that is, between labour and the ordinary capitalist. Next, we can find q_1 and q_4 from (8) and (11). It is interesting to note that the response of q_1 and q_4 to variations in w can be positive or negative. Recall that monopoly capitalists receive q_1 and q_4 in addition to ordinary profits. So they need not oppose a rise in wage rate if the associated fall in ordinary profit is more than compensated for by the rise in super profit. It is also conceivable that there will be conflicts between the two monopoly capitalists themselves.

There are two alternative perceptions about rent. In the Ricardian version, shown above, rent is a passive residual with no bearing on the uniform rate of ordinary profit. By contrast, in the Marxian theory, rent is an active element in the sense that it affects the ordinary profit rate as described below. Instead of (12), suppose that $q_3 = 0$, but q_2 is a given positive parameter. From (9) and (10) we get

$$1 + r = (1-wb_3)/[a_2 + (a_3b_2 - a_2b_3)w + a_3m_2q_2] \qquad (13)$$

Clearly, a rise in q_2 would reduce the ordinary profit rate r. Now what happens to the rent on specific factor 1 that is used in activity 1 of the machine industry, as q_2 varies? With (8) – (10) and $q_3 = 0$, we find

$$m_1q_1 = A + m_2q_2 \qquad (14)$$

where $A = [a_2-a_1 + (a_3b_2-a_2b_3+a_1b_3-a_3b_1)\ w]/a_3$ (15)

Hence q_1 rises with q_2.

In the light of the above model one can think of a scenario where activity 1 of the machine industry is operated by a domestic monopoly capitalist, and activity 2 of the same industry by a foreign monopoly capitalist, say, a multinational corporation. If the latter is allowed to exercise its monopoly power to extract a higher super profit, the rate of ordinary profit prevailing in the economy will fall by (13). But the domestic monopoly capitalist in the same industry, operating activity 1, would realise a higher amount of super profit by (14). On balance, therefore, the latter may find it worthwhile to support a government policy that strengthens the hands of foreign monopoly capitalist. However, the ordinary capitalist in the cloth industry will oppose such a policy. Now that the Indian economy is being globalised, this model will receive an added relevance.

4. INDUSTRY AND FINANCE

The financial sector is a very important part of the economy. We have seen recently the wealth-churning power of the stock market. In the fifteen-month period ending April 1992, the stock price boom in

India created paper wealth of some one trillion rupees *(The Economic Times,* Calcutta, 11 July 1992). For comparison let us note that India's GNP in one whole year is of the order of four trillion rupees. To take another example of the magnitude of the financial sector, the world-wide volume of foreign exchange trading is estimated currently at $500 trillion a year. By comparison, the volume of world merchandise export is minuscule; only $3.36 trillion as of 1990; even the world GDP at $22.30 trillion is not much.

Marx (1894, p. 438) observed that, with the rise of joint-stock companies, a new breed of capitalists had sprung up. He called them 'financial aristocracy' – 'a new variety of parasites in the shape of promoters, speculators and simply nominal directors; a whole system of swindling and cheating by means of corporation promotion, stock issuance, and stock speculation.' In his analysis of class struggle in France, 1848–50, the bourgeoisie is divided into two incongruous parts – the industrial bourgeoisie and the financial aristocracy. Contradictions between these two sections can be seen from the following statement. The financial aristocracy

> sat on the throne, it dictated laws ... it distributed public offices, from Cabinet portfolios to tobacco bureau posts ... The industrial bourgeoisies proper formed part of the official opposition ... Its opposition was expressed all the more resolutely, the more unalloyed the autocracy of the finance aristocracy became. (Marx, 1850, p. 206.)

Below we present a model where the stock market is a medium for distributing surplus product in a form that resembles the Ricardian rent. We shall use the scaffolding of a modern economy with managers, industrial bourgeoisie, and the financial aristocracy, but then strip away risk and uncertainty in the name of scientific abstraction. The economy will be visualised in the image of a representative firm that is run by a manager with the principle of profit maximisation. All prices and the interest rate are given as parameters. Capital goods last for one period. Gross profit is defined as the excess of revenue over expenditure (wages, materials and depreciation). Net profit is gross profit after interest charges.

Let R denote gross profit, K capital, and P net profit. On the basis of McFadden's duality theorem we stipulate the profit function[2] as follows:

$$R = R(K), \quad R(0) = 0, \ R'(.) > 0, \ R''(.) > 0 \qquad (15)$$

For the purpose of this study we adopt a quadratic specification of (15):

$$R = aK - bK^2 \qquad (16)$$

For example, Dow (1993) constructs what he calls a surplus function that is conceptually equivalent to our profit function. Dow's surplus function is quadratic in output. Now, the average gross profit function is as follows:

$$R/K = a - bK \qquad (17)$$

For illustration we (Sau 1991, p. 7) have estimated (17) with financial data from the corporate sector of India, 1973–89. The result is given below:

$$R/K = 3.7005 - 0.0038\ K,\ r^2 = 0.74 \qquad (18)$$
$$(6.5517)$$

where the figure in parentheses is the t-value, and the variables are measured in Rs. 100 million at constant prices. Of course, (18) does not exactly correspond to (17) as K in (18) is net fixed assets; Indian companies do not work with circulating capital alone. But in (17), K denotes capital with the life of only one period. While (18) does not prove the empirical validity of (17), in the Indian economy the estimate nevertheless indicates that the concept of profit function is not entirely out of place.

Given the rate of interest i the firm maximises net profit P with reference to K.

$$P = R(K) - iK \qquad (19)$$

In equilibrium, keeping in view (16), we find

$$i = a - 2bK \qquad (20)$$

The difference between average and marginal gross profits is a rent.

How is the total profit distributed? Our model will mimic only some features of a modern economy. The actors will not play all their realistic roles here. Risks and uncertainty being assumed away, even the rationale of their presence here may be questioned. To recall, a manager runs the firm. There is a capital fund owned and operated by the industrial bourgeoisie. Managers duly borrow from the fund in the beginning of the period, and return the principal along with the interest at the end.

There is a stock market where financial capitalists operate. Every firm issues equities which are bought by these capitalists. Each share represents one unit of capital and entitles the owner to receive dividends. By the law – a structural feature – of this wonderland, the remaining part of the gross profit is given out as a dividend. There is no risk or uncertainty. The stock market functions without speculation. Yet this economy will have erratic movements over time as we shall see in a moment.

The industrial capitalists consume, at the end of the period, a part of the capital fund, and plough back the rest as investment in the next period. Let s be their propensity to save out of the capital fund.[3] With t denoting time we thus have

$$K(t+1) = s[K(t) + iK(t)] \qquad (21)$$

Like the Ricardian landlords, our financial capitalists have nothing to do with the capital fund; they consume their dividend income entirely. The rate of interest is determined by the managers' demand for investment and the available supply of capital. Now (17), and (19)–(21) yield

$$K(t+1) = s[(1+a)K(t) - 2bK^2(t)] \qquad (22)$$

Evidently (22) is a parabola in $[K(t), K(t+1)]$ – space. It passes through the origin. The axis of the parabola is vertical, and the vertex is at $[(1+a)/4b, s(1+a)^2/8b]$. So

$$\text{max-}K(t+1) = s(1+a)^2/8b \qquad (23)$$

By the same token we must have $K(t+1) = 0$, where $\text{max-}K(t)$ occurs. Then it follows from (22) that

$$\text{max-}K(t) = (1+a)/2b \qquad (24)$$

We know that $K(t)$ and $K(t+1)$ belong to the same set, say, S. Set S is bounded from above and it has a unique supremum. Therefore

$$\text{max-}K(t) = \text{max-}K(t+1) \qquad (25)$$

In view of (23)–(25) we get

$$s(1+a) = 4 \qquad (26)$$

The significance of (26) will be apparent soon.
    Multiply both sides of (22) by $2b/(1+a)$ to get

$$z(t+1) = \theta.z(t)[1 - z(t)] \qquad (27)$$

where
$$z(t) = 2bK(t)/(1+a) \qquad (28)$$
$$\theta = s(1+a) \qquad (29)$$

From (24) and (28) we realise that

$$z(t) = K(t)/\text{max-}K(t) \qquad (30)$$

We know that if $K(t)$ reaches $\text{max-}K(t)$ then $K(t+1)$ becomes zero; and the economy ceases to exist. So we shall assume that $K(t)$ never attains the value of $\text{max-}K(t)$ that is otherwise permitted by the parabola. In other words

$$(1+a)/2b > K(t) \qquad (31)$$
Therefore: $$0 < z(t) < 1 \qquad (32)$$

It is a standard theorem in non-linear dynamics that (27), subject to the provision of (32), can generate a diverse menu of trajectories depending upon the value of θ. Here, necessarily in view of (26) and (29):

$$\theta = 4 \tag{33}$$

Hence the time path of (27) is chaotic. Starting from an arbitrary position the economy may not reach the steady state value of $z = 3/4$ (Day 1983, p. 208; Devanay, 1989; Goodwin, 1990; Hoppensteadt and Hyman, 1977; Kelsey, 1988, pp. 8–11).

Let y denote dividend per share.

$$y = (R - iK) / K \tag{34}$$

From (16), (20) and (34), we get

$$y = bK \tag{35}$$

Thus share price will follow the course of K which, as proved above, is necessarily chaotic.

In this model capital accumulation reaches a point where the marginal profit turns negative, but the rigid saving function continues to work. One need not be surprised. In a modern economy, as Keynes emphasised, saving and investment are done by two independent groups of agents. Evidently, positive saving takes place even when the *real* rate of interest is negative. The chaos is partly a reflection of this anomaly. In a concrete situation perhaps other variables such as prices will adjust. However, 'there [is] now ample evidence that almost all systems which are multidimensional, nonlinear and time dependent are endogenously unstable' (Minsky, 1986, p. 10n). Goodwin (1986, p. 209) once said: 'In economics, unlike physics, the problem of instability is not very serious. The economy is bounded on the high side by given resources, particularly labour, and on the low side by a variety of rigidities in expenditure, particularly unemployment benefits.' But later he seems to have changed his mind (Goodwin, 1990). Even the two-class growth-cycle model of earlier-vintage Goodwin (1967), with a small modification, can be shown to generate chaotic dynamics (Pohjola, 1981). Simple interaction between multiplier and accelerator can also have the same consequence (Boldrin, 1988).

Referring to (17) and (18) we find that our estimate of constant a is 3.7005. By (29) and (33) it implies that $s = 0.85$, which is quite reasonable.[4] We could have taken separate saving propensities with respect to income and wealth in (21). But then the algebra would become rather untidy without any qualitative benefit. In any case, if the result of our theoretical model and econometric exercise has any relevance for India then we can conclude that the economy has an underlying tendency for chaotic movements.

5. CONCLUDING REMARKS

In the works of Kosambi (1970), Mitra (1967, 1977), and Myrdal (1968) taken together, one can see a certain paradigm: the economy maintains several modes of production. The payoffs of dominant classes are so interwoven that they cannot be neatly partitioned. Hence there is no clear polarisation at the political plane. It is difficult to mobilise massive support for change. The economy displays a syndrome of relative stagnation. This low-level equilibrium will be displaced most probably as a result of a forceful onslaught from outside. If and when that happens the response of comparatively backward segments of the economy will have an overtone of religious fundamentalism and outright superstition. It is our judgment that the recent history of India meets this description remarkably well.

The models of the preceding three sections constitute a sample of what, in our perception, ought to be the essence of structuralist macroeconomics. The models rigorously demonstrate, in theory the existence of a *criss-cross* of class interests, and thereby reconfirms the structure of the above paradigm. The dominant classes are so intricately bound up with each other that sharp alignments are inconceivable at this stage. Furthermore, we have shown that the economy is inherently unstable. Which means that the State must have a pivotal place in the economy so as to keep some semblance of order.

The following is a sketch of the contemporary Indian scene as viewed from this perspective. In 1981 the government negotiated the largest loan – SDR five billion – made by the International Monetary Fund (IMF) to any country up to that date. Much like 'a forceful onslaught from outside' a series of conditions came along with the loan. India was thus launched on a path of economic liberalisation. But it was a hesitant beginning. Only in early 1985, just for a few moments, did the movement gather some momentum. But, in May 1985, the then Prime Minister, Rajiv Gandhi, failed to obtain a ratification of an economic policy statement from the Congress party. As a result, the pace of reform slackened thereafter. Thus the decade of 1980s was a period of stop-and-go liberalisation. Yet it had a visible effect. By way of a reaction to the reform programme the so-called *Hindutva* phenomenon with its trident of religious fanaticism sprang up from the dark depths of India's political economy.

Historically speaking,

> the dominant class in India and India's urban life bears the stamp
> of the foreigner who imposed the bourgeois mode of production.

> ... [T]he countryside at large and Indian religious institutions
> carry the indelible mark of their primitive origins because
> primitive modes of life have been and are still possible in many
> parts of India. (Kosambi, 1970, pp. 22–3.)

Accordingly, one possible hypothesis could be that the recent rise of
religious fundamentalism and the cry for *swadeshi* in India is a
particular response of the relatively conservative remnants of the
old order to the imposition of a foreign mode of production. Iran
under Western-style modernisation by the Shah, can possibly be
cited as a similar example.

The balance-of-payments crisis of 1991 was basically a reflection
of the secular stagnation of the Indian economy; it was more of a
crisis of confidence. There is evidence that while the outside world
has been taking long strides in technology, the factor productivity in
India's industry has shown a negative trend. The little growth in
national product that has taken place so far is mostly 'extensive' in
nature, rather than 'intensive'. It was difficult to mobilise massive
support for any radical change. The most 'forceful onslaught from
outside' has come this time in the wake of the payments crisis in
June, 1991, in the form of conditions again, from the IMF and the
World Bank. The government of the country, as we have seen
above, is structurally assigned the task of stabilising the economy. It
is, therefore, perfectly understandable from a functional point of
view why the government accepted those terms and conditions. The
dominant classes, on the other hand, are as usual divided in their
approach with respect to economic liberalisation. And, if history is
any guide or if our theory has any substance, this time, too, the
ongoing external shock would probably be absorbed into another
top layer on the economy of India.

NOTES

The author gratefully acknowledges the perceptive comments of an anonymous referee on
an earlier draft. The usual caveat applies.

1. By no means does (7) indicate any possible policy rule for the individual landlord or
    capitalist farmer. To infer micro behaviour from macro relations is always hazardous.
    For instance, it is a standard proposition in macro economics that the price level is
    determined by the demand and supply of money. It would be idle to search for the
    price level, on this ground, from an individual's demand function for money. A
    somewhat similar situation obtains in physics: 'the laws that regulate the behaviour of
    the microcosm differ fundamentally from those of the macrocosm' (Elyashevich, 1987,
    p. 12). For the inconsistency between quantum mechanics and the general theory of
    relativity see Hawking (1988, pp. 12–13).
2. McFadden (1966) has extended the concept of cost functions to revenue functions, and
    has proven a duality theorem which is the profit function analogue of the
    Shepherd–Uzawa duality theorem on cost and production functions. The McFadden
    theorem assures that the correspondence between the specified profit function and the

underlying production function is unique. The literature on this subject is quite large (Cowing 1978; Fuss, McFadden, and Mundlak, 1978; Lau, 1978; McFadden, 1966, 1978; Shepherd 1953; Uzawa, 1964).

In McFadden's profit function the arguments are factor prices normalised by the product price. Since the price of a factor is a function of the quantity, we have taken the quantity of capital as the argument. Our version of the profit function is a particular *reduced form* that subsumes all other inputs. See also Dow (1993).

3. It is a standard assumption that saving depends upon income and wealth, and that the respective propensities are constant. Our s can be construed as a weighted average of the two propensities.

4. Suppose the propensity to save with respect to wealth is unity, the capital–output ratio is 4, and the weighted average of the two saving propensities is 0.85 as it is in our estimate. Then the propensity to save out of income works out to be 0.25 which is approximately the figure for India.

REFERENCES

Bergman, L., D.W. Jorgenson, and E. Zalai (1990), *General Equilibrium Modelling and Economic Policy Analysis*, Oxford: Basil Blackwell.

Boldrin, M. (1988), 'Persistent Oscillations and Chaos in Dynamic Economic Models: Notes for a Survey', in P.W. Anderson, K. J. Arrow, and D. Pines (eds), *The Economy as an Evolving Complex System*, Redwood City, CA: Addison-Wesley, pp. 49–75.

Cowing, T.G. (1978), 'The Effectiveness of Rate-of-Return Regulation: An Empirical Test Using Profit Functions', in Fuss and McFadden, pp. 215–46.

Day, R. (1983), 'The Emergence of Chaos from Classical Economic Growth', *Quarterly Journal of Economics*, pp. 98, 201–13.

Dervis, K., J. de Mellow, and S. Robinson (1982), *General Equilibrium Models for Development Policy*, New York: Cambridge University Press.

Devaney, R.L. (1989), *An Introduction to Chaotic Dynamical System*, 2nd edn, Redwood City, CA: Addison-Wesley.

Dobb, M. (1967), *Papers on Capitalism, Development and Planning*, London: Routledge & Kegan Paul.

Dow, G.K. (1993), 'Why Capital Hires Labour: A Bargaining Perspective', *American Economic Review*, 83(1), pp. 118–34.

Dutt, A.K. (1984), 'Rent, Income Distribution and Growth in an Underdeveloped Agrarian Economy', *Journal of Development Economics*, 15, pp. 185–211.

Elyashevich, M.A. (1987), 'Quantum Theory: Origins and Growth', in *Physics of the 20th Century: History and Outlook*, Moscow: Mir Publishers, pp. 12–96.

Fuss, M. and D. McFadden (eds) (1978), *Production Economics: A Dual Approach to Theory and Applications*, 2 vols, Amsterdam: North Holland Publishers.

Fuss, M., D. McFadden and Y. Mundlak (1978), 'A Survey of Functional Forms in the Economic Analysis of Production', in Fuss and McFadden (1978), pp. 219–68.

Goodwin, R.M. (1967), 'A Growth Cycle', in C. Feinstein (ed.), *Socialism, Capitalism and Economic Growth*, London: Cambridge University Press.

Goodwin, R.M. (1986), 'Swinging along the Turnpike with von Neumann and Sraffa', *Cambridge Journal of Economics*, 10, pp. 203–10.

Goodwin, R.M. (1990), *Chaotic Economic Dynamics*, Oxford: Clarendon Press.

Hawking, S.W. (1988), *A Brief History of Time: From the Big Bang to Black Holes*, Toronto: Bantam Books.

Hoppensteadt, F. and J. Hyman (1977), 'Periodic Solutions of a Logistic Difference Equation', *SIAM Journal of Applied Mathematics*, 32, pp. 73–81.

Kelsey, D. (1988), 'The Economics of Chaos or the Chaos of Economics', *Oxford Economic Papers* 40, pp. 1–31.

Kosambi, D.D. (1970), *The Culture and Civilization of Ancient India in Historical Outline*, Delhi: Vikas Publishing House.

Lau, L.J. (1978), 'Applications of Profit Functions', in Fuss and McFadden (1978), pp. 133–216.

Marx, K. (1850), 'The Class Struggle in France, 1848–50', in K. Marx and F. Engels, *Selected Works*, Vol. 1, Moscow: Progress Publishers, 1969

Marx, K. (1862–63), *Theories of Surplus Value*, Part III, Moscow: Progress Publishers, 1971.

Marx, K. (1894), *Capital*, Vol. 3, Moscow: Progress Publishers, 1966.

Marx, K. and F. Engels (1965), *Selected Correspondence*, Moscow: Progress Publishers.

McFadden, D. (1966), 'Cost, Revenue and Profit Functions: A Cursory Review', Institute for Business and Economic Research Working Paper, No. 86, Berkeley: University of California.

McFadden, D. (1978a), 'Cost, Revenue, and Profit Functions', in Fuss and McFadden (1978), Vol. 1, pp. 3–110.

McFadden, D. (1978b), 'The General Linear Profit Functions', in Fuss and McFadden (1978), Vol. 1, pp. 269–86.

Minsky, H.P. (1986), *Stabilizing an Unstable Economy*, New Haven, CT: Yale University Press.

Mitra, A. (1967), 'Class Relations and Growth of Output', in B. Singh and V.B. Singh (eds), *Social and Economic Change*, Bombay: Allied Publishers, 1967, pp. 451–8.

Mitra, A. (1977), *Terms of Trade and Class Relations: An Essay in Political Economy*, London: Frank Cass.

Myrdal, G. (1968), *Asian Drama: An Inquiry into the Poverty of Nations*, Vol. 2, New York: Random House.

Pohjola, M.T. (1981), 'Stable, Cyclic and Chaotic Growth: The Dynamics of a Discrete-Time Version of Goodwin's Growth Cycle Model', *Zeitschrift für Nationalökonomie*, 41, pp. 27–38.

Sau, R. (1986), 'Ground Rent and Super Profit in the Sraffa System', *Indian Economic Review*, 21, pp. 51–60.

Sau, R. (1988), 'A Theory of Underdeveloped Capitalism', *Economic and Political Weekly*, 23, pp. 1797–803.

Sau, R. (1990), 'Surplus Profit and Class Relations in Two Stages of Capitalism', *Science and Society*, 54(2), pp. 179–92.

Sau, R. (1991), 'Profit, Interest and Trade in a Keynes–Ricardian Perspective', *Economia Internazionale*, 44(4), pp. 409–24.

Sau, R. (1992), 'Making of Payments Crisis: India 1991', *Economic and Political Weekly*, 33, pp. 1741–5.

Shepherd, R.W. (1953), *Cost and Production Functions*, Princeton, NJ: Princeton University Press.

Sraffa, P. (1960), *Production of Commodities by Means of Commodities*, Cambridge: Cambridge University Press.

Taylor, L. (1983), *Structuralist Macroeconomics*, New York: Basic Books.

Taylor, L. (ed.) (1990), *Socially Relevant Policy Analysis: Structuralist Computable General Equilibrium Models for the Developing World*, Cambridge, MA: MIT Press.

Uzawa, H. (1964), 'Duality Principles in the Theory of Cost and Production', *International Economic Review*, 5(2), pp. 216–20.

12

Planning in India:
Retrospect and Prospects

A. Vaidyanathan

INTRODUCTION

Planned development of the kind that India has been pursuing since independence is now under severe attack. The attack centres not so much on the objectives as on the way planning has worked and on the role that the State has sought to play in the process. There has never been much disagreement on the necessity for sustained rapid expansion and diversification of economic activity or about the State's responsibility to ensure that everyone has access to means of satisfying basic minimum needs. Planning is criticised for not accomplishing these aims in the last four decades; for consistently failing to fulfill its targets; and for not checking the deterioration of the fiscal position and the balance of payments position during the 1980s.

These failures are attributed variously to (a) the wrong strategies (specifically preoccupation with heavy industry to the neglect of agriculture, over-protection of domestic industry, and insufficient concern for increasing exports); (b) the way these strategies were sought to be implemented, particularly the excessive reliance on the public sector and the stifling effects of the control system on the private sector; and (c) weaknesses in the process of formulating and implementing the plans. Much has been written on the first two aspects.[1] This paper is largely concerned with the third aspect.

Indian planning is characterised by a strong interventionist role for the State within the framework of a mixed economy and a federal system of government. Initially the government was seen, even by the leading private industrialists, as essential to undertake direct investments, to develop infrastructure and basic industry which were beyond the competence and resources of the nascent private sector and thereby stimulate and support the growth of private sector.[2] State intervention in the form of direct public ownership of key sectors, regulation of the private sector and controls over allocation of scarce resources came to be considered as essential for achieving growth with social justice. Apart from the ideal of socialism, which appealed to a sizable segment of political opinion, the Directive Principles of State Policy in the Constitution spelled out some of the major social concerns which should guide policy.

INDIAN PLANNING: DISTINCTIVE FEATURES[3]

The nature and effectiveness of interventions are conditioned by several factors of which two are fundamental: (1) the federal structure of government; and (2) the fact that governments, both central government and state governments, are democratically elected and have to renew their mandate periodically.

Planning in a federal setup

The domains over which the centre and the states may exert authority are clearly defined in the constitution. Some (such as heavy industry, railways, atomic power) are exclusively in the centre's jurisdiction, while others (including agriculture, land reform, irrigation, electricity, education, health and roads) are in the domain of the states.

Securing a consensus on the national plan, and ensuring the consistency of programmes and policies pursued by different constituents of the federation with the objectives and priorities of the overall plan, are major problems. The political consensus on plan-related matters is sought to be achieved formally through the National Development Council (where the central and the state governments are represented) and informally through the party conclaves. The Planning Commission plays a crucial role in articulating the overall plan and working out the size and content of programmes at the centre and in the states through an extended consultative process. Various instruments have been used to get the states and departments to comply with the plan. These include the central government's power to make policy on subjects in which the centre and the states have concurrent jurisdiction; earmarking parts of central assistance to state plans for specified programmes; and special central funding for programmes conceived by the centre in areas that formally fall under the exclusive jurisdiction of the states.

These worked reasonably well, though not always and not uniformly successfully, for nearly two decades after independence when the Congress Party held sway at the centre and in most states. Once this pattern was broken, achieving and enforcing consensus on development plans has become increasingly difficult.

The political environment

Vision and farsightedness are essential to planning. Both were very much in evidence for some time after independence thanks to the undisputed leadership of Nehru and the supremacy of the Congress Party. Even so, in a democratic system, politicians in power tend to be preoccupied with immediate survival, or at the best with the next elections. They are therefore not particularly interested in the long-term consequences of their actions. This tendency has become progressively more acute with the passing of Nehru, the end of Congress supremacy and the growing fluidity of politics.[4] Altogether, the working of the political and the administrative system has become strongly biased in favour of promises and actions which have electoral appeal in the short run, even when it is known that they will turn out to be unsustainable or harmful over the long run. The Planning Commission has been unable to check this tendency.

Thus even though actual growth has fallen consistently short of targets, suggestions that it would be prudent to lower targets and trim the size of the plan to a realistic assessment of the capacity to mobilise resources were seldom accepted.[5] It is considered a cardinal political sin to set targets lower than in earlier plans or those proposed by the party that held power earlier. That promises of land reform and other means of reducing inequality have proved to be empty rhetoric has not prevented them from being repeated ritually in every plan. The shift of emphasis from reduction of relative inequality to removal of absolute poverty – reflected in the emergence and spread of various poverty alleviation programmes – no doubt reflects the compulsion of democratic politics and is not wholly based on its inherent merits. Being convenient instruments for distributing patronage on a wider scale, such programmes also serve the interests of politicians in power. This adds to their political appeal.

By the same token there is unwillingness to take action which is necessary for the stability of the economy but which may hurt the interests of one or other powerful or numerically strong groups in the society. This fear is heightened by the compulsions of electoral politics and the precariousness of power and largely explains the reluctance to implement measures acknowledged to be necessary to restore fiscal stability – be it strict enforcement of tax laws, raising prices of publicly provided goods and services to meet costs, reducing subsidies which benefit the well-to-do, or improving efficiency of public agencies and enterprises.

Attitudes of the politicians and the bureaucracy are also strongly coloured by the fact that control over decisions on the scale and location of projects (be it a road, school, hospital, irrigation work or factory), the award of contracts, the appointment of personnel or determination of which individuals or groups will benefit from a poverty alleviation or welfare scheme are all instruments for securing the political support base and simultaneously a convenient source of much-needed funds for party and personal purposes. Gradually offices in public institutions (public corporations, cooperatives and the like) have come to be seen and used as part of what has become virtually a 'spoils system'.

Independent professional advice, public scrutiny of major investment decisions, enforcement of rules and regulations (intended to ensure that projects are designed and executed to achieve the end result at the lowest cost) and the functioning of Public Accounts Committees and Estimate Committees of the Parliament and State legislatures, the Comptroller and Auditor General, the judiciary and other watchdog institutions (which are meant to ensure that public funds are handled with probity and in the public interest) have all been compromised, softened and made increasingly ineffective in various ways. The cumulative effect of all this has been to give planning a bad time.

Changes in political environment

Political configurations and processes have also been changing rapidly and this naturally affects the planning as well. On the one hand there is a significant trend towards centralisation reflected in the progressive expansion of the 'concurrent list' to include areas which were originally in the exclusive jurisdiction of the states; the worsening financial status of the states making them more dependent on the centre and also more amenable to taking up central and centrally sponsored programmes; and the growing tendency for the centre to influence the scope and content of state-level programmes through various types of special programmes funded by it.

This centralising tendency is manifest at the state level too. Local government institutions have been weakened by supercession, postponement of elections and meagre resources and powers. The staff under the control of local governments have in most cases agitated successfully to have themselves incorporated as part of the State government bureaucracy. Politicians in power at the state level have tightened their control over the funds available for development and also over the public institutions (like co-operatives and public corporations) for use as instruments of patronage.

Even as these centralising tendencies have gained ground at the governmental level, there has been a progressive loosening of centralised political control. This control, which was characteristic of the heyday of Congress Party hegemony, began to change with the death of Nehru. Since then, the Congress Party has split; new political parties like the BJP and Janata Dal have emerged at the national level, even as purely regional parties gained ascendency in some states (notably Tamil Nadu and AP, Punjab). The tension between the centre and the states has intensified with the states becoming increasingly resentful of attempts by the centre to unseat duly constituted state governments in arbitrary ways and to use its superior access to financial resources to secure its political interests. Competitive electoral politics has sponsored competitive populism, making it more difficult to achieve the minimal consensus necessary to ensure effective collection of taxes, efficient running of public services and keeping subsidies in check.

The balance of political forces has also been changing. Being a vast and diverse polity, regional, linguistic and caste differences have always been important factors weighing on the side of pluralism. Unlike in many other developing countries, neither the capitalist, nor a modernising managerial élite, has been able to establish undisputed hegemony over State power. On the contrary, electoral politics gave an opportunity for the relatively large landed classes from rural areas and the urban professional and middle classes to enter the legislatures and the government. Some observers characterise these groups as part of a distributive coalition running the State. Workers in the organised sector, including the government and the public sector, have also been influential because of their strategic positioning in the economy and the emergence of powerful trade unions.

However this is arguably an oversimplification. One of the most striking developments of the past two decades is the rapid growth in scale and variety of poverty alleviation programmes designed to woo the electoral support of the poor. The poor, though not organised to press their interests directly in the political arena, are numerous. In an electoral system based on universal adult franchise, almost every party finds it necessary (following the dramatic demonstration that 'Garibi Hatao' is a very effective vote-catching platform) to demonstrate their interest in and concern for the welfare of the poor. While this has, at one level, led to unrestrained populism, it can also been seen as an indication that the democratic process is an effective means of forcing the powers-that-be to pay attention to the interests of the poor. Moreover, these programmes have increased the awareness of the poor of their importance in the political process and the potential for more active pressing of their claims. The emergence of OBC-minorities–SC alliances, and the sharp increase in political tensions in several parts of the country on this account, could be read as a reflection of this.

This loosening of central power is accompanied by the emergence of religion as a more primary and contentious issue in politics, and the erosion of the consensus of the Nehruvian era on the planning and the role of the State in fostering economic development and social justice. The cumulative effect of all this is hardly conducive to planning which is dependent on forging a wide enough political consensus to make policy informed by a coherent long-term vision and to ensure that the policies needed to realise the vision are made and implemented consistently.[6] The recent economic reforms, which are as much the result of ideological shifts as of the compulsions created by the failures of the past, and the resources crisis have called into question the original concept of planned development, the role of the State and the functions of the Planning Commission.

The functioning of the Planning Commission

The Planning Commission, appointed by the central government in 1950, has a wide mandate including the determination of the overall strategies of development, the quantum of resources to be devoted for that purpose and their allocation between different programmes. It is supposed to review all major projects before clearance, advise on important policy matters and monitor the performance of the plan as a whole and of individual programmes. Its composition was designed to give it sufficient political weight in the councils of government. The National Development Council, comprising key central ministers and all state chief ministers, provided the forum for discussing important issues concerning the national plans and development policy.

So long as there was political commitment to planning and the government was stable – as was the case during the 1950s and early 1960s – the Commission did play an important role in all the above respects. The first two plans presented a long term vision and a coherent strategy to realise it. The Commission emerged as a bridge between the centre and the states. It mediated the competing claims of the centre and the states, of different states for central assistance and of various central ministries. But after Nehru's death, the weakening of the Congress and the emergence of governments ruled by parties other than Congress in several states, led to the gradual erosion of the role of the Commission as an independent professional body focusing on the medium and long-term problems in a wide, national perspective.[7]

The Planning Commission has successfully persuaded the states to set up their own overall planning organisation. Although most states now have planning boards or commissions of their own, few are equipped to play an effective role in devising overall plans appropriate to the needs of each state. In most cases they are no more than ornaments; they are not accorded the status and power to play anything like an important role in determining development priorities and allocations in the state plans within a coherent long-term perspective of their growth.

The Commission however has not taken the same degree of sustained interest in strengthening sectoral planning. Occasionally sectoral studies have been commissioned either from individual experts or expert committees. Some useful detailed studies on transport, energy, fertilisers, and steel – to mention a few examples – have come out of this process.[8,9] These serve rather as *ad hoc* exercises without any arrangement for monitoring actual developments in relation to projections and the changing conditions of resources, technology and market conditions. It is also difficult to see evidence of their findings shaping, in any systematic or sustained way, investment priorities, technology choices, price policy and technology development and the policy framework to realise them. Neither the Commission, nor the ministries and the concerned public enterprises, have done much to build design organisations and promote forward-looking research and technology development on their own or in collaboration with research laboratories. The situation in the states – which are responsible for electricity, water resource development, and roads – is, if anything, worse.

As for its role in decision-making, the executive ministries, and to some extent the states, had from the beginning looked again at the Commission's role and its power to influence decisions which were in their domain.[10] The ministries have been zealously guarding their prerogative in policy making. While the Commission was usually consulted on major policy and investment decisions, its views were not always decisive. The technical sophistication of the five-year plans in articulating implications of overall goals for investment allocation, production targets and resource mobilisation is indeed remarkable.[11] But the Commission has been less than successful in working out, and getting the government to accept, a coherent set of policies needed to implement the programme.[12]

The Commission's effectiveness in respect of specific investment decisions was also compromised by the reluctance of departments to provide the information needed to evaluate the viability of particular projects or programmes and track their actual progress fully, accurately and promptly. The Commission had no independent channel for such information. The creation of the Project Appraisal Division within the Commission, and making it the secretariat to the Public Investment Board, gave it some power but not enough.

Soon after its constitution, the Planning Commission created a Programme Evaluation Organisation to obtain an independent assessment of the working and impact of various programmes. This organisation has shown remarkable candour and objectivity in its reports, which are also published. However, the evidence of their impact in terms of improving the design of interventions is much less striking. Most states also have their own evaluation organisations. Their reports not being in the public domain, it is difficult to assess their impact. A notable and serious gap in post-evaluation exercises is the conspicuous absence of systematic critical reviews of the performance of large investment projects in terms of the deviation of actual time schedules, costs, utilisation of facilities, and impact on production from the original assumptions.

Until recently Indian planning was based on the understanding that direct and detailed firm and product specific controls over allocation of foreign exchange, capital and other scarce inputs, as well as controls over production, creation of new capacities and pricing are necessary in the larger social interest. The control system however has grown in a piecemeal fashion, rather than as a well-thought-out, coherent set of instruments to achieve clearly stated goals. The elements constituting the control system were introduced and altered to meet particular exigencies. The resulting incoherence and inconsistency is at least part of the reason why rationing and price controls did not achieve their ostensible aims.[13]

India's experience, and the experience of the centrally planned economies, has also shown that the central authority simply cannot get the relevant information in necessary detail, promptly and without any distortion, from individual enterprises and agencies. And attempts to digest this information and reach decisions on who is to get what material in what quantities, what is to be produced, by whom, and how, have simply failed. Such decisions as have been made could not be enforced. The shroud of secrecy surrounding project approvals and policy decisions, and the fact that the public does not have access to the relevant information or the opportunity to raise objections and seek reviews has also compromised the accountability of public authorities for their decisions.

REORIENTATION OF PLANNING

It is for these reasons that we see a strong swing of opinion against central planning and in favour of dismantling the control régime, freer access to imports, foreign capital and technology; and other liberalisation measures. The search for fewer, simpler impersonal and indirect mechanisms – operating via fiscal policy – as a way of creating an incentive environment conducive to efficient but decentralised decisions by both public and private enterprises is understandable and justified. The need for planning is not, however, eliminated in the process.

Planning in its widest connotation calls for anticipation of longer term significance and consequences of emerging social, economic and technological trends; and taking action soon enough in advance to ensure that agreed basic social objectives (particularly meeting basic needs for everyone and equality of opportunity) are realised and that bottlenecks do not impede the progress of the economy.

Some problems are obvious enough. The country's endowment of several key natural resources (like land, forests, water and oil) is not only limited in absolute terms but is also rather modest in relation to the population. Some of these resources (like oil) are rapidly depleting in the rest of the world too. More effective use of these resources (by increasing their productivity, conservation and by the use of cheaper/more abundant substitutes preferably based on renewable resources) is therefore imperative. Major technological developments need to be constantly monitored, developments which are of significance in the Indian context need to be identified, and their acquisition and/or future development need to be encouraged. There is also the wider, long-term problem of 'sustainable' development. Action on all these fronts must be informed by a clear understanding of the interconnected implications of broadly defined social goals in terms of mutual consistency, potential conflicts, trade-offs, etc.

Both past experience and the reforms currently in process call for major changes in the organisation and processes of planning. The Planning Commmission has to adapt its organisation and functioning in the light of the inevitable changes in the nature and scope of the State's role both directly and in regulating the private sector. It needs to build up a wider, stronger information base, acquiring, if need be, the power and the capacity to establish its own channels for collecting data on key aspects of the economy. Instead of devoting so much of its staff and time to discussing details of innumerable individual schemes of the central government and the states, the Commission should focus more on evolving long-term strategy and policy for key sectors, evaluating major investment decisions and their actual implementation records, expert evaluation of selected important sectoral and regional programmes consisting of a large number of small schemes and questions concerning long-term technology and resource management for sustainable development. It should hand over detailed planning at the state level to state planning agencies, and confine itself to providing an independent critical review of the overall performance of states and of key sectors of the economy. The Commission cannot and should not attempt to perform all these activities with its own staff but should rely more and more on outside experts either by commissioning them to carry out studies on selected, well-defined problems or by inducting them for such tasks within the Commission.

Second, the Commission should pay special attention to widening and deepening the competence for sectoral and regional planning. This is particularly important in energy, transport, water and some major industries, as well as in activities (like urban planning) which involve (a) large long-gestating investments; (b) a high degree of inter-sectoral linkage; (c) rapid technological change; and (d) depletion of non-renewable resources and/or high pollution risks. Institutions need to be strengthened at the sectoral level to periodically assess future needs and alternative ways of meeting the needs in the long term as a basis for guiding pricing, investment and technology policies in respect of key sectors (like energy, land and water, transport, environment and important raw materials). Such assessments are best organised under the auspices of the Planning Commission whose function is to view sectors and projects in a comprehensive economy-wide perspective. The Commission should also take an active interest in assessing the nature and scale of specialised design-engineering organisations needed at the centre, in the states and outside the government and to recommend policies to encourage the formation of such organisations.

Both link up with building long-term technological capabilities through programmes for making up current gaps, for the adaptation and improvement of available technology, and for developing new technologies. Here again the Planning Commission is, in principle, best placed to provide the wide and long-term perspective and get the sectoral specialists from the public and private sector, research institutions, design-engineering organisations and technology experts into a creative interaction on a continuing basis. This does not mean that the Planning Commission should become a mammoth organisation. Rather, it should play the kind of role that MITI plays in Japan – it should be a forum of strategic thinking, a medium for getting the relevant expertise from concerned enterprises, universities, and laboratories together to examine the problems and come up with solutions, and an interlocutor with the government to establish appropriate policies and institutional arrangements.

The third major task is to improve the performance of public sector institutions and agencies both in setting up new facilities and in operating them. This calls for fundamental changes in the way government and its enterprises work. We need credible and effective mechanisms to ensure that investment decisions are made after objective techno-economic appraisal by professionals and that the political considerations in such decisions are made explicit and kept to a minimum. Greater autonomy and flexibility for the enterprises to plan their operations in the light of market conditions must be an essential part of reforms to improve efficiency. But efficiency is not only a function of allowing enterprises to adapt flexibly to market signals; it depends equally on how the non-market institutions function. One crucial aspect of this concerns the relation between the enterprises, the political executive, the Parliament and the watchdog institutions. The other relates to the internal structure and functioning of enterprises.

Not all decisions on resource allocations are made with reference to the market. Within each firm – irrespective of whether it is publicly or privately owned and whether its ownership is concentrated or diffused – such decisions are invariably made in the framework of a hierarchical organisation, each with its own rules, procedures and control systems to ensure efficient operation. This would suggest that the central issue is not ownership but internal structures, procedures and incentive systems within the firms. Transferring a part – even a substantial part – of the equity in PSUs to the private sector will not automatically solve the problem unless these questions are addressed. Devising a programme for such institutional reform is therefore one of the major tasks of planning and planners.

The fourth area of reform in planning has to do with setting up and managing facilities to develop common production resources used by a large number of users. The most important examples of this are land development, irrigation, research, and credit. The present system whereby such programmes are conceived, set up and operated by the State without much, if any, interaction with the beneficiaries leaves a great deal to be desired. In the case of land, water and credit the success of the programmes depends crucially on the beneficiaries agreeing to certain discipline in terms of the allocation of the resources between uses and users, and an effective mechanism for ensuring compliance.[14]

The State alone cannot accomplish this; nor can such facilities be left wholly to user organisations (especially in relatively large projects). What we need is an arrangement whereby the users are made to acquire a stake in the facility and are actively involved along with State officials and professional managers of the facilities in evolving a set of generally acceptable rules and enforcement mechanisms. In the case of research and extension, again, the problem is to evolve incentive systems to promote active interaction between the research workers, extension agents and the farmers; to ensure that the research system is responsive to the needs of users; and to make the researchers accountable for their performance.

Finally, the institutional arrangements for planning and implementation in the states need a thoroughgoing reorganisation. Apart from strengthening the state-level planning agencies and getting them to play a more active role in providing an overall perspective, there is much scope for improving the content and efficacy of programmes. Apart from power, major irrigation, major roads and road transport, the bulk of state-level development outlays happen to be on local development activities which are widely dispersed in space. Their efficacy is seriously impaired by three features: (a) a great deal of overlapping and duplication between different schemes; (b) the top-down approach designing programme content and deciding how the resources are to be allocated in space; and (c) ensuring that programmes targeted at particular groups do in fact reach them in full measure.[15]

The solution, as has been widely recognised, involves rationalisation of programmes to minimise duplication. More importantly, in respect of all local development activity, state-level schemes of standardised design should give place to integrated local-level plans whose content reflects the specific needs, opportunities and priorities of each district, block and village. The funds allotted to such local development projects should be pooled and allocated across districts (possibly blocks) on the basis of the magnitude of unemployment and poverty and the deficiency in basic amenities with due allowance for the potential for further resource development. And democratically elected local government institutions should be given the opportunity and the necessary support to plan the content of these local development programmes and to implement them.

The passage of the 74th constitutional amendment on Panchayati Raj sets the stage for such reforms. But it would take much patient and sustained effort before those who exercise power under the existing, highly centralised political system and bureaucracy can be persuaded, perhaps even forced, to accept a different role in a more decentralised arrangement. This institutional reform is crucial to the success of investment and other interventions by the public sector for promoting rural development and protecting the vulnerable.

Some of these reforms are now on the agenda. Significant progress has been made in dismantling central government controls over industry and in rationalising foreign trade and exchange rate policies; some subsidies have been cut; forcing public undertakings to mobilise their own resources has increased pressure on them to improve efficiency; and the 74th constitutional amendment creates space for better regional planning with meaningful local participation in development. But all these initiatives are limited to the centre; the states have been largely left out of the process and no serious effort has been made to enlist their active involvement and co-operation. Without the latter, the reforms under way, which are already facing resistance, cannot go far. The Planning Commission has a key role to play in promoting, through the NDC, a minimal political consensus on the necessary reforms in the above areas and also on the way planning has to be reoriented in the changed context. That this has not happened, and that the Planning Commission has chosen to play a passive role, is therefore regrettable.

NOTES

1. For recent critiques of Indian planning see Ahluwalia 1985, Lucas and Papanek (eds) 1988, Adiseshaiah (ed.).
2. The need for a strong government role in India's development was emphasised by Visveswarayya and by the Bombay Plan prepared by industrialists (Thakurdas, 1944).
3. An excellent historical review of the evolution of Indian Planning – both at the level of concept and implementation – up to the mid 1960s is available in Hanson, 1966. For a critical assessment of the functioning of the planning process see Paranjape, 1975.
4. For a political economy interpretation of Indian Planning see Frankel, 1978; Rudolph and Rudolph, 1987; and Bardhan, 1982.
5. The controversy between 'bold planning' and 'realistic planning' has of course been characteristic of all plans. But while, in the first three plans, the debate centred around the relative merits of alternative strategies and their feasibility, the political pressure for over-pitching targets and for approving large plans came into prominence from the late 1960s and early 1970s. There was a public controversy over the wisdom of the Planning Commission yielding to such pressures in the early 1970s, leading to the resignation of one of the members of the Commission (see Minhas, 1974, for one view of this controversy). Although this issue has kept surfacing since, successive governments and the Planning Commission have been most reluctant to reduce the overall growth targets below 5–5.5 per cent a year even though actual growth (until the 1980s) averaged 3.5 per cent per year.
6. This is part of the wider debate on centre–state relations which intensified in the 1970s and led to the appointment of the Sarkaria Commission (GOI, 1987–88). .
7. For a brief overview of this process see Krishnaswamy *et al.*, 1992.
8. The Perspective Planning Division in the early 1960s prepared a series of papers spelling out the main tasks involved in translating long-term targets for sectors like

transport, electricity, steel, fertilisers and machinery into concrete projects and the nature and scale of specialist organisation needed. These papers are unpublished. Pant, who headed PPD, repeatedly drew attention to this aspect in the Commission, the working groups, and the ministries. Attempts to develop indigenous design organisations in steel and fertilisers ran into difficulties. One can obtain some idea of the kind of problems involved, and the reason for the slow progress in this field, from Desai's study of Bokaro Steel Plant (Desai, 1979).

9. During the early 1960s, some pioneering studies were done to determine the optimum location, scale and time phasing of capacity in key industry (such as fertilisers and cement) within the framework of an overall perspective plan (Manne (ed.) 1967). The reports of the Energy Survey Committee (GOI, 1965); the working group on Energy Policy (GOI, 1979); the National Transport Planning Committee (GOI, 1980) and recent (unpublished) studies on long-term plans for energy and steel commissioned by the Planning Commission are examples of such work. The lack of continuity, the weak institutional memory, and the failure systematically to review actual experience in relation to earlier analyses and recommendations as a basis for subsequent sector studies are conspicious weaknesses.

10. It needs recalling that John Mathai resigned as Finance Minister soon after the Planning Commission was set up in 1950 on the ground that the commission was an extra constitutional body which would become a 'parallel Cabinet'.

11. A variety of planning models ranging from the simple Harrod–Domar type macro models, to multisector, multiperiod optimisation models have been constructed and estimated in India. For an excellent review see Rudra, 1975.

12. Gadgil (1967) appropriately called it as 'planning without a policy frame'.

13. For a critique of the control system see GOI, 1967, 1979 and Jha, 1980.

14. The rationale of this approach in the case of large surface irrigation works has been discussed at length in the report of a committee on Irrigation Pricing set up by the Planning Commission (GOI, 1992).

15. For a powerful statement of the case for decentralistion see Jain, 1985.

REFERENCES

Ahluwalia, I. J. 1985. *Industrial Growth in India; Stagnation since the Mid-Sixties* (OUP, New Delhi).
Bardhan, P.K. 1984. *The Political Economy of Development in India* (OUP, New Delhi).
Desai, Padma. 1979. *Bokaro Steel Plant: A Study of Soviet Economic Assistance.*
Frankel, Francine R. 1978. *India's Political Economy 1947–1977: The Gradual Revolution,* (Princeton University Press, Princeton).
Gadgil, D.R. 1967. 'Planning without a Policy Frame', *Economic and Political Weekly*, Annual Number, February 1967.
GOI. 1987. Report of Commission on Centre–State Relations, Parts I and II (GDI Press, New Delhi).
GOI. 1988. *Centre–State Relations,* Parts I and II (GOI, Press, New Delhi).
GOI. Planning Commission. 1965. *Energy Survey of India.*
GOI. Planning Commission. 1967. *Report of the Industrial Planning and Licensing Policy Inquiry Committee, Main Report.*
GOI. Planning Commission. 1979. *Report of Working Group on Energy Policy.*
GOI. Planning Commission. 1980. *Report of the National Transport Planning Committee.*
GOI. Planning Commission. (Undated). *Perspective Planning for Transport Development: Report of Steering Committee.*
GOI. Ministry of Finance. 1979. *Report of the Committee on Controls and Subsidies.*
GOI. Ministry of Energy and Coal. 1980. *Report of the Committee on Power.*
Hanson, A.N. 1966. *The Planning Process* (OUP, London).
Jain, L.C. 1985. *Grass without Roots* (Sage, New Delhi).
Jha, L.K. 1980. *Economic Strategy for the 80s* (Allied, New Delhi).
Krishnaswamy, K.S., I.S.Gulati and A.Vaidyanathan. 1992. 'Economic Aspects of Federalism in India', in Mukherjee Nirmal and B. Arora (eds), *Federalism in India:*

Origins and Development (Vikas, New Delhi).

Lucas, Robert and Gustav, Papanek (eds). 1988. *Indian Economy. Recent Development and Future Progress* (West View, London).

Manne, A.S. (ed.). 1967. *Investment for Capacity Expansion Size Location and Land Time Phasing* (George Allen & Unwin, London)

Mukherjee, Nirmal and Balveer Arora. 1992. *Federalism in India: Origins and Development,* (Vikas, New Delhi).

Paranjape, H.K. 1964. *The Planning Commission: A Discriptive Account* (Indian Institute of Public Administration, New Delhi).

Rudra Ashok. 1975. *Indian Planning Models,* Allied Publishers, New Delhi.

Rudolph Lloyd and Suzanne Rudolph. 1987. *In Pursuit of Lakshmi: The Political Economy of the Indian State* (Orient Longman, Bombay).

Thakurdas, Purushothamdas and others. 1964. *Plan for Economic Development of India.*

EXPERIENCE:
THE COMPARATIVE DIMENSION

13

The Need for the Comparative Method in the Social Sciences: An Essay with the Agrarian Question in India in Mind

Terence J. Byres

1. ANALYSIS INFORMED BY COMPARISON

This is not an essay about Ashok Mitra, whose importance and many contributions to our understanding of post-1947 India are captured elsewhere in the volume. There is, however, an aspect of the distinctiveness of his intellectual approach to which I would draw attention, since it is one to which the present essay responds. This is a clear historical sense, theoretically informed, allied to an awareness of the need to view India in relation to other societies and other experience. It is one of his numerous strengths.

This might be taken to imply a comparative approach. But that would be to imply too much and to set up, perhaps, expectations at once excessive and unrealistic. I shall come, presently, to the comparative method as a distinct field of enquiry.

Ashok Mitra nowhere spells out in detail, nor does he anywhere even identify (to my knowledge), the need for a comparative approach. There is no reason why he should. It is only where systematic comparative work is attempted that such a programmatic methodological statement might be anticipated – and even then it is not always forthcoming. He does not pursue a comparative approach systematically, and nor would one expect him to. Few social scientists do. It is unnecessary, and it would be tiresome if they did. He nowhere articulates, then, the importance of the comparative approach as a methodological principle. Yet, he displays a recurring perception that, if India's political economy is to be grasped and if sense is to be made of it, it cannot be seen in isolation – cannot be viewed simply in its own terms, or hermetically. It must, indeed, be assayed theoretically, but it needs a comparative dimension to give it perspective and significance. This is one of the several ingredients which give his writing authority, insight and depth.[1]

The need for a comparative dimension, ultimately, in any attempt to understand the structure and functioning of individual economies or social formations, and to grasp the nature of transitions between social formations, is a principle to which I strongly subscribe. Thus, even if one's sole interest lies in analysing a single economy or social formation, or even a part or region thereof, over a narrow range of time, it is desirable that the analysis be informed by comparison. There is a general sense in which this is clearly so.

Whether at the most general level or at the disaggregated level, comparison can be a fertilising influence. It can open analytical perspectives. It can clarify and make more secure the analytical judgements which political economists – and more narrowly based economists, and other social scientists including historians – make. It can do so by establishing criteria independent of a particular context.

Those significant analytical judgements, which are routinely made, are many, and they are familiar. They lie at the very heart of the everyday practice of political economists and economists. They fall into certain broad categories, of which we may identify three. They concern, firstly, the nature of performance, and what constitutes satisfactory performance: for economists, obviously, economic performance. They relate, secondly, to the character and manner of change – crucially, for economists, structural change; to lack of change; and to what comprises desirable, or possible, change. They encompass, thirdly, what determines performance, change, or lack of change; that is, they are about causality.

Clearly, such judgements cannot be simply empirical. They need to be ordered by, and rooted in, theory, as I have already suggested, and as Ashok Mitra clearly recognises: in the ideal types which theory establishes, and the hypotheses which theory suggests. The theory which Ashok Mitra (and I) favour is that of Marxian political economy, and I believe that body of theory to be especially appropriate to the pursuit of comparison. Analysis must, further, be grounded, as Ben Fine has recently put it, 'in secure theoretical foundations that remain sensitive both to diversity and historical contingency' (Fine, 1993, p.2). That seems to me to be crucial. Marxist political economy provides such secure theoretical foundations. The sensitivity to diversity and historical contingency, I posit, must come, in part, from carefully pursued comparison. There are, I need hardly say, no guarantees as to the outcome. That, however, does not preclude the statement of principle.

It is, in part, by comparison that one might make the relevant, sensitive judgements about performance. How might one judge the adequacy of performance without some comparative yardstick? Comparisons suggests what is reasonable, and even necessary. It is, to a degree, in comparative terms that one might conceive of change in a suitably nuanced manner, How, otherwise, might one understand the nature, the scope, and the likely direction of change? Comparison, moreover, may point to the possibility of a substantive diversity of outcome. It is in a comparative perspective that one might reach for possible lines of causality. Comparison has the power to widen the range of possible hypotheses.

2. THE DESIRABILITY OF OPEN AND EXPLICIT COMPARISON, CAREFULLY MADE, AND SUITABLY PURSUED IN HISTORICAL TERMS

Comparison, then, in the workaday practice of economists and other social scientists, can, suitably pursued, prevent analytical closure by keeping one alive to the diversity and historical contingency insisted upon by Ben Fine. What, then, does one mean by 'suitably pursued'? There are three simple and obvious, but none the less significant, senses to which I would draw attention.

Comparison, of course, exists pervasively. It may be open. It may be perfectly explicit whether in passing (which is not uncommon), or in considerable detail. It may, however, be hidden; or it may wear a disguise. Such comparison may be implicit, with no actual comparison made.[2] The investigator may be only dimly aware of it, if aware of it at all. It may be none the less real for that. Its suitable pursuit requires, I suggest, firstly, that it be open and explicit. That should be a binding analytical principle.

Comparison may be essentially empirical – with another actual country's or economy's experience, either in the past or currently. One can think, say, of a comparison of contemporary India with Meiji Japan, or contemporary China or other east Asian countries. Such comparisons are commonly made. They may, however, be partial, fragmentary or casual. We may posit that it need not be part of a systematic comparative enquiry. But it should, secondly, be serious. It is necessary that the comparison, if it is to be useful, be less than casual and be made with some care.

Implicitly or explicitly, it may be comparison against a purely theoretical construct – say a contemporary developing country against a fully capitalist social formation, or one that is feudal, or semi-feudal. The comparison, in such terms, may, indeed, be excessively demanding. But that is not my point here. The theoretical construct, expressed in abstract theoretical terms, may derive, in effect, from a particular historical experience; one recalls, for example, the extent to which Marx draws upon the English experience in *Capital*. Or it may be comparison against a stylised version, a 'model', of a particular country's experience; for example, in one terminology, the 'Prussian path' or, in another, the 'Japanese model'. It is important that a crude rendering of the historical experience in question – in the extreme, historical caricature – be avoided. Comparison should be suitably pursued in historical terms.

3. SYSTEMATIC COMPARATIVE WORK AND THE COMPARATIVE METHOD

A well-established tradition of comparative work is the best way of meeting these requirements, or, at least, of securing a sensitivity to them. For an awareness of the kind displayed by Ashok Mitra to be truly effective, those guided by it need to be able to draw upon an established and constantly revitalised corpus of comparative work. I would reiterate the distinction between 'analysis informed by comparison' (such as Ashok Mitra's) and systematic comparative analysis. The former is desirable for all social scientists. The latter is a distinct branch of enquiry of its own, with discernible methodological principles.

Such systematic comparative analysis will address, *inter alia,* those issues of performance, change and causality to which I have drawn attention. Pursued systematically and rigorously, comparative work entails a comparative method. I will draw attention below to certain aspects of that comparative method, including the different ways in which it is practised, and to possible matters of contention. Before that, however, we may briefly consider what is claimed on its behalf and what it may deliver.

The authors of an influential work on comparative economic development, *Patterns of Development, 1950–1970,* Hollis Chenery and Moises Syrquin, make part of the case for the practice of the comparative method in systematic comparative work – in this instance in economics:

> Intercountry comparisons play an essential part in understanding the processes of economic and social development. To generalize from the historical experience of a single country, we must compare it in some way to that of other countries. Through such comparisons, uniform features of development can be identified and alternative hypotheses as to their causes tested. (Chenery and Syrquin, 1975, p. 3.)

Barrington Moore, another practitioner of the comparative method, who has written one of the classics of the comparative approach, a magisterial and powerful work of comparative history[3] also argues the value of a systematic comparative approach.

> In the effort to understand the history of a specific country a comparative perspective can lead to asking very useful and sometimes new questions. There are further advantages. Comparisons can serve as a rough negative check on accepted historical explanations. And a comparative approach can lead to new historical explanations. (Barrington Moore, 1966, p. xiii.)

As we shall see, we here confront two very different approaches to the comparative method. Yet the arguments made in favour of that method, by these exponents who differ markedly in their analytical procedures, are very similar.

The comparative principle enunciated by these authors is as valid for any of the social sciences as it is for economics or history. The claim made is, I suggest, perfectly justified. At the broadest possible level, it has the power to unblock analytical channels. This (in the briefest and broadest possible compass) it may do in four essential ways. Firstly, it may reveal significant historical regularities. It may, indeed, identify 'uniform features of development'. That, in itself, is immensely valuable. Secondly, the potential clarifying power of an adequately practised comparative approach – its capacity to cast new light – is great. A variety of historical patterns may be demonstrated. That, too, is of great potential value. Thirdly, it may, indeed, lead to the questioning of stereotypes. Fourthly, it may generate exciting new hypotheses via a questioning of 'accepted historical explanations' and by generating 'new historical explanations'. It would be difficult to exaggerate the significance of this. All in all, to use my earlier formulation, it has the power to diminish analytical closure.

Such a comparative method, I submit, needs to be an integral part of political economy (and, indeed, more broadly, of history and the social sciences). Political economists (or economists, or social scientists) of whatever persuasion, will not necessarily self-consciously embrace it. Yet, I believe, their work will be enriched and strengthened, will be given greater precision and enlarged scope, and will be made more analytically open by its adequate pursuit within the social sciences. This needs to be done as a distinct branch of each discipline. There are, however, general principles that might be explored.

In what remains of this brief essay I offer some observations on the comparative method. It is the systematic pursuit of the comparative method that is my concern here. It is some of the aspects of a fully crystallised comparative approach, which imply a comparative method, that I wish to consider. For the last few years I have been involved with comparative work in relation to the agrarian question and agrarian transition. My observations derive from that work. I can, perhaps, best proceed now by explaining why a major excursion into comparative work seemed to me to be desirable. This may clarify some of the points made previously. I had, after all, been a regionalist, in the sense that my major concern had been with India. I had, it is true, been involved with Peter Nolan, in a comparison of India and China (Byres and Nolan, 1976). But that was something of a diversion. The more recent concern has been altogether more serious and lasting.

Before so proceeding I would stress the following. I attach great importance to the need for the comparative method. It cannot, in my view, be argued for strongly enough. But if, in this essay, I concentrate on the considerable potential of the comparative method, and embrace, perhaps, in this respect, a kind of methodological optimism, I assuredly would not wish to deny the many, and often formidable, difficulties associated with adequate pursuit of comparison. Here is a demanding discipline. I note some of the difficulties below.

Moreover, while comparison has the potential to illuminate powerfully, there is, of course, no guarantee that it will do this. Indeed, as with any methodology inappropriately pursued, practice may be crass, unhelpful and even disastrous. That goes almost without saying. It is not my intention here to consider thoroughly bad examples of the method. Since space forbids detailed consideration of instances of such treatment I have not mentioned them in the present essay. Clearly their existence does not invalidate the principle being suggested.

4. THE AGRARIAN QUESTION IN INDIA AND EXCURSION INTO THE COMPARATIVE METHOD

My work on India has been largely concerned with the agrarian question, with the prospects for agrarian transition, and with the forms that such transition might take. Moreover, I have acquired a wide perspective on that work, as editor of the *Journal of Peasant Studies* since its inception in 1973. I have been drawn inexorably towards comparative economic history by a growing dissatisfaction with the way academics resort to a limited number of paths of capitalist agrarian transition, apparently traversed in the West, whose essential features are identified and made to constitute the elements of possible models of agrarian transition.

These 'models' have been influential in at least two significant senses. Firstly, certain crucial interventions have been made, both in the colonial past and in the post-colonial era, in apparent conformity with them, while some of them are at present used prescriptively. Then, secondly, current realities in poor countries are often judged against them: they have become models which embody criteria by which one may judge whether, and in what form, a capitalist agrarian transition is being negotiated.

It gradually seemed to me that practice in this respect is defective and misleading in two important ways. The first is that the paths in question – the 'models' being taken to contemporary reality – are too few. The full range of historical instances of successful transition is not referred to.

Not only that but, secondly, the conception of these paths is too stereotyped and too narrow. So it is that, with these models as reference points, the processes at work in contemporary poor countries may be seriously misunderstood: they may not be fully recognised, or they may even go wholly unrecognised because a set of limited and rigid criteria are not met.

It appeared desirable to me to try to establish, more thoroughly than is usually the case, what was involved in certain major paths of agrarian transition before bringing stylised versions of these paths (that is, 'models') to bear upon contemporary poor countries as standards of judgement. If, explicitly or implicitly, we are to use such 'models' as embodying criteria by which to judge whether or not agrarian transition is proceeding and to establish the nature of that transition, then we incur a responsibility.

It behoves us to try to determine the exact contours of the paths in question and to consider the processes which were at work in each case. Before committing ourselves to conclusions about whether or not variants of a particular path are being followed, or are likely to be followed, we need to be sure that what we have in mind is not a caricature. We need, further, to avoid the analytical closure involved in assuming that the few 'models' we have in mind exhaust the relevant possibilities.

This can only be pursued through some form of comparative economic history. Such was the impulse which drew me to comparative economic history; and not only to comparative economic history but to processes that worked themselves out over long stretches if time – i.e. to long-term economic development.

My own perspective, I suppose, might be suggested as 'European models: do they exist? And if they do, what are they?' The paths chosen for study suggested themselves easily enough. Analytical influence and possible relevance determined choice. Here were countries from whose apparent history influential models have been abstracted, or whose history seemed relevant. They are England, Prussia, France, North America, Japan, and (in the modern era) South Korea and Taiwan. It is from my preoccupation with these that my observations on the comparative method derive.

The English path has had great analytical impact among both Marxist and non-Marxist scholars. It was the first successful capitalist agrarian transition. It was the one treated with such power by Marx in *Capital*. It was in relation to it that the relevant analytical categories were first seriously deployed. It was looked at longingly by certain intellectuals in other countries, for example by the Physiocrats in eighteenth-century France. Their analysis of their own situation had a strong comparative element. An apparent reading of it underpinned one great agrarian intervention by the State in eighteenth and nineteenth century colonial India, which continues to have repercussions in South Asia. The English path has been, and continues to be, the subject of intense debate. Any treatment of agrarian transition must start with it. But what is the English path? That is not as clear as one might assume – nor as is commonly assumed. Much historical work has been done in recent years that demands that stereotyped views of the 'English path' need to be discarded. One of my aims, then, was to review that evidence and obtain a more nuanced view of the 'English path'.

The Prussian path was negotiated relatively early, and differed markedly from the English one. Unique in Easter Europe, by the late nineteenth century, it attracted the attention of Engels and Lenin, and figured prominently in Kautsky's classic text on the agrarian question, *Die Agrarfrage* (Kautsky, 1899, 1900, 1988). It is portrayed, justifiably, as a reactionary way of negotiating agrarian transition. It has been influential among those seeking to chart possible transitions in contemporary poor countries. Variants of the Prussian path are often said to be in motion in certain poor countries, although knowledge of what actually transpired in Prussia seems, at best, to be shadowy. Again, much new historical writing exists, which permits a far fuller view of the 'Prussian path'.

The American path is another early one: clearly visible by the end of the nineteenth century, although not necessarily predictable in the course it would follow. It is sometimes held out as a desirable model, as it was by Lenin for Russia: far more desirable, it is postulated, than any possible modern variation of the reactionary Prussian path. The 'initial conditions' obtaining in North America were very different from anything seen in a poor country today.

Nevertheless, the major characteristics of the North American path do need to be investigated. This path enters discourse on contemporary poor countries less frequently than does either the English or the Prussian path, but often enough to require examination. But what is the 'American path'? It turns out to have characteristics very different from those expected. These need to be identified and distilled within a comparative framework.

Both Marx and Engels displayed an interest in the realities of the French countryside, although not as part of an example of successful transition. On the contrary, it was what seemed to have failed to happen in France, rather than any transition that had obviously taken place, that attracted their attention. The French path has not been influential in the manner of the other paths already identified: that is analytically, prescriptively, and as a formal model taken to contemporary realities. It is, however, of considerable interest and has been the subject of scrupulous investigation by French historians; a rich body of secondary evidence now exists, to attract the comparativist. It may, in fact, have a significance for some contemporary poor countries that needs emphasis. First, however, it needs to be investigated in comparative terms.

The Japanese path was not one envisaged by Marx when he wrote *Capital*. It was the first case in Asia of thoroughgoing capitalist agrarian transition. It is, therefore, of very great interest. It is also frequently suggested, by orthodox development economists and by others, as a paradigm for Asian countries to follow. It is sometimes bracketed with the Prussian path, and may, indeed, be seen as reactionary in its characteristics. Its reactionary nature may not be in doubt, but it is, in fact, quite distinctive in its features. Its nature has been the subject of intensive investigation and powerful debate among Japanese scholars. That debate has long been available only in Japanese. Fortunately, some of it, at least, may now be seen in English. We may now be able to portray the 'Japanese path' far more accurately than previously.

More recently, in the post-1945 era, Japan has been joined by Taiwan and by South Korea as examples of successful Asian capitalist agrarian transition. Not only that, but these agrarian transitions were deeply marked by Japanese influence – especially by Japan's needs and action as a colonial power. The groundwork was laid, in a colonial setting, before 1945. These transitions, too, are held by some – especially by orthodox development economists – to contain important lessons for other poor countries. Whether such lessons can be so easily drawn must depend on what, precisely, the nature of the Taiwanese/South Korean path has been. That does not always seem to have been established clearly. It needs to be.

These, then, have been the objects of my investigation. Some preliminary results have been published (Byres, 1986, 1991). A detailed study is on the way to completion (Byres, forthcoming). I hope my account may have illustrated why a concern with the comparative method may have significance. What I shall now do – after what I hope has been a useful diversion – is return to the main thread of my argument with some observations on the two main approaches to comparison, variants of those approaches, and possible difficulties and weaknesses associated with them.

5. DIFFERENT APPROACHES TO COMPARISON: THE VARIABLE-ORIENTED APPROACH, THE CASE-ORIENTED APPROACH, AND SOME VARIATIONS

I have cited two major exponents of the comparative method – Chenery and Syrquin, on the one hand, and Barrington Moore, on the other – and have indicated that they represent very different approaches to comparison. We may identify the broad nature of the difference and distinguish some variations of approach, before turning, in the next section, to a critical view.

Chenery and Syrquin (Chenery and Syrquin, 1995, p. 3) follow, avowedly, in the tradition of Colin Clark's pioneering *Conditions of Economic Progress* (Clark, 1940) and Simon Kuznets' remarkable 'Quantitative Aspects of the Economic Growth of Nations' (Kuznets, 1956–67, 1966). With structural change as their central concern, they practise a particular, and well-developed, form of comparative analysis: that based upon cross-national data sets, using econometric analysis in order to test, for a large number of countries (in their case 101 countries), various hypotheses and to establish certain generalisations rigorously. This has been identified (although not with respect to Chenery and Syrquin) as the variable-oriented approach (Ragin, 1987, p. ix and *passim*). It is commonly practised in the social sciences, being part of 'the trend in mainstream social science towards the application of ever more sophisticated multivariate [statistical] techniques to all types of social data' (Ragin, 1987, p. viii). That it can be powerful and illuminating is clear. That it has possible shortcomings is equally clear, as we shall see.

Barrington Moore employs a very different approach to comparison. It proceeds via a limited series of carefully conducted case studies (in his case six),[4] pursued in depth: each one taken separately, and then with the comparison carefully made on a basis of the case studies. This has been termed the case-oriented approach (Ragin, 1987, p. ix and *passim*). There are now several notable instances of it. One notes, in different traditions but using the case-study approach in broadly similar fashion, for example, Eric Wolf's *Peasant Wars of the Twentieth Century* (Wolf, 1969 – six case-studies);[5] Perry Anderson's outstanding *Lineages of the Absolutist State* (Anderson, 1974b – 10 cases);[6] Theda Skocpol's *States and Social Revolutions* (Skocpol, 1979 – three cases);[7] Clive Trebilcock's *The Industrialization of the Continental Powers, 1780–1814* (Trebilcock, 1981 – three separate cases and three taken together);[8] and Colin Mooers's *The Making of Bourgeois Europe* (Mooers, 1991 – three cases).[9] Again, the analytical power that can be deployed in such an approach and the immense insight that it can bring are obvious. It does, however, have certain possible weaknesses, which need to be identified.

There are recognisable variants of these two approaches which do not, however, precisely follow the lines suggested. We may briefly note some of them, without attempting to be exhaustive.

We may take, for example, Michael Lipton's *Why Poor People Stay Poor* (Lipton, 1977), in which his thesis of 'urban bias' is expounded. This, one might say, is a non-rigorous variant of the variable-oriented approach. Here, a particular argument is expounded, and the evidence from a large number of countries is trawled in order to support it (see Byres, 1979, pp. 217–18). But there is no systematic use of a cross-national data set.

Robert Brenner's immensely stimulating writing on agrarian class structure and economic development in pre-industrial Europe is an important illustration of the comparative method (Brenner, 1976, 1977, 1978, 1982, 1989). This is, surely, a powerful example of comparative history, which is case oriented. But it differs from the examples of the case-oriented approach already cited. As with Lipton (if we make that comparison), a particular argument is made and runs through the whole presentation. Here, however, Brenner does not seek to bolster the argument by citing evidence from as large a number of countries as possible but neither does he present discrete and separate case-studies to provide the basis for an eventual set of conclusions and generalisations. Rather, the argument is presented at some length and then illustrated by a reading of the evidence of a limited number of cases, back-to-back, so to speak: now England, now France, now Germany; or now Eastern Europe and now Western Europe; and so on.

E.L. Jones, in two works of comparative history that have attracted much attention, is different again (Jones, 1981, 1988). He develops a wide-ranging argument, drawing examples from a bewildering variety of times and places, and now and then focusing on a case-study that catches his attention.[10] Jones is neither systematic nor rigorous.

Then, there is what one might term the 'running comparison': a straight comparison from start to finish. Patrick O'Brien and Caglar Keyder's *Economic Growth in Britain and France, 1780–1914* (O'Brien and Keyder, 1978), is such a comparison. Two cases are chosen and they are compared, as far as possible, indicator by indicator, before conclusions are drawn. The study by Byres and Nolan, *Inequality: China and India Compared, 1950–1970* (Byres and Nolan, 1976) is a further example of such a comparison.

Attempts have been made to combine the two methods (as pointed out by Ragin (Ragin, 1987, pp. xiii–xiv and 69–84)). These (Paige, 1975; Stephens, 1979; Shorter and Tilly, 1974), however, have not been especially successful as examples of a combined approach. To the extent that they have had strengths, they have been those of one or other of the two broad approaches: 'each tends to be dominated by one [research] strategy' (Ragin, 1987, p. xiv). A 'more synthetic approach to comparative research' (Ragin, 1978, p. xiv) has not emerged in any decisive or useful sense.

No doubt other variants might be identified. Space forbids such an exercise. We may now turn to further aspects and possible weaknesses of the comparative approach, in its different manifestations.

6. FURTHER ASPECTS AND POSSIBLE WEAKNESSES OF VARIANTS OF THE COMPARATIVE APPROACH: (A) THE VARIABLE-ORIENTED APPROACH

If we start with the variable-oriented approach, we note, firstly that, by its very nature, it abstracts from complexity and diversity in its search for the general. Its strengths are many,[11] but if one's aim is to capture complexity, historical contingency and substantive diversity, then it has clear deficiencies. It cuts a swathe through complexity, abhors historical contingency and discounts diversity. It seeks the general at the expense of the particular and the specific. It would be of very limited use in addressing the issues relating to the agrarian question and agrarian transition which I discuss in Section 4. Only a case-oriented strategy could possibly begin to do that.

Secondly, it is prey to an absence of data and to the problem of data of uneven quality. If a full data set does not exist, or if only data of very uneven quality are available, then it cannot proceed properly. At the very simplest level: 'A seemingly large set of more than one hundred nation-states can be reduced by half if there are problems with missing data. Often the remaining cases are not representative of the original hundred-plus nation states' (Ragin, 1987, p. 10). This is true of the historical record of the advanced capitalist countries and it is true, also, of contemporary developing countries. If, in these circumstances, the method *is* deployed it will yield results of very limited value; or, worse, results which may be positively misleading. This is an obvious point, but an important one which is not always recognised as fully as it should be.

Thirdly, if it is to be practised, it needs to be comprehensive, systematic and rigorous. The Lipton version of the variable-oriented approach has clear deficiencies. It is not done sufficiently systematically or rigorously: partly, but not wholly, because of the data problem just noted. The argument, therefore, cannot be sustained.[12] The moral seems to be obvious. The argument would have gained immeasurably, had it been supported either by a properly rigorous variable-oriented approach, or, failing that (perhaps because of the data problem), as I argued when I reviewed the book, 'had [it . . . proceeded] . . . on the basis of a few properly chosen case-studies placed within a careful comparative framework, along the lines, let us say, of Barrington-Moore's famous work' (Byres, 1979, p. 217). A full-blooded rendering of one or the other was called for. The Lipton variant does not commend itself as a desirable example of the comparative approach.

7. FURTHER ASPECTS AND POSSIBLE WEAKNESSES OF VARIANTS OF THE COMPARATIVE APPROACH: (B) THE CASE-ORIENTED APPROACH

The case-oriented comparative approach has its own problems. We may best identify these by considering one important area of comparative work: comparative history. The difficulties that emerge are, however, likely to be general: to be inherent in the case-oriented approach.

One such problem relates to the reservations, suspicion, or hostility that comparative history frequently encounters among those working historians who are not themselves comparativists. Such historians may spend their lives working on a particular country, or region, over a narrow range of time. They may blink in surprise at the efforts of comparative historians. Thoroughly familiar with their sources and with the literature relating to their period, they may resent efforts to make what may seem to them to be sweeping generalisations (although, from the viewpoint of the variable-oriented approach, they may be far from that).

As Eric Hobsbawm observed in his review of Anderson's two volumes (Anderson, 1974a, 1974b), professional historians are 'increasingly shackled by the double fetters of primary research and specialised knowledge. Like animals outside their own territory, historians feel neither confident nor secure once they leave the shelter of "my period"' (Hobsbawm, 1975, p. 177). These feelings will, of course, be aroused by the comparativist; and they may translate into hostility when the comparative historian gets on to their individual territory, even if there is recognition of the possible value of comparative history outside of that territory. But they do reflect a genuine predicament for the comparativist.

I recall, in the 1960s, when Barrington Moore's book was being reviewed, the observation on more than one occasion that it was a remarkable piece of work, displaying immense historical and sociological imagination and so on, except that it got country *x* wrong (country *x* being the country on which the reviewer was a specialist). We do have a real problem here.

The problem relates, in part, to the kind of evidence used by the comparative historian, and whether it is representative; how, from a perhaps vast sea of evidence, the comparative historian chooses; what the comparative historian does with counter-evidence. Given an inevitable need to be selective, I wonder what working principles exist or might be established for comparative historians in this respect?

I have mentioned Brenner. One notes Heide Wunder's waspish and dismissive comment on Brenner, and on comparative historians in general: 'It is the lot of the comparative historian to have to rely on textbooks and secondary literature, but unfortunately Brenner has fallen victim to the Prussian myth (*Hohenzollernlegende*) with all its contradictions and inconsistencies' (Wunder, 1985, p. 91). I think that this may be unfair on Brenner. But how, then, does the comparative historian cope with this problem? To which particular textbooks and secondary literature does he or she resort?

It is a problem which demands immense vigilance on the part of the comparativist. It also required certain qualities. The comparativist, having displayed, perhaps, the necessary 'foolhardiness' in confronting large themes, as Hobsbawm has it, requires 'an enormous appetite for reading' and a 'notable capacity for synthesis' (Hobsbawm, 1975, pp. 177 and 178). The comparativist, then, may be doubly foolhardy in not only addressing large themes but in risking judgement according to such standards.

8. A COMPARATIVE APPROACH INVOLVING BOTH THE EXPERIENCE OF ADVANCED CAPITALIST COUNTRIES AND CONTEMPORARY POOR COUNTRIES CAN BE MUTUALLY ENLIGHTENING

Finally, I have long felt that a consciously pursued comparative approach, involving both the experience of advanced capitalist countries and contemporary poor countries, can be mutually enlightening. It can and should, I think, be a genuinely two-way process. This I cannot pursue in detail. But it is a matter of some significance.

The usual Eurocentric assumption – made quite blithely, I hasten to add, in poor countries themselves – is that we derive insight about processes of development from the European/North American and Japanese experiences. Perhaps we do, if we proceed with care. Equally, however, economic historians of Europe – certainly of Britain – may be led to ask new questions, or pursue new lines of enquiry, through an awareness of the rich body of work done in, and in relation to, contemporary poor countries.

Let me give some examples, which seem to me to be striking, and which suggest questions that need to be addressed in European history. As it happens, much of the relevant literature relates to India.

The first relates to sharecropping: its persistence, its rationale, its apparent absence in Britain, and so on.[13] European work on sharecropping would gain immensely from a familiarity with the relevant work. Secondly, a close reading of the literature on the inverse relationship between output per acre and size of holding, and its seeming breakdown with the advent of 'new technology' would be of great benefit. Thirdly, an awareness of the rich literature on the inter-sectoral terms of trade, and the relationship of movements therein to the process of industrialisation, might be very revealing. We started with Ashok Mitra. Let us finish with the observation that Ashok Mitra's excellent book on the inter-sectoral terms of trade (Mitra, 1977a) is likely to be especially enlightening for those European historians who might wish to do serious work on this most neglected problem in European economic history.

NOTES

I am grateful to an anonymous referee for comments which led to the insertion in the text, at various points, of some cautionary remarks. If I have avoided some of the more difficult and, indeed, more interesting issues raised by comparative analysis, and if I have been less critical than I might have been, this was intentional in what is a modest, exploratory essay. I can only promise to address some of these issues in a future treatment.

1. This is displayed, for example, in his paper on agricultural taxation (Mitra, 1963) and in his *Terms of Trade and Class Relations* (Mitra, 1977a). It is obvious in his *Calcutta Diary,* which has appeared regularly in the *Economic and Political Weekly* since 1972. For a selection of the early contributions see (Mitra, 1977b).
2. O'Brien and Keyder, authors of an interesting study in comparative history, draw attention to Tom Kemp's 'extensive writings on French economic history', in which 'although Kemp is not engaged in comparative history, there is no doubt that his judgements on the performance of the French economy over the nineteenth century are permeated by implied references to British standards' (O'Brien and Keyder, 1978, p. 17). Many other such examples might be adduced. O'Brien and Keyder, in fact, go on to argue, on a basis of the evidence which they muster, that Kemp is quite wrong in his implied judgement that French performance in the nineteenth century was significantly inferior to British.
3. While Barrington Moore's book is clearly a classic, and a work of some power, it is not without a serious blemish. Thus, for example, the ignoring of colonialism and imperialism, in a work on the early industrialisers in Europe, and, of course on Japan, and on an ex-colony and a former semi-colony, like India and China, represents a significant shortcoming. But this, we must stress, is not a defect of the comparative method *per se*. It is, rather, a weakness in the manner of its pursuit.
4. His cases are England, France, America, China, Japan and India.
5. Wolf's six case studies are: Mexico, Russia, China, Vietnam, Algeria and Cuba.
6. The ten cases are: Spain, France, England, Italy, Sweden, Prussia, Poland, Austria, Russia and the House of Islam (i.e. the Ottoman Empire).
7. Here, France, Russia and China are examined in depth.
8. The three separate cases are Germany, France and Russia; and the three together, Italy, Austria-Hungary and Spain.
9. Mooers investigates France, Germany and England.
10. In his first book, *The European Miracle* (Jones, 1981), the Ottoman Empire, India and China are examined; and in the second, *Growth Recurring* (Jones, 1988), Japan.
11. These strengths are identified and discussed in (Ragin, 198, pp. 53–68). They are obvious enough. I will not repeat them here.
12. This I argue in detail in Byres (1979).
13. On aspects of this see Byres (1983).

REFERENCES

Anderson, Perry, 1974a, *Passages From Antiquity to Feudalism,* London: New Left Books.
Anderson, Perry, 1974b, *Lineages of the Absolutist State,* London: New Left Books.
Brenner, Robert, 1976, 'Agrarian Class Structure and Economic Development in Pre-Industrial Europe', *Past and Present,* February, no. 70. Reprinted T.H. Aston and C.H.E. Philpin, eds, 1985, *The Brenner Debate. Agrarian Class Structure and Economic Development in Pre-Industrial Europe,* Cambridge: Cambridge University Press.
Brenner, Robert, 1977, 'The Origins of Capitalist Development: A Critique of Neo-Smithian Marxism', *New Left Review,* July–August, no. 104.
Brenner, Robert, 1978, 'Dobb on the Transition from Feudalism to Capitalism', *Cambridge Journal of Economics, 2.*
Brenner, Robert, 1982, 'The Agrarian Roots of European Capitalism', *Past and Present,*

November, no. 97. Reprinted in T.H. Aston and C.H.E. Philpin, eds, 1985, *The Brenner Debate. Agrarian Class Structure and Economic Development in Pre-Industrial Europe*, Cambridge: Cambridge University Press.

Brenner, Robert, 1989, 'Economic Backwardness in Eastern Europe in Light of Developments in the West', in Daniel Chirot, ed., 1989, *The Origins of Backwardness in Eastern Europe: Economics and Politics from the Middle Ages until the Early Twentieth Century*, Berkeley: University of California Press.

Byres, T.J., 1979, 'Of Neo-Populist Pipe-Dreams: Daedalus in the Third World and the Myth of Urban Bias', *Journal of Peasant Studies*, January, vol. 6, no. 2.

Byres, T.J., 1983, 'Historical Perspectives on Sharecropping', in T.J. Byres, ed., *Sharecropping and Sharecroppers*, London: Frank Cass. Originally published as special issue of *Journal of Peasant Studies*, vol. 10, nos 2 and 3, January/April.

Byres, T.J., 1986, 'The Agrarian Question, Forms of Capitalist Agrarian Transition and the State: An Essay with Reference to Asia', *Social Scientist*, November–December, nos 162–3.

Byres, T.J., 1991, 'The Agrarian Question and Differing Forms of Capitalist Agrarian Transition: An Essay with Reference to Asia', in Jan Breman and Sudipto Mundle, eds, *Rural Transformation in Asia*, Delhi: Oxford University Press.

Byres, T.J., forthcoming, *Paths of Agrarian Transition: The Diversity of Capitalist Resolution of the Agrarian Question*.

Byres, T.J. and Peter Nolan, 1976, *Inequality: India and China Compared, 1950–70*, Milton Keynes: The Open University Press.

Chenery, Hollis and Moises Syrquin, 1975, *Patterns of Development, 1950–1970*, Oxford: Oxford University Press for the World Bank.

Fine, Ben, 1993, 'Towards a Political Economy of Food', typescript, Department of Economics, School of Oriental and African Studies, University of London.

Hobsbawm, Eric, 1975, 'From Babylon to Manchester', review (of Anderson, 1974a and 1974b), *New Statesman*, 7 February.

Jones, E.L., 1981, *The European Miracle. Environments, Economies, and Geopolitics in the History of Europe and Asia*, Cambridge: Cambridge University Press.

Jones, E.L., 1988, *Growth Recurring. Economic Change in World History*, Oxford: Clarendon Press.

Kautsky, Karl, 1899, *Die Agrarfrage. Eine Uebersich uber die Tendenzen der modernen Landwirtschaft un die Agrarpolit u.s.w.*, Stuttgart: Dietz.

Kautsky, Karl 1900, *La Question Agraire. Étude Sur Les Tendance de L'Agriculture Moderne*, Paris: V. Giard and E. Briere. Republished by Maspero in facsimile, Paris, 1970.

Kautsky, Karl, 1988, *The Agrarian Question*, first English translation by Pete Burgess, 2 volumes, London: Zwan Publications. First published in 1899 in German.

Kuznets, Simon, 1956–1967, 'Quantitative Aspects of the Economic Growth of Nations, I–X', *Economic Development and Cultural Change*, vols V (1956, no. 1, October, and 1957, no. 4, Supplement, July); VI (1958, no. 4, Part II, July); VII (1959, no. 3, Part II, April); VIII (1960, no. 4, Part II, July); IX (1961, no. 4, Part II, July); X (1962, no. 2, Part II, January), XI (1963, no. 2, Part II, January); XIII (1964, no. 1, Part II, October); XV (1967, no. 2, Part II, January).

Kuznets, Simon, 1966, *Modern Economic Growth. Rate, Structure and Spread*, New Haven and London: Yale University Press.

Lipton, Michael, 1977, *Why Poor People Stay Poor. A Study of Urban Bias in World Development*, London: Temple Smith.

Mitra, Ashok, 1963, 'Tax Burden for Indian Agriculture', in Ralph Braibanti and Joseph J. Spengler, eds, *Administration and Economic Development in India*, Durham, NC and London: Duke University Press and Cambridge University Press.

Mitra, Ashok, 1977a, *Terms of Trade and Class Relations*, London: Frank Cass.

Mitra, Ashok, 1977b, *Calcutta Diary*, London: Frank Cass.

Mooers, Colin, 1991, *The Making of Bourgeois Europe. Absolutism, Revolution, and the Rise of Capitalism in England, France and Germany*, London: Verso, New Left Books.

Moore Jr., Barrington, 1967, *Social Origins of Dictatorship and Democracy. Lord and Peasant in the Making of the Modern World*, London: Allen Lane, The Penguin Press.

O'Brien, Patrick and Caglar, Keyder, 1978, *Economic Growth in Britain and France 1780–1914. Two Paths to the Twentieth Century*, London: Allen & Unwin.

Paige, Jeffrey, 1975, *Agrarian Revolution. Social Movements and Export Agriculture in the Underdeveloped World,* New York: Free Press.

Ragin, Charles C., 1987, *The Comparative Method. Moving Beyond Qualitative and Quantitative Strategies,* Berkeley and London: University of California Press.

Shorter, Edward and Charles Tilly, 1974, *Strikes in France, 1830–1968,* Cambridge: Cambridge University Press.

Skocpol, Theda, 1979, *States and Social Revolutions. A Comparative Analysis of France, Russia and China,* Cambridge: Cambridge University Press.

Stephens, John, 1979, *The Transition from Capitalism to Socialism,* London: Macmillan.

Trebilcock, Clive, 1981, *The Industrialization of the Continental Powers, 1780–1814,* London and New York: Longman.

Wolf, Eric R., 1969, *Peasant Wars of the Twentieth Century,* New York, Evanston and London: Harper & Row.

Wunder, Heide, 1985, 'Peasant Organization and Class Conflict in Eastern and Western Germany', in T.H. Aston and C.H.E. Philpin, eds, *The Brenner Debate. Agrarian Class Structure and Economic Development in Pre-Industrial Europe,* Cambridge: Cambridge University Press.

14

Alternative Strategies of Agrarian Change in Relation to Resources for Development in India and China

Utsa Patnaik

A comparative study of Indian and Chinese development strategies and achievements is of obvious interest to all those who are concerned about Third World development problems. India and China achieved effective political independence from imperialism and started planned economic growth at about the same time, though under very different socio-political systems. Both were poor, populous, with long traditions of artisan skills but little modern industry, still primarily rural and agrarian in terms of employment, and both were characterised by a high degree of concentration of land ownership deriving from a long history of pre-capitalist landed property. Important differences and dissimilarities lay in the social structure (the absence of caste in China and greater ethnic-linguistic cohesiveness than in India), and in the more profound impact of two centuries of direct colonisation in India compared to a century of semi-colonial status in China. Nevertheless, there seem to be enough similarities in the initial conditions, despite all the differences, to make a meaningful comparison of the two countries' strategies of development. The relative performance of the two economies could in turn be interpreted as a test of the efficacy of the vastly differing strategies followed in the two countries with regard to economic growth and distributive egalitarianism.

The purpose of this paper is to argue that a major element of the difference in development strategy in the two countries, lay in the treatment of the agrarian sector and in the contribution of that sector to resources for investment and development. The topics of 'land reforms' and 'rural institutional change' do not usually figure in development economics and, when they do, they are treated simply as desirable, but not essential, facilitating factors in the transition to a modern industrialised economy. A study of the Chinese and Indian development experiences in the last half a century suggest to us, however, that the specific context of agrarian labour surplus imparts an immense importance to these factors – land reforms and institutional change – which is still insufficiently appreciated at the theoretical level. We would go so far as to argue that the higher rate of capital formation in China compared to India, the consequent higher rate of growth of the domestic economy, the better performance on social welfare indicators and the more recent higher rate of growth of participation in the world economy, are all closely related to the initial basic measures of land reforms and comprehensive agrarian institutional change put in place by the early sixties. These measures certainly created the conditions for an expansion of the mass internal market for manufactured goods, of great importance in the post-War, post-colonial world for large economies trying to break free from colonial patterns of export specialisation and exchange. But we would argue that these measures did much more than that: they were innovative in that they widened the internal social base of investment immensely by breaking away from the reliance on a well-to-do minority of the rural population to serve as agents of investment, and drawing, instead, the entire population into the process of capital formation, both through the direct contribution of labour and through the pooling of resources. It is with respect to the narrowness of the social base of investment that the Indian experience appears to us to be crucially different from the Chinese one.

It might be argued that there exists an alternative pattern of growth in which there are no radical redistributive land reforms widening the internal market, but exports serve to stimulate internal demand and hasten the accumulation process, as with silk exports in post-Meiji Japan, and textiles exports in South Korea and Japan in the 1960s. These cases, however, are not really germane to the problems and potential of the large labour-surplus economies which we are considering. Post-Meiji exports in the 1870s and 1880s benefited from a unique conjuncture hardly likely ever to be repeated: the outbreak of silkworm disease in Europe and at the same time the shifting of a number of European countries away from the silver standard to gold, leading to a sharply depreciating price of silver which greatly improved the competitiveness of countries like Japan; while in the post-Second World War world only those countries (South Korea, Japan) which were politically and militarily allied with the USA in its bid to 'contain communism' could ride on huge US military and related expenditures in the Korean War and later the Vietnam War, and be given access to capitalist markets. Countries like China and India were automatically excluded, and by their own historical choice, from the dubious largesse accorded to client states. For these countries the model of 'export-led growth' and inflow of foreign funds as an initial strategy was an irrelevant one; a substantial internal investment effort was the only alternative. The question in labour surplus economies was what form this investment could take.

In order to pursue this argument it is necessary to develop a framework of concepts, including some which are already familiar and others which, while familiar, have not been formalised so far. In the first two sections we briefly develop the analytical framework which we believe is not only useful but indispensable for the project of understanding the different development strategies in the two countries. The next section looks at the tentative results of applying this framework to the question of mobilising resources for development. This section is, however, more in the nature of suggesting an agenda for future work rather than a set of finished conclusions.

ACTUAL AND POTENTIAL ECONOMIC SURPLUS AND THE PROBLEM OF MOBILISATION IN THE COURSE OF DEVELOPMENT

The special characteristic feature of populous, labour surplus economies which has been long recognised is that while there may be little explicit open unemployment, there is pervasive underemployment of labour amongst petty producers in the tertiary and agricultural sectors in particular. The idea that surplus labour could be mobilised for capital formation at little extra cost was discussed at great length in the literature on development economics in the 1960s and 1970s (Nurkse, Rao, Dobb, Sen, Schultz, Viner, Kumar and others) and a number of empirical estimates of the extent of surplus labour were also attempted (for India, see Rudra, Majumdar, Mehra *et al.*). There were certain conceptual limitations to that discussion, however, in that the logical implications of the successful mobilisation of surplus labour – implications with regard to the necessary institutional changes – were not discussed explicitly. No policy measures for large-scale mobilisation were ever seriously contemplated in India despite the intensity of the theoretical discussions. In China, on the other hand, while the theoretical discussion which may have taken place is not available to us, the basic principles of the surplus labour question appear to have been clearly grasped by the policy makers. The entire strategy of institutional change in the agrarian sector appears to have been highly conducive to the effective mobilisation of surplus labour for near-costless capital formation and to have helped both in the self-financing of a higher rate of rural investment and in providing a good part of the initial resources for building up rural industry.

Surplus labour arising from underemployment may be regarded as constituting a *potential economic surplus* which is 'potential' because it cannot be used straight away without certain necessary changes in the way production is organised, and which nevertheless does constitute 'surplus' in the economic sense because its very existence does embody the possibility of producing more than the existing output level without raising the consumption bill much. This potential surplus inherent in underemployment is quite different from Paul Baran's idea of 'potential surplus' in an advanced capitalist economy (Baran, 1957). We find it difficult to think of a different term which would capture the essence of the surplus potentially inherent in underemployment, hence we retain the term 'potential surplus' despite its prior use with a different meaning. It has to be distinguished from what might be termed the *actual economic surplus,* which is already being produced as part of the given level of output over a given time period in the economy concerned, and which, from the income side of national income accounting, constitutes the sum of all property incomes (profit, rent, trading commission and interest). Let us first consider the question of the economic surplus actually produced and its forms from the point of view of resources for development.

It is particularly important to be clear about the distinction between actual economic surplus already being produced and what we have termed the 'potential economic surplus' which is inherent in the underemployment of labour, giving rise to the existence of 'surplus labour', because of the possibility of conceptual and terminological confusion. The actual economic surplus, part of the actually produced output, itself embodies 'surplus labour' in the sense of labour over and above that required for producing the necessary consumption of the workers. However this surplus labour which is embodied as part of the existing level of output already being produced, and which is equal to the sum of property incomes, is clearly conceptually quite different from that 'surplus labour' which is inherent in the existence of underemployment. The latter arises from the difference between the work that can potentially be performed by the worker if suitable opportunities for work were available, and the work actually being performed. It is only a potential and not an actual source of economic surplus since, at any given point of time within the existing organisation of production it is not actually being used for production, nor is its large-scale mobilisation for production an automatic part of the normal functioning of the economy. (The Lewis model on economic growth with unlimited supplies of labour indeed implicitly assumes that the normal functioning of the labour market would automatically draw underemployed labour into more productive employment at a constant real wage, but apart from that segment of the underemployed which is landless and mobile, we would argue this is not in fact a realistic assumption to make for reasons we will discuss below.)

The Actual Economic Surplus

The definition of the actual economic surplus generated in the agricultural sector at the macro-economic level may be set out as follows:

$$S = Y - V$$

Where $\qquad Y = Q\,(1 - k)$
and $\qquad V = Wc + Uc$

Q is the gross value of agricultural output, k is the proportion of output going as all material costs and amortisation, hence Y is net value added. V is the consumption of hired labour and dependants Wc plus the subsistence consumption of self-employed producers Uc, so that actual economic surplus S from agriculture is value-added Y less consumption of all agriculture-dependent workers and their dependants V, whether they are wage-paid or own-account workers. (Another possible definition of surplus would be on the basis of a minimum consumption norm for workers and dependants, such as is used for poverty estimates, rather than actual consumption. This would give a smaller estimate of surplus if there were a high proportion of the population at below minimum nutritional levels.)

From the incomes side, the net value added in agriculture Y is disbursed as the wage bill of hired workers W, the retained income (after payment of rent, interest, and so forth) of the wholly family-labour based, self-employed cultivators U, and the sum of property incomes profit P, rent R and interest I, as follows:

$$Y = (U + W) + (P + R + I)$$

If we assume that all wages are consumed and that the retained income of the self-employed is identical with their subsistence consumption, then $(U + W) = V$ and $(P + R + I) = S$.

For most purposes this simplification is admissible, since savings of labouring households and wholly self-employed rural households are generally negligible and positive savings of the better-off among them are offset by negative savings of the others.

Many of the discussions of development have centred, in one way or another, on the problem of redirecting the existing, or actual economic surplus into investment of a productive and socially useful kind so as to raise the rate of productive investment out of national income substantially. To the extent that a large fraction of the actual economic surplus is currently not productively invested, there is evidently scope for raising the rate of productive investment without squeezing consumption too much.

What do we mean by productive investment here? Typically, at the start of the development process, the composition of the actual economic surplus is not conducive to a high rate of investment of the modern type. The major part of the actual economic surplus out of the given level of national income accrues as (a) land rent, (b) usury interest, or (c) commercial profits, and only a minor part accrues as (d) profits of capitalist agricultural enterprise, and manufacturing and industrial profit, which may be expected to be ploughed back into expanding material production. This is but another way of saying that the underdeveloped economy in general, and its agrarian sector in particular, is dominated by landlords, moneylenders and traders. Their surpluses are invested 'productively' from their respective individual points of view, since they obtain a return by way of rent, interest and trading profits; but their surpluses are not necessarily invested 'productively' from the social point of view, since such investment does not usually add to output flows. (Traditional money lenders generally finance consumption or productive inputs required only for maintaining current output levels; rentiers mainly consume their rents; traders by definition are seldom concerned with production expansion.) Such returns essentially represent the gains of one group of people who monopolise property in various forms, in the form of income transfer, sometimes at the expense even of dis-saving, from other groups of people who produce.

The productively invested part of economic surplus – namely manufacturing and industrial profit and capitalist profit in agriculture – is too small a fraction of the whole to sustain the higher rate of investment required for achieving target growth rates. The problem then, to begin with, is how to transform the socially unproductive forms of actual economic surplus into socially productive forms in such a manner as to widen the social base of investment to the maximum possible extent. The historical experience of dealing with this problem has differed markedly from country to country, but the broad conceptual distinction between the 'revolutionary' and the 'conservative' paths of transition remains a useful one. The former has been marked by an outright elimination, from the economic point of view, of the social classes appropriating surplus in unproductive forms and hence the elimination of these forms as economic categories, through a seizure without compensation and a radical egalitarian and free distribution to the peasantry, of the landed property so seized. The conservative path has been marked by a compromise with landlordism: their right to rent is recognised and the capitalised value of rent is paid as compensation for the acquisition of land rights from them; these rights are then redistributed to the peasants through a market mechanism – that is, by asking for a price per unit of area, which automatically limits the acquisition to a minor segment of the peasantry which is able to pay. Historically the bourgeois revolutions in Europe and, in particular, the French Revolution are thought of as representing the 'revolutionary' path since they resulted in confiscation and free distribution to the peasants, while the conservative path is classically the 'Prussian Junker path' in Europe. This conservative path is represented in Asia, arguably, by the Meiji land reform after 1868, which capitalised *daimyo* rents into interest-bearing bonds as compensation to the feudal lords while abolishing their tenures (Norman, 1975). In the present century the 'revolutionary path' is represented by the bourgeois democratic programme of free land redistribution after confiscation in Russia after the 1917 Bolshevik Revolution, and a similar process in China after 1949. The land reform in Japan after the Second World War, administered by the US occupation regime, was not the outcome of a domestic revolutionary movement but was extremely radical in content since it virtually expropriated all non-resident landlords, allowed resident landlords to retain only 1 *cho* (2.45 acres) and conferred ownership, at nominal prices for land, to the tenants.

The land reform strategies in modern India and China have differed very markedly, the radical path of abolition of feudal tenures without compensation being followed in China while a conservative path of abolition with compensation has been followed in India. Certain logical implications regarding the consequent degree of equity in land and resource control, the tax burden on the peasants and the ability to raise resources from agriculture, were inherent in these different strategies. Let us look at an estimate of the contribution of land reform to development finance in China (Lippit, 1974) for the period immediately after liberation, and consider the possible results of a similar exercise for India.

MOBILISATION THROUGH LAND REFORM, OF THE ACTUAL
ECONOMIC SURPLUS IN AGRICULTURE FOR DEVELOPMENT

The case of China

In an interesting pioneering study, Victor Lippit estimated the one-shot contribution of land reform to development finance in China during the early 1950s, although the estimation of the continuing contribution was not attempted. At the factual level let us note that land reform in the initial phase consisted of the identification of the class affiliation of rural cultivating households in terms of the overall guidelines laid down by the CPC and in particular by Mao Tse-tung for defining the landlord, the rich peasant, the middle peasant, the poor peasant and the labourer. This identification was carried out by the village-level committees which included peasants and CPC cadres. Invaluable insights into the actual process of identifying class affiliation is provided by the account in William Hinton's now classic *Fanshen*.

Lippit estimates the share of rent, profit, interest and (Kuomintang) taxation in the net output produced in agriculture in 1952. The share of rent and profit in agricultural value added is arrived at on the basis of data on the share of cultivated land under tenant and hired labour cultivation respectively, and an estimate of the value added per acre (which is assumed to be the same for both types of land). Rent and profit work out at 10.7 per cent and 3.4 per cent of agricultural net output. The share of interest on outstanding loans to net output is estimated at 2.8 per cent and the share of official taxation on peasant proprietors under the Kuomintang regime at 2.1 per cent of net output. (Landlord taxes are already included in their income.) At a conservative estimate, therefore, the share of all these property incomes and taxation combined was 19 per cent of net domestic product in agriculture in 1952 and amounted, in absolute terms, to 9.39 billion yuan at current prices. (This is likely to be a substantial underestimate as illegal taxation, exactions by local gentry and 'warlords', traders' commissions and interest payments in kind could not be included probably owing to the lack of data.) An alternative estimate which could also serve as a check on this estimate in terms of the broad order of magnitude could have been provided if the consumption bill of the agriculture-dependent population had been estimated and deducted from the value added to give the surplus, but this was not done, again presumably owing to the lack of reliable data on consumption. Expressing Lippit's figures in terms of our earlier notation and adding T for taxation,

$$S = (P + R + I + T) = 0.034\ Y + 0.107\ Y + 0.028\ Y + 0.032\ Y$$

$$= 9.39 \text{ bn. yuan at } 1952 \text{ prices.}$$

The Kuomintang was defeated at the end of the civil war in early 1949. The abolition of rent, interest and most profit was complete by 1953 as, under the agrarian reform, landlords, moneylenders and traders ceased to exist at all, and most rich peasants ceased to cultivate with hired labour as their control over land was reduced. Of the total cultivated area of 107.9 m. ha. it is estimated that about 44 per cent was redistributed through seizure without compensation and allotment by village committees without taking any payment, to the landless and the land-poor peasants. This is an extremely comprehensive and thoroughgoing order of redistribution, which despite some errors of classification and some abuses, meant the effective 'levelling' of the rural population and the securing of a highly egalitarian distribution of resources. Along with land, other durable assets both productive and consumable, were also redistributed (for a description see W. Hinton's *Fanshen*).

The surplus released partly went to raise the incomes of the beneficiaries of the reforms, and was partly mopped up through fiscal and relative pricing measures by the new government of the PRC. According to Lippit's estimate, a little less than half of the actual economic surplus released by the land reform went to augment peasant's incomes, while the State mopped up 1.16 bn. yuan or about one-eighth of the surplus through direct taxation. This tax income from agriculture amounted respectively to 8.0 per cent and 10.3 per cent of the total net and gross domestic investment in the economy in 1952.

More important than direct taxation, however, was the use of the terms of trade mechanism. Through an initial policy of maintaining high margins over cost for the essential manufactured goods, and hence keeping their prices high (on average about 25 per cent higher than would otherwise have prevailed) a substantial part of the remaining surplus, or about two-fifths, was mopped up. This was possible because, unlike agricultural production, manufacturing production was more immediately socialised and, by 1951, both state-owned and collectively owned enterprises were subject to administrative pricing of their products and taxation of their profits. We will return to the terms of trade question later. Suffice it to say here that maintaining higher prices for manufactured goods entering into rural consumption than would have prevailed without State administrative pricing led to a diversion of the agricultural surplus released by the land reform in the form of enhanced profits for the manufacturing enterprises which were then mobilised by (a) direct investment of a part of these additional profits in expanding these enterprises and (b) by the State taxing the enterprises. The 'terms-of-trade' avenue of mobilising the actual surplus in agriculture released by the land reform is estimated by Lippit to have contributed 26.7 per cent and 34.5 per cent gross and net domestic investment in 1952.

Thus the total contribution of land reform to development finance, adding up the contribution of direct taxation and the terms of trade contribution, came to an estimated 34.7 per cent of gross and 44.8 per cent of net capital formation in the economy in 1952. While the exact figures need not be taken as sacrosanct, they do indicate the broad order of magnitude involved, which is certainly very substantial. It appears to have been achieved, moreover, without any great sense of sacrifice or deprivation being imposed on the majority of the rural population which, on the contrary, gained materially from the land reform both in terms of assets and in terms of the higher incomes immediately obtained with the abolition of all rents, illegal warlord taxation and interest claims of usurers. A minority of the rural population consisting of the latter groups, who were expropriated, did of course suffer loss of assets and of incomes as they were reduced by and large from landlord and rich peasant status to middle peasant status. The terms of trade mechanism continued to be an important one for mopping up rural savings for the duration of the first three plans (1952–70).

This was quite consistent with the observed slow improvement which took place in the barter terms of trade with base 1952 in agriculture's favour, bearing in mind that after the ravages of the Depression and war, compared to base 1930–36 = 100 the index had moved sharply against agriculture and was only 60 in 1948, improving to 82.3 in 1952, and climbing back to 99.0 only as late as 1957. The improvement after 1952, when economic activity and urban absorption of wage-goods was rising fast, would certainly have been much faster without the deliberate overpricing of manufactured goods. By 1972 the net barter terms of trade, with base 100 in 1952, had improved to 149.06 or only by about half, which is a very slow rate of improvement over two decades (see Table 14.1). The initial rural–urban income disparity remained untouched even while household real earnings in both rural and urban areas were rising owing to improved employment.

More recent studies of resource transfer from agriculture to industry in various developing countries, including China (by Ishikawa, Sheng, Karshenas) all suffer from a common conceptual problem in defining positive real resource transfer from agriculture, primarily in terms of an 'export surplus on merchandise account' at constant prices, from agriculture to non-agriculture where the two sectors are thought of as trading with each other. 'Agriculture' as a sector in these studies does not include the non-crop production activities of the very same persons in peasant households who are working in crop production, while 'non-agriculture' does not include the crop-related activities of the rural artisan households. Thus no idea can be obtained of the 'burden on the peasants' imposed by industrialisation in such an activity-specific approach as opposed to a social-class specific approach.

Since it turns out that, in China, there was an 'import surplus' for agriculture activity (this, in fact, arose from the systematic over-valuation, owing to high administered prices as mentioned earlier, of agriculture's imports from the organised non-agricultural sector), 'financed' by non-agriculture incomes (generated mainly by the peasant households within the rural sector itself) these authors conclude that the net resource flow was into agriculture from non-agriculture. This may be technically correct given the activity-specific definitions adopted, in which 'agriculture' is not coterminous with 'rural', but it can be seriously misleading for the tendency is inevitably to slip from the activity concept to the 'agricultural sector as the source of industrial finance' concept, which is in fact a much broader one customarily interpreted as the 'burden on the peasants'.

Two facts are ignored in the activity-centred definitions of intersectoral flows: first, the fact that in centrally planned socialist economies prices have played a qualitatively different role from their role in private-enterprise market economies and have been used as a mechanism of both stabilising urban costs of living and extracting resources. If organised sector manufactured goods prices entering rural consumption are deliberately kept about 25 per cent higher as a matter of State policy (on Lippit's estimate) than they otherwise would have been, and the resulting larger surpluses of the relevant socially owned manufacturing enterprises are then taxed or directly reinvested, then this, by any sensible conception, does mean a resource transfer out of agriculture, not the other way around. We would thus differ from Ishikawa, Karshenas *et al.* and argue that a uniform interpretation of what constitutes 'resource transfer' for all countries, regardless of the crucial differences in the social nature of asset ownership, is a misconceived and misleading exercise.

The activity-centred approach to measuring inter-sectoral flows does not permit us to answer the question of to what extent particular social classes, such as those comprising the peasantry, helped to finance investment in the economy. This is the relevant question, and not much light is cast upon it by separating the agricultural and non-agricultural activities of the same economic agent and saying that the agricultural sector saw a net inflow from 'non-agriculture' when the latter in fact represents mainly the non-crop activities of the very same rural workers who are located in peasant households engaged in crop production.

The case of India

The conception of land reform in India, from the beginning, was a conservative and legalistic one in which certain types of tenures were sought to be abolished with compensation, with no reference to the economic status of the people concerned and, hence, with no reference to the effects on the agrarian classes. Thus *zamindari* tenure in its various forms was to go on payment of compensation, and it made no difference whether the person or family holding land under *zamindari* tenure held thousands of acres of land or only a fraction of an acre. Similarly tenants were conceived of as a blanket legal category, who would have the optional right of purchase of land taken over from *zamindars,* and it made no difference whether the tenant was a rich cultivator with a hundred acres, part of which was leased, or a very poor tenant with only one acre of fully leased land. Moreover those holding land under intermediary tenures did not have the whole of that land taken over but only that part which they did not claim as their 'own-cultivated' (*khud-kasht*) land.

The 'conservative' path of land reform followed in India was thus conservative with regard to several related aspects: in the payment of compensation to the *rentiers,* in ignoring economic status completely in favour of juridical status, in explicitly allowing large areas of land to be retained by the former *rentiers* (*zamindars, jagirdars* and other intermediaries) provided they claimed to cultivate with hired labour – with no mechanism for checking if they actually did – and, finally, in demanding cash payment from tenants for optional purchases of ownership of land vested with government. Moreover, all this was done through a long drawn-out and cumbersome legal process giving ample time for those who wished to retain large areas to do so through concealment, paper partitioning, and paper conversion of land to exempt categories like orchards, co-operatives, and so forth, while implementation of the laws was 'from above' by the district-level administration.

Other than in the few areas of the country where there had been militant peasant struggle (as in Telengana) there was no information system for the rural poor about the provisions of the laws which were utilised by the literate minority. In every respect there is a sharp contrast with Chinese land reform, which was explicitly based on the identification of economic class status, and which did not permit the concealment and retention of substantial areas by the landlords and rich peasants because implementation was decentralised to the village-level committee which was familiar with every detail of relative resource possession and which organised the direct seizure and redistribution of land, houses and durable goods on the basis of criteria worked out at meetings of the general body of the village within the broad overall guidelines of the Agrarian Reform Law.

The proportion of the total cultivated area in India which was redistributed, mainly through the legal mechanism (although there were some specific cases of landlord flight from the land, such as in Telengana) during the two decades following 1950, can be put roughly at about one-twelfth at a maximal estimate on the basis of the sample survey data on the distribution of owned and operated land by size-classes of holdings. A reverse process of widespread small tenant evictions also took place and partly counteracted the decline in the concentration of operated land. At the beginning of the land-reform process in India as a whole, the top 15 per cent of all households, ranked by area owned, had 70 per cent of the owned area while the bottom 60 per cent had six per cent of the total owned area. After 20 years the net decline in owned area with the top 15 per cent of all rural landowning households was about four per cent of the total area owned and the net decline for the next 25 per cent of households was 3.5 per cent of total area owned while the gain for the lowest 60 per cent of households was around 7.5 per cent. This is a very small order of redistribution of land, and the bulk of the gain in the last category was for the better-off cultivators who could afford to purchase land. During the process of land reform the smaller and weaker tenants suffered eviction and the proportion of hired labourers in the rural workforce rose substantially, a slight counteracting factor being provided by the free distribution of ceiling-surplus land to landless labour, without which the proportion would have risen even more. This figure of around one-twelfth of the total cultivated area undergoing redistribution contrasts sharply with the Chinese one of more than two-fifths.

If we were to carry out an exercise similar to that done by Lippit for China with regard to the contribution of Indian land reform to development finance, what would we be likely to find? The estimation procedure would be more difficult owing to the long drawn-out and evolving nature of the reforms, for one thing, and the outcome would be ambiguous owing to the fact that the actual extent of change in the share of the unproductive forms of surplus such as rent in the total surplus is not captured adequately by the data owing to doubts about the *de facto* extent of decline of land under tenancy and increase in cultivation with hired labour.

We may distinguish between the contribution of land reform to (a) increased private investment by the landlords turned capitalists, comprising investment both in agriculture and in the non-agricultural sector (in construction, agro-processing and other manufacturing and so forth) and (b) investment by the State out of resources obtained, if any, through taxation and terms of trade movements. As regards the first, the decline in the share of rent income in net value added, can serve as a proxy measure on the assumption that profit incomes are productively invested. According to the first National Income Committee's Report of 1951, land rent in kind plus seed comprised about 15 per cent of gross output in agriculture. Since the proportion of total operated area under recorded tenancy was just above 20 per cent according to the 8th round of the NSS on landholding, and the share of rent in gross output from tenanted land was one-half on average, it seems realistic to suggest that about 10 per cent of gross output was the rent bill on a minimum estimate (without taking account of unrecorded tenancy). The actual rent bill would have been higher; assuming under-reporting by around a quarter we may tentatively add another 2.5 per cent of gross output on this account. There is no specific estimate for interest and commercial profit but these, together with illegal tax exactions, are unlikely to have been less than another five per cent or so of gross output value. So from 15 to 17.5 per cent of gross output value comprised unproductive forms of surplus in agriculture. On the assumption that net output was about 55 to 60 per cent of gross output (as indicated by the NSS studies on the cost of material inputs for the major crops), the total unproductive surplus S(u) would correspond to between 25 to 29 per cent of net output:

$$S(u) = R + I = (0.10 \text{ to } 0.125) \, X + 0.05 \, X$$
$$\text{Assuming } Y = 0.60 \, X,$$
$$S(u) = (0.166 \text{ to } 0.208) \, Y + 0.083 \, Y$$
$$= (0.25 \text{ to } 0.29) \, Y$$

The steady decline in recorded area under tenancy, taken at face value, would imply a corresponding decline in the share of land rent in net output generated in agriculture. Taking the leased in area decline from over 20 per cent to about seven per cent of total operated area from the early 1950s to the late 1970s as a proxy for the corresponding increase in direct cultivation, one can say that land reforms contributed to raising the share of profit from the pre-existing level to about seven per cent to nine per cent of gross output value, corresponding to 11.7 to 15 per cent of net output value, over the duration of the two decades concerned. While land rent declined relatively, there is no evidence that the activities of rural moneylenders and traders altered in any significant way.

As regards (b), direct taxation, the second avenue of possible contribution to investment finance, the direct taxation of agriculture was actually considerably reduced in real terms after independence because the cash rates of land revenue remained unchanged despite the high rate of inflation in the Second World War and the period of the Korean war boom. Land revenue and other taxes (such as government canal irrigation levies) provided a steadily declining share of total tax revenues and formed a sharply declining share of value added in agriculture. Starting at nine per cent in 1950, by the 1960s land revenues contributed only two to three per cent of total tax revenues compared to 12–15 per cent in China. By the 1980s it had declined to less than one per cent of total tax revenues. The source of the revenue altered partly since a larger part of it now came from those tenants who had ceased to be tenants of the *zamindars* and now held land from government directly without right of transfer (such as the *sirdars* in Uttar Pradesh). The *zamindars* on the other hand became the new owners with rights of transfer over most of the land they had earlier held since they claimed it as their *khud-kasht*. The compensation paid to the *zamindars* for the minor part of the land they did give up had to come out of the revenues, so the net change in revenues available to the State should be obtained after deducting this compensation, estimated at 670 crore rupees in total (Report of the National Commission on Agriculture, 1976, p. 51), of which 360 crore rupees had been already paid out by 1975, and payment was continuing as ceiling laws were implemented.

The compensation of Rs.360 crores, disbursed mainly in the 1950s and 1960s, may not seem very high today but it has to be considered in relation to a total first plan outlay of Rs. 5000 crores, and against a background of falling prices until 1957–58 after the collapse from 1953 of the Korean War boom, which meant a rising real value to those compensated. Thus the Rs. 360 crores compensation to *zamindars* and other intermediaries, amounted to about 7.2 per cent of the total five-year plan outlay for the entire country and over four-fifths of the compensation accrued to only a minuscule proportion making up the landed rich who accounted for about 0.02 per cent of the country's population. (It is arguable that a really comprehensive land redistribution is only possible without compensation and through seizure, if one considers the burden on the exchequer, ultimately passed on to ordinary taxpayers, of a commitment to compensate for up to half of the cultivated area, assuming India had the same order of redistribution as China did. In short the commitment to compensate limits the feasible extent of redistribution severely.)

THE POTENTIAL ECONOMIC SURPLUS AND ITS MOBILISATION

The potential economic surplus is inherent in the existence of underemployment, the fact that workers in certain sectors in particular are not working full-time but only for part of the time they are capable of working. For those without any productive resources of their own, such as landless rural labourers and resourceless artisans, this may be because there is insufficient demand for their labour. For those who do have some land and resources, it may be because the land and resources are too little relative to the family size and working capacity, so that even with the most intensive possible use of the existing resources to maximise their income, they remain underemployed. (We are obviously using the term potential economic surplus in a different sense from the use by Paul Baran who, in the context of advanced capitalist countries like the USA, used it to denote that part of the actually produced economic surplus which was unproductive from a social point of view.)

The mobilisation of surplus labour for infrastructural investment was much discussed in India in the 1960s and 1970s following Rao and Nurkse's initial formulation of this possibility. The extent of surplus labour was empirically estimated, using methodology differing in detail but based on the same principle (the difference between work actually done and work capable of being done) by different authors for various areas, at below one-third to as high as two-fifths. The existence of a potential economic surplus is, however, a very different matter from its realisation in the sense of successful mobilisation. The latter depends very crucially on institutional change. The Indian and Chinese strategies of investment have differed radically in that, owing to the lack of an adequate degree of land redistribution and the absence of co-operation in production, India has not achieved an extensive process of the direct transformation of unutilised labour reserves into physical capital. China has depended heavily on precisely this avenue of investment, starting from the inception of co-operative production from the mid-1950s and consolidating it during the phase of people's communes from 1958–59 to the end of the 1970s, which broadly represents the expression of Maoist strategy in the rural sphere. Why land reform followed by small peasant co-operation is essential for a comprehensive mobilisation of surplus labour for capital formation will be explained below.

Let us consider a simple model of a population of underemployed cultivators in a village consisting of H identical households operating H holdings of identical size to produce a single good, staple grain. Each household has n working members, so the total workers in the community $N = nH$. Every worker puts in d hours of labour per week in cultivation and related tasks, but can work d* labour hours per week where $d^* > d$, if work is available. (We abstract from seasonality for the time being; d* is thus an average work norm as contrasted with the work actually being put in.) The total weekly hours of work being performed is dN and this, we assume, is necessary for maintaining the existing output level of X quintals of grain produced on a per week basis (that is, an annual output of 52.X qtls). In short, we assume that there is no inefficiency in the system. This implies that if the total labour input were to be lowered below dN per week then output would go down from the existing level of X qtls. grain.

The total required work input of dN days can be performed in principle by only dN/d* number of workers, rendering $N [1-(d/d^*)]$ workers superfluous, if each worker agrees to work up to the work norm of d* days. To take a numerical example, suppose that, in a village, the number of what are taken to be identical households and land holdings H is 30; that there are two workers per family of five members, giving $N = 60$ workers for the community; and that the current input of labour days per week per worker d is 4, so that the total actual labour input for producing the existing weekly output level of say 10 quintals of grain is $dN = 4 \times 60 = 240$ days. By assumption, this total number of days' labour input is necessary to produce 10 qtls. grain; in short there is no inefficiency. Suppose that the workers say that they are prepared to work six days a week if work is available, so that the norm d* is six days. Although the labour days actually worked per holding are 2×4 days $= 8$ days per week, the labour days capable of being worked are $2 \times 6 = 12$ days. The potential surplus is $(12-8) = 4$ days per holding, or half of the actual labour input. For the community as a whole, the total required labour-time input of $dN = 240$ days can potentially be performed by $dN/d^* = 240/6 = 40$ workers, each working harder by two days a week instead of the 60 workers engaged at present, making $[N-dN/d^*] = [60-40] = 20$ workers superfluous to agricultural production, thus releasing one-third of the work-force for other work. This one-third of the workers could potentially contribute $20 \times 6 = 120$ days or an additional half of the work currently being performed, for capital formation.

Parenthetically, it may be mentioned that the question of underemployment and surplus labour appears to have been conceptually misunderstood by authors like Schultz, Viner and others who thought that inefficient production was being discussed. They implicitly thought of a situation where more labour-time was being worked than was necessary for producing a given level of output, so that 'surplus labour' was constituted by the difference between the longer labour time actually worked and that required for producing the given output level. This would be the case, in terms of our numerical example, if we drop the explicit assumption we have made, that initial production is efficient and assume, instead, that the output level of X qtls. grain can be produced, say, with only 180 days as opposed to the 240 days actually being worked by the 60 workers, rendering 60 days of work unnecessary. In short, each worker is putting in one day which is quite unnecessary to production because it adds nothing to output – in other words, production is inefficient. Since this was the concept of 'surplus labour' they adopted, it is not surprising that Schultz, Viner and others emerged as strenuous opponents of the existence of labour surplus in this sense in underdeveloped countries. Schultz argued that traditional agriculture was efficient, and therefore no 'surplus labour' existed; while Viner argued that he could not conceive of a situation in practice where more work in terms of careful weeding, irrigating and watching crops, would not add to output. These arguments are germane to the question of efficiency, but they are not germane at all to the quite different concept of surplus labour arising, not from inefficiency, but from underemployment, the concept under discussion here. In this case the work time currently being put in cannot be cut down without affecting output; but nevertheless workers embodying additional work time can potentially be released if each worker works harder than before in an institutional structure which permits this.

We have been careful to talk about 'potential' additional work throughout because, without some form of pooling and co-operative production, actually mobilising the potential surplus in practice would prove to be virtually impossible. This is because, as long as atomistic petty production in separate smallholdings, as in our example, continues to prevail, the potential surplus always exists in terms of labour-time of so many days constituting fractions of person-years, while the workers are, of course, discrete and indivisible and cannot be 'withdrawn' in fractions! Thus in terms of our example above, if even a single worker is 'withdrawn' from a farm, that farm would experience labour shortage, since the required weekly input for maintaining current output is eight days but the worker remaining behind can only work for a maximum of six days, the norm.

The existing labour market cannot take care of the problem except under highly specific circumstances. Withdrawing workers from some holdings and compensating for the resulting shortfall in required work input on farm by hiring underemployed workers from other farms would involve a wage cost, for it is doubtful if workers would work free on others' farms in the prevailing environment of private atomistic operations, even if they are underemployed. Even supposing that workers could somehow be withdrawn, while they could in principle be fed out of food supplied by the remaining workers who now work harder to maintain output, unless the capital formation projects were located nearby a direct provisioning would not be feasible and, in practice, some form of taxation of the workers remaining in agriculture to finance the provision of food for workers withdrawn for project work would be necessary. But in such a case it would be unreasonable to expect that the remaining workers would not only work harder to maintain output but also submit to additional taxation from an outside authority which did not exist earlier.

While costless capital formation basically required a system of 'deferred wages' for project workers and peasants alike, that is, it required all workers to put in more labour days without this being immediately rewarded, it seemed very difficult to operate such a system. All these issues were discussed threadbare in the course of the debates on surplus labour in India, and the consensus was that 'everything else remaining the same', costless capital formation on any significant scale was not feasible despite the existence of labour surplus (what we have termed the 'potential surplus') amounting, on various estimates, to a quarter to a third of the existing workforce. It was pointed out by K.N. Raj in his (1960) study of the Bhakra Nangal project that over 60 per cent of the labour force required for a single big project had to be recruited from outside Punjab; at the same time a state-wise estimate for India showed that, in Punjab, surplus labour amounted to 18 per cent of the existing labour force (Mehra, 1966).

These problems were, in practice, resolved in China, we would argue, owing to the fact that 'everything else' did not remain the same and, following the egalitarian land reform, co-operative

242

Economics as Ideology and Experience

production was established at a fairly rapid pace. The pooling of the units of production meant in the first place that the contradiction between the existence of surplus labour in terms of labour time, and the requirement of mobilising it in terms of discrete workers, was resolved. Going back to the simple numerical example given earlier, it is evident that if the community of 30 households pool their land and equipment, and operate jointly, then the necessary labour input for maintaining existing output can be performed by 40 workers out of 60 on the new large joint area (with no problems of labour exchange or labour hiring as when individual small holdings are retained) with each worker working more days in regular existing tasks while the remaining workers 'released' by the former's fuller employment, focus on building up productive assets which, with a lag, raises the entire community's income or standard of life in real terms. Initially the extra work is 'unrewarded' and is performed in the expectation of a sharing of future higher incomes.

It is possible to implement such a system of more work without immediate additional payment, or what would be called a system of 'deferred wages' under capitalism, only with an egalitarian policy of providing for everyone's basic needs while they work harder, and in a structure of ownership which ensures that the assets created by the extra work belong by and large to the people putting in the extra work. It would be virtually impossible to motivate people to work harder than they are initially doing, no matter how underemployed they might be, unless the initial low incomes are equitably shared in order to ensure a subsistence for all, and unless the fruits of their extra work belong to them and benefit them in the long run. This is the economic and social essence of the egalitarian strategy. We would argue that the strategy in practice proved to be highly successful, after some initial operational problems, and that even though the arguments for egalitarianism were put forward in mainly political terms, there was the sound underlying economic rationale of raising the rate of productive investment through the direct transformation into capital, of the potential surplus inherent in surplus labour arising from underemployment. The explicit objectives of growth and equity were the same whether in India or in China; but the specific policies of achieving the objectives differed radically primarily on account of the retention of atomistic private production in a substantially unreformed agrarian structure in one case as contrasted with a radical redistributive land reform followed by pooling of the investment effort in the other.

A successful mobilisation on a small scale could take place with pooling even in the primary level co-operatives comprising 20–40 households (formed from 1952 onwards out of the mutual aid teams) where the right of property in land and equipment was retained through payment out of common income against members' contributions of these assets. What matters is the physical amalgamation of myriad tiny plots for the purpose of operation regardless of the title under which this is done. The Indian delegation to China in its report on rural co-operatives published in 1955 expressed favourable reactions on the ability of even these rather small units to complete irrigation works on a larger scale than would have been possible under private investment. In the event these 'semi-socialist' co-operatives had been merged and upgraded to advanced co-operatives comprising 100–300 households by 1956, where the 'return to land and equipment' element was done away with and a system of distribution of income according to work was established. A noticeable acceleration in the rate of capital formation within agriculture resulted because surplus labour was thrown into building up vital productive infrastructure (notably small scale irrigation works), into afforestation and land reclamation, and into setting up and expanding agro-processing, handicrafts and small-scale rural manufacturing industries. A part of this is measured in the official data but a substantial part remains unmeasured. Investment in education and health was stressed from the beginning and the construction of public facilities like primary schools and clinics, and combating disease-bearing pests in the hitherto badly neglected villages, were equally important outcomes of the mobilisation of potential economic surplus.

Was this the result of a more-or-less 'blind' adherence to the objective of promoting socialised ownership of the means of production, or was it the outcome of conscious theorising? We do not have access in the English language to the views of other leaders in China, but certainly a reading of the writings of Mao Tse-tung, the main architect of the push towards rapid formation of co-operatives followed by collectives in the late 1950s, leaves no room for doubt that there was a very clear grasp of the new productive possibilities inherent in co-operatives from the point of view of mobilising labour for capital formation and rural enterprises of every type by the peasants. Writing in 1954 in a note to a piece entitled 'An outlet has been found for surplus labour power', based on specific examples of newly formed co-operatives, Mao says the following:

> under present conditions of production there is already a surplus of roughly one-third of labour power. What required three people in the past can be done by two after co-operative transformation, an indication of the superiority of socialism. Where can an outlet be found for this surplus labour power of one-third or more? For

the most part, still in the countryside . . . The masses have
unlimited creative power. They can organize themselves to take
on all spheres and branches of work where they can give full play
to their energy, tackle production more intensively and
extensively and initiate more and more undertakings for their
own well being. (*Selected Works* (*SW*) 5, p. 269)

The undertakings being considered were land reclamation,
irrigation, afforestation, rural handicrafts and industry (agro-
processing and other), infrastructure (roads, bridges and so forth),
the energy sector, and social investment which required pest
eradication and building schools, clinics and entertainment facilities
for the peasants. The possibilities were indeed myriad given the
abysmally low level of material, educational and health
development in the countryside. In the 'Debate on Co-operative
Transformation', dated 1955 Mao stressed the need for 'state
organized land reclamation by settlers using machinery (the plan
being to bring 400 to 500 million mou of waste land under
cultivation in the course of three five year plans)' (p. 197), and also
the need for taking on the daunting task of reversing deforestation
and land degradation:

I think the barren mountains in the north in particular should be
afforested, and they undoubtedly can be. Do you comrades from
the north have courage enough for this? Many places in the south
need afforestation too. It will be fine if in a number of years we
can see various places in the south and north clothed with
greenery. This will benefit agriculture, industry and all other
spheres. (*SW* 5, p. 219)

Conservationist principles were being articulated and
implemented in China three decades before they were seriously
discussed in India, and for the very good reason that China started
its development with much higher indices of deforestation and land
degradation than did India, and with a much more severe land
availability constraint (see Sanghvi, 1969). In the event, the targeted
additions to total arable area proved difficult; cultivated area
expanded but from the mid-1960s it started contracting as
industrial, commercial and residential construction grew.
Afforestation targets were better met and in the following two
decades the very low proportion of remaining forest area in China
had been nearly doubled, very largely through co-operative and
later collective, deferred-income labour, with technical help by
specialised forestry experts.

Even before the formation of the much larger communes from 1958, it was expected that, in the advanced co-operatives (size on average 200 households), the annual number of days employed per man would nearly double and that the figure for women would increase substantially. In some areas, owing to absorption of existing underemployment in productive work, labour shortage had already emerged as early as the mid-1950s, resulting in the drawing of more women into the workforce. Commenting on an article on the impact of co-operative formation, Mao says:

> Things in this country also show us that an outlet can be found in the villages for rural surplus labour-power. As management improves and the scope of production expands, every able-bodied man and woman can put in more work-days in the year. Instead of over one hundred work days for a man and a few score for a woman as described in this article, the former can put in well over two hundred work days and the latter well over one hundred or more . . . (*SW* 5, p. 270)

Again:

> Before the cooperative transformation of agriculture, surplus labour-power was a problem in many parts of the country. Since then many cooperatives have felt the pinch of a labour shortage and the need to mobilize the masses of the women, who did not work in the fields before, to take their place on the labour front ... For many places the labour shortage becomes evident as production grows in scale, the number of undertakings increases, the efforts to remake nature become more extensive and intensive and the work is done more thoroughly. (*SW* 5, p. 268)

According to the data in Schran (1969), the annual number of days each person was employed in rural China rose by more than half from 119 to 189 during the period 1950 to 1959 (Table 14.3) with most of the rise coming after the formation of the advanced co-operatives. While the earlier extremely severe underemployment no longer existed, these figures indicate the persistence of fairly severe underemployment – 176 idle days a year – and hence a continuing scope for mobilising potential surplus. It may be noted that, in India, the average annual number of idle days for casual rural labourers in the 1955–56 rural labour enquiry was 120 – that is underemployment was substantially less severe than in China.

From 1952 to 1957 the estimated accumulation rate in rural areas in all agriculture-related sectors, as a percentage of total national investment, actually registers a decline from 13.3 per cent to 8.6 per cent according to Riskin (1987; see his Table 10.6, p. 239). This is implausible in the extreme as a considerable increase in the direct transformation of labour into asset formation was taking place at this time in the co-operatives: we suspect that these percentages reflect monetised investment alone, leaving out evaluation of such direct use of surplus labour. Generally such projects would have a largely non-monetised component (the use of unpaid surplus labour) plus a more-or-less important monetised component (mainly equipment and energy). It is likely that there is a substantial underestimation of actual capital formation in value terms both in this period and later, even in the official Chinese sources, leaving out much of the non-monetised portion in rural areas, as there are clearly severe problems in valuing the direct transformation of unpaid surplus labour into collective capital without mediation through markets, as was taking place at this time. The existence of valuation problems, however, does not alter the fact that there were large real additions to assets which are not being captured fully in the data. There are interesting questions of national income accounting here and the possibility of building up entirely new series of capital formation.

The co-operatives themselves provided not value but physical indicators of additions to assets, in terms of acreage of wasteland reclaimed, acreage terraced or afforested, capacity of irrigation reservoirs constructed, number of schools and clinics set up, and so on. During the first plan period (1952–56) 'close to 200 mn. mou were added to the total irrigated area, nearly half of this during 1955–56 by the co-operatives. In addition there was much terracing of the (hillside) fields and large-scale tree planting' (Wheelwright and McFarlane, 1970). During 1958 to 1979 the number of rain-water harvesting systems (water reservoirs) constructed was reportedly about 46,000 with an average capacity of 0.87 million cubic feet, adding a total of 40 billion cubic feet of water storage capacity at the level of the commune to the irrigation capacity created by central investment in conventional large multi-purpose irrigation projects.

By early 1958 it seems to have been felt particularly by Mao Tse-Tung that the scope of even the advanced co-operatives had been nearly fully utilised and further progress required an even larger scale of operation, enabling the mobilising of larger masses of people for projects, especially in water conservancy, which would accelerate the supply of food grain and raw materials for industry, and speed up the environment, literacy and health campaigns in the rural areas. According to Mao:

> If we cannot basically solve the problem of agricultural cooperation within roughly three five-year plans (1952–67), that is to say, if our agriculture cannot make a leap from small-scale farming with animal-drawn farm implements to large-scale mechanized farming ... then we shall fail to resolve the contradiction between the ever increasing need for commodity grain and industrial raw materials and the present generally low output of staple crops, and we shall run into formidable difficulties in our socialist industrialisation and be unable to complete it. (*SW* 5, p. 197)

Further, comprehensive rural planning would also run into difficulties if the productive and administrative units were not large enough.

The size of each of the people's communes which were set up through the administrative merger of 25 or more advanced producer co-operatives from 1958 onwards was such as to permit much more ambitious schemes of capital formation than before, since each comprised at least 5,000 households and most were much larger. Each commune, like the co-operatives earlier, operated a welfare fund and an accumulation fund, together amounting on average to about nine to 13 per cent of total annual net income (net of all material production costs); each commune paid in addition from four to six per cent of net income as tax to the State, the remaining 81 to 87 per cent being distributed as personal incomes to the members (Lippit, 1987, p. 175).

Values of nine to 13 per cent of total net income may not seem a very high rate of saving, but it has to be borne in mind that these were institutional savings entirely used for on-commune common productive investment and welfare, and excluded the personal savings out of distributed income, which the households might use to purchase durable goods, invest in their private plots and in better housing for themselves. It has also to be remembered that the peasants' contribution to the State was not limited to taxation alone but was also inherent in the fact that their output was procured by the State at low administered prices, carefully monitored to ensure urban price stability while giving a slow but steady rate of improvement in the terms of exchange to the farmers.

The peasants were not losing out, however, relative to workers in organised industry, for the real wage rate for manufacturing workers actually declined marginally, while the earnings per family of workers rose in real terms owing to a rise in employment both in terms of days per employed worker and in terms of much higher female participation rates. Workers in industry, no less than the peasants, were shouldering the burden of raising the rate of investment in the economy via a slower planned rate of rise in their real incomes than in labour productivity during the first three plans. In view of this, the coverage of both peasants and workers by systems of almost free health care and free education, and the provision of basic consumption goods, housing and fuel at fixed low prices were important elements in standards of living which were in fact rising faster than is indicated by the rise in incomes. Estimates of real incomes obtained by the usual procedure of deflating money incomes by changes in the price index do not give an accurate picture of living standards because the low expenditure weights of vitally important elements such as a cleaner environment, accessible health care and basic education, understate the extent of the rise.

The complete coverage of all households in rural areas and the pooling of the savings of thousands of families in the commune investment fund meant that a big investment thrust was possible; in the course of this there was a drive to incorporate women in the workforce to an even larger extent than before. The almost 'war mobilisation' approach to production, the virtual creation of a series of land armies gong out in platoons to tackle big projects of terracing hills, building reservoirs and planting trees, cleaning up snail-infested canals, filling up mosquito-breeding sites and so on, represented an unprecedented degree of labour mobilisation, not only for China but anywhere in the world in this century in times of peace. Young nations have, potentially, a degree of energy and enthusiasm that cannot be generated in old and tired nations; and though ancient in civilisational terms, China at this time was a young nation. The big thrust on the front of irrigation and rural industry, and the thrust on the front of health care, were both the products of the new strategy from 1958. The monetised investment in equipment and energy became more important in this period as a necessary complement to use of surplus labour, and matching financial aid was extended to collectives by government.

This strategy is best viewed as a sharp acceleration – perhaps far too sharp in the beginning, judging by Table 14.2 – of the already existing trends of mobilising surplus labour, now on an even larger scale, plus mobilising complementary savings mainly via the collective 'accumulation fund' out of the increasing incomes arising from past investments. By their very nature, such very large-scale mobilisations cannot be sustained for longer than a decade or two; but provided they do the intended job this need not matter. It is arguable that the scale of the problems was such that they could only be tackled by bold initiatives; which is not to deny that there were heavy social costs involved too in such a major organisational upheaval, compounded by inexperience, and initial over-optimism about immediate results which, given the nature of the investment gestation lags, were simply not realistic.

The timing from 1958 to 1961, of the transition to communes as part of the 'Great Leap', in retrospect, was not propitious. There were a series of bad harvests, attacks of pests in some parts of the country and floods in other parts; total food grain output fell by over a quarter during the period. It is difficult to say how much the radical organisational shift to large-scale communes at this time, and the initial inevitable management problems, might have contributed to the food output decline. Those who are hostile to the very concept of large scale socialised agriculture have tended to attribute the entire output fall to this institutional shift alone; this is difficult to accept since crop output does fluctuate and after a series of good years a large dip is not uncommon – India, for example, experienced a decline of nearly 20 per cent in food output in 1964–65 without any organisational changes at all.

It is likely that, in China, a substantial decline would have taken place anyway, but might have been of a smaller magnitude and the effects on the rural population less severe, had the transition to the communes not coincided with it, and had it taken place a few years later. There was an overestimation of production by cadres under pressure to report instant results from the switch to large-scale production, whereas in reality three-to-five-year lags were involved given the type of projects being initiated, and initial disorganisation and management problems were severe. The failure to appreciate the magnitude of the output decline in time appears to have led to monumental bungling by government, which engaged in excessive procurement of grain from the rural areas in 1959 (Riskin, 1987; see Table 14.2) and further lowered grain availability for peasants – which no doubt aggravated the noticeable rise in the crude death rate over this three year period. The birth rate also fell very drastically, probably through a combination of the effects on fertility and the decision by peasant households to postpone having babies in these three bad years, so the difference between the birth rate and death rate, or the rate of natural increase actually became negative in 1960 and was much lower than normal in the preceding and following years. After 1962 the birth rate soared to levels higher than in even the early 1950s, as though there was a bunching of reproduction decisions and peasants were scrambling to compensate for the earlier decline.

The methodology adopted of estimating 'famine deaths' during this period by many scholars, by simply comparing actual population during these years with population projected on past trends in the rate of natural increase, however, is a very dubious one. There is a great deal of difference between a population shortfall arising from babies not being born at all and one arising from a rise in the death rate of people already there, associated with a fall in their nutrition levels. The latter can be legitimately called 'famine' death while the former cannot: it will not be contested that a necessary condition for dying in a famine is to be born in the first place. Wildly exaggerated and sensationalised estimates of 'famine deaths' in China have been circulating, based on following the dubious methodology of not adjusting for the decline in the birth rate. On such logic we would have to talk about massive 'famine' in all European countries during and after the Second Word War, arising from the difference between the projected rate of natural increase on past trends, and the actual rate of natural increase which was lower not only owing to direct mortality but also owing to the effects on the birth rate. What is a more realistic order of magnitude? From Table 14.2, if we take the 1957 death rate as the benchmark and calculate the excess over this rate in the following four years, we get 10.5 m. as the rough estimate of excess mortality, of which 6.5 m. is in the year 1960 alone when the death rate rose by nearly ten per thousand. This estimate would rise if instead of a benchmark year, the declining death rate trend is projected for the years 1959 to 1961. This order of excess mortality is, of course, bad enough and is a permanent blot on the otherwise impressive record of the Maoist period. To see it in perspective, however, we have to bear in mind that India's 'normal' crude death rate in 1960, the peak year of China's famine, was 24.6 or only 0.8 less than China's, while in the preceding and following years it was eight to ten per thousand *higher* than in China, without attracting the slightest opprobrium from those who are highly censorious of the Chinese experience.

The new system appears to have settled down by 1962; the experience of 1958–61 had dramatically underlined the absence of food security and gave an urgency to Mao Tse-Tung's slogan of 'taking grain as the key link' which was associated with the stress on regional self-sufficiency in basic food grains. An intensification of production through raising output from irrigated and hence multiple cropped areas, combined with a policy of rapidly increasing the supply of industrial inputs, contributed to sustaining a growth rate ahead of continuing high population growth rates. The use of industrial inputs – power, petroleum, chemical fertiliser, cement – and of machinery – irrigation and drainage equipment, tractors, power tillers, and other machinery – rose at annual compound rates of over 20 per cent between 1957 and 1978:

Annual growth rate (per cent)

Rural power consumption 1957–78	21
Small scale cement output 1962–77	23
Chemical fertiliser output 1957–78	22
Tractors (horsepower) 1957–78	20
Power tillers (Hp.) 1970–78	50
Irrigation and drainage equipment	25
Total Hp. of all machinery 1957–78	24

Source: Rawski (1982).

The communes put the labour released from crop production not only into infrastructural and social investment but also into manufactured intermediate goods. The efficiency of operation and quality of output of the iron mills, small cement plants and fertiliser plants may well not have compared with world levels but, in the situation of an abysmal lack of these inputs in rural areas for uses which did not necessarily require the best quality specifications, it made economic sense to pursue the policy of 'walking on two legs' and permitting a range of techniques of varying labour intensity for the production of a given intermediate. The small-scale industries on the communes contributed a considerable share of national output for a number of inputs.

Per capita food grain availability (already about a third higher than in India in 1950) was raised steadily – the only period of declining availability being 1959 to 1961, discussed earlier – despite a high rate of population growth up to 1970.

The number of participants in the 'winter works campaign' for land reclamation, terracing and contour bunding, constructing and maintaining irrigation reservoirs and water management systems was at different phases 8 to 15 million in 1963 and rose year by year to 90 million by 1971, and averaged 100 million between 1972 and 1977 (Rawski, 1982). All this was slack-season labour plus workers released by the combination of pooled operation and agricultural mechanisation which was going on at an accelerated pace during these 15 years. The enormous scale of the mobilisation is evident since, at its peak, it accounted for a quarter to a third of the entire labour force, the size of the latter itself being larger owing to higher female participation rates. Owing to labour-saving technical change there was thus what might be termed a dynamic potential labour surplus over and above the existing, or static labour surplus. It made sense to augment the labour surplus further in this manner through mechanisation because this was linked to a policy of setting up a range of labour-intensive rural industries (initially catering largely for the growing local demand and the national market but with the possibility of linking up to the export market, as happened after 1979).

The proportion of cultivated area under irrigation rose from 20 per cent in 1950 to 27 per cent by 1957 and to 46 per cent by 1978, a peak level which has not been added to after that owing to the introduction of household contracts from 1979 (indeed there has been a slight decline in area irrigated after that date). About 46,000 reservoirs with a total capacity of 40 billion cubic feet were reportedly constructed up to 1978, and permitted the intensification of cultivation through increased multiple cropping, absorbing more labour in the process. These are meso-level systems, the average capacity of a reservoir working out to 0.87 million cubic feet, much larger than the largest scale of private tubewell-pumpset investment by rural capitalists in India, and are not damaging to the environment, being designed for local conditions and serving up to a dozen villages.

By and large it is reasonable to say that labour mobilisation and savings mobilisation within the commune system transformed the agricultural production base, realised Mao Tse-tung's aim of solving the problem of a high enough rate of supply of both 'commodity grain and raw materials' to industry, and did so while giving a rising standard of life to the peasants (except between 1959 and 1961), albeit one rising at a slow rate. An unprecedented order of primitive socialist accumulation was made compatible with rising peasant living standards precisely because of that policy of egalitarianism which is so reviled today.

Rural agro-processing units, as well as a very large range of other intermediate and final goods industries (iron, cement, power generation, brick and tile, implements and machinery, textiles and brocades, bedding and ready-made garments, woollen goods, herbal medicines, toys, handicrafts, and so forth) were set up on the communes on a small-to-medium scale and using meso-level techniques, employing a combination of seasonal and full-time labour depending on the type of enterprise, and catering in the case of light manufacturing to both the domestic and the international market, again depending on the product. By 'meso-level technique' we refer to the fact that these were not restricted to traditional artisan skills and methods but used simple powered equipment and a division of labour appropriate to medium scale enterprises. The number of enterprises per commune appears to have ranged from 25 to 45. This possibility of investing in such a large range of agro-processing and other manufactures without affecting basic crop production, which grew adequately, arose from two related factors: (a) the release of labour time from crop production through continuing mobilising of surplus labour, in two forms: seasonal labour time for seasonally operating enterprises, and permanent shift of workers to full-time non-crop work (the extent of surplus labour itself was being increased through mechanisation) and (b) the regular reinvestment of part of the increasing collective investment funds generated through the past mobilisation of surplus labour to build up productive manufacturing assets and raise incomes. In many fast-developing coastal areas by the 1970s the surpluses of the rural enterprises in turn became large enough to help in diversifying agricultural output, thus reversing the flow of funds between activities within the collective.

These rural industries helped to reduce underemployment further and to raise value added per worker and hence per capita rural incomes for everyone, since the principle of distribution was not activity specific but remained that of work points earned by team and brigade members. In some highly developed coastal areas by the end of the 1970s non-agricultural incomes already accounted for the major share of total net income on rural communes. The combination of more labour intensive wet cultivation, sidelines and rural industries, also obviated (to a considerable extent though not completely) the problems of unplanned urban migration, and the resulting overcrowding, slum housing and poor sanitation which other developing countries face.

We do not propose to discuss the post-1979 policy changes introducing individual production and household contracts, except to note that, as might be expected, many gains of the era of collectivist egalitarianism and of high accumulation rates started being reversed, even as growth rates in rural areas spurted. It is arguable that the objective of narrowing the rural–urban income gap and raising consumption rates by lowering accumulation could have been achieved without breaking up the producing unit to the atomistic household, by introducing the same price and taxation changes that were actually made, but within a reformed collective structure: an across-the-board rise in procurement prices by a quarter in 1979 followed by a further rise altered the terms of exchange by a half in agriculture's favour, effective taxation was reduced by lowering procurement quotas and paying a 50 per cent higher price for above-quota output, and a mass consumption boom was initiated in rural areas, stimulating domestic manufacturing production. None of these desirable changes in fact logically required decollectivisation, consequent loss of the economies of scale, 'collapse of infrastructural investment' and re-emergence of unemployment; but, as is often the case with a major shift in policy regime motivated by an ideological vision, some changes which are desirable are made the validating factors for other, more fundamental changes, in the social relations of production, which may well lead to severely negative outcomes in the long run and be of an irreversible nature.

There is evidence that rural infrastructure was no longer maintained adequately after 1980; the State's capital construction expenditure on agriculture as a percentage of total capital construction, declined sharply to six per cent in 1981–84 and further to only three per cent in 1985 to 1989, compared to 10 per cent during the two decades of the communes, and this was a decline in absolute terms too; farm mechanisation received a setback, and as the collective economy declined unemployment emerged as a major problem from the early 1980s. From 1979 to 1985 the growth rate of agricultural production was high, traceable mainly to a very fast increase in fertiliser application, trebling in less than a decade, on the existing wet area, while overall sown area has been contracting. After the mid-1980s, however, capital construction has declined further and since little slack existed by way of scope for further intensification of private current inputs application, growth has slowed down; trend in this respect are remarkably similar to those in India. Rural unemployment has surfaced as a very major problem and subject for discussion; the analysis of its causes is generally superficial, talking of Maoist policies having 'suppressed' unemployment by promoting 'inefficiency', whereas the real reason lies in the decline of the earlier winter works and other collective labour mobilisation programmes. Whether it is particularly 'efficient' to let vital irrigation and other productive infrastructure decline by destroying collective institutions and at the same time eliminate employment and income-generating rural programmes, is a question that deserves more serious discussion than has been seen so far. The removal of restrictions on labour mobility also came more-or-less at the time when the cohorts born during the years of very high birth rates of 40 and more per thousand in 1964–67 have started joining the workforce from 1984–87; massive unplanned migrations of the rural unemployed have started, which is already likely to recreate slums in Chinese cities. The rural health care system has deteriorated, reflected in a rise in the infant mortality rate and further declines in the sex-ratio in a direction adverse to women.

The strong export performance of the Chinese economy after the 1979 'opening up' has capitalised to a very large extent on the existing solid base of rural industry, which could expand further as domestic and overseas markets grew, and which required only the administrative linkage to the State-operated export bodies which could assess overseas market demand and feed back specifications to the rural enterprises, now renamed 'township and village enterprises'. The competitive strength of these enterprises derives from low overheads and wages in rural and semi-urban areas, keeping the cost structure of exportables low while benefiting the rural enterprise workers through additional employment and rising incomes.

The commune structure had also given great fiscal manoeuvrability to the Chinese State until 1979, as it was comparatively easy to collect taxes from around 50,000 communes compared to several lakh co-operatives earlier (while the prospects of taxing even the top one-twentieth of individual households in rural India, comprising some 4.5 million households, has defeated the Indian State). The tax structure in rural China was moderate but, owing to the complete coverage of every single rural household (paying the tax out of its commune collective fund), it was a much larger source of revenue for the government than in India. After 1979 the policy of 'relinquishing revenue' has resulted in a self-imposed fiscal squeeze for the Chinese State.

Ultimately both the rate growth of an economy as conventionally defined as well as the society's performance on human development indicators depend on the rate of investment in productive capital formation and in health, education and the environment. The basic argument here is that the remarkable performance of the Chinese economy for nearly 30 years from 1950 to 1978 and particularly in 1962–78, both with regard to output growth and with regard to education and health care, was possible very largely owing to the strategy of sharply raising the rate of investment of both types. The very large increase in the investment rate (an increase which has not been correctly estimated so far) was in turn possible through the mobilisation, within the framework permitted by co-operatives and later communes, of the large potential surplus inherent in acute underemployment. Combined with egalitarian distribution, this mechanism permitted a transformation of the rural productive base, and allowed peasant real incomes to rise at the same time. The raising of the productive base in turn raised the rate of growth of the actual economic surplus. Unemployment in the form of underemployment, which constitutes a near intractable problem in labour-surplus, initially predominantly agricultural economies, was thus turned into a means of capital formation, of diversification into rural industries, and of achieving higher rates of development.

The economic rationale of the egalitarian strategy has not been appreciated at the analytical level by the present Chinese planners, who in implementing the new economic policies from 1979 are surprised when they have to face problems of a massive re-emergence of underemployment, combined with a decline of rural infrastructure and a reversal of social development indicators.

TABLE 14.1
AGRICULTURE–MANUFACTURING TERMS OF TRADE IN CHINA, 1952–78

Period	Index of Next Barter Terms of Trade (Pa/Pna)		
(base 1926=100)			
1926	100.00		
1933	68.27		
(base 1930–36=100)		(base 1952=100)	
1944	38.0	1952–54	104.73
1948	60.0	1955–57	107.98
1951	82.3	1958–60	115.27
1952	84.0	1961–63	138.51
1957	99.0	1964–66	133.86
1962	115.8	1967–69	142.76
1965	118.5	1970–72	149.08
1975	144.4	1973–75	155.56
1978	143.1	1976–78	158.43
1979	183.2	1979–81	181.91
		1982–83	178.65

Source: Riskin, 1987, Ishikawa, 1967 and Sheng, 1992.

TABLE 14.2
VITAL RATES, GRAIN OUTPUT AND PROCUREMENT, 1955–65

Year	Crude birth rate	Crude death rate	Rate of natural increase	Grain output m.t.	State procurement of net output, Per cent
1955	32.60	12.28	20.32	183.9	19.7
1956	31.90	11.40	20.50	192.7	14.9
1957	34.03	10.80	23.23	195.0	17.4
1958	29.22	11.98	17.24	200.0	20.9
1959	24.78	14.59	10.19	170.0	28.0
1960	20.86	25.43	−4.57	143.5	21.5
1961	18.02	14.24	3.78	147.5	17.5
1962	37.01	10.02	26.99	160.0	16.1
1963	43.37	10.04	33.33	170.0	17.0
1964	39.14	11.50	27.64	187.5	17.0
1956	37.88	9.50	28.38	194.5	17.3

Source: Adapted from Riskin, 1987, Table 6.5 on p.137.

TABLE 14.3
CHINA: PEASANT LABOUR DAYS PER ANNUM IN AGRICULTURE, 1950–59

Year	Total annual labour days (billion)	Average annual labour days
1950	26.489	119.0
1951	26.835	119.0
1952	27.168	119.0
1953	27.537	119.0
1954	28.155	119.3
1955	29.439	121.0
1956	38.084	149.0
1957	41.518	159.5
1958	47.474	174.6
1959	58.420	189.0

Source: Peter Schran, *The Development of Chinese Agriculture 1950–1959*, p.75, quoted in Lippit (1974).

Note: The sharp increases from the large-scale mobilisation for rural water conservancy in the winters of 1955–56 and 1957–58 are reflected above. The estimates cited for 1959 appear somewhat improbable as demobilisation was proceeding throughout the year.

TABLE 14.4
RATE OF ACCUMULATION OUT OF NATIONAL INCOME, 1952–79

Year	Rate of Accumulation	Year	Rate of Accumulation
1952	21.4	1966	30.6
1953	23.1	1967	21.3
1954	25.5	1968	21.1
1955	22.9	1969	23.2
1956	24.4	1970	32.9
1957	24.9	1971	34.1
1958	33.9	1972	31.6
1959	43.8	1973	32.9
1960	39.6	1974	32.3
1961	19.2	1975	33.9
1962	10.4	1976	30.9
1963	17.5	1977	32.3
1964	22.2	1978	36.5
1965	27.1	1979	34.6

Source: State Statistical Bureau, 1984, p. 32.

TABLE 14.5
LABOUR ABSORPTION IN AGRICULTURE, 1957 AND 1975

Type of Work	1957	(Billion man-days) 1975 Estimate A	Estimate B
A. Farm work	27.4	71.2	49.7
1. Cultivation	n.a.	49.7	33.1
2. Organic manuring	n.a.	21.5	16.6
B. Subsidiary work	6.2	9.9	9.9
C. Construction	2.3	8.3	8.3
1. Winter works	n.a.	5.0	5.0
2. Other	n.a.	3.3	3.3
D. Other	0.9	0.0	0.0
TOTAL	36.9	89.4	67.9
Annual work days per worker	159.0	272.0	207.0
As ratio of full employment	0.58	0.99	0.75

Source: Rawski, 1982.

TABLE 14.6
STATE INVESTMENT IN AGRICULTURAL CAPITAL CONSTRUCTION, 1953–89
(annual average in million Yuan, constant values)

Period	(1) State investment in agriculture	(2) Total state investment	(3) Per cent of (2) to (1)
1953–55	602.67	9,624.17	6.26
1956–58	1,667.0	18,841.90	8.85
1959–61	3,168.67	28,906.30	10.96
1962–65*	2,221.25	12,323.88	18.02
1966–74*	3,366.25	33,932.23	9.92
1975–77	4,039.67	38,935.20	10.38
1978–80	5,443.00	52,815.72	10.31
1981–83	3,292.67	53,091.78	6.20
1984–86	3,603.00	99,974.95	3.60
1987–89	4,631.00	147,741.18	3.12

Source: Adapted from Ash, 1992.

REFERENCES

Ash, R. F. 1991. 'The Peasant and the State', *The China Quarterly*, No. 127, September.
Ash, R. F. 1993. 'The Agricultural Sector in China: Performance and Policy Dilemmas during the 1990s', *The China Quarterly*, No.131, September.

Baker, R., Sinha, R. and Rose, B. (eds). 1982. *The Chinese Agricultural Economy* (Westview Press, Colorado).

Baran, P.A. 1957. *The Political Economy of Growth* (Monthly Review Press, New York).

Chen Nai-Ruenn. 1966. *Chinese Economic Statistics* (Edinburgh University Press, Edinburgh).

Dobb, M. H. 1951. *Some Aspects of Economic Development* (Delhi, The Delhi School of Economics).

Govt. of India. 1976. Report of the National Commission on Agriculture 1976, Part XV Agrarian Reforms (Min. of Agriculture and Irrigation).

Hinton, W. 1967. *Fanshen* (Random House, New York).

Ishikawa, S. 1988. 'Patterns and Processes of Inter-sectoral Resource Flows: Comparison of Cases in Asia', in G. Ranis and T.P. Schultz (eds), *The State of Development Economics* (Basil Blackwell, Oxford).

Karshenas, M. 1995. *Industrialisation and Agricultural Surplus: A Comparative Study of Economic Development in Asia* (Oxford University Press, Oxford).

Kumar, D. 1957. 'The Transfer of Surplus Labour from the Rural Sector', *Indian Economic Journal*, Vol. 4, No. 4.

Lewis, W.A. 1954. 'Economic Growth with Unlimited Supplies of Labour', *The Manchester School of Economic and Social Studies*, Vol. 22, May.

Lippit, V. I., 1974. *Land Reform and Economic Development in China* (M.E. Sharpe, White Plains, New York).

Lippit, V.I. 1987. *The Economic Development of China* (M.E. Sharpe, Armonk, New York/London).

Majumdar, N.A. 1961. *Some Problems of Underemployment* (Allied, Bombay).

Mao Tse Tung. 1967. *Selected Works*, Vol. 5 (Foreign Languages Press, Peking).

Mehra, S. 1966. 'Surplus Labour in Indian Agriculture', *Indian Economic Review*, Vol. 1, No. 1, April.

Mundle, S. 1981. *Surplus Flows and Growth Imbalances* (Allied, New Delhi).

Nickum, J.E. 1974. 'A Collective Approach to Water Resources Development: The Chinese Commune System 1962–1972' (Ph.D. Dissertation, University of California at Berkeley).

Nickum, J.E. 1977. *Hydraulic Engineering and Water Resources in the People's Republic of China* (US–China Relations Program, Stanford, California).

Norman, E.H. 1975. 'Japan's Emergence as a Modern State', in J.W. Dower (ed.), *Origins of the Modern Japanese State – Selected Writings of E.H. Norman* (Pantheon Books, Random House, New York).

Nurkse, R. 1953. *Problems of Capital Formation in Underdeveloped Countries* (Blackwell, Oxford).

Raj, K.N. 1960. *Some Economic Aspects of the Bhakra Nangal Project* (London).

Rao, V.K.R.V., 1952. 'Full Employment and Economic Development', *Indian Economic Review*, Delhi.

Rawski, T.G. 1979. *Economic Growth and Employment in China* (Oxford University Press, New York).

Rawski, T.G. 1982. 'Agricultural Employment and Technology', in Barker, Sinha and Rose (eds).

Riskin, C. 1987. *China's Political Economy – The Search for Development since 1949* (Oxford University Press, New York).

Rudra, A. 1973. 'Direct Estimation of Surplus Labour in Agriculture', *Economic and Political Weekly*, Vol. 8, Annual No.

Sanghvi, P. 1969. *Surplus Manpower in Agriculture and Economic Development* (Allied, Delhi).

Schran, P. 1969. *The Development of Chinese Agriculture 1950–1959* (University of Illinois Press, Urbana).

Schultz, T.W. 1964. *Transforming Traditional Agriculture* (Yale University Press, New Haven).

Sen, A.K. 1966. 'Peasants and Dualism with and without Surplus Labour', *Journal of Political Economy*.

Sen, A.K. 1975. *Employment, Technology and Development* (Clarendon Press, Oxford).

Sheng, Y. 1992. *Intersectoral Resource Flows and China's Economic Development* (Macmillan, London).

Wheelwright, E.L. and McFarlane, B. 1970. *The Chinese Road to Socialism* (Monthly Review Press, New York and London).

15

Capital Flows and Macro-Economies: A Historical View

Jayati Ghosh and Abhijit Sen

The vulnerability of national economies in the face of a massive increase in international private financial flows now dominates the concerns of economists and policy-makers across the world. Two types of reactions are evident in developing countries that have recently experienced substantial inflows of direct investment and portfolio capital. In one particularly optimistic vision, the sudden and substantial increase in foreign capital inflows is seen as part of a broader – and welcome – process of 'globalisation', whereby all the various national economies are becoming increasingly integrated through trade, through capital flows, through the geographical dispersion of phases of production, and through technology which facilitates all of these as well as creating a greater homogeneity of culture through the universalising role of the newer forms of media. According to this perspective, the increase in cross-border capital flows reflects a new buoyancy in the global economy, reduces developing countries' dependence upon high-conditionality borrowing from multilateral financing institutions in order to deal with balance of payments problems, and allows for substantial investment increases in such countries which will contribute to faster growth.

The second type of reaction is more guarded, even pessimistic, pointing to the volatile nature of much of these capital flows, emphasising the speculative element especially in increased securitisation, and arguing that the attendant loss of autonomy in monetary policy may be compounded by exchange-rate effects resulting from capital inflows, which may augur badly for the current account balance. In this position there is no necessary positive relation between capital inflow and economic growth or industrial dynamism – an argument that has some bearing on tendencies in the major industrial capitalist countries since the mid-1980s as well as the post-1990 experience of several Latin American and South Asian countries.

Despite their differences, both points of view are united in treating the recent spurt in international private capital flows (and especially in portfolio investment) as qualitatively *new,* representing a major departure from earlier tendencies, which results from both the general rise of finance capital and the nature of technological change, and which is characteristic of the greater international economic integration, an essential part of late capitalism in its phase of global resurgence. It will be argued in this paper that this presumption – of novelty and lack of precedent – is a mistaken one, and that the current level of integration of the world economy, while significant by post-war standards, is none the less not as impressive as that which had already been achieved a century earlier. However, other changes in international production, distribution and investment imply that present levels of integration may have more far-reaching results. It is further argued in this paper that a comparison of recent features of international capital flows and financial expansion with the earlier period is instructive in that it provides an insight into the mechanisms which relate the growth of finance to economic growth and development in general. One particular causal process is highlighted as of especial interest.

In the next section, long-term trends in international economic integration are considered, and it is argued that, if anything, a variety of indicators show a *lower* degree of 'globalisation' and openness of national economies in comparison with the late nineteenth century. In the subsequent section, two relatively short periods – the last decade of the nineteenth century and the period since 1980 – are compared. The growth of finance and capital markets as well as increased international capital flows are observed to characterise both periods; the difference is that in the late nineteenth century these occurred in a context of overall economic boom while in the late twentieth century they have thus far been associated with aggregate stagnation and even recession in the developed countries and in a number of developing countries. The last section is devoted to trying to analyse the reasons for this critical difference, and an explanation is suggested for the observed association of financial boom with real sector recession in a number of countries in the late twentieth century.

I

The nineteenth century witnessed the full-fledged and unhindered expansion of capitalism as a global system. The process was aided by the various forms of colonialism that were spread by the European powers, and especially by the extension of the British Empire, which in turn had a crucial role in the establishment of British supremacy in the world economy. In the early part of the century, the creation of different triangular trade patterns and the nature of labour and capital flows were all significant in creating a certain division of labour internationally, as well as ensuring British domination of the world.[1] By the late nineteenth century, these were still important, but the emphasis had shifted essentially to capital flows. In this period the predominance of the City of London in international money and capital markets (along with the fact that London was also the entrepôt for the international trade in commodities) was critical in underpinning the success of the gold standard as well as determining the extent, pace and direction of international capital flows.[2]

By the last few decades of the nineteenth century (the period until the First World War, which is commonly seen as the heyday of the gold standard) the process had culminated in an international economic system that was characterised by quite a remarkable degree of integration, perhaps the most 'free' trade that has been witnessed historically, and a clearly marked division of the world into richer and poorer countries that would persist in basic contour for a century. In several ways, the world economy of that period evidenced very close interlinkages between national economies. Among such indicators must be counted the importance of labour flows, which remained significant until the end of the century. The great waves of migration that have marked the expansionist phases of capitalism (including the movement of white settlers to the areas of temperate settlement in North America and Oceania, and the movement of indentured labour, particularly from south Asia, to western locations) all continued well into the late nineteenth century. These were relatively large shifts of populations, to the extent that commensurate movement would be simply unthinkable in the late twentieth century.

Along with this, the late nineteenth century was noted for the explicit pursuance of *laissez faire* trade policies by Britain and several other countries whose purposes were served, involuntarily, by colonies. This meant that according to trade indicators, this period was characterised by a high degree of 'openness'. The very process of capitalist penetration meant that most of the smaller economies, including almost all of what are now known as developing economies, had shares of trade in national income that were significantly higher than today.[3] Interestingly, the same is true of what was the largest and most important economy then – Britain – which in 1870 had a share of trade in national income of close to 30 per cent, as compared to around 20 per cent in 1990.[4] Further, not only were tariffs in general much lower than those prevailing across the world today, but non-tariff barriers were rare and confined to a few cases and a few countries (most notably, in this period, Japan). In a number of colonies, of which India was perhaps representative, external trade in this period was virtually unconstrained by any kind of State-imposed control, and the resulting pattern of trade – with such countries mainly exporting primary commodities and importing manufactured goods – meant that the implications of foreign trade filtered down to direct producers and consumers in ways more direct than the mediated mechanisms evident today.

The most blatant indicator of greater international economic integration in the nineteenth century was the sheer extent and direction of cross-border capital flows. These were proportionately very large not only for the major exporting economies, but also for recipient economies which could therefore maintain prolonged deficits on the external current account.[5] Indeed, these capital flows were necessary for maintaining the stability of the gold standard as an international monetary regime, with an actual pattern of adjustment which was very different from the classic price-specie flow mechanism envisaged by Hume. The role played by international capital flows was to allow certain countries to maintain deficits or surpluses for fairly sustained periods even as others (typically those less-developed countries on the periphery of the system) were forced to adjust without such a cushion. The burden of adjustment was thus effectively placed on exporters of primary commodities, who faced fluctuating export prices as well as inadequate access to capital inflows which could reduce the need for adjustment. Since Britain was the major capital exporter, and indeed dominated international capital outflows throughout this period, changes in the discount rate of the Bank of England could be used to regulate the outflow of capital, thus allowing the monetary authorities effectively to control the movement of gold-backed sterling.[6]

One measure of the proportionate importance of such international capital flows is the size and longevity of current account surpluses or deficits of particular countries. It should be noted that these flows – which emanated primarily, although not solely, from Britain – were directed only towards certain countries, and it is this which contributed in no small measure to the subsequent division in the world economy between capital-rich and capital-poor countries. Essentially, the greater part of such capital flows followed the movement of people migrating from Britain, with which they can be linked both in direction and in volume over time. The long swings that have been identified in British capital export over the nineteenth and early twentieth centuries correspond very closely with long swings in British labour emigration.[7]

The concentration of most of the flows towards the regions of European settlement allowed these countries to maintain quantitatively significant current account deficits. Thus, the US had current account deficits of more than four per cent of national income for the better part of the nineteenth century, while Canada's deficit was as high as 13 per cent in the period of five years before the outbreak of the First World War. Meanwhile Britain ran a current account surplus of between five and 10 per cent of GNP for more than four decades averaging eight per cent over the two decades prior to the First World War. As a result of such continuous outward capital flows, on the eve of the First World War, Britain's total foreign assets were equal to almost twice the country's national income.[8] Such large and extended surpluses and deficits find no parallel in modern times, with the much-talked-of US current account deficit since 1984 amounting to less than three per cent of GNP, peaking at 3.6 per cent in 1987, and declining to less than one per cent by 1993. The largest capital exporter of modern times, Japan, has run current account surpluses averaging only 2.8 per cent of GDP over the decade 1984–93.[9]

Another way of considering the same issue is to look at the savings-and-investment behaviour of major countries over time. Obviously, a low correlation between domestic savings and investment would suggest a higher current account imbalance and thus proportionately greater capital flows, while higher savings–investment correlations would indicate the lesser quantitative significance of such flows. Here, the Feldstein and Horioka (1980) study of domestic savings and international capital flows indicated that the divergence between domestic savings and investment rates within economies has actually declined over a long time span, suggesting that capital flows have commensurately declined in importance over time. A later study by Zevin (1992) involving regressions of investment ratios by savings ratios for eight important capitalist countries, also provides similar results, as exhibited in Table 15.1A. A comparison of Tables 15.1A and 15.1B (which deals with our estimates for the period 1980–91) indicates that, in the 1980s, such divergences once again became noticeable, approaching the levels of the late nineteenth century, although they were not as substantial as in the early part of this century when international capital flows were at their peak.[10]

TABLE 15.1
REGRESSIONS OF INVESTMENT RATES AGAINST SAVINGS RATES

A: Historical

Time Span	Constant	Savings rate	Adjusted R2
1870	.013	.836	0.23
	(.064)	(.50)	
1880	-0.27	1.179	0.65
	(.048)	(.34)	
1890	.045	.668	0.26
	(.052)	(.36)	
1900	.049	.603	0.35
	(.045)	(.28)	
1910	.051	.625	0.00
	(.109)	(.64)	
1920	.043	.767	0.60
	(.040)	(.26)	
1960–69	.059	.779	0.82
	(.022)	(.19)	
1970–79	.047	.843	0.67
	(.036)	(.19)	

Notes: 1. Dependent and independent variables throughout are rates of gross savings and gross investment to GNP, for Britain, France, the USA, Canada, Italy, Sweden and Australia. For Germany, the figures used relate to net saving and net domestic capital formation as ratios of GNP.
2. Standards errors are in parentheses.

Sources: For all rows but the last: Zevin (1992), page 57; UN National Accounts Statistics.

B. 1980–1991

Year	Constant	Savings rate	R2
1980	-1.11	1.08*	0.73
1981	-4.10	1.21*	0.76
1982	3.48	0.82**	0.48
1983	6.14	0.66**	0.48
1984	10.46	0.47	0.21
1985	10.87	0.46	0.18
1986	11.89	0.39	0.26
1987	11.81	0.41***	0.39
1988	13.69	0.35	0.30
1989	15.33	0.29	0.29
1990	13.06	0.36**	0.59
1991	9.09	0.49*	0.73

Notes: * Significant at 1% level
** Significant at 5% level
*** Significant at 10% level
Countries are the same as in Table 1A.

Source: UN National Accounts Statistics.

Directly examining the exports of long-term capital (direct foreign investment plus portfolio capital) from industrial countries as a group (which includes exports of capital to other industrial countries) also reveals a very similar pattern. The peak of such long-term capital flows was precisely in the period 1870–1913, the gold standard years. In Table 15.2, an estimate of such long-term capital exports as a proportion of GNP at current prices for all developed countries is provided. From this it is evident that after the First World War such flows declined drastically. Subsequently there was an increase in such flows in the mid- to late-1980s (which is also supported by the indirect evidence of Table 15.1B). Even so, this fairly substantial increase (most of which relates to flows between industrial countries) has still not implied the higher ratios of long-term capital export to national income achieved earlier.

TABLE 15.2
EXPORTS OF LONG-TERM CAPITAL FROM INDUSTRIAL COUNTRIES
(As per cent of GNP at current prices)

Year	Percentage of GNP
1840	3 to 4
1870	3.8
1913	4.9
1929	1.0
1938	neg.
1953	0.7
1960	1.1
1986	2.85
1988	2.20
1992	2.61

Sources: All except the last three years: M. Panic (1988), page 172. Last three years calculated from IMF Balance of Payments Yearbooks and World Bank World Development Reports.

To put things into perspective, it should be remembered that these proportionately declining capital flows have occurred in the broader historical context of increasing capital intensity of production, whereby the capital flows themselves have lesser impact on increasing output and income; and a continuous and long-term process of the concentration of the world's economic resources within a fairly small number of countries and large multinational firms. Thus, not only are international long-term financial flows (which here are defined to include portfolio capital flows) of the recent past quantitatively of lesser significance than at some points in the past, but they are also qualitatively less effective in generating more output and employment growth in the host countries, given the ways in which production processes and forms of control over resources have altered.

Yet there must be some basis to the generalised sense of greater fluidity of finance capital which pervades economic appraisals today. This stems from the fact that, long-term trends notwithstanding, there has been a significant increase in international financial flows in the past two decades compared to the period, say, after the Second World War. Indeed, cross-border capital flows effectively collapsed after the period of hectic speculative activity between the two World Wars, and were further restricted by fairly stringent capital controls operating in most countries. They only revived substantially after the investment by OPEC countries of their surpluses with Eurocurrency banks, which gave a major boost to transnational banking in the 1970s. Subsequently, deregulation of financial markets as well as the emergence of large macro-economic imbalances within developed industrial countries have meant the rapid expansion of financial markets, including those for securities, both within and across borders. Recent trends in international finance and the growth of capital markets worldwide thus represent a move towards a situation similar to that prevailing a century earlier, after a period of several decades during which both national and international capital markets were under fairly tight governmental control in most countries of the world.

One important caveat to this needs to be noted. The criteria used above, in terms of ratios of current account deficits to GNP or the correlation between domestic savings and investment rates, essentially reveal the extent of *net* capital flows. But one obvious feature of the past decade and more is the substantial growth of *gross* flows across countries (and in particular between the industrial countries). This is clear from the volume of transactions in the international money markets: more than $1 trillion is estimated to change hands daily in New York alone. These gross flows, many of which would cancel out over a period of a year, would not therefore be reflected in balance of payments statistics yet they represent a substantial increase in purely speculative flows. These have major destabilising potential, and are also responsible for the much increased volatility of international currency markets. The point is that the increase in total international capital flows in the recent past is primarily of this variety, and long-term net flows have only just begun to reach the levels of a century earlier.

II

The last two decades of the operation of the full-fledged gold standard (effectively, the last decade of the nineteenth century and the first decade of the twentieth) had some important similarities with the past decade in this century, in terms of the nature of financial expansion and capital flows. In fact, there were several areas of correspondence, and some very critical areas of difference, which will be elaborated below. The comparison of these two time periods is particularly relevant because it serves to illuminate a feature which, in our view, is fundamental in explaining the relationship between finance and economic growth in general.

The first broad analogy relates to the nature of the capitalist system prevailing in these two periods. The 1890s was part of the first period of the glory of capitalism as a world system, with unconstrained growth and few legal or institutional hindrances to the achievement of expansionary aims as far as the industrial countries were concerned. This was the period of the cementing of the international division of labour which prevailed for the better part of this century.[11] Despite the quantitative predominance of nationally oriented capital, the essence of the system was international and this was often recognised explicitly, for example by the Paris Convention of 1883 on the issue of protecting intellectual property through patents. The 1990s are witness to the global resurgence of multinational capital after a period of relative constriction stemming from the combination of increased energy and other commodity prices and shifting power balances within developed countries resulting in rising real wages and profit squeezes. The last decade of this century is conceivably one of the most favourable from the point of view of the untrammelled expansion of capitalism in its various forms – financial, industrial and trading. The current hegemony of international capital stems from many factors including its much increased leverage over domestic working groups through the spread of unemployment in developed countries; greater bargaining power *vis-à-vis* most developing countries as a result of the fall in relative prices of primary products following changes in demand patterns; and the integration of formerly socialist economies into the capitalist system. This hegemony is expressed in, and strengthened by, international agreements such as the recent GATT treaty and the mode of functioning of the multilateral financial institutions.

The second similarity relates to the nature of the capital flows that were dominant in the two periods. In the latter half of the nineteenth century, net outward capital flows (which were overwhelmingly those of Britain) were dominated by the purchase of long-term negotiable securities.[12] In fact, from 1865 to 1913, as far as Britain was concerned, both the trend and the longer sweep of new overseas issues and total net capital outflows were quite close, with the former often accounting for more than 95 per cent of the latter. This period thus witnessed the first great wave of securitisation, both nationally and internationally. This was accompanied by a high degree of capital market integration in that period, as confirmed by the changes in stock prices and movements in short-term interest rates in the major industrial countries.[13] The period since 1990 has also been marked by a renewal of portfolio investments resulting from international securitisation. In 1992, such portfolio investments made up around 70 per cent of all net private foreign investment, representing a growing part of aggregate cross-border capital flows, although they are still not quite as dominant as they were in the late nineteenth century.[14]

The wave of securitisation and the substantial movement of cross-border capital reflected a general boom in finance and capital markets in the late nineteenth century, which is very similar to the boom we have witnessed over the past decade-and-a-half, first in developed countries and subsequently in a range of developing and formerly socialist countries. In the 1880s and 1890s this was part of the general increase in sophistication of financial institutions and growing reliance on financial intermediation that characterised this phase of capitalist development. In the 1980s and 1990s, the financial boom has been associated with the processes of government deregulation and liberalisation of financial markets that have occurred to a greater or lesser extent in almost all industrial countries since 1980, and subsequently in developing countries.

The major recipients of international capital in the late nineteenth century were countries like the US, Canada and Australia (as mentioned earlier, primarily the regions of European settlement), but certain developing countries also received a share, albeit substantially smaller.[15] Foremost among these were Argentina, Brazil and South Africa, which were all able to finance current account deficits of between three and five per cent of GNP in this period.[16] In the 1990s, the dominant share of such flows has in fact been directed towards the so-called 'emerging markets' in developing countries.

These similarities across the two time periods cannot obscure some very critical differences which are of special interest in analysing present patterns. One obvious difference is the lack of a clearly defined 'leader' of the world economy in the sense in which Britain played the role during the years of the gold standard. Although the world is currently seen as unipolar in geopolitical terms, with the US clearly dominant, the US economy today does not have the commanding position that Britain had then by virtue of its capital exports, its role as financial centre and trade entrepôt, and as colonial power over a large part of the globe. Although the US is still the single largest economy in the world, its share has been declining and is currently lower than that of the European Community. Nor does the US exercise the qualitative control that came to it during the Bretton Woods era, when it could effectively determine the supply of liquidity in the world economy through the release of dollars. In effect, today the world economy has no real leader, but instead it has competing blocs. In turn, the dominance of multinational companies has meant that these players have reduced, to some extent, the role of national governments in affecting even international economic relations. The internationalisation of production, with roughly one-third of global marketed output now estimated to be under the control of around 100 large multinational companies, has drastically changed the nature of capitalism.

For our purposes, another very significant difference relates to the fact while the explosion of finance in the late nineteenth century occurred in the context of stable and growing aggregate output and income in the industrial countries, high and rising investment rates and a general boom in world trade,[17] the recent spurt in finance and capital markets does not have such a favourable background. Rather, the contemporary financial expansion across the world has been associated with recession in the major industrial countries, falling investment rates, a slow-down in the growth of international commerce, and an inability to translate financial growth into real sector growth. It is clear from Table 15.3 that the post-1988 recession in industrial countries has involved both decelerations/falls in real fixed capital formation and reduced fiscal stances in the important industrial countries.

TABLE 15.3
ECONOMIC INDICATORS FOR SEVEN INDUSTRIAL COUNTRIES
(% change over previous year)

	1988	1989	1990	1991	1992	1993
Real GDP	4.5	3.2	2.4	0.8	1.7	1.3
Per capita GDP	3.8	2.6	1.6	0.0	1.0	0.6
Real GFCF	7.2	4.0	1.8	−2.9	2.5	3.2
*Fiscal impulse	−0.1	−0.7	+0.3	0.0	+0.3	−0.5
Employment	1.9	1.8	1.2	−0.5	0.3	1.0
**Unemployment rate	6.3	5.8	5.7	6.6	7.2	7.1

Notes: Data refer to the United Kingdom and Canda.
      * Fiscal impulse refers to the change in the general government fiscal balance over the previous year as a percentage of GDP; '+' is expansionary and '-' is contractionary.
      ** Refers to the proportion of declared unemployed to total workforce; typically underestimates actual unemployment.

Sources: OECD Economic Survey 1993; IMF World Economic Outlook 1993.

Further, even as the industrial economies have been in recession, the value of stock market capitalisation has increased dramatically and the prices of certain other assets (typically real estate and other financial assets) have soared in speculative booms. In those developing countries where the growth of financial sector and capital markets has been especially marked (Mexico, Chile, Argentina are obvious Latin American examples; Turkey and Pakistan could also be mentioned) the capital inflows that have fed stock market booms have also meant appreciating exchange rates, and have been associated with recession in the manufacturing sector, declining rates of investment to national income, and stagnant or declining per capita incomes in the aggregate.[18] It is this uneasy coexistence between effulgent finance and real economies in depression which is examined in the following section.

III

There are three possible ways of interpreting the observed tendency of the deepening of the financial sector alongside real sector stagnation or shrinkage. The first, and most optimistic, position is to treat the financial boom as a precursor of a forthcoming real boom, as an indication of a high degree of 'animal spirits' among entrepreneurs and general investor confidence in the economy. In this perception, the rise in asset market prices generally is not inimical to growth but, rather, heralds a future phase of growth, which is supposedly just around the corner. This rather Panglossian view characterises at least the public pronouncements of most regimes in countries where this occurs, although possibly the private perceptions of those involved may be less sanguine. In essence, this view amounts to the assumption that the price of financial assets is an accurate 'leading indicator' of economic activity in the real sector. For this to be true, asset prices should not only always be close to their fundamentals, with insignificant bubble elements, but these fundamentals themselves should also be determined more by expectations of future levels of economic activity than by anything else. In fact, expectations of falling raw material and unit wage costs during a recession could cause expected profits to rise even without any expectation of an increase in activity, and a similar effect could follow tax cuts and privatisation of public assets at prices below their replacement cost. Most importantly, however, it is simply untrue that asset prices always track fundamentals and that the bubble component can be ignored. Indeed, it can be plausibly be argued that periods of financial innovation (such as the recent period which has seen a massive increase in new derivative financial instruments designed to reduce individual risks) are those which lengthen the period during which asset prices can diverge from fundamentals without correction.

The second view involves taking an opposite position, which attributes the blame for any recessionary tendencies to the very expansion of the financial sector, arguing that such expansions, to the extent that the bubble element dominates, actually serve not to intermediate between savings and investment in an economy, but only to divert existing savings from productive to non-productive uses. From this perspective, rising asset markets offer very high returns through capital gains, which cannot be matched by productive investments in the real economy. The consequent diversion of savings leads to declining investment rates and lower aggregate demand, and thus can have recessionary implications for the real economy.

While the latter position has some plausibility, it suffers from two problems: first, an implicit conception of some kind of 'savings fund' in the economy from which all forms of investment activity have to occur; and second, an inability to explain why the financial boom occurs in the first place, independent of any real sector impetus. Indeed, the argument comes under strain once it is recognised that financial sector deepening and expansion can also be associated with phases of sustained and general growth in output and employment. Historically, there have been several such phases, including the late nineteenth century and early twentieth century described above. Thus, in itself, this argument is not a valid explanation for the recession in many industrial and developing countries; nor is it an adequate description of the nature of links between finance and development.

This suggests that there may be a third possible explanation of the phenomena under consideration. In this the causation actually works in the other direction, from patterns in the real economy to the financial sector. The behaviour of finance becomes a reflection of a primary change in real variables, although obviously financial variables may subsequently take on a life of their own. The process can be envisaged as follows. There occurs some shift, or 'dislocation'[19] in the real economy, which operates to reduce the rate of return on productive investment. This shift may come in the form of an exogenous shock, or it may be a reflection of internal social dynamics, such as an organised working class which is able to increase the wage share of national income, or sociopolitical pressures which change the amount and pattern of government expenditure. The fact that productive investments are no longer as profitable induces a search for other avenues of investment, within the domestic economy and outside it. The stock market can provide such a vehicle, as can various other asset markets, especially in periods during which financial deregulation and liberalisation allow for a range of financial innovation.

Once the shifts in investible resources occur, because of the perceptions of agents that the newer financial investments will be more profitable, such expectations can become self-fulfilling and these markets rise in a self-propelled way. This then makes such investments even more profitable, and speculative activity in these markets is fuelled by the rapid capital gains to be made. At such a stage the existence of these rapidly rising financial markets may hinder new productive investment in the way described above, but it must be remembered that here the 'primary sin' occurs *in the real sector,* with the decline in investment opportunities there. The constraint upon further productive investment comes from the higher returns to be found in the financial sector, which redirect investible resources towards the holding of financial assets rather than the creation of new real assets. One piece of evidence supporting such a conclusion comes from the fact that real rates of return on capital investment in the business sector have risen sharply to more than 15 per cent by 1992–93 from around 12 per cent at the beginning of the 1980s, even as real rates of investment have fallen.[20] This suggests that only the most profitable investment opportunities are taken up, given the alternative lure of financial assets.

This mechanism bears a close relationship to Kindleberger's theory of financial crisis,[21] although of course Kindleberger argues that the initial displacement may be financial or real. The critical thing about his theory is that money is completely endogenous: when the macro-economic system is constrained by a tight supply of money relative to requirements, it creates more, at least for a time.[22] The provision of liquidity to meet any needs – speculative or 'real' – is thus not a problem. If this is so, then it is evident that 'tight money' policies of the State, in a situation in which there is a demand for holding assets, will not suppress such demand for finance and therefore increases in financial asset markets, but will in fact fuel them. The process involves rational behaviour by individuals, but in such a way that 'the sum total of all people reacting to opportunity is excessive'. The upward process continues until it becomes clear to some individuals, and then to more, that credit positions are extended beyond sustainability, and that maintenance of capital gains requires getting out of assets rising in prices faster than others. This leads to the period of 'financial distress'. Such distress may abate, or it may intensify into a rush-panic-crash, or it may be dealt with through the intervention of the lender of last resort; which of these occurs depends upon various factors including especially governmental responses.

For this argument to be applicable to the behaviour of financial markets in the past 15 years, there must be indications of some real sector 'dislocations' which then lead to shifts in different markets, in such a way as to involve substantial increases in financial activity without real growth in the economy. It is our contention that such dislocations are to be found in the culmination of certain long-term tendencies within capitalism, that are particularly acute today. Monopoly capitalism is marked by the contradictory pulls of stagnation and exclusion that come from its organisational and class structures, and technological dynamism that comes from competitive pressures, But the actual progress of capitalism has been closely linked throughout its history to forces 'external' to it, in particular the existence of non-capitalist hinterlands that can be incorporated, dominated and exploited, as well as the activities of the State. The present phase of capitalism is one that exhibits a reduced positive impulse from both of these forces.

Thus, the late nineteenth century was marked by the rapid creation and penetration of markets in the 'periphery' of the system as well as the exploitation of raw materials and resources from the hinterland that proved to be absolutely crucial in the expansionist phase. In the late twentieth century there are greater constraints to such use of the hinterland – and also less of a hinterland to be exploited in this manner, although it could be argued that the current penetration of markets and acquisition of assets in the formerly socialist economies represents one such 'new' hinterland. Certainly, while control over resources, and in particular energy sources, remains a matter of some importance, the impulse to growth that comes from expansion into new economic territory is significantly less today than it was a century earlier.

The other change of substance is the recent one in the nature of State involvement in the macro-economy in capitalist countries. This is one real sector shift that has marked several of the major industrial economies since 1880 and many developing and formerly socialist countries. This is often referred to as the 'withdrawal' of the State from the arena of productive activity, although in essence it represents not a withdrawal so much as an altered pattern of intervention which is still directed towards favouring the interests of particular groups within society, and in particular the interests of large multinational capital in its various forms. The thrust of the ideological, political-economic and class configuration changes of the past decade-and-a-half has been to encourage the reduction of active productive investment by the State, and to encourage the free and unhampered the operations of supposedly 'free markets' of private agents, both at home and abroad. By contrast, the States of expansionary capitalist countries a century earlier were actively involved in providing conditions for the increase in capitalist profitability in production and trade, as well as in large public infrastructural investments which had positive demand-and-supply implications. The military expenditures of the time were also critical, not only for their direct demand effects, but because they played enabling roles for capitalist activity through the enforcement of politico-economic control over the hinterland. Thus, in the earlier period, despite the overt rhetoric of *laissez faire,* various national governments provided essential positive stimuli for the expansion of capitalism nationally and globally.

In the recent past, for the reasons enumerated above, such a productive impetus from the State has been far more limited, if not non-existent. Thus the fiscal impulse (which can be defined as the change in the fiscal deficit as a proportion of national income) has been negative or close to zero in the major capitalist countries since the mid 1980s, as is evident from Table 15.3 above. The processes of disinvestment and privatisation may have led to windfall gains and rents accruing to some agents in society, but in the aggregate they have had deflationary implications. The running down of public infrastructure – both physical and social – has affected growth prospects in all of these economies through the obvious demand and supply linkages.[23] The essential point is that it is not the total quantitative dimension of government expenditure that is important – for this is very high, and indeed has never been higher historically – but the changes in its amount and pattern at the margin, which impart either a positive or negative impulse. The one common factor in practically all the capitalist economies that are today experiencing either stagnation or recession is this changed pattern of State involvement. To some extent this reflects the very successes of such intervention in the past, which led to such large quantitative increases in State expenditure that further increases are much more constrained if not politically impossible.

The limits to national and global Keynesianism thus come as much from within different societies as from the inflationary surges that they may involve. And insofar as these lead to qualitatively different types of State involvement in the economy, they can easily be seen as contributing in important ways to the rise of finance. In this argument, therefore, the relationship between finance and growth cannot be easily straightjacketed: it depends critically upon the role of the State, which itself is determined by a range of political and economic forces.

NOTES

We are grateful to Prabhat Patnaik, Utsa Patnaik and C.P. Chandrasekhar for comments.

1. For descriptions of some of these patterns, see S.B. Saul (1960) and Latham (1978). Hobsbawm (1977) discusses the role of these patterns of trade and payments in maintaining the stability of the Empire as well as the international economic system.
2. Triffin (1964) illustrates this very graphically, but there are other, equally telling assessments to be found in Eichengreen (ed.) (1990).
3. See Latham (1960). The continents of Asia, Africa and Latin America accounted for about one-fourth of world trade, but their role was qualitatively even more significant because of the pattern of triangular and more complex systems of payments.
4. See Deane and Cole (1969) for a description of the importance of trade in the British economy in the nineteenth century.
5. See Jenks (1963), de Cecco (1974) and Davis and Huttenback (1988, Chapter 2) for descriptions of the pattern of British capital flows.
6. The importance of capital flows in altering the pattern of balance of payments adjustment between countries during the period of the gold standard is now well documented. See Triffin (1974) and Eichengreen (ed.) (1990).
7. See Brinley Thomas (1972) and Edelstein (1982) for details. W.A. Lewis (1977) provides an insight into the implications of this for the opportunity cost of labour in different countries and the consequent pattern of technological transformation and development.
8. See Nurkse (1944) and Yeager (1977) for details.
9. IMF (1993).
10. The inclusion of Japan would have improved the R2s for the 1980s since Japan had very high rates of saving *and* investment. However, the study here does not include Japan, which was a country with a large savings-investment imbalance in the 1980s, because it was not among the countries considered in the earlier study by Zevin.
11. See Bairoch and Levy-Leboyer (eds) (1981).
12. Edelstein (1982) provides estimates of both the annual outflow of British savings into foreign assets and the purchase of foreign securities by British residents.
13. See Zevin (1992) especially Table 3.1.
14. Portfolio investment in the late nineteenth century none the less had a very different character from that current today. In the earlier period, such investment (essentially defined as shareholding less than 25 per cent of total equity of the company) could still imply some degree of control because of the institutional structures that were involved. In the recent past, most of the growth in portfolio capital flows has come from non-bank financial institutions such as mutual funds which are much less interested in controlling the enterprises concerned and more concerned with capital gains.
15. The direction of aggregate new British portfolio investment in the 50 years up to 1914 was a follows: 21 per cent went to the US and 13 per cent to Canada, 17 per cent went to South America, 14 per cent to Asia, 13 per cent to Europe and 11 per cent each to Africa and Australia (Latham, 1978, p. 51).
16. The case of India, which also received a certain amount of inflow, both in the form of government backed securities and bonds for railway construction and Indian government holding of external debt, is special in this regard. This is because any capital inflows must be balanced against the (largely current) outflows resulting from the fact of colonial domination, which imposed a variety of foreign exchange expenditures including the infamous 'Home Charges', and which amounted to a substantial resource outflow. See, among others, Ganguly (1965) and Sen (1992).

17. This period of the nineteenth century was known as the 'Great Depression' in prices, primarily resulting from the substantial expansion in supply of both primary and manufactured commodities. Yet this was a 'depression' only in the most nominal sense, since it was accompanied by historically high rates of output and trade growth.
18. It is obvious that India in the period 1991–94 also falls in this category.
19. A term favoured by Kindleberger and Paul Davidson (1982).
20. See OECD (1993).
21. Elaborated in Kindleberger (1977, 1984).
22. It is interesting that Kindleberger sees this not as the result of recent technological advances which facilitate financial innovation, but because of the innate social ability to innovate financially and create forms of liquidity when the need arises. Similar perceptions can be found in Zevin (1992) who points out that 'the essence of money is that it is an idea. It exists within and between human minds.'
23. In this context it is instructive to note that the only major country experiencing very rapid economic growth over the current period – China – is one which has had major increases in State infrastructural spending, concentrated in the 'favoured' regions.

REFERENCES

Bairoch, Paul and M. Levy-Leboyer (eds) (1981) *Disparities in Economic Development Since the Industrial Revolution,* London: Macmillan.
Bordo, Michael (ed.) (1992) *Financial Crises,* 2 vols, Aldershot: Edward Elgar.
Buckley, Peter J. (ed.) (1990) *International Investment,* Aldershot: Edward Elgar.
Davidson, Paul (1982) *International Money and the Real World,* London: Macmillan.
Davis, Lance E. and Robert A. Huttenback (1988) *Mammon and the Pursuit of Empire: The Economics of British Imperialism,* Cambridge: Cambridge University Press.
Deane, Phyllis and W.A. Cole (1969) *British Economic Growth, 1688–1959: Trends and Structure,* London, Cambridge University Press.
De Cecco (1974) *Money and Empire: The International Gold Standard: 1890–1914,* Oxford: Basil Blackwell.
Edelstein, M. (1982) *Overseas Investment in the Age of High Imperialism: The United Kingdom, 1850–1914,* London: Methuen.
Eichengreen, Barry (ed.) (1990) *The Gold Standard in Theory and History.*
Feldstein, M. and C. Horioka (1980), 'Domestic saving and international capital flows', *Economic Journal.*
Ganguly, B.N. (1965) *Dadabhai Naoroji and the Drain Theory,* Bombay: Asia Publishing House.
Hall, A.R. (ed.) (1968) *The Export of Capital from Britain 1870–1914,* London: Methuen.
Hobsbawm, E.H. (1977) *Industry and Empire: From 1750 to the Present Day,* Harmondsworth: Penguin.
International Monetary Fund (1993) *World Economic Outlook,* Washington DC.
Jenks, H.L. *The Migration of British Capital up to 1870.*
Kindleberger, Charles P. (1978) *Manias, Panics and Crashes: A History of Financial Crises,* New York: Basic Books.
Kindleberger, Charles P. (1984) *A Financial History of Western Europe,* London: George Allen & Unwin.
Latham, A.J.H. (1978) *The International Economy and the Underdeveloped World, 1865–1914,* London: Croom Helm.
Nurkse, Ragnar (1944) *International Currency Experience,* League of Nations.
OECD (1993) *Economic Survey.*
Panic, M. (1988) *National Management of the International Economy,* London: Macmillan.
Saul, S.B. (1960) *Studies in British Overseas Trade, 1870–1914,* Liverpool: Liverpool University Press.
Sen, Sunanda (1992) *Colonies and Empire,* Delhi: Orient Longman.
Simon, Matthew (1968) 'The Pattern of New British Portfolio Investment 1865–1914', in A.R. Hall (ed.).

Thomas, Brinley (1972) *Migration and Urban Development: A Reappraisal of British and American Long Cycles,* London.

Triffin, Robert (1964) *Evolution of the International Monetary System – Historical Reappraisal and Future Perspectives,* Princeton: Princeton University Press.

Yeager, Leland B. (1978) *International Monetary Relations: Theory, History, Policy,* second edition, Bombay: Allied.

Zevin, Robert (1992) 'Are World Financial Markets More Open? If so, why and with what effects?' in Tariq Banuri and Juliet Schor (eds) *Financial Openness and National Autonomy,* Oxford, Oxford University Press.

16

Privatising the Third World: The Role of Ideology in the Bretton Woods Reform Agenda

Rehman Sobhan

INTRODUCTION

One of the by-products of the end of history appears to be the growing disbelief in the role of the public sector and the ascendancy of the private sector as the principal agent of economic activity. This reconfiguration in intellectual fashions owes in part to the fallacious belief that the public sector was the institutional surrogate for a socialist system whilst private enterprise was the embodiment of the liberal democratic paradigm. A considerable body of literature as well as historical experience has persuaded us that large public sectors co-exist with private ownership of the means of production and the ascendancy of market forces while private ownership may be quite consistent with a dominant state machine having policies quite subversive to the concept of market competition. Contention over the role of the public and private sectors as proxies for the conflict between capitalism and socialism has thus been somewhat redundant.

Societies categorising themselves as socialist did, however, have large areas of the means of production under various forms of social ownership. The modes, however, varied widely from centralised government–owned enterprises to the village enterprises or even enterprises owned co-operatively by groups of people. Areas of private property ownership varied with these societies. In the reform era of socialism the area of private ownership, the scope for private enterprise without ownership rights, and the reconfiguration of the corporate persona of the State, has shown considerable flexibility. Socialist institutions and attitudes to property rights are still evolving in particular countries such as China and Vietnam so that we are a long way from having a definitive concept of what constitutes a socialist mode of production.

Whilst socialists are going through their own rethinking process, the liberal school, now reinvigorated by the post-socialists of Eastern Europe and the former USSR, seems much less evolutionary in its approach to forms of property ownership. It is now argued as an axiomatic proposition that public ownership is manifestly undesirable on grounds of inefficiency and must be replaced as soon as possible by private forms of production. Where state owned enterprises (SOEs) exist this must be seen as a transitional form of ownership. This rather categorical position on public and private property rights has graduated from the text books of Hayek, Von Mises and Friedman into the political agendas of the big powers such as the United States and into the investment related policy prescriptions of international bodies such as the Bretton Woods Institutions (BWI), the World Bank and the IMF, as well as the reform programmes of both post-socialist and developing economies.

Whilst there may be much scepticism over the need for a diminished role for the State as opposed to a reconfiguration in its role, and whilst the commitment to market reforms may be much less axiomatic than the BWI believes, there is a general agreement that the public sector as an agent of production needs to diminish its role in the economy. It is this belief that has driven the global move towards the disinvestment in, and privatisation of, former SOEs and the drive to expand the role of the private sector. The immediate circumstances, conceptual assumptions and outcomes of this drive towards privatisation in the Third World constitute the basis of this paper.

At the outset we need to establish what we mean by 'privatisation'. For the purposes of this paper the term 'privatisation' will be used to denote the disinvestment of publicly owned and/or managed assets/enterprises to private ownership. This particular definition is thus more limiting than the wider concept of promoting the private sector or the development of capitalism which can take place, and indeed has taken place, in many countries without prejudice to the productive role of the public sector.

The 1980s, and early 1990s, have been the era of privatisation of economic activity. Between 1980–91, 6,832 public enterprises (PE) were privatised around the world (Kikeri, Nellis and Shirley, 1992). However, 66 per cent of this figure is accounted for by the massive privatisation programme in East Germany and 12 per cent by the rest of Eastern Europe. The OECD countries' share of this global process was only 20 per cent leaving 20 per cent of the privatised enterprises in the Third World. Chile, under the Chicago-inspired leadership of General Pinochet, led the way in the Third World, privatising 75 per cent of its enterprises between 1973–81.

Chile had already launched a major drive towards privatising various public enterprises after the military seized power in 1973, but the more pervasive moves towards privatising the economies of the world date from the advent to power of the more ideologically motivated regimes of Ronald Reagan in the USA and Margaret Thatcher in Britain. The ambitious privatisation programme under Mrs Thatcher in the UK was followed by similar, albeit less ambitious, programmes of divestiture in other European countries such as France, Germany and Italy. It was, however, in Eastern Europe and the Third World where a much more decisive structural shift in the ownership of productive assets began to manifest itself in the 1980s. Today, there are few developing countries left that have not already initiated a process of divestiture of some of their public holdings, or have not at least made strong public commitments to do so.

This paper limits itself to a summary discussion of the privatisation process in Third World countries. It discusses the circumstances leading to this shift in policy, its ideological assumptions, and its socio-political and economic implications for Third World countries. Whilst the paper draws upon some of the limited empirical evidence on the privatisation experience in some Third World countries there is as yet very little empirical work at hand evaluating the actual outcomes of the privatisation process. Our paper will thus remain more conceptual in its scope and remain designed to stimulate professional and, more importantly, political debate on the subject as well as suggest areas for more empirical research.

DECOLONISATION AND THE GROWTH OF THE PUBLIC SECTOR IN THE THIRD WORLD

Whilst socialist literature, and practice in some of the socialist economies, suggested that public ownership was the touchstone of socialism, few post-colonial policy-makers in the Third World embraced the socialist paradigm as part of a holistic guide to their development. Most such régimes were guided by more pragmatic concerns.

In the post-colonial era of the 1960s and even the 1970s, very few Third World countries debated the divide between the public and private sectors. In most such cases the public sector grew without prejudice to the role of the private sector. Indeed the public sector was seen by even the private sector as an essential pillar of support for their development, as a provider of infrastructural support, a supplier of capital and intermediate goods and, in some cases, as a market.

In the early period of development, nationalisation of enterprises meant exactly what it does in the Chambers dictionary:

> to make national, to make the property of the nation, to bring
> under national management, to naturalise[.]

The targets for nationalisation were thus the foreign-owned enterprises or in some cases, as in parts of Africa and Malaysia, enterprises owned by a non-indigenous bourgeoisie. Thus nationalisation was seen not as an integral part of a socialist agenda for development but as the unfinished business of the decolonisation process where nationalist regimes were seeking to recover control over natural resources, productive assets and business space that had been monopolised by a metropolitan bourgeoisie for the profit of the colonising country.

In most developing countries the takeover of the business space occupied by a metropolitan bourgeoisie meant the extension of the role of the post-colonial State into that space since in few countries of the Third World was there any evidence of an adequately mature indigenous bourgeoisie who could take over the mines, plantations, oil wells, large processing plants and even such utilities as power generating systems and railways which had been monopolised by the metropolitan bourgeoisie. Where, indeed, such a class had evolved over the years in India, parts of Latin America and East Asia, in the interstices left open to such entrepreneurship by the metropolitan bourgeoisie, it was this very class that became one of the mainstays of the nationalist movement, seeking to expand into areas of business occupied by metropolitan capital during the colonial period.

The rhetoric of post-colonial regimes about capturing the commanding heights of the economy and even invocations to socialism must have sounded exciting to radical intellectuals and generated frissons of alarm within the breasts of a fledgling domestic bourgeoisie. But the targets of the nationalisers always remained fixed on expatriate capital. This same goal moved otherwise non-radical regimes such as the Iranians, the Saudis, the Venezuelans, the Indonesians, even the Gulf Arabs to nationalise oil production and even to move upmarket into distribution and downstream processing of their energy resources. It is no surprise that in the Third World the biggest contribution of public enterprise to GDP is not in India or Tanzania, or in other state-centric regimes, but in the oil-exporting countries and particularly the former and extant monarchies of the Middle East where the State-owned oil companies became the vehicle of choice for recovering control over natural wealth from expatriate ownership. It was this same dynamic which gave Zambia one of the largest public sectors in the Third World when it took over the copper mines from foreign ownership. It was this same dynamic which extended the State sector in Algeria where the target was French-owned wealth, in Indonesia, where it was Dutch-owned assets, in Malaysia, where the goal was to promote the Malaysian ownership of productive wealth, or in Angola and Mozambique where the State took over assets abandoned by their Portuguese owners in the post-independence period. It was the same set of circumstances which prevailed in Bangladesh, where the State sector expanded its control of fixed manufacturing assets from 34 per cent to 77 per cent through the takeover, after liberation in 1971, of the 728 enterprises abandoned at the time by non-Bengali business houses who had hitherto monopolised industry and commerce in that region (Sobhan and Ahmad, 1980).

It was only in a very few Third World countries where we have evidence of the growth of public enterprise as part of a conscious socialist agenda designed to transform the relations of production. Countries which come to mind, such as the erstwhile USSR, China, Vietnam, North Korea or Cuba, are few and far between. In only very few countries of the Third World, apart from those which declare themselves to be socialist, did public enterprise expand itself at the expense of a national bourgeois. Even where this happened, as in India when life insurance was nationalised in the 1950s and the commercial banks in the 1960s, or in Pakistan when President Bhutto took over the main assets of the 22 families who had dominated the economy, or when the post-liberation government in Bangladesh nationalised Bengali-owned textile and jute mills, or in Sri Lanka when the Bandaranaike government took over the tea plantations, the actual share of the 'socialised' sector was small compared to the public sector directly set up by the government or taken over from expatriates. In all these countries, even after the nationalisations had taken place, the public enterprise/GDP ratio rarely exceeded 15 per cent. Indeed quite a sizeable private sector remained alive and well, in all walks of the economy – particularly in agriculture, small industry and trade.

It was mostly in the South Asian countries that anything resembling an ideological debate took place over the respective size of the public and private sectors, since it was precisely in these countries that some assault, however modest its dimensions, had been made on the modest holdings of an indigenous bourgeoisie. In most of Africa, Latin America, South East and East Asia, the size of the public sector, or the issue of its frontiers with the private sector was rarely an issue of public debate.

THE BRETTON WOODS INSTITUTIONS (BWI) AND THE PRIVATISATION AGENDA

Questions on the size of the public sector or a regime's lack of support for the private sector were thus hardly under discussion before the 1970s and usually originated in policy dialogues between Third World governments and the World Bank (World Bank, 1974). The bank often appeared to be less concerned with promoting an indigenous entrepreneurial class, which in many Third World countries may have been non-existent, but remained concerned with making Third World countries more receptive to expatriate capital. However, in the 1960s and 1970s, hang-ups about the predatory role of foreign capital still coloured the perceptions of the post-colonial leadership in most Third World countries. The World Bank, even in the 1970s, was less inclined to debate the public-private mix and was more inclined to focus on making public enterprises more efficient through enterprise reforms and liberalisation of pricing policy.

In most Third World countries seeking to recapture control over the economy, the colonial encounter had aborted or frustrated the growth of an indigenous entrepreneurial class. Where such a class existed it did so in the areas of trade and small industry usually catering to the local market. Where bigger entrepreneurs emerged, survived, and grew they had to demonstrate exceptional entrepreneurial skills to do so. Such a class emerged in some Third World countries, such as Brazil, India and among the Chinese populations of East Asia. In most Third World countries the State was the only agent capable of running the large mines, plantations or refineries which were 'nationalised' from their expatriate owners. In most of these countries, what existed of an educated middle class was concentrated in public administration or the professional and academic community, rarely in business. Thus it was this class, located within or around the machinery of State, who were the best available custodians of such large assets. Thus the evolution of a large public sector in most Third World economies in the areas of mineral development, industry, infrastructure, external trade, even banking, was an inescapable outcome of the decolonisation process. Where, as in some Francophone African countries such as the Ivory Coast, the post-colonial State chose to preserve its colonial inheritance and leave the economy in the hands of an expatriate business elite, the role of the State remained more limited.

In these circumstances, the assault by the BWI on the edifice of the public sector, built up in the course of the decolonisation process, has a curious a historical dimension to it which may explain the indiscriminate way in which the privatisation agenda has been pushed in every country within the thrall of the BWI, whether in South Asia, Sub-Saharan Africa or Central America.

THE CHANGING CIRCUMSTANCES LEADING TO BWI DRIVEN PRIVATISATION AGENDAS FOR THE THIRD WORLD

The move by the BWI to dictate systemic changes in the development agenda of many Third World countries involving, *inter alia* a divestment of public enterprises, remains largely a phenomenon of the 1980s. Its ideological impulse appears to have originated in the regime changes in the USA and UK. However, the BWI's capacity to push an ideological agenda owed in no small way to the changed circumstances of the 1980s.

It was the impact of the first oil price shock, in 1973/74, and then again in 1979/80, that contributed to an aggravation of macro-economic imbalances on budgetary and external account in most Third World economies. The build up of massive external debt in a number of Third World countries and the collapse in access to commercial capital left the BWI as the principal source of new capital or as an intermediary for rescheduling commercial debts. At the outset of the 1980s, the BWI were moving into a more political phase in their relations with their clients. The BWI thus used these changed circumstances to push their own agenda of structural adjustment reforms where the reduction of the size of the State sector figured at the top of their programme.

The initial attack by the BWI was directed at the contribution of public enterprise deficits to the size of the overall budgetary deficit of a particular developing country. Their immediate goal was to reduce the size of the budget deficit, which was deemed by the World Bank/IMF to be unsustainable. To the extent that budgetary imbalances demand cuts in public expenditure, the presence of fiscal deficits of public enterprises as a charge on the budget was indeed a matter of legitimate concern. The BWI approach to public sector deficits went well beyond policy measures to make public enterprises more solvent and sought to reduce the deficit by reducing the overall share of the public sector in the economy. This suggested that the solution to a painful limb was to cut it off, rather than to diagnose why the limb was suffering pain and whether various therapeutic prescriptions might not cure the pain.

THE WORLD BANK'S PRIVATISATION AGENDA

There is an elaborate literature on the pathology of public enterprises and ideas for remedial action to address their various illnesses. Even the more recent literature about clientist coalitions pressuring the State to appropriate the surplus from public enterprises does not suggest that eliminating public enterprises would eliminate the clientist coalition (Khan, 1989). This class could simply go on extracting resources from other segments of the State, including the public development finance institutions (DFIs).

There is enough evidence to show that public enterprises can be made both efficient and profitable under an appropriate political and policy dispensation (Jones, 1979; Amsden, 1989; Wade, 1991). Nor is there any reason to believe that transferring the ownership of a sick public enterprise to private hands would eliminate its sickness rather than transfer its therapy from the budgets to the banks through the accumulation of debt defaults.

The World Bank has, however, now committed itself to the position that reform of PEs can, at best, be a stopgap arrangement. They have committed themselves, 'to the conclusion that ownership itself matters' (Kikeri *et.al.,* p. 21). Thus, on first principles, States should prefer the private sector and, where the public sector is to remain intact, 'the burden of proof is on those who favour the creation or maintenance of SOEs' (ibid., p. 21). The World Bank thus appears to have taken the debate beyond the issue of some rational division of labour between the public and private sectors based on issues of externalities and market imperfections and come down in favour of an axiomatic belief in the superiority of private enterprise. Unfortunately, as with much of the applied economic analysis, their empirical work to support this hypothesis remains weak. The Bank report cites evidence from a limited in-depth country study of the UK, Chile, Mexico and Malaysia – all middle-income or developed economies chosen for their strong presumption of success in their privatisation projects. Otherwise they pick-up episodic information of particular countries, Argentina in 1989–91, some sub-Saharan countries, China in 1991, Mexico in 1982, and Guinea. The country, the years evaluated, the measures of performance, productivity, profits, investment, all appear to be chosen at random without any conceptual framework of reference or any intertemporal measure of comparison. It looks as if any information, from any country, at any time, which would prove the inefficiency of public enterprise, is invoked by the Bank. Similarly, evidence of the failure of PE reform remains ahistorical and without any conceptual premise.

In the same way, to validate the argument for improved performance after privatisation, any available evidence to sustain the hypothesis seems acceptable to the Bank. Thus the Bank quite fallaciously categorises the output of 'non-State enterprises' in China as 'private produced industrial output' (ibid., p. 20), even though these 'non-State enterprises' are in fact owned by a variety of local administrative entities and under various forms of collective property rights. This categorisation is used to positively correlate the index of factor productivity in different provinces with the share of 'non-State enterprises' in industrial output under the head of 'productivity-ownerships links in China by produce, 1985–87' (ibid., figure 2).

This slipshod argumentation in support of the World Bank's privatisation agenda is unfortunately backed up by a considerable investment of Bank resources in persuading developing countries to connect themselves to a programme of privatisation. Between 1981–92, 182 bank lending operations to 67 countries (over half in Sub-Saharan Africa) committed the respective borrowing countries to programmes of privatisation. Indeed over 70 per cent of the Bank's structural adjustment loans, in one form or another, support privatisation. This investment of bank resources has thus become for most developing countries, particularly in Sub-Saharan Africa, the main engine for privatisation in the Third World. This is not to rule out that Mexico, Chile, Argentina, and possibly the South Koreans, Thais, and Malaysians moved down the road to privatisation driven by their own perceived needs and changing objective conditions. But for most other countries it remains an open question as to whether and to what extent they chose to privatise their economies of their own volition or because the Bank had the capacity to twist their arms. What remains noteworthy, however, is that all this proselytising and power-play by the Bank in favour of the private sector is based on very flimsy theoretical grounds or empirical evidence or on any serious well-researched evidence of the outcomes of privatisation in a broad range of developing countries but which have been picked at random across the globe.

OUTCOMES FROM THE PRIVATISATION PROCESS

Considering the politically driven and globally ambitious nature of the BWI privatisation agenda, attempts to evaluate its outcome have been negligible. The bank commissioned studies of 12 enterprises drawn from the four countries cited above to look at the success stories of privatisation. Such a loaded sample which omits the privatisation experiences of Sub-Saharan Africa, Bangladesh (which is second only to Chile in the Third World in the compass of its privatisation programme), and many countries in Latin America, reflects either weak research competence or malfeasance in avoiding looking at countries where the privatisation experience may have been less than satisfactory.

To back up their own study on privatisation the Bank report once again draws upon episodic evidence to support a case for positive outcomes from privatisation. It thus cites one study to argue that, 'In Bangladesh privatised textile mills were more profitable than public sector mills.' But there are at least two studies citing evidence to the contrary in this same textile sector (Sobhan, 1990; Bhaskar, 1991). Nor does the Bank cite evidence from Bangladesh that a special survey of 290 of the 690 privatised enterprises reported that 54 per cent of their enterprises had closed down (Sobhan, 1991). In the same way, the Bank report cites a 62-enterprise study of privatised petrochemical and autopart firms in Mexico and reports improvement over three years in financial management and upgrading of technological processes, but makes no reference either to the base year of comparison or other indicators such as profitability and total factory productivity. Where they refer to Sub-Saharan Africa, the report says, *en passant,* that in Guinea, only four out of 28 privatised firms continue to operate profitably. In order to cover up the possibility of losses after privatisation the Bank report argues that 'bankruptcies and closures do not indicate that the policy was misguided, the demise of loss-making firms, public or private, can free assets for more productive use.' But this *a priori* assertion by the Bank shows no evidence that such liquidated assets have in fact found their way into new investments or generated additional employment in particular developing countries.

IDEOLOGICAL IMPERATIVES TO PRIVATISATION

It must thus be recognised that the issue of privatisation in the Third World has in the Reagan–Bush–Thatcher era graduated from a pragmatically motivated attempt to reduce the exposure of an over-extended State machine, into an ideologically driven agenda underwritten by aid funds of the BWI, other regional development banks, some UN agencies such as the UNDP, USAID and the ODA in the UK. The US director on the World Bank or other international financial institutions exposes most loan applications from a Third World country to the litmus test of whether this project promotes private enterprise.

It is not clear whether under the Clinton administration, such ideological zeal will continue to be demonstrated by US representatives at a bilateral or multilateral level, but the legacy of this messianic phase in US policy still continues to linger on in the corridors of the BWI whose officials continue to push aid-dependent Third World governments along the road to privatisation without reference to the outcomes of recent episodes of privatisation, the general capability and efficacy of the resident private bourgeoisie, or the consequences for the future growth and diversification of the economy.

THE IMPLICATIONS FOR THE THIRD WORLD

This consistent and pervasive exposure to privatisation in many Third World countries has implications for both policy making and politics in many Third World countries. In the countries of East and now South East Asia, in India, in Turkey, in some of the bigger Latin American economies, a native industrial bourgeoisie has evolved over the last half century and even longer. The class has, in these countries, demonstrated a capability for running larger enterprises, including infrastructure projects, in adapting and innovating new technology, and even exporting it. In these countries the mix between public and private enterprises must be driven by optimising considerations about which institutions are best able to produce public goods and best spread the benefits from project externalities. Here there is an element of political economy involved, where smaller, regional entrepreneurs, or those from a particular ethnic background, may in fact look to public enterprises as a countervailing power to the larger private entrepreneurs who have come to control the commanding heights of some Third World economies. Where in particular these smaller but numerically larger class of entrepreneurs have a political voice the liquidation of the public sector in the absence of a capable local bourgeoisie may not be that imminent.

In countries where the industrial bourgeoisie is much more embryonic and heavily dependent on financial underwriting by the State, more complex issues of political economy arise. The goal of policy remains evolutionary with the State encouraging local private enterprise through some loan financing. This policy would require that these local entrepreneurs stake their own equity in commissioning enterprises within their managerial reach. In this situation, the State will still expect to play a decisive role not just in the development of the physical and social infrastructure of the economy but in setting up industries beyond the financial and managerial reach of the local bourgeoisie. This strategy allows for the local bourgeoisie to mature into larger entrepreneurs in the years ahead and take over industries initially set up by the State.

The more serious problem however remains when an ideologically motivated policy moves to disinvest as much of the productive public sector as it can, pre-empts all public sector growth in industry and pushes DFI money at the private sector to set up industries, without reference to their equity stake, managerial capability or the business background of the entrepreneurial class. This has indeed been a guiding force in the disinvestment policies of such countries as Bangladesh, sub-Saharan Africa, and recently some East European and post-USSR economies. The consequences of such politically motivated privatisation agendas could be dangerous for the growth of the economy. This would be manifest in a high closure rate or losses of the disinvested enterprises, default to lending institutions and considerable malfeasance and lack of transparency in the disinvestment process. The possibility that a small fraction of the State bourgeoisie, or those with connections to the political élite, would appropriate command of large public assets, with a low equity stake of their own, and use these enterprises to extract rents, could lead to micro-economic inefficiency aggregating into macro-economic failure in production and investment. Downward trends in manufacturing investment and output in a number of Third World countries in sub-Saharan Africa, Latin America, and Bangladesh suggests that this argument has some empirical backing.

In such societies there is the added moral hazard that divesting public assets to a selective fraction of the bourgeoisie leads to a delegitimisation of the social order. The arbitrary selection process, with low accountability and poor performance outcomes, creates a sense of unfairness within the less-privileged segments of the bourgeoisie operating outside the patronage of the State, within the more numerous constituency of the working class, within the informal sector and within the peasantry. All these excluded classes may in fact have all the qualities associated with productive entrepreneurship but remain outside the purview of the disinvestment process.

Thus a new coalition between the residual machinery of the State, a new State-sponsored bourgeoisie, underwritten financially and ideologically by the World Bank, may degenerate into an arrangement of collusive criminality, where, in the name of private enterprise, substantial State-created assets are divested without any commensurate gains in national output, investment and productivity. This suggests that the privatisation process cannot just operate in a historical vacuum driven by the ideological compulsions of the donors and the political power of a new élite. For such a privatisation strategy to take root it has to emerge out of a national political debate which spells out the distributive and productivity implications of a disinvestment strategy, relates this to the capabilities of a local entrepreneurial class, disperses the ownership base of State-created assets as widely as possible and ensures fuller democratic controls over the disinvestment and evaluation process. Such a strategy should leave space for an active, purposeful, efficient and similarly accountable public sector.

REFERENCES

Amsden, A., *Asia's Next Giant: Late Industrialisation in South Korea,* Oxford University Press, 1989.

Bhaskar, V., *Privatisation and the Developing Countries: The Issues and the Evidence,* UNCTAD, Working Paper No. 47, Geneva, August 1992.

Chang, H. and Singh, A., *Public Enterprises in Developing Countries and Economic Efficiency,* UNCTAD Discussion Papers No. 48, Geneva, August 1992.

Galal, A., *Public Enterprise Reform,* Working Papers, World Bank, Washington DC, 1990.

Galal, A., Jones, L.P., Tandon, P. and Vogeisang, I., *World Bank Conference on Welfare Consequences of Selling Public Enterprises: Case Studies from Chile, Malaysia, Mexico and the UK,* Country Economics Department, Public Sector Management Private Sector Development Division, World Bank, Washington DC, June 1992.

Gardels, Nathan P., 'Auctioning off the National Patrimony', *New York Times,* 12 Nov. 1989, New York.

Hemming, R. and Mansoor, Ali M., *Privatisation and Public Enterprise,* IMF, Working Paper, Washington DC, 1987.

Jones, L.P., *Public Enterprise and Economic Development: The Korean Case,* KDI, Seoul, 1975.

Khan, M., *Clientelism, Corruption and Capitalist Development: An analysis of state intervention with special reference to Bangladesh,* Ph.D. Dissertation, Cambridge University, 1989.

Kikeri, S., *Bank Lending for Divestiture,* Working Paper, World Bank, Washington DC, 1990.

Kikeri, S. and Shirley, M., *Privatisation: Lesson of Experience,* World Bank, Washington DC, 1992.

Kornai, J., *Road to a Free Economy,* W.W. Norton, New York, 1990.

Ljunggren, B., *Market Economies under Communist Regimes: Reform in Vietnam, Laos and Cambodia,* HIID Development Discussion Paper, No. 394, Cambridge MA, Aug. 1991.

Sobhan, R. and Ahmad, M., *Public Enterprise in an Intermediate Regime: A Study in the Political Economy of Bangladesh,* BIDS, Dhaka, 1980.

Sobhan, R., 'The State and the Development of Capitalism: A Third World Perspective', *Perspectives on Capitalism,* K. Bharadwaj and S. Kaviraj (eds), Sage, New Delhi, 1989.

Sobhan, R., *The Development of the Private Sector in Bangladesh: A Review of the Evolution and Outcome of State Policy,* BIDS Research Report, No. 124, Dhaka, 1990.

Sobhan, R., 'An Industrial Strategy for Industrial Policy: Redirecting the Industrial Development of Bangladesh in the 1990s', *Bangladesh Development Studies,* Dhaka, March–June 1991.

Wade, R., *Governing the Market: Theory and Role of Government in East Asian Industrialisation,* Princeton University Press, Princeton, 1990.

World Bank, *Bangladesh Development in a Rural Economy,* Washington DC, 1974.

World Bank, *World Development Report: Challenges of Development,* Washington DC, 1991.